Social Identifications

Michael A. Hogg and Dominic Abrams

Social Identifications

A SOCIAL PSYCHOLOGY OF INTERGROUP
RELATIONS AND GROUP PROCESSES

Routledge · London and New York

First published in 1988 by
Routledge
11 New Fetter Lane, London EC4P 4EE

Published in the USA by
Routledge
in association with Routledge, Chapman and Hall, Inc.
29 West 35th Street, New York, NY 10001

Printed in Great Britain by
Biddles Ltd, Guildford

British Library Calatoguing in Publication Data

Hogg, Michael A.
  Social identifications: a social psychology of intergroup relations and group
  processes.
  1. Social groups 2. Interpersonal relations 3. Social psychology
  I. Title II. Abrams, Dominic
  302.3 HM132

  ISBN 0-415-00694-5
  ISBN 0-415-00695-3 Pbk

Library of Congress Cataloging in Publication Data

Hogg, Michael A., 1954–
  Social identifications: a social psychology of intergroup relations and group
  processes/Michael A. Hogg and Dominic Abrams.
  p.   cm.
  Bibliography: p.
  Includes index.

  ISBN 0-415-00694-5   ISBN 0-415-00695-3
  1. Intergroup relations. 2. Group identity. 3. Collective behavior.
  I. Abrams, Dominic, 1958–   II. Title, HM131, H594 1988
  302.3—dc19   87-30779 CIP

To Bee, Seth, and Ellen

Contents

Foreword

Social identity theory – the topic of this book – refers to a body of ideas that has been evolving continuously and sometimes very rapidly since the beginning of the 1970s. The first published paper that introduced these ideas appeared in 1972 (Tajfel 1972a), but the tradition of work may be dated from the initial research on the effects of social categorizations on intergroup behaviour already begun by Henri Tajfel and his colleagues (Tajfel, *et al.* 1971). The results of these studies were unexpected and in terms of conventional theories unexplicable. As Tajfel put it, they were 'data in search of a theory'. Social identity theory began as an attempt to make sense of these data. Many researchers around the world have since been influenced by the social categorization findings. The 'minimal group paradigm' which Tajfel and his colleagues created has now become a standard procedural tool of experimental research on intergroup behaviour. Social identity theory remains distinctive as being the only major theoretical tradition deriving from this work.

The initial ideas (those subsequently published in a few pages at the end of the 1972 article) had already been formulated by Henri when I arrived to work with him in Bristol in 1971. He argued that social groups needed to establish a positively valued distinctiveness from other groups to provide their members with a positive social identity. He illustrated this hypothesis by pointing to the results of the minimal group experiments (my first work as his research student in 1971 was to use the hypothesis to generate a systematic explanation of social categorization effects and related forms of intergroup discrimination; Turner 1975). Originally, then, and at the time that the term was fixed upon (about 1978) in preference to others that were also current (Henri himself used it only rarely and much later) social identity theory referred to a specific analysis of basic processes in intergroup discrimination and its application to the explanation of real-life social conflict and change. However, this is no longer the case: other ideas have made their appearance, relying on, developing, transforming the earlier thinking, but always in some way related to it. Strictly speaking, there are now in fact two social identity theories: the original intergroup theory, which is an analysis of intergroup conflict and social change and focuses on individuals' need to maintain and enhance the positively valued distinctiveness of their ingroups compared to outgroups to achieve a positive social identity (Tajfel 1972a, 1981a; Tajfel and Turner 1979, 1986; Turner 1975), and the more recent self-categorization theory (Turner 1982, 1984, 1985; Turner et al. 1987), which represents a general theory of group processes based on the idea that shared social identity depersonalizes individual self-perception and action. Correspondingly, the term social identity theory is now sometimes used to refer to the intergroup theory, sometimes to refer to both theories and sometimes to the family of ideas shared by social identity researchers. The fundamental hypothesis shared by both theories is that individuals define themselves in terms of their social group memberships and that group-defined self-perception produces psychologically distinctive effects in social behaviour.

It is a mistake, therefore, to think that the theory is simply about intergroup relations or that research on it has remained within any one empirical paradigm. On the contrary, one of its hallmarks has been the vigour with which it has extended itself into many different areas of social psychology. To summarize all the issues to which it has been applied would be tedious because there are now so many, but a selective survey would have to include the effects of social categorization on intergroup relations, intergroup conflict and ethnocentrism (including racial prejudice and inter-ethnic contact), social change, the social psychology of language, identity and the self-concept, psychological group formation, the distinction between inter-personal and intergroup behaviour, group cohesion, social attraction, social influence and conformity, social co-operation (e.g. 'social dilemmas' and social interaction in mixed-motive settings), crowd behaviour, group polarization, social stereotyping, attribution theory, equity theory and the metatheory of social psychology. Some of its most exciting recent implications have to do with social perception/cognition and, being a part of the development of social psychology in Europe, it has implied from the beginning an emphasis on 'the social dimension' of social psychology (Tajfel 1984) and a rejection of individualism. Many researchers have been attracted to the fact that the theory has always espoused a combative anti-individualistic metatheory. Jaspars (1986), for example, in discussing whether social psychology in Europe has produced any genuinely different intellectual focus for the subject points to the social identity idea 'that the individual often acts as a representative of a social category and employs such categories to achieve a social identity and self-evaluation' (p. 11) as the key theme of the 'social' emphasis in European work.

Much of the excitement of the theory lies in the fact that it has proved so readily applicable to such a wide variety of problems and fields. Social identity processes are beginning to emerge as major and pervasive aspects of human social psychology, with a relevance that extends way beyond the conventional and artificial limits of intergroup behaviour or group interaction. This book, then, is most timely. There is a definite need for a single source that can serve to summarize and introduce the main ideas, findings and applications of social identity theory and show how it has become an important new approach to social psychology. Michael Hogg and Dominic Abrams have taken on a large and difficult task. They have deliberately adopted a carefully balanced (and the only workable) approach, both presenting social identity theory as a working perspective in the field and outlining their personal views. The theory is not an orthodoxy or dogma (which is one reason why after eighteen years it is more alive than ever, still developing and its impact still growing) and it would be wrong to try to present it as such. The authors have done a thorough and excellent job in providing a comprehensive overview of what has been achieved.

John C. Turner
Sydney, October 1987

Preface

This book is about social groups: about what happens between them and what happens within them. It is about intergroup behaviour and group processes. It is also about the psychological bases of being a group member – of 'belonging' to a group. In considering these issues we discuss traditional social psychological approaches, and in this sense the book is a text. However, we are intentionally partisan. The aim is to highlight limitations and shortcomings of these approaches, and to argue for an alternative *social identity* approach, an approach which has its roots in research into intergroup relations conducted in the late 1960s and early 1970s by Henri Tajfel and his colleagues at the University of Bristol. The book thus provides an introduction to and overview of the social identity approach in social psychology.

Our book is primarily written for social psychologists, their students, and critics. We had a readership in mind: graduate and senior undergraduate students of social psychology, and more broadly social scientists interested in what social psychology might have to offer as regards the explanation of intergroup relations, prejudice, discrimination, and group processes.

The book is intended to fill a gap. There are already many books which report research stemming from the social identity perspective, but none which integrates the various insights and advances into a single and developed argument. Some are highly technical and detailed (e.g. Doise 1978; Tajfel 1978a; Turner et al. 1987), some rather restricted in focus (e.g. Hewstone 1983; St Clair and Giles 1980; Turner and Giles 1981), while others are simply collections of chapters by different authors without any concerted attempt to fuse the messages of each (e.g. Tajfel 1984). There are also textbooks which report some of the research, but which do not incorporate the theoretical critique from which the research has emerged. Some merely report the phenomena associated with social identity, such as intergroup discrimination (e.g. Deaux and Wrightsman 1984), others restrict their coverage to a few topics, and are intended more as general social psychology texts (e.g. Brown 1986; Eiser 1986). What is lacking is an integrated and comprehensive exposition of the social identity approach, which is accessible to people who are interested in but not necessarily familiar with, well versed in, or wedded to, the approach. We hope to have provided just such a book.

We recommend that it be read from beginning to end as an unfolding story. However, it has been structured so that those who like to 'dip' may do so: Chapters 1 and 2 are essential reading, but can be read in conjunction with any one of the subsequent chapters because pivotal theoretical points are reiterated. We have deliberately shied away from including boxed examples, cartoons, anecdotes, test-yourself questionnaires, and other devices often used to haul the reader through general textbooks. Nor are we concerned with the minutiae of every experiment conducted using the social identity perspective, but rather with the themes, directions, and discoveries which it provides. We limit ourselves to describing a few experiments and paradigms where it is necessary for understanding the arguments. Our concern is to show the utility of the theoretical approach, and this is best done through the reinterpretation and analysis of evidence from established social psychology. We have chosen to refer to a large number of primary sources and texts in order to illustrate and back up points, and to assist the reader who wishes to delve more deeply into relevant literature. The book is thus also an introduction to and overview of the social psychology of intergroup behaviour and group processes.

This, then, is the first *social identity text*: the first book to integrate the diverse applications and approaches of the social identity approach. Naturally, in such a limited space it is impossible to convey every twist and turn, every theoretical nuance, every empirical uncertainty. The book presents an argument and illustrates the way it can be supported. For more detailed accounts the reader is directed to other sources (see the end of each chapter).

Having read this book, the reader should be ready and able to enquire further. We provide the structure, set the questions, and promote the social identity approach to the answers.

The book was conceived one rainy afternoon in one of our offices at the University of Bristol Department of Psychology. Its progress from that day in 1984 was slow but steady, and was aided by innumerable and various contributions from friends, relatives, and colleagues. Our first debt is to those who provided the initial climate of encouragement and support necessary to get us going on the idea in the first place – in particular, John Edwards for his stoic calm, and Sonia Jackson for the invigorating mayhem of Henleaze Gardens. Without their prompting and questioning we might never have entertained the possibility of writing a book, even though the need for it was staring us in the face. We would also like to thank Tory Higgins for his encouragement given at a later stage in the enterprise. Our second debt is to our students, whose interest in the social identity perspective and whose eagerness to discuss and debate its implications increasingly made us aware of the need for a text on the subject. From them we learnt a great deal. Our third debt is to our teachers: those who originally introduced us to the social identity approach, fired us with their enthusiasm, and inspired us throughout – John Turner, Rupert Brown, Howard Giles, Mick Billig, and the late Henri Tajfel. Our contemporaries have also been our teachers, and are owed a debt: John Colvin, Susan Condor, Karen Henwood, Penny Oakes, Nick Pidgeon, Steve Reicher, Phil Smith, Margaret Wetherell, Jennie Williams, and numerous others associated with the 'Bristol school' of intergroup relations research. Discussions late into the night in Bristol and Canterbury will not soon be forgotten.

Shortly after deciding to write the book, Michael Hogg moved to Australia to take up a Postdoctoral Research fellowship at Macquarie University in Sydney, working with John Turner. A year later he moved to the University of Melbourne to take up a lectureship in psychology. In the meantime Dominic Abrams had moved to Scotland to take up a 'new blood' lectureship at the University of Dundee. Progress on the book was inevitably delayed. We are grateful to the British Council, who came to the rescue: Dominic Abrams was awarded an academic-travel grant, which enabled him to visit the University of Melbourne for three months in 1986. During this time we completed the work, further assisted by an Arts Faculty special-research grant to Michael Hogg from the University of Melbourne.

We would like to thank those who helped prepare various drafts of the manuscript: Anna Shewan, Mair Rowan, and Margaret Grubb at Dundee, and Trish Cochrane, Gabby Lyon, and Sylvia Negro at Melbourne. Special thanks must go to Susan Condor, Helen DeCieri, Tim McNamara, and Kevin Grady for taking the time to read carefully the manuscript, or parts of it, and provide us with specific comments and general advice to Diane Houston for preparing the subject index, and to Mary Ann Kernan, our editor, for her constant encouragement, pragmatic guidance, and unfailing tolerance. The final version, is however, solely our responsibility.

Finally, this book could never have been written without the support of our personal friends and relatives: Eve Hogg, Marion Meade, Sonia Jackson, Tilli Edelman, Angie and Nick Emler, and particularly Bridget Hogg and Diane Houston. We would simply like to thank them all.

Michael Hogg and Dominic Abrams
Melbourne, July 1987

1

Introduction

> There was here a Nazi extermination camp between July 1942 and August 1943. More than 800,000 Jews from Poland, USSR, Yugoslavia, Czechoslovakia, Bulgaria, Austria, France, Belgium and Greece were murdered. On 2 August 1943, the prisoners organized an armed revolt which was crushed in blood by the Nazi hangmen.

This chilling message is inscribed in six different languages on six large stones which stand sentinel in the silence of the forest near the small village of Treblinka in Poland. It documents the systematic premeditated extermination of human beings at the rate of 2,200 each day. While the gas chambers were reaping their grim harvest of human life at Treblinka, so too were they at Maidanek, Sobibor, Chelmo, Belzec, Dachau, Bergen-Belsen, Buchenwald, and many others. In Auschwitz alone, more than 2,000,000 people were exterminated between January 1942 and the summer of 1944. The magnitude of human suffering is simply beyond comprehension; it is mind-numbing in its enormity.

This is genocide – the ultimate expression of prejudice and discrimination. It is intergroup behaviour at its most horrific extreme: the attempted annihilation of an entire race. But it is only the tip of the iceberg of people's inhumanity toward their own kind: hatred, domination, subjugation, exploitation, degradation, oppression, and extermination are the hallmarks of history. And yet, people are perhaps the most sociable of all creatures: delighting in and thriving upon the company of others. They not only spend the overwhelming part of their waking lives in the presence of others, but more fundamentally they are products of history, culture, and society. They are socially constructed. Their views, opinions, values, activities, and means of communication are learnt or acquired from others. Their behaviour is largely governed by norms, or agreements between people, concerning appropriate or acceptable ways to behave and opinions to hold under particular circumstances. Without such agreement, communication, which lies at the core of human existence, would be impossible – it depends upon the existence of an agreed-upon set of rules, or a grammar.

How can we explain the apparent paradox of how the cohesion required for social existence can coexist with the divisions in society? In this book we confront the issue by focusing upon the social psychological nature of group membership. We try to understand the social psychology of people in groups – their intergroup and their intragroup behaviour. In particular, we present a specific approach to this analysis which we feel represents a promising advance on existing social psychological approaches. This is the *social identity approach.*

Let us return to the paradox. The key to a solution lies in the fact that, while a society is made up of individuals, it is patterned into relatively distinct social groups and categories, and people's views, opinions, and practices are acquired from those groups to which they belong. These groups can be considered to have an objective existence to the extent that members of different groups believe different things, dress in different ways, hold different values, speak different languages, live in different places, and generally behave differently. Some groups endure over many generations, others are relatively transitory; some are vast with many many millions of members, others are extremely small; some are very prestigious, others are treated with contempt. There are often striking differences between national groups (Italians, Germans), religious groups (Buddhist, Muslim, Protestant, Catholic), political groups (socialist, conservative), ethnic groups (Tamils and Singalese in Sri Lanka), sex groups (male, female), tribal groups (Karen, Lahu, Akha in Thailand), youth groups (punk, skinhead), university faculty groups (Science, Arts, Law), and so on. Small decision-making groups also have their own relatively unique ways of operating and norms of conduct, as do occupational groups. The important point is that the groups to which people belong, whether by assignment or by choice, will be massively significant in determining their life experiences.

It is now only a small step to recognize that groups have a profound impact on individuals' *identity.* That is, people's concepts of who they are, of what sort of people they are, and how they relate to others (whether members of the same group – *ingroup* – or of different groups – *outgroup*), is largely determined by the groups to which they feel they belong. While this may be very vivid in the case of, for example, Catholics and Protestants in Northern Ireland, it can also be observed at the level of short-lived decision-making groups in business organizations, relatively transient committees, and in the instant comaraderie felt among strangers brought together on a package tour. The question that arises is *how* do people identify with a group, and precisely what are the consequences of such identification?

This is essentially a social psychological question as it pivots on the issue of how society bestows self-conception; how it constructs individuals through the mediation of groups represented by normative or consensual practices, and how in turn individuals recreate these groups. It addresses how 'Each of us changes himself, modifies himself to the extent that he changes and modifies the complex relations of which he is the heart' (Gramsci 1971: 352). It asks what are the psychological and social psychological processes involved in the relationship between individuals and groups, and what factors govern the form taken by relations between groups. What determines whether intergroup relations are hostile, competitive, and antagonistic or whether they are co-operative and relatively amicable? These questions lie at the very heart of social psychology, and address perhaps some of the most important phenomena of human existence, such as identity, the self, group solidarity, international relations, prejudice, discrimination, stereotyping, conformity, and collective behaviour (riots, demonstrations, etc.).

Although, as we show in this book, social psychology tackles these issues and has advanced our understanding, it tends to make a distinction between the study of, on the one hand, large-scale social categories (race, sex, nation, etc.), and, on the other, small collections of individuals who are in the same place at the same time and who are all interacting mutually with each other. Traditionally, social psychology only considers the latter to constitute a group. It explains group behaviour in terms of interaction between individuals, and largely fails to consider the way that groups furnish individuals with an identity. That is, the emphasis is on the *individual in the group*. Of course, this perspective makes it very difficult to deal with large-scale group phenomena and with the societal construction of self. We are, however, very optimistic, since over the last fifteen years or so a new approach has gradually developed in social psychology which turns the traditional perspective on its head and focuses on the *group in the individual*. This is the *social identity approach*.

The central tenet of this approach is that belonging to a group (of whatever size and distribution) is largely a *psychological* state which is quite distinct from that of being a unique and separate individual, and that it confers *social identity*, or a shared/collective representation of who one is and how one should behave. It follows that the psychological processes associated with social identity are also responsible for generating distinctly 'groupy' behaviours, such as solidarity within one's group, conformity to group norms, and discrimination against outgroups. Furthermore, this perspective has enormous potential for improving and extending the explication of an array of phenomena which have traditionally been approached by social psychology from a more 'interpersonal' perspective. The purpose of this book is to show how the social identity approach can dramatically enhance and enrich an understanding of social groups.

In Chapter 2 we focus on *theory*. We describe the social identity perspective in terms of its various assumptions and its specific theoretical propositions. The main aim of this chapter is to provide the foundation on which all subsequent chapters build. A second and very important aim is to locate the social identity perspective in the broader framework of social psychology and the social sciences. We therefore spend some time at the outset discussing contrasting perspectives on human behaviour in both social psychology and social theory, and identifying their relative strengths and weaknesses. On this basis we furnish an historical context for the social identity approach, spell out its metatheoretical underpinnings, and propose ways in which it represents an advance on other social psychological approaches.

While later chapters can be read in isolation, they are designed to be read always in conjunction with Chapter 2 and assume a familiarity with the critical context of the approach and its theoretical premises. Each chapter is designed to show how the social identity perspective contributes to our understanding of a specific psychological issue, and to extend and elaborate those aspects of theory relevant to that issue. The general format of these chapters is one in which the issue and its importance in social psychology and everyday life is stated, traditional social psychological approaches are described and critically discussed, limitations are located in a relatively general critique of certain approaches to social psychology (spelt out in detail in Chapter 2), the contribution of the social identity approach is discussed and evaluated both theoretically and empirically, and prospects and future directions for the social identity perspective in the area and in related areas are considered. However, it should be noted that each of these later chapters can stand on its own as a relatively detailed critical overview of social psychological theory and research in the area covered by the chapter. Taken together they cover a large portion of the social psychology of group phenomena.

Chapter 3 deals with *intergroup behaviour*: the manner in which individuals relate to one another as members of different groups. This chapter discusses intergroup discrimination, relative deprivation, competition and co-operation, status and power, and other intergroup phenomena. Chapter 4 extends the analysis of intergroup relations by examining *stereotyping*: the way groups are perceived. We discuss the shared nature of social stereotypes and the way in which people can assign these stereotypes to themselves. We examine the way in which stereotypes are embedded in social representations or ideologies associated with social categories and how they are related to causal attributions. We also discuss the structure of stereotypes, the stereotypic content of social beliefs, and the nature of prejudice.

We then shift emphasis to what goes on inside groups, that is on *intragroup behaviour*. Chapter 5 addresses the question of what determines group solidarity or cohesiveness, and confronts the question of how, in a psychological sense, a group comes into being. What transforms an aggregate of unrelated individuals into a distinct social group with its own defining characteristics? In dealing with these issues we discuss communication networks and structures in small groups, leadership patterns, group productivity, decision-making groups, and the impact of group norms on all these.

Chapter 6 continues the emphasis on life within the group, but this time we discuss *social presence* and *social performance*; the focus is on the person in the group and the impact of the psychological presence of group members on the motivation and behaviour of the individual, rather than on intragroup processes. We examine how theories of social facilitation, social impact, self-awareness, and self-presentation contribute to our understanding of individuals' behaviour in group contexts, such as negotiation and bargaining.

In Chapter 7 we deal with the social behaviour of the group as a whole. We explore the bases of *collective behaviour*: protests, demonstrations, riots, revolutions, and examine the extent to which classical theories of the crowd, theories of de-individuation, self-awareness, numerical distinctiveness, and blind conformity are successful in accounting for forms of collective behaviour.

Right at the heart of social behaviour lies *social influence*, the process through which people affect each others' opinions and behaviours. This important issue is discussed in Chapter 8, where we focus specifically upon the influence process associated with *conformity* to group norms. After discussing the contribution of traditional perspectives on conformity, we show how the social identity perspective changes our understanding of social influence and an array of conformity phenomena: group polarization in decision-making groups, leadership, brainwashing, and active minorities sponsoring social change.

The major vehicle of social influence is communication. In Chapter 9 we discuss communication but principally dwell upon *language*. Speech style and language can function as some of the most potent symbols of identity, so it is not at all surprising that the social identity perspective is of great utility in understanding an array of sociolinguistic phenomena.

The final chapter (Ch. 10) functions as a short summary and overview, in which we integrate the various themes and strands of the social identity approach and then illustrate it with, and apply it to, a concrete intergroup context, that of the relations between the sexes. We are brief and descriptive – painting a broad canvas in bold strokes, rather than constructing a detailed technical drawing – because the aim is to convey something of the way in which the social identity approach as an integrated whole can be, and is, employed to explicate the behaviour of 'real' social categories. The chapter closes with some *conclusions* concerning the relative advantages of the social identity approach in comparison to other approaches discussed in the book. We also specify those areas where we feel current and future initiatives in social identity theory and research are being taken.

2

The social identity approach: context and content

The group spirit, the idea of the group with the sentiment of devotion to the group developed in the minds of all its members, not only serves as a bond that holds the group together or even creates it, but . . . it renders possible truly collective volition.

(McDougall 1921: 63)

The group spirit, involving knowledge of the group as such, some idea of the group, and some sentiment of devotion or attachment to the group, is then the essential condition of all . . . collective life, and of all effective collective action.

(ibid.: 66)

There is no psychology of groups which is not essentially and entirely a psychology of individuals. Social psychology . . . is a part of the psychology of the individual.

(Allport 1924: 4)

To answer the question where this mental structure of the group exists, we must refer . . . to the individual. [It is] learned by each individual from the specific language and behaviour of other individuals. Where such continuity of social contact ceases the organized life of the group disappears. Were all the individuals in a group to perish at one time, the so-called 'group mind' would be abolished forever.

(ibid: 9)

These extracts deal with what has been called the 'master problem' of social psychology, namely the relationship between the individual and the group. The prototypical opposing positions are represented above by William McDougall and Floyd Allport: group behaviour is qualitatively different from individual behaviour, and the group is somehow contained in the mind of the individual group member and influences behaviour accordingly; *versus*, group behaviour is individual behaviour among many individuals who are in the physical presence of each other – the group is a nominal fallacy.

In discussing intergroup behaviour and group processes we confront this controversy head on. Are groups merely aggregates of individuals in which the normal processes of interpersonal behaviour operate in the usual way but among a larger number of people, or do groups represent modes of interaction and thought which are qualitively distinct from that involved in interpersonal interaction? In the present chapter we introduce the concept of *social identity* as a means of resolving this issue.

Introduction

Social identity is defined as 'the individual's knowledge that he belongs to certain social groups together with some emotional and value significance to him of the group membership' (Tajfel 1972a: 31), where a social group is 'two or more individuals who share a common social identification of themselves or, which is nearly the same thing, perceive themselves to be members of the same social category' (Turner 1982: 15). These quotations convey some fundamental aspects of the social identity approach. Identity, specifically *social* identity, and group belongingness are inextricably linked in the sense that one's conception or definition of who one is (one's identity) is largely composed of self-descriptions in terms of the defining characteristics of social groups to which one belongs. This belongingness is *psychological*, it is not merely knowledge of a group's attributes. Identification with a social group is a psychological state very different from merely being designated as falling into one social category or another. It is phenomenologically real and has important self-evaluative consequences.

In this chapter we present the social identity approach, its assumptions, its theoretical propositions, and its scope. This is intended to be a theory chapter to equip the reader for subsequent chapters which explore specific topics that the approach addresses. In turn, these later chapters will provide the empirical findings which have bearing on the theory and will dwell in more detail and elaborate upon those aspects of theory relevant to the topic. However, before doing this we shall spend some time contextualizing the approach. We feel it is very important to show where the social identity perspective fits in social psychology: how it differs from other perspectives, what assumptions it shares. Here we are really concerned with metatheory, with what *type* of theory the social identity approach represents. In order to do this we will need not only to define social psychology and explore the implications of our definition but also to examine the historical milieu and intellectual climate in which the approach has its origins. This contextualizing exercise will broaden out to include the metatheoretical location of the social identity approach with respect to cognitive psychology, general psychology, psychoanalysis, philosophy, and perhaps more importantly sociology and other social sciences.

Social psychology

DEFINING SOCIAL PSYCHOLOGY

What is social psychology? Although there are almost as many definitions as texts, it is not unduly difficult to detect a common underlying theme: social psychology is the *scientific study of human social behaviour*. As a working definition this will suffice, as it describes both the method and the focus of what passes as social psychology, or what *most* social psychologists do as social psychologists. They study human social behaviour scientifically. This is, however, a very general and bland definition, and a closer look reveals important disagreements, controversies, and differences of emphasis.

Social psychology is a science by virtue of its use of scientific method; this distinguishes it from, for example, philosophy, which employs a largely rationalistic method of enquiry. The model of science adopted is exemplified by Newton's *Philosophiae Naturalis Principia Mathematica*, of 1687, and by classical theoretical physics in general. Human beings are law-governed machines that react to stimuli very much like any physical object, and so to understand human social behaviour we need only isolate the various stimuli and establish the laws which determine their effects. Laboratory experimentation is the ideal method because it best permits the isolation and examination of individual causal agents. So it is not surprising to learn that the 'founder of experimental psychology', Wilhelm Wundt, who created the first psychological laboratory in 1879 in Leipzig, and the 'father of modern experimental social psychology', Kurt Lewin, who set up the Research Center for Group Dynamics in the 1940s in the United States, both had a background in physics.

Even at the outset, social psychology's candidature for science has had its critics. Wundt believed that laboratory experimentation and the scientific method was not necessarily the optimal way to gain an understanding of the dynamic relationship between the individual and society (Wundt 1916), which he considered to be the defining focus of social psychology (called 'folk psychology', or *Völkerpsychologie*, by Wundt). Introspection might play an important role. While always present, objections to 'excessive' scientism attained a particularly high profile in the 1960s and 1970s as a part of the so-called 'crisis' of confidence in social psychology (Elms 1975; Israel and Tajfel 1972; Rosnow 1981; Strickland, Aboud, and Gergen 1976).

One reaction to this 'crisis' is a rejection of experimentation and an emphasis upon the study of the individual as a unique whole person. Attention is focused on subjectivity as an historically constructed and meaningful experience of oneself, which can best be accessed by analysing the accounts people give of themselves and their experiences. This perspective can be represented by a number of labels: social constructionism (e.g. Gergen 1973, 1982a), humanistic psychology (Shotter 1984), ethnomethodology (Garfinkel 1967), ethogenics (Harré 1977, 1979; Potter,

Stringer, and Wetherell 1984), the dramaturgical model (Goffman 1959), and 'post-structuralist' approaches (e.g. Henriques et al. 1984).

The other reaction has been to retain faith in experimental methods, but competent and carefully conducted experiments (see Campbell 1957; Kruglanski 1975; Turner 1981a). This approach argues for a plurality of methods for testing hypotheses, and the careful selection of that appropriate to the question. Laboratory experiments are not condemned outright, they are the appropriate empirical method for certain research questions. It is in this spirit that research in the social identity tradition has developed.

While one aspect of the 'crisis' concerns the methods of social psychological research, another focuses more upon the type and quality of understanding of human social behaviour that the discipline furnishes. Although the roots of experimental social psychology are in Kurt Lewin's emphasis upon the construction and testing of theories (e.g. Lewin 1952), the discipline has become strikingly deficient in precisely this area. There are empirical relationships aplenty, which have been experimentally tested to exhaustion with increasingly sophisticated and complicated experimental methods and statistical and computational techniques, and yet there is remarkably little to show for all this activity as regards theoretical advances. Social psychological knowledge often appears to be simply a collection of isolated short-range empirical generalizations which lend it a strangely disjointed and unintegrated feel. It appears to lack unity at the level of broad perspective or general theory (see Cartwright 1979; Festinger 1980). Perhaps one reason, one might even argue the reason, for this shortcoming is that social psychology has been looking in the wrong direction. It has set itself the wrong question to answer. No amount of smart methodology can salvage anything from research that fails to ask the correct question. In a moment we shall argue that social psychology may have largely misinterpreted the term social, and has thus been unable to ask itself the questions appropriate to social psychological theorizing.

But first let us briefly finish unpacking our definition of social psychology, by focusing upon its target: human social behaviour. While the careful and systematic study of animal social behaviour in naturalistic settings (i.e. ethology) may have some relevance for our understanding of people (see Crook 1980; Hinde 1979, 1982), the study of rats or pigeons, for example, pressing levers in cages is considered to be of little value. The focus is humans. In addition, by including the term behaviour we are simply acknowledging that social psychological theories of the operation of the human mind can only be constructed from what people do and say: the mind is not directly observable. This does not, however, entail behaviourism, which either denies the existence of mind or claims its study to be relatively fruitless. On the contrary, social psychology is concerned to study the mental processes and structures which mediate the dialectical relationship between stimuli and behaviour. How people behave, what they do, generates the relevant stimuli to which they react, and this is mediated by mental processes and structures.

Our portrait, then, of 'good' social psychology characterizes it as an empirical science which adopts an array of methods to discover the mental processes involved in the complex dialectical relationship between stimuli and human behaviour. But what of 'social'? What does the term mean? How has it been interpreted in the past? Herein lies the debate of principle concern to us. What is social about social psychology?

THE 'SOCIAL' IN SOCIAL PSYCHOLOGY

Credit for conducting the first social psychology experiment is traditionally given to Triplett, who investigated the effect of the physical presence of others on the performance of various tasks, such as winding in fishing line or peddling a bicycle (Triplett 1898), and thus initiated a continuing tradition of social psychological research into the social facilitatory or inhibitory effect on behaviour of the mere physical presence of others (see Ch. 6 below, and also reviews by Guerin 1986; Paulus 1983; Sanders 1981). Perhaps, then, psychology is *social* to the extent that it examines the way individual behaviour is affected by the physical presence of others. It is not surprising to learn that a large proportion of social psychology is concerned with face-to-face encounters between small numbers of individuals, for example, research into non-verbal communication (Argyle 1973; Scherer and Ekman 1982), group decision-making and small-group dynamics (Golembiewski 1962; Shaw 1981), conformity and social influence (Allen 1965, 1975) see also Ch. 5 and 8 below). Furthermore, since, according to James, 73 per cent of naturally formed groups are dyads (James 1953), much of social psychology focuses on the dyad as the ultimate or prototypical unit of social psychological analysis (e.g. Kelley and Thibaut 1978; see also Ch. 5 below).

This sort of definition cannot, however, encompass another large portion of social psychological concerns, for example research into values, attitudes, opinions, and beliefs (e.g. Rokeach 1973; Cooper and Croyle 1984) and their change (see Cialdini, Petty, and Cacioppo 1981), and also into stereotypes (see Ashmore and Del Boca 1981) and social representations (Farr and Moscovici 1984). What is needed is a broader definition such as perhaps Gordon Allport's description of social psychology as 'an attempt to understand and explain how the thought, feeling, and behaviour of individuals are influenced by the actual, imagined, or implied presence of others' (Allport 1968: 3). Attitudes are *social* psychological because they orient people with respect to other people, events, and/or physical objects. Without other people, attitudes would very likely not exist at all. At very least they depend on language, and language as a consensual means of communication between human beings cannot exist without there being other human beings (see Ch. 9 below). Attitudes can be carried away from face-to-face encounters in the mind of the individual, and thus there is a sense in which they represent the *implied presence* of other people.

Associated with this conceptualization of *social* is one, or perhaps *the*, core controversy of social psychology. The issue concerns whether there is or is not something *fundamentally* different about the behaviour of an individual alone and in a group. There are many ramifications to this issue. Is an individual alone behaving socially? Is the behaviour of a group simply an aggregate of the behaviour of individuals on their own? Is group behaviour psychologically distinct and qualitatively different from individual behaviour? The fundamental paradox lying at the heart of these questions addresses the theoretical relationship between psychological and sociological contributions to social behaviour (see Turner and Oakes 1986). We shall discuss this issue in some detail as its resolution has dramatic consequences for the type of social psychology that emerges, and it is the critical background within which the social identity perspective is framed.

Early non-experimental social psychology confronted the paradox in studying large-scale collective events such as crowds, riots, demonstrations, and mobs. In particular, it was French revolutionary crowds, magnificently described by Emile Zola (e.g. *Germinal* and *La Débâcle* – see the extract at the beginning of Chapter 7), which were studied. Gustav Le Bon's observations of these crowds led him in his classic work on the crowd to conclude that in crowds the thin veneer of socialized behaviour is stripped away to lay bare the baser human instincts (Le Bon [1896] 1908). That is, in groups people's behaviour regresses to a more primitive level at which instinctive impulses are indulged in the absence of the usual internalized checks originating in social conventions and norms. This perspective still underlies much contemporary social psychology of collective behaviour (e.g. Zimbardo 1970; see also Ch. 7 below). Based heavily upon Le Bon, Freud (1922) spoke of the way in which the crowd releases *id* impulses, and then went on to construct his psychodynamic analysis of the social group in general, which has served as the basis for much very influential theorizing on collective behaviour, intergroup relations, prejudice, and discrimination – for example, Adorno *et al.*'s (1950) 'authoritarian personality', and Dollard *et al.*'s (1939) 'frustration-aggression hypothesis'; see also Ch. 3 below.

In contrast to this perspective, William McDougall made no assumption about the deep motives of human beings being expressed under conditions such as the crowd. Instead, he introduced the concept of *group mind* (McDougall 1921). McDougall believed that group behaviour is different from individual behaviour because out of the interaction or aggregation of people emerges a group mind that has a reality and existence which is independent of and qualitatively distinct from that of its individual members. It was never intended that the concept should refer to some free-floating extra-psychological entity (Turner and Oakes 1986), and yet there has been a tendency to interpret it as such and therefore treat it as lying outside the domain of psychology. Nevertheless, McDougall's perspective can still be detected in some early classics of experimental social psychology, such as

Sherif's (1936) study of social norms and Asch's (1952) approach to social psychology (see Ch. 8 below).

However, it is with Floyd Allport's proclamation that psychology occurs in the mind of the individual and that therefore 'there is no psychology of groups which is not essentially and entirely a psychology of individuals' (Allport 1924: 4), that the dominant social psychological perspective on the relationship of individual to group is to be found. Individuals behave differently in groups because the usual interpersonal factors which affect individuals' behaviour are present in greater number and/or greater strength. In short, there is nothing qualitatively different about groups. This traditional perspective on groups is discussed in detail in Chapter 5.

While this may be the dominant perspective in social psychology, it has as its critics those who feel that it is 'reductionist', a metatheoretical shortcoming which hinders proper understanding. Since this critical stance is the background of the social identity perspective it is important that we spend some time explaining what is meant. 'Reductionism' refers to the tendency to explain a phenomenon in terms of the concepts and languages of a 'lower' level of explanation: for our purposes, the hierarchy of analysis is, for example, (from top to bottom) social history, sociology, small-group dynamics, individual psychology, physiology, biology, chemistry, physics. That is, social history can be explained by sociology, sociological phenomena by group dynamics, group dynamics by the properties of individuals, and so on. The implication seems to be that finally it should be possible to use physics (social psychology's prototype of science) to explain *all* higher-level phenomena.

Although it would clearly be absurd to claim that knowledge about the workings of the atom can inform us (in any way other than metaphor) about the workings of society (but see Kellerman 1981; also Ch.5 and 7 below), a smaller reduction from say chemistry to physics may not be so implausible. The basic point is that too great a reduction of level of analysis makes it impossible to answer many of the important questions posed at the original higher level. For example, an environmental enthusiast enquiring into forest conservation would find little of use in an explanation articulated in terms of osmotic pressure, ion pumps, and so on, when the question requires (in this example) an analysis in terms of the interests of capital. Likewise, putting one's arm out of the car window to indicate an intention to turn can be explained in terms of muscle contraction, nerve impulses, understanding of and adherence to social conventions, and so on. If the level of explanation does not match the level of the question, then the question is essentially left unanswered.

Much of traditional social psychology is reductionist, in that it explains the social group in terms of properties of the individual; that is, it is individualistic, and has been ever since the time of Floyd Allport (Cartwright 1979; Pepitone 1981; Sampson 1977, 1981). By dissolving the group into individuals, the concept of 'group' no longer has any separate conceptual status from that of the individual, and social psychology no longer studies the social group; it merely focuses on interaction between individuals – see Steiner's comments (Steiner 1974, 1983, 1986) and especially Ch. 5 below.

In large part, social psychology's crises can be attributed to its reductionist theorizing. This critique has been articulated by a number of people, but its most forceful and integrated presentation is from European social psychologists, particularly those working in Europe during the late 1960s and early 1970s (e.g. Billig 1976; Doise 1978, 1986; Israel and Tajfel 1972; Moscovici 1972; Tajfel 1981a; Taylor and Brown 1979). It is not exclusively a European critique by any means (see, for example, Cartwright 1979; Festinger 1980; Gergen 1973; Pepitone 1981; Sampson 1977, 1981; Steiner 1974, 1983, 1986; Triandis 1977; Zander 1979), but it was perhaps Europe that most eagerly took up the gauntlet thrown down by the critique. At this time a European approach to experimental social psychology was born, and was nurtured and guided by a small group with the late Henri Tajfel in Britain and Serge Moscovici in France emerging as perhaps the leading figures. The *European Journal of Social Psychology* was created and an association formed to bring together people in Europe – to allow them to meet and exchange ideas. (See Doise 1982; Jaspars 1980, 1986; Tajfel 1972b for some of this historical background.) The principal and explicit aim was to forge a non-reductionist social psychology which would be able to deal with the dynamic relationship between individual and society without sociologizing or individualizing it: that is, to explore the *social* dimension of human behaviour (Hogg and Abrams 1985; Tajfel 1984).

It is in this context that the social identity approach has developed as a spearhead of this attack on individualism in social psychology. Its initial focus was the study of intergroup relations – an assault on the hollowness of explanations of international conflict, genocide, and so on, purely in terms of individuality without any consideration of sociohistorical factors (see Ch. 3 below). Over the years the approach has broadened out to include a widening variety of group phenomena and to become an attempt to reintroduce the concept of 'group' as a distinct explanatory tool in social psychology (e.g. Turner et al. 1987). Social identity is a *perspective* and an *approach* in that it is a particular *type* of theory, a particular way of approaching social psychology. It is also a *theory* in that it comprises a set of interrelated propositions from which empirically testable hypotheses can be generated. These two aspects are considered to be interrelated: theory can only be developed within the context of a distinct and explicit metatheory.

For the remainder of this chapter we shall discuss the social identity approach: first at the level of metatheory (what kind of a theory is it?), and then at the level of theory (what does the theory itself say?). At this point it is important to differentiate between two uses of the term 'social identity'. In the strict sense outlined above social identity is a formally defined and theoretically integrated set of processes and assumptions explaining the relationship between sociocultural forces and the form and content of individual social behaviour. It is used in a coherent theory formulated within a specific critique and specific model of the social world and is represented in a relatively clearly circumscribed literature (e.g. Tajfel 1978a, 1981a, 1982a; Turner and Giles 1981; Turner *et al.* 1987). The second, broadly descriptive usage of the term 'social identity' does not share our perspective, conceptual language, or theoretical propositions, and above all does not refer to the same literature (cf. Baumeister 1986, Sarbin and Scheibe 1983). However, this is not to say that the latter has no relevance to the former; it is merely that we believe that the former goes some if not a long way towards the development of a more theoretically integrated and truly *social* social psychology.

Social identity: themes, questions, and context

The social identity approach rests upon certain assumptions concerning the nature of people and society, and their interrelationship. Specifically, it maintains that *society comprises social categories which stand in power and status relations to one another*. 'Social categories' refers to the division of people on the basis of nationality (British/French), race (Arab/Jew), class (worker/capitalist), occupation (doctor/welder), sex (man/woman), religion (Muslim/Hindu), and so forth, while 'power and status relations' refers to the fact that some categories in society have greater power, prestige, status, and so on, than others. Categories do not exist in isolation. A category is only such in contrast with another. For example, the social category 'Black' is meaningless unless it serves to differentiate between those who *are* 'Black' and those who are not – that is, a contrasting category. Any individual is at once a member of many different social categories (e.g. a male Buddhist Australian surfer), but is unlikely to be a member of mutually exclusive categories, such as Protestant *and* Catholic in Northern Ireland.

The nature of the social categories and their relations to one another lend a society its distinctive social structure, a structure which precedes individual human beings. Individual people are born into a particular society and thus social categories are largely pre-existent *vis-à-vis* individuals. However, the social structure is not a static monolithic entity. On the contrary, it is constantly in flux, constantly changing (gradually or very rapidly) as a consequence of forces of economics and history, categories come and go (prior to the mid-twentieth century there was no such occupational category as 'computer programmer'), their defining features alter (historical modifications to stereotypes of North American Blacks), their relations with other categories change (intergroup relations between the sexes), and so on.

The social identity perspective has, in keeping with all theories or approaches, it progenitors, its intellectual pedigree. In characterizing society as structured in terms of social categories it shares with much of sociology a structuralist perspective (cf. Durkheim [1893] 1933; Parsons 1951; Merton 1957; Marx [1844] 1963; Weber 1930). However, in emphasizing (as we shall see later) the forces and pressures upon social groups to differentiate themselves from other groups rather than strive for similarity, we can detect a greater intellectual debt to 'conflict' theorists such as Marx and Weber than 'consensus' theorists such as Comte (1877), Durkheim [1893] (1933), Parsons (1951), Spencer (1896), and Merton (1957). That is not to say that there are *no* 'consensus' themes embraced by the social identity concept, merely a greater emphasis on conflict. In Chapter 8 we shall see how the consensus theme surfaces in Sherif's (1936) treatment of norms, Moscovici's (Farr and Moscovici 1984) notion of 'social representations', and the social identity approach to conformity.

Consensus structuralists tend to characterize society as a structured whole in which, although there is role differentiation between groups, there are no deep ideological divisions. There is instead a broad social consensus or agreement on the 'rules of the game', on what is socially acceptable and what is not. Order and stability is the normal state of affairs, and those who do not share society's values or do not fit society's roles are considered deviant; where 'deviants' are not just different but abnormal in that the socialization process responsible for transmitting society's values to the child has been ineffectual. Furthermore, the structural functionalist (literally 'social structure serves an adaptive function') use of the 'organism' metaphor for society characterizes the deviant as dysfunctional in the sense that a disease or diseased organ may kill the organism.

Marx and Weber (conflict structuralists), on the other hand, draw attention to profound differences in ideology, values, beliefs, and so forth which can characterize different groups in a society. They focus upon the intrinsically competitive or conflictual nature of relations between groups, which they trace to pervasive intergroup power and status differentials. Order, stability, and stasis is a frail and transient state of affairs in a world of dynamic social flux. This perspective opens the way for an examination of how dominant groups can create and enforce (materially and/or ideologically) a *status quo* that masks, submerges, or inhibits overt conflict (e.g. Beynon 1975; Parkin 1971). The social identity approach is firmly wedded to this 'conflict' view of society.

Although there is a tendency among structuralist sociologists (Durkheim in particular) to reify social structure, to treat it as a material *thing* rather than a pattern of relationships, sociological theory, in plotting its parameters, almost always has something to say (albeit often only implicitly) about its assumptions concerning the relationship between individual and society. Durkheim believes society affects individuals by creating, through common ways of acting, a 'collective consciousness' that acts as a moral constraint upon behaviour. In a similar vein, McDougall introduced his concept of 'group mind' (McDougall 1921) which we discussed earlier. A similar notion has been used by Sumner to describe how social groups create their own distinctive customs or 'folkways' (Sumner 1906). In general, sociology and early non-experimental social psychology leave unanswered the question of precisely how, through what psychological process, society or the group actually installs itself in the mind of the individual and thereby shapes behaviour. It is not enough to simply say that society or groups create a collective consciousness or a group mind. As social psychologists we need to know how and why the individual's mind accomplishes this task.

Freud's attempt to address this question focuses on the instinctive sexuality of the child which brings it into conflict with the same-sex parent (Freud 1922). Both wish to possess sexually the opposite-sex parent. The resolution of this crisis is achieved by the child internalizing (or symbolically becoming) the same-sex parent, and thus simultaneously taking on board all the values and norms of the society. This event becomes the process whereby individuals are influenced by all groups. Freud's approach has been influential in Parsons' sociology (Parsons 1951), and much contemporary social psychology of small group dynamics (see Blumberg et al. 1983; Kellerman 1981).

A very different approach is adopted by symbolic interactionism (Mead 1934; Meltzer, Petras, and Reynolds 1975). Here, society's influence on the individual is mediated by self-conception, where the 'self' itself initially arises and is constantly modified through life by interaction between individuals. This interaction is largely symbolic since behaviour is not only *functional* but overwhelmingly *expressive* (Goffman 1959): for example, wearing glasses is functional in that it improves vision, and is expressive in that it can communicate wisdom, 'bookishness', senility, and so on. Symbols are above all consensual or shared (they must be in order to fulfil their communicative function), and thus by symbolizing ourselves as others do, or taking the role of the other, we have constructed ourselves as social objects, as microcosms of the society in which we live. This approach assigns great importance to language as perhaps the medium *par excellence* of symbolic interaction (see Ch. 9 below). It has also been used to study the child's acquisition of language (Lock 1978), and under the broad rubric of 'labelling theory', to examine the social processes which create 'deviant' identities such as drug addicts (Becker 1963), the insane (Lemert 1951; Scheff 1975; Szasz 1961), and institutionalized identities (Goffman 1968).

Sharing a slightly different emphasis on self or identity is Marx, who argues that there is a difference between a statistical or demographic category and a social class (we must remember that Marx was primarily concerned with social divisions in terms of class). Social categories, which are essentially statistical entities (e.g. 'people with red hair'), become human groups, that is psychological entities, through recognition of a common plight. Social action arises in terms of this identity (literally *identical* plight, experience, etc.). This distinction is also highlighted by the social identity perspective –

Tajfel's use of 'social categories' and 'human groups' in the title of one of his later books (Tajfel 1981a). The social identity concept, however, directly addresses the psychological processes involved in translating social categories into human groups, in creating a psychological reality from a social reality.

In so far as traditional approaches in social psychology tend to focus upon the *individual in the group* (but see Weigert 1983), the social identity approach can be considered to be much more closely linked to sociological perspectives. It turns the traditional social psychological approach on its head, to use a familiar phrase, and examines the *group in the individual*. By redefining the fundamental problematic of social psychology in this way it 'socializes' (or resocializes) social psychology. In keeping with Marx and the symbolic interactionists (especially labelling theorists) rather than Parsons, it considers identity and self-definition to mediate between social categories, as statistical or historical entities, and individual behaviour. However, it goes further: as a social *psychological* approach, it explores the psychological processes involved in translating social categories into human groups.

These processes create identity and generate behaviours which have a characteristic and distinctive form, that of group behaviour. Sumner writes:

> a differentiation arises between ourselves, the we-group, or in-group, and everybody else, or the others-groups, out-groups. The insiders in a we-group are in a relation of peace, order, law, government, and industry to each other. Their relation to all outsiders, or others-groups, is one of war and plunder, except so far as agreements have modified it.
>
> (Sumner 1906: 12)

Sumner coins the term 'ethnocentrism' to capture this essential 'form' taken by group behaviour, and it is this (though not necessarily to quite such an extreme degree) that the social identity approach seeks to explain.

There is also a functionalist strand to the social identity approach in that the psychological *processes* involved in self-conceptionalization and group behaviour are considered to be largely trans-historical and universal because they fulfil a fundamental adaptive function for the human organism (e.g. Doise 1978; but see Billig 1985, for a different view). They are essentially processes of simplification and evaluation that serve to pattern experience and provide direction to behaviour, without which we would not be able to act at all. We would be overwhelmed and paralysed by overstimulation. In keeping with many of the dominant perspectives in social psychology – for example, cognitive consistency (Abelson et al. 1968), attribution (Harvey and Smith 1977), and social cognition (Fiske and Taylor 1984) – the social identity perspective assumes that the human organism seeks to impose order upon the potential chaos, William James' 'blooming, buzzing confusion', of raw experience (James 1890). There is, as Bartlett puts it, 'effort after meaning' (Bartlett 1932).

This assumption that groups are functional to both individual and society because of the adaptiveness of underlying psychological processes should be clearly distinguished from the 'social Darwinist' (e.g. Herbert Spencer – see Andreski 1971) doctrine that *specific* social structures and hence groups and relations between groups have evolved to represent the optimal social order for the times. The latter view simply serves to legitimate the status quo and, in the presence of mechanical laws of social evolution, emasculate human agency in social change. The organismic model of society which underpins much consensus structuralism (e.g. Parsons, Durkheim) facilitates this stance, though some sociologists, such as Merton, do raise the question of to whom particular societal organizations are functional.

In contrast, the social identity approach simply states that social groups are inevitable because they are functional – they fulfil individual and societal needs for order, structure, simplification, predictability, and so forth. All the rest *must* incorporate an historical analysis. It is not possible to predict or explain content or culture by recourse to psychological processes alone. Psychological processes ensure that groups are inevitable, but do not directly govern what type of groups they are, what characteristics they have, or how they relate to other groups. Functionalism of this sort is more in keeping with that to be found in social anthropology, for example the work of Malinowski (e.g. 1926), where social structure is treated as developing to fulfil basic human needs such as food, sex, shelter, and protection.

We have gone to some lengths in this section to state the general stance taken by the social identity approach and its relationship to other perspectives in social science. We have done this because we feel that theory out of context is like a ship without a helm, aimlessly cruising in circles over the same ground. If social psychology is to make systematic and cumulative advances, then it must stop going in circles, it must avoid 'reinventing the wheel'.

Before moving on to discuss the specific content of the theory of social identity, we should summarize the model upon which it rests (Table 2.1). Society is treated as a heterogenous collection of social categories which stand in power and status relations to one another, and whose dynamics are

Table 2.1 Social identity perspective in context

	Society	Individual
Assumptions	Hierarchically structured into discrete social categories which stand in power, status, and prestige relations to one another.	Cognitively simplifies and orders perceptions and experiences in order to be able to understand and act.
Sources	Conflict social theorists, e.g. Marx, Weber.	Cognitive psychology, e.g. Bartlett, Bruner.

subject to the forces of economics and history. People derive their identity (their sense of self, their self-concept) in great part from the social categories to which they belong. The group is thus in the individual, and the psychological processes responsible for this are also responsible for the form that group behaviour takes (e.g. ethnocentric). Individuals belong to many different social categories and thus potentially have a repertoire of many different identities to draw upon. It is inconceivable that two person's life experiences can be identical, so it is inevitable that we all have our own unique and distinct repertoires (similar to those of others to varying degrees). In this way we can account for the apparent uniqueness of each individual human being: every individual is *uniquely* placed in the social structure and is thus unique (Berger and Luckmann 1971). Georg Simmel describes it thus:

> The groups with which the individual is affiliated constitute a system of coordinates, as it were, such that each new group with which he becomes affiliated circumscribes him more exactly and more unambiguously. . . . [T]he larger the number of groups to which an individual belongs, the more improbable it is that other persons will exhibit the same combination of group-affiliations, that these particular groups will 'intersect' once again (in a second individual).
>
> (Simmel 1955: 140)

Here we have uniqueness and individuality constructed out of identity (literally out of being *identical* to others, but a unique combination of others), and so have no need for the concept of an *a priori*, innate, or unconscious unique self which is often invoked by more individualistic treatments of the self (e.g. Erikson 1959; Freud 1922; Jung 1946; Rogers 1951; Maslow 1954).

Social identity: theory

CATEGORIZATION

When you look at a rainbow you see seven relatively discrete bands of colour, and yet what is actually there is a continuous distribution of light of different wavelengths. Your cognitive apparatus has automatically divided the continuum into seven perceptually distinct colour categories, each encompassing (or obscuring) a range of different wavelengths. The cognitive process of categorization simplifies perception. It is fundamental to the adaptive functioning of the human organism, as it serves to structure the potentially infinite variability of stimuli into a more manageable number of distinct categories (Cantor, Mischel, and Schwartz 1982; Bruner 1958; Doise 1978; Rosch 1978). Effectively, it brings into sharp focus a nebulous world, by accentuating similarities between objects within the *same* category and differences between stimuli in *different* categories. That is, the process of categorization produces an accentuation effect (Tajfel 1957, 1959).

The classic experiment is by Tajfel and Wilkes (1963), who found that subjects who were judging the length of individual lines from a continuous series where the four shorter were labelled 'A' and the four longer 'B' significantly exaggerated the difference in length between A-type and B-type lines (Tajfel and Wilkes 1963). They also tended to overestimate the similarity in length of lines having the same label. If the label, which is an A–B dichotomy or categorization, was unrelated to line length, then no accentuation effect occurred. Tajfel reasoned that the accentuating effect of categorization is only a special case of a more general effect arising from people's dependence on peripheral dimensions (whether a line had the category label A or B in this case) which they believe to be correlated with the focal dimension which they are to judge (line length in this case). (This accentuation effect is discussed in more detail in Ch. 4 below; see also Doise 1978; Eiser 1986; Eiser and Stroebe 1972; and Tajfel 1981a.)

The accentuation effect also occurs in the judgement of social stimuli, that is people. For example, Secord, Bevan, and Katz (1956) and Secord (1959) presented their subjects with a series of photographs of faces ranging on a continuum from pure Caucasian to pure Negro and asked them to rate each face for degree of physiognomic and psychological 'negroness'. They found that the subjects generated their own peripheral dichotomy of black *versus* white and tended to accentuate similarities within and differences between those faces falling in the two categories.

Attitude statements are also social stimuli, and Eiser and colleagues (see Doise 1978; Eiser and Stroebe 1972; Eiser 1980; Eiser and van der Pligt 1984) have explored the ways in which categorization produces accentuation here as well. It seems, then, that the categorization process produces the same kinds of cognitive distortion in the perception of both physical and social stimuli, though our interest clearly lies mainly with the latter.

Categorization generates accentuation only on those perceptual dimensions which are believed to be associated (or correlated) with the categorization (Doise, Deschamps, and Meyer 1978; Tajfel, Sheikh, and Gardner 1964). So, if the focal dimension were 'sense of rhythm', then quite possibly the categorization black/white might produce accentuation whereas male/female would not. If it were 'nurturant', then categorization by sex would be likely to cause accentuation, while race would not. Basically, the categorization process produces stereotypic perceptions, that is the perception or judgement of all members of a social category or group as sharing some characteristic which distinguishes them from some other social group. The particular dimensions on which this occurs are those *subjectively believed* to distinguish between categories, where the origin of these beliefs are to be found in the relevant cultural history of the society in which one lives (see Ch. 4 below for details).

The final point to make concerning the accentuation effect is that it is more pronounced when the categorization is important, salient, of immediate relevance, of personal value, etc. to the individual. Tajfel incorporated this expectation in his theory (Tajfel 1959), and Marchand has provided empirical support from individuals' perception of the area of various shapes (Marchand 1970). As regards social categories, there is abundant evidence that those who place a greater importance on a particular categorization tend to stereotype more extremely than others – perhaps we might call these people 'prejudiced' (see Chs. 3 and 4 below).

In order to explain this last point, we ought to remind ourselves that the categorization of people is rarely, if ever, conducted in the dispassionate and objective manner in which, say, an ornithologist classifies birds. The categorization of people – social categorization – is overwhelmingly with reference to *self*. We are also people, so categorizing others must have direct implications for ourselves in so far as it says something about the category relations between self and other. People tend to classify others on the basis of their similarities and differences to *self*; they constantly perceive others as members of the same category as self (ingroup members) or as members of a different category to self (outgroup members). To explain how the involvement of self in social categories can account for variations (temporal, situational, inter-individual) in the degree of accentuation or stereotyping, we have to introduce a second process: *social comparison*.

But first, we must look at the cognitive consequences of the involvement of self in the categorization process. Just as we categorize objects, experiences and other people, we also categorize ourselves (Turner 1981b, 1982, 1985; Turner *et al.* 1987). The outcome of this process of self-categorization is an accentuation of similarities between self and other ingroupers and differences between self and outgroupers, that is self-stereotyping. To be more precise, self-categorization causes self-perception and self-definition to become more in terms of the individual's representation of the defining characteristics of the group, or the group *prototype* (but see Chs. 4 and 8 below for specialized use of this term). Stereotyping is considered to occur on *all* dimensions subjectively believed to be correlated with the relevant intergroup categorization, that is attitudes, beliefs and values (the traditional foci of stereotyping research – see Ch. 4), affective reactions (see Ch. 5), emotions (see Ch. 7), behavioural norms (see Ch. 8), styles of speech and language (see Ch. 9), and so on. Thus self-categorization at once accomplishes two things: it causes one to perceive oneself as 'identical' to, to have the same social identity as, other members of the category – it places oneself in the relevant social category, or places the group in one's head; and it generates category-congruent behaviour on dimensions which are stereotypic (in the broad sense above) of the category. Self-categorization is the process which transforms individuals into groups (see Ch. 5).

SOCIAL COMPARISON

Statements about how good, intelligent, musical, clean, tall, well-dressed, and so on, people are, are comparative. Whether someone is considered to have a great deal of a quality or very little of it depends upon who this person is compared against – that is, the *subjective frame of reference* that is being employed. The subjective frame of reference refers to the set of comparison others that is subjectively available to the individual in making a particular judgement, and it is this that governs the judgement made (Turner 1985; Turner *et al.* 1987). While society as a whole, or at least one's range of experiences in society, dictates the subjective frame of reference, people can exercise a certain degree of control over this by choosing a restricted range of comparison others. One instance where this is very likely to occur is when we are making comparisons between *ourselves* and others – called *social comparisons* by Festinger (1954; Suls and Miller 1977).

The meaning attached by social identity theorists to the term 'social comparison' (e.g. Tajfel 1972a, 1978a) is somewhat different from that first intended by Festinger. Festinger's theory of social comparison processes states that we have a need to establish the veracity of our beliefs, opinions, and abilities in order to have confidence in them, and that usually we do this by direct comparison with physical reality: if we believe a priceless porcelain urn is fragile we can always drop it on the concrete to see. However, when no such direct physical reality checks are readily available (there is a heavily armed guard watching over the urn), then we resort to making comparisons with the opinions of others – social comparisons. In contrast, the social identity perspective holds that *all* knowledge is socially derived through social comparisons, and this includes knowledge about the physical world. One's confidence in the truth' of one's views is provided by the establishment of consensus – agreement between people. Physical reality appears objectively given, indisputable and non-problematic because there is a widespread and extremely firm consensus, which ensures that we rarely, if ever, encounter any disagreement to challenge our perceptions. This is *not* to say that reality does not exist, rather that one's perceptions of it are socially structured. In Chapter 8 we discuss these ideas much more fully (see also Hogg and Turner 1987a; Moscovici 1976; Tajfel 1972a).

Through social comparison we learn about ourselves and obtain confidence in the veracity and utility of our beliefs. That is, we are motivated to make social comparisons in order to be confident about our perceptions of ourselves, other people, and the world in general. However, we also like to feel that our perceptions, rooted in one consensus, are better and more correct than other possible perceptions rooted in other consensuses. If we treat different consensuses as defining the parameters of different groups, then we can see that people strive to hold the views of their own group and see the world in the same way as do other ingroup members, and that ingroup perceptions are positively evaluated as providing 'true' understanding. In fact, we can go even further to reveal that in general there will be a tendency to positively evaluate *all* stereotypic properties of the ingroup (the phenomenon of ethnocentrism) as they distinguish the consensus to which one subscribes from that to which one does not. Let us pursue this evaluative theme.

When making an intergroup social comparison, that is between self as ingroup member and other as outgroup member (or between in and outgroup as a whole), there is a tendency to maximize intergroup distinctiveness – to differentiate between the groups as much as possible on as many dimensions as possible. However, this automatic accentuation effect is guided by an important self-evaluative motivational consideration. Since dimensions of social comparison are overwhelmingly evaluative (Osgood, Suci, and Tannenbaum 1957), it is important to accentuate intergroup differences especially on those dimensions which reflect favourably upon ingroup. By differentiating ingroup from outgroup on dimensions on which the ingroup falls at the evaluatively positive pole, the ingroup acquires a *positive distinctiveness*, and thus a relatively *positive social identity* in comparison to the outgroup. Since self is defined in terms of the ingroup (self and ingroup are identical), this selective differentiation accomplishes a relatively positive self-evaluation that endows the individual with a sense of well-being, enhanced self-worth and self-esteem.

The social identity approach proposes the existence of a fundamental individual motivation for self-esteem (e.g. Tajfel and Turner 1979; Turner 1981b, 1982), which is satisfied in an intergroup context by maximizing the difference between ingroup and outgroup on those dimensions which reflect positively upon ingroup. There is some direct experimental evidence for the self-esteem hypothesis, namely that intergroup differentiation elevates self-esteem (Hogg et al. 1986; Oakes and Turner 1980). That people have a need for self-esteem is supported by clinical investigations which show the dire consequences of acutely low self-esteem (e.g. Martin, Abramson, and Alloy 1984). However, in Chapter 10 we return to this issue to raise some questions concerning different levels at which motivation underlying self-conception and group behaviour may operate.

Categorization and social comparison operate together (see Turner 1981b) to generate a specific form of behaviour: group behaviour. This involves intergroup differentiation and discrimination, ingroup favouritism, perceptions of the evaluative superiority of the ingroup over the outgroup, stereotypic perception of ingroup, outgroup, and self, conformity to group norms, affective preference for ingroup over outgroup, and so on. *Categorization* leads to stereotypic (in the broad sense introduced here) perceptions of self, ingroup and outgroup, and also a degree of accentuation of intergroup differences. *Social comparison* accounts for the selectivity of the accentuation effect (accentuation mainly occurs on self-enhancing dimensions) and the magnitude of the exaggeration of intergroup differences and intragroup similarities.

SOCIAL IDENTITY AND THE SELF-CONCEPT

Thus far we have discussed 'process'. We shall now discuss structure, cognitive structure. The self-reflective nature of human beings entails that self is both object and subject, that there is a 'me' for the 'I' to reflect upon. Although there has been and still is endless debate over the nature of and relationship between the 'me' and the 'I', we shall merely assume that the 'I' is cognitive process (largely automatic but occasionally deliberate) and the 'me' is cognitive structure in the form of the self-concept. There is a tension or dialectic between 'I' and 'me', in that while 'I' is responsible for constructing 'me', it is constrained and guided in its task by the specific content of the 'me' it has constructed. For example, if my 'me' is 'punk', my 'I' will not very easily be able to construct a 'solicitor' 'me' for me!

The social identity approach adopts a particular model of self, or how the 'me' is structured, which is based on ideas of Gergen (1971) and distinctions made in social identity research between qualitatively different types of behaviour (e.g. Tajfel and Turner 1979; Tajfel 1972a, 1974). This is most completely described by Turner (1982) (see Fig. 2.1). The self-concept comprises the totality of self-descriptions and self-evaluations subjectively available to the individual. It is not just a catalogue of evaluative self-descriptions, it is textured and structured into circumscribed and relatively distinct constellations called *self-identifications*. There is no reason to assume that self-identifications should be mutually exclusive – it is quite possible that one self-identification may contain some self-descriptions that are contradictory, and some that are congruent with those subsumed by another self-identification. For example, the self-identification 'soldier' may include self-descriptions as loyal, tough, aggressive, dedicated, selfless, and willing to kill on others' behalf, while the self-identification 'Christian' may include loyal, strong, *gentle*, dedicated, selfless, and *unwilling* to kill at all.

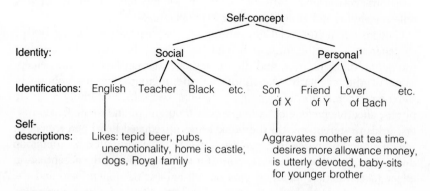

Figure 2.1   The structure of self

[1]Personal identifications are almost always grounded in relationships with specific individuals (or objects).

THE SOCIAL IDENTITY APPROACH 25

This is possible because people do not *subjectively* experience the self-concept in its entirety but rather as relatively discrete *self-images* which are dependent on 'context'. Different times, places, and circumstances render different self-identifications 'salient' self-images. The self is thus both enduring and stable, and also responsive to situational or exogenous factors.

Self-identifications can be described as falling into one of two relatively separate subsystems of the self-concept: *social identity* or *personal identity*. Social identity contains *social identifications*: identity-contingent self-descriptions deriving from membership in social categories (nationality, sex, race, occupation, sports teams, and more short-lived and transient group memberships). Personal identity contains *personal identifications*: self-descriptions which are 'more personal in nature and that usually denote specific attributes of the individual' (Gergen 1971: 62) (e.g. idiosyncratic descriptions of self which are essentially tied to and emerge from close and enduring interpersonal relationships).

The social identity approach primarily focuses upon the concept of social rather than personal identity. It simply maintains that under certain conditions social identity is more salient than personal identity in self-conception, and that when this is the case behaviour is qualitatively different: it is group behaviour. There is a continuum of self-conception ranging from exclusively social to exclusively personal identity (but see Stephenson 1981 and 1984, and Chapter 6 below, for a slightly different interpretation), which is associated with a behavioural continuum ranging from ethnocentrism, or *group behaviour*, to idiosyncratic *interpersonal behaviour*. The specific *content* of behaviour depends on which particular social or personal identification is subjectively salient (Fig. 2.2).

Continua	Person pole		Group pole	
(1) Self-conception:	Personal identity	⟷	Social identity	
(2) Person-perception:	Idiosyncratic	⟷	Stereotypic	
(3) Social behaviour:	Personal interindividual behaviour	⟷	Intergroup and intragroup behaviour	

Figure 2.2 Person–group continua

Since social self-identifications are essentially social self-categorizations, it is not difficult to generate a *principle* governing their salience. Within any given social frame of reference that social categorization will become salient which best 'fits' – using Bruner's terminology (Bruner 1957) – the relevant information available to the individual; Oakes (1987) and Turner (1985) hypothesize that social categories fit the available 'data' to the degree that they maximize the contrast between intercategory differences and intracategory similarities. In other words, the cognitive system processes information in a given context so as to explain the relevant similarities and differences in the most parsimonious way possible; that is, it generates a categorization which accounts for the maximum amount of variance. In this way the simplest meaning for the context is generated.

So, for example, if one is engaged in a discussion with three other people in which one agrees with you while the other two agree with each other but disagree with you and your supporter, then sex may become salient if you and your supporter are male and the other two are female. Self-conceptualization is likely to be in terms of sex-category membership (Hogg 1985a, and Hogg and Turner 1987b, find empirical support for this). If the relevant agreements and disagreements (similarities and differences) correspond to race, then race will be salient and self-conceptualization will be in terms of race, and so on. This 'goodness of fit' process does not depend on other people being *physically* present. It can occur when others are cognitively present, and hence can occur when one is on one's own.

Individual motivations to adopt certain self-categorizations and avoid others feed into this seemingly mechanical process via the individual's ability to subjectively redefine the context or negotiate behaviourally a new context for all to see. The individual is trying to select a different subjective frame of reference. Let us return to our four-person discussion group above. Relevant agreements and disagreements initially render sex salient; however, self-categorization in terms of sex may be considered undesirable by, say, one of the females. In order to avoid this identity she might present arguments and opinions and behave in such a manner that relevant agreements and disagreements are not explicable in terms of sex, but rather in terms of political affiliation: she and one of the males are now in agreement while at odds with the other two, who are in agreement with each other. Political affiliation is now rendered salient and self-conceptualization is in terms of political identity. As you can see, there is a dialectical relationship between cognitive processes and motivations or goals. There is a dynamic negotiation of self-conceptualization.

SOCIAL IDENTITY AND SOCIAL STRUCTURE

The social identity approach makes an important contribution to an understanding of the dynamics of large-scale group relations: intergroup conflict, collective action, social movements, and so forth (Tajfel and Turner 1979; Taylor and McKirnan 1984; see especially Ch. 3 below). This macro-social emphasis is particularly important since it directly addresses the relationship between social processes and individual behaviour – the dialectical relationship between society and the individual, mediated by social identity. In many respects it was to deal with this feature that the concept of social identity was originally fashioned by Tajfel (e.g. 1974).

Societies comprise large-scale social categories (race, sex, religion, class, occupation, etc.) which stand in power, status, and prestige relations to one another. The dominant group (or groups) has the material power to promulgate its own version of the nature of society, the groups within it and their relationships. That is, it imposes the dominant value system and ideology which is carefully constructed to benefit itself, and to legitimate and perpetuate the status quo (see Larrain 1979, for discussion of perspectives on ideology). Individual human beings are born into this structure, and by virtue of their place of birth, skin colour, parentage, physiology, and so forth, fall into some categories and not others. To the extent that they internalize the dominant ideology and identify with these externally designated categories, they acquire particular social identities which may mediate evaluatively positive or negative self-perceptions.

Subordinate group membership potentially confers on members evaluatively negative social identity and hence lower self-esteem, which is an unsatisfactory state of affairs and mobilizes individuals to attempt to remedy it. They can accomplish this in various different ways, depending in part upon *subjective belief structures*, that is the individuals' beliefs concerning the nature of society and the relations between groups within it. Subjective belief structures usually reflect the dominant ideology (after all, it is initially through social consensus about one prefabricated version of reality that the dominant group hopes to retain its privileged position), *but* the dominant ideology does not necessarily have to coincide with the 'true' nature of society.

There are two broad types of subjective belief structure: *social mobility* and *social change* (Table 2.2; see Fig. 3.1). Social mobility refers to a belief that the boundaries between groups are permeable. Individuals can with ease 'pass' from one group into another. They can as individuals by dint of hard work, connections, and so forth, become redefined (along perhaps with their immediate family) as members of the dominant group. A belief in social mobility simply leads subordinate group members to adopt individualistic strategies to attempt to cast aside their subordinate social identity with its

Table 2.2 Subjective social belief structures and strategies for positive self-image

	Subjective Social belief structure Mobility	*Change*
Strategies for positive self-image	Individual mobility or passing into the dominant group	(a) Social creativity (select different dimension of comparison, redefine existing dimension, select different comparison group) (b) Social competition

Note: See Chapter 3 and Figure 3.1 for further details.

potentially negative connotations and material inferiority in favour of the dominant group's social identity and concomitant material advantage and positive evaluation. Since this strategy leaves the status quo unchanged, in terms of the power and status relations between groups, and inhibits collective action such as riots and demonstrations on the part of the subordinate group, it is clearly very much in the interests of the dominant group to promulgate an ideology of social mobility. This is the 'myth' of individual freedom which characterizes some contemporary western capitalist societies. It is a 'myth' because individual mobility is not easy to accomplish, it is in fact extremely difficult to successfully 'pass' from subordinate to dominant group. Those few who do, do so almost by special dispensation in order to perpetuate the myth, to become the token woman truck driver, or token black solicitor.

Social change is rather an unfortunate term as it does not necessarily refer to social change in its common parlance usage to denote *radical* change. Instead, it refers to a belief that the boundaries between groups are rigid, fixed and impermeable. They cannot be crossed. It is not possible as an individual to simply cast aside the mantle of subordinate group membership and take up that of the dominant group. You are stuck with your potentially negative low-status group membership and can only resort to strategies aimed at improving your *group's* social status. These are group, not individualistic, strategies, and they are of two kinds: *social creativity* and *social competition*.

Social creativity strategies are adopted if the individual cannot subjectively conceive of *cognitive alternatives* to the status quo. That is, the individual is unable to envisage any other possible social arrangement to that which already exists. The dominant group can create an ideology to enforce this view: e.g. genetic arguments enshrined in a reverence for science which serve to subordinate women, or religious ideologies that attribute group membership to destiny (e.g. the Hindu caste system). Social creativity strategies do not alter the status quo, yet they do render the social identity of the subordinate group relatively more positive. For example, the subordinate group can select and try to gain recognition for different dimensions of intergroup comparison, on which the subordinate ingroup can be positively evaluated. This strategy is nicely illustrated by a study by Lemaine in which two groups of children were set the task of building a hut, but one group was handicapped by being provided with substandard materials (Lemaine 1966). They of course lost the competition, but they rationalized it by stressing how much nicer their garden was than that of their opponents.

Another creativity strategy involves the evaluative redefinition of traditionally negative characteristics. For example, the use of the slogan 'black is beautiful' by American blacks in the 1960s, or the positive re-evaluation by women of traditionally negatively valued stereotypic characteristics of women (see Condor and Henwood 1986).

A third strategy involves the choice of a different comparison group altogether. Rather than make social comparisons with the dominant group where the outcome is inevitable and immutable (relatively low self-esteem for subordinate group members), comparisons can be made with other subordinate groups or, better still, with even lower-status groups. This is the phenomenon of working-class sexism (Firestone 1970) or 'poor white racism': low-status groups expressing more overt and extreme prejudice towards other low-status groups than is expressed by high-status groups.

These social creativity strategies are most likely to be used in combination with historical circumstances dictating their relative predominance, in order to improve the self-image through positive social identity of members of low-status groups. The reaction of the dominant group would depend on the strategy being adopted. Lateral social comparisons among subordinate groups would invite no response as this essentially constitutes the very successful 'divide and rule' approach to domination. If, however, the subordinate group chooses to adopt different *dimensions* of comparison with the dominant group or else to redefine the poles of existing dimensions, then the dominant group must ensure that the process doesn't go too far. It must either challenge and repudiate (by ideological means) a subordinate group's attempts or else simply shift to, and legitimate, other dimensions of intergroup comparison. Dominant groups, by virtue of their material control of the media, can often do this very easily.

Real confrontation between subordinate and dominant groups (*social competition*) only arises when the subordinate group can conceive of cognitive alternatives. The legitimacy of the status quo is called into question, it is no longer seen to be stable and immutable, and alternative social arrangements and means of bringing them about are easily envisaged and articulated. Real social change is possible. The subordinate group need no longer remain subordinate. A radical alternative ideology – see Parkin's 'radical value system' (Parkin 1971) – is developed and projects the subordinate group into direct competition with the dominant group. This can involve relatively constitutional politicization of discontent (e.g. the black civil rights movement of the 1960s), violent terrorism (e.g. the Black Panther, and Bader–Meinhof movements of the 1970s), civil war (e.g. Northern Ireland), revolution (e.g. Iran), and passive resistance (e.g. Gandhi).

The macro-social application of the social identity approach will be covered in further detail in Chapter 3, and will also be returned to in later chapters where extensions and empirical evidence will be discussed.

Conclusion

In this chapter we have outlined the basic assumptions and specific theoretical constructions of the social identity approach. We have introduced the language of the social identity approach so that subsequent chapters need not be unnecessarily burdened with the ground-work and can move immediately into more detailed elaboration and exploration of specific aspects of the approach. We have provided the bare bones. Subsequent chapters will add the flesh. A second crucial role of this chapter has been to furnish a context for the social identity approach. We have tried to relate it to or locate it in a broader discussion of what we feel should constitute *social* psychology. We have outlined the questions the approach seeks to address and tried to describe what *type* of theory it is and how it relates to other perspectives on people, society, and their relationship in social psychology and some relevant other social sciences. We strongly urge the reader to relate later chapters to this one. Let us now go on to address such questions as: What evidence is there for this approach? In what areas has it been applied? What are its limitations? What are its strengths? In the course of the ensuing chapters we hope to answer some of these.

Each of the following chapters deals with a separate aspect of group behaviour, and each has the same format: a detailed critical review of traditional social psychological approaches, often occupying as much as two-thirds of the chapter, is followed by a discussion and evaluation of the contribution already made, and that yet to be made, by the social identity approach.

Recommended reading

There is no text relevant to this chapter in general. However, Israel and Tajfel (1972), and Strickland, Aboud, and Gergen (1976) provide good coverage of the 'crisis' literature, and Israel and Tajfel (1972), Billig (1976), and Doise (1978) all deliver excellent critiques of reductionism. For an overview of perspectives in sociology we would recommend Cuff and Payne (1984). As regards the social identity approach, Tajfel (1978a, 1981a, 1982a) has edited a series of detailed and specialist books. The recent book by Turner et al. (1987) focuses more on self-categorization, while Tajfel and Turner (1979) is the best account of macro-social aspects. Turner and Giles (1981) is a good edited collection of contributions from researchers using the social identity perspective to examine intergroup behaviour.

3

Intergroup behaviour

Two mighty powers have . . . been engaged in a most obstinate war for six and thirty moons past. It began upon the following occasion. It is allowed on all hands, that the primitive way of breaking eggs before we eat them, was upon the larger end: but his present Majesty's grand-father, while he was a boy, going to eat an egg, and breaking it according to the ancient practice, happened to cut one of his fingers. Whereupon the emperor his father, published an edict, commanding all his subjects, upon great penalties, to break the smaller end of their eggs. The people so highly resented this law, that our histories tell us, there have been six rebellions raised on that account; wherein one emperor lost his life, and another his crown . . . It is computed that, eleven thousand persons have, at several times, suffered death, rather than submit to break their eggs at the smaller end. Many hundred large volumes have been published upon this controversy: but the books of the Big-Endians have been long forbidden.

(Jonathan Swift, *Gulliver's Travels*, 1726)

A considerable part of the Negro's efforts of the past decades has been devoted, particularly in the South, to attaining a sense of dignity. For us, enduring the sacrifices of beatings, jailings and even death was acceptable merely to have access to public accommodations. To sit at a lunch counter or occupy the front seat of a bus had no effect on our material standard of living, but in removing a caste stigma it revolutionized our psychology and elevated the spiritual content of our being. Instinctively we struck out for dignity first because personal degradation as an inferior human being was even more keenly felt than material privation.

(Martin Luther King Jnr, *Chaos or Community*, 1967)

These two very different extracts illustrate some of the themes to be explored in this chapter. The first describes how intergroup conflict can arise out of the categorization of people into two groups on the basis of a relatively meaningless and arbitrary criterion. It describes how such small beginnings can result in extreme intergroup conflict, and how individuals fashion an identity from the category in which they fall: Big-Endians. The second extract also highlights the role of identity in intergroup behaviour: it illustrates how strategies of intergroup behaviour serve a psychological motive, that of positive self-evaluation, which can be more fundamental than more material goals.

Introduction

Intergroup behaviour refers to the way in which people behave towards one another as members of different social groups. For example, as negotiators in industrial disputes, as supporters of different teams, as members of different ethnic groups, or nations, as representatives of different tiers of an organization, and so on. In practice, research in this area tends, not surprisingly, to focus on more extreme forms of intergroup behaviour: intergroup prejudice, racism, sexism, nationalism, conflict, and political violence. It is in the study of intergroup behaviour and the relations between large-scale groups that social identity theory has its origins (Tajfel 1963).

We have already outlined the social identity perspective as a whole. In this chapter we elaborate those aspects which are particularly relevant to an explanation of intergroup behaviour. However, in order to establish the proper theoretical and historical context for the contribution made by the social identity approach it is necessary first to provide a detailed critical review of other social psychological approaches. This exercise occupies the first two-thirds of the chapter. We begin by examining early psychodynamic explanations of prejudice and discrimination, then show how some of these were developed into theories of relative deprivation and political conflict. We discuss Sherif's explanation of intergroup behaviour (Sherif 1962), which dwells on realistic conflict of interests between groups, and then describe how the social identity approach helps to resolve some of the ambiguities and limitations of these earlier perspectives. We describe the minimal group paradigm and explore some of the macro-social implications of social identity theory.

Psychodynamic approaches

THE AUTHORITARIAN PERSONALITY

One of the main problems for psychologists studying intergroup relations is to explain how individuals come to adopt a prejudiced view of outgroups. Perhaps the classic work is Adorno et al's study of The Authoritarian Personality (1950). The authors were convinced, in the light of post-war revelations of the extent of Nazi war atrocities, that prejudice (and by implication, discrimination) was the product of a particular kind of personality structure – that of authoritarianism. As Horkheimer and Flowerman, in their foreword to The Authoritarian Personality, pointed out, the problem was to

> explain the willingness of great masses of people to tolerate the mass extermination of their fellow citizens. What tissues in the life of our modern society remain

cancerous, . . . and what within the individual organism responds to certain stimuli in our culture with attitudes and acts of destructive aggression? . . . [and more specifically] What is there in the individual that renders him 'prejudiced' or 'unprejudiced'?

(ibid.:v)

Adorno *et al.* adopted Freud's psychodynamic model of the human mind to pursue the idea that racial prejudice is a symptom of individual sickness or abnormality of psychological functioning. They argued that children who are subjected to the child-rearing practices of overly harsh and restrictive parents develop an authoritarian-personality syndrome. Freud believed that the self was at least partly constructed by introjecting (that is, psychologically internalizing or incorporating) the parents. Such 'status anxious' parents who are obsessed with rules, duty, convention, and authority, secure dependence and obedience by emotional blackmail which makes their children both revere and despise them. The parents are idealized and hatred for them is *repressed*, to find its expression elsewhere. Identification with parents becomes generalized to all authority figures, and just as criticism of parents is repressed, so is that of these authority figures. The criticism is *projected* instead, onto outgroups, which lie beyond the individual's ego boundaries, and are of lower status and power than the ingroup. Repressed aspects of the personality, such as sexuality and malice, are attributed as outgroup characteristics and serve to rationalize the selection of outgroups as legitimate targets for aggression. Thus, repressed aggression towards authority is *displaced* onto the outgroup. The authoritarian personality syndrome is one in which the individual respects and defers to authority figures, is obsessed with rank and status, is intolerant of ambiguity and uncertainty, has a need for a clearly defined and rigidly structured world, and expresses hatred and discrimination against weaker others. The authoritarian is someone who is predisposed to be prejudiced.

Adorno *et al.* administered questionnaires to measure directly the attitudes and the personality of over 2,000 predominantly white middle-class individuals. The questionnaire contained a number of different scales. The Anti-Semitism (A–S) Scale measured hostility towards Jews. The psychological imbalance of the anti-Semite was reflected by endorsement of seemingly incompatible attitudes such as regarding Jews as being both too seclusive ('Jews keep too much to themselves, instead of taking the proper interest in community problems and good government') and too intrusive ('There are too many Jews in the various federal agencies and bureaus in Washington and they have too much control over our national policies'). There were also scales to measure anti-negro attitudes, Political and Economic Conservatism (PEC), and finally, general Ethnocentrism (E), from which Adorno *et al.* were able to show that individuals differed in their *general* hostility towards ethnic outgroups of all varieties. Ethnocentrism, a concept borrowed from

Sumner (1906), was conceived as the tendency to be inflexibly tied to one's own group, and to reject all things associated with other groups, or as Adorno et al. described it, a 'need for an outgroup' (Adorno et al. 1950: 148). Since outgroups are perceived as threatening and power-seeking, the survival of the ingroup (and hence oneself) depends on the elimination of all outgroups.

Adorno et al. went on to examine the *personality* structure (as distinct from attitudes) of the ethnocentric individual, by administering projective tests and interviews, and developing the now familiar F (tendency towards Fascism) Scale. This comprised items based on clinical interviews and it tapped components of the syndrome of authoritarianism, such as adherence to conventions, submission to authority figures, aggression against underlings, superstitious and stereotyped beliefs, obsession with power, and sexual guilt. Adorno et al. interpreted their findings as supporting the theory. Individuals who were highly authoritarian were also more ethnocentric, and evidence from the various questionnaires, interviews, and tests converged to suggest that the origins of this syndrome were in the child-rearing practices to which they had been exposed.

These findings have subsequently been subjected to considerable scrutiny, much of which has been summarized excellently by Roger Brown (1965) and Michael Billig (1976). Some criticisms focused on methodological and measurement problems, including response acquiescence (Cohn 1953), 'yea-saying' and 'nay-saying' (Couch and Keniston 1960), limitations of sampling (Hyman and Sheatsley 1954), and insufficiently rigorous coding of data (Brown 1965). Others argued that the rigid cognitive style of authoritarianism was not restricted to those holding right-wing ideologies but could equally well characterize *extremists* of both the left and right. Members of both groups may be tough-minded (Eysenck 1954) or dogmatic (Rokeach 1960). However, these criticisms do not question the idea that the source of prejudice is personality, nor that the appropriate level of explanation is that of individual differences. It is assumed that 'personality may be regarded as a determinant of ideological preferences . . . [although it] evolves under the impact of the social environment' (Adorno et al. 1950: 5). The search for behavioural and attitudinal manifestations of authoritarianism continues in some current research (e.g. Heaven 1980; Ray 1980; Ray and Lovejoy 1983).

Another source of criticism stems from evidence that cultural factors can outweigh personality factors in accounting for prejudice and discrimination. For example, Prothro found that while there were wide individual differences in anti-Semitism amongst Louisiana whites, they all displayed highly consistent anti-black attitudes (Prothro 1952). In addition, MacKinnon and Centers provide evidence of a correlation between low socioeconomic status and high authoritarianism (MacKinnon and Centers 1956). Such evidence undermines the idea that personality, rather than culture, is at the heart of the 'syndrome'.

Pettigrew systematically examined the authoritarian personality hypothesis in the context of anti-Black prejudice in South Africa, and the north and south of the United States (Pettigrew 1958). He found that anti-Semitism and authoritarianism were not significantly correlated with anti-Black prejudice. Rather, the presence or absence of racial prejudice was more parsimoniously explained in terms of the existence or absence of a culture of prejudice against Blacks. Personality factors tend only to augment prejudice against a specific social group if there exists an ideology which targets that group for prejudice. Subsequent research confirms this finding (e.g. Duckitt 1983). It is also generally the case that perceptions of relations between one's own and specific other groups determine more of the variation in intergroup hostility than does the underlying disposition to be prejudiced (Bierly 1985; Heaven 1983). Thus those defining themselves as 'Christians' may be particularly intolerant of homosexuals (Bierly 1985). Prejudice therefore appears to be largely a matter of conformity to norms (see Ch. 8 below). This conclusion is nicely supported by Minard's research in a West Virginian coal-mining community where there existed two sets of norms: black/white segregation above ground, and equality and integration below ground (Minard 1952). Sixty per cent of miners adhered rigidly to these contextual norms, while only 20 per cent were prejudiced both below and above ground, and 20 per cent attempted integration in both contexts. The changes in intergroup behaviour of the other 60 per cent cannot easily be explained in terms of the miners' personalities. More recently, large-scale studies (e.g. Campbell 1971) reveal that whether or not whites maintain social distance from blacks is largely determined by situational constraints and is not based on generalized attitudes (Seeman 1981).

The most damaging objections to the explanation of prejudice in terms of the authoritarian personality stem from the more general critique of individualism (described in Ch. 2 above). The fundamental point is that this form of explanation reduces large-scale social phenomena to the psychological make-up of individuals, and does this by recourse to intra-psychic dynamics responsible for individual differences. The critique is thoroughly elaborated by Billig (1976; see also Tajfel 1978b, and Milner 1981). With regard to personality, the point is not that psychological constitution is irrelevant, but that relationships between groups would be fixed and invariant if they were simply products of the stable and unchanging personalities of their constituent members. In reality, intergroup antipathy can arise and dissipate within dramatically short spaces of time. For example, the British government regarded Argentina as being so friendly that it sold arms which Argentina later used against Britain during the Falklands conflict. This phenomenon presents a problem which cannot be explained at the level of personality. The problem is to account for culture-wide, or collective, shifts in intergroup attitudes, and to explain how hostile intergroup relations might arise and decline.

THE FRUSTRATION–AGGRESSION HYPOTHESIS

In contrast to Adorno *et al.*, Dollard *et al.* (1939) considered prejudice to be a product of the *normal* everyday functioning of the human mind. Still within a psychodynamic framework, their frustration–aggression hypothesis seemed to provide an answer to the problem of *when* intergroup behaviour would become hostile. They maintained that 'frustration always leads to some form of aggression', and that 'aggressive behaviour always presupposes the existence of frustration' (ibid.: 1). It was argued that psychic energy is mobilized in order to pursue individual goals and is dissipated by achievement of the goal. Goal achievement is *cathartic*: it restores psychological equilibrium. If goal achievement is prevented (i.e. frustrated) by the blocking of goal-directed action, the mobilized, and undissipated energy is experienced as psychic tension and arousal (i.e. there is an 'instigation to aggress') which can only be relieved by aggression, usually against the agent or cause of frustration. An important feature of the theory is that the frustrating agent may not always be the recipient of the consequent aggression. When the true agent is unavailable, or when direct aggression might incur punishment, the aggression becomes redirected onto an alternative target. This occurs in one of two ways.

The first is by *stimulus generalization*, in which case the target is as similar as possible to the frustrating agent. The less similarity there is between the frustrator and the target, the less aggression the target will receive. Thus a child who is bullied by a peer may then vent his or her anger on another peer. The second mechanism by which the instigation to aggress becomes redirected is termed *displacement*. In this case a completely different, substitute target receives the full force of the aggression which is 'meant' for the frustrator. Thus the bullied child may kick the cat rather than retaliating against the bully or another similar child.

While most of the ensuing research explored interpersonal aggression, Dollard *et al.* developed an explanation for *intergroup* prejudice as being *displacement* of aggression towards ingroup members onto those of dissimilar outgroups. They proposed that the rise of anti-Semitism in Germany, following the First World War, was due to displaced aggression which stemmed from the continuing frustration of economic goals following the Treaty of Versailles. Hovland and Sears (1940) developed a more comprehensive theory of *scapegoating*, proposing that frustrated majority-group members who cannot easily aggress against (or identify) the frustrating agent displace their aggression onto relatively defenceless minority groups, especially if there is a consensus about the appropriateness of antipathy towards that group. For example, Gordon Allport quotes the political agitator who proclaims, 'When will the plain, ordinary, sincere, sheeplike people of America awaken to the fact that their common affairs are being arranged and run for them by aliens, communists, crackpots, refugees, renegades, socialists, termites, and traitors' (Allport 1954: 69).

In support of their theory, Hovland and Sears showed how increased lynchings of blacks in the United States between 1882 and 1930 were linked, presumably via the mediation of frustration, to a decline in cotton prices experienced by white farmers. This kind of evidence, as well as experimental evidence which shows a link between frustration and intergroup hostility (Miller and Bugelski 1948) has been criticized extensively by Billig (1976). The main problem has been to explain why any particular group should be a more obvious target for displaced aggression than any other (why were Jews or blacks the scapegoat for economic decline?). Moreover, it is often very difficult to determine in advance what dimensions are critical for determining dissimilarity or similarity of others (Worchel and Cooper 1979), and hence to know whether prejudice has resulted from the dynamic process of displacement or the more learning-based process of stimulus generalization (Milner 1981). In addition, the theory does not enable us to distinguish between the instantaneous aggression which may follow receiving an insult and the simmering prejudice that stems from thwarted economic goals (Billig 1976). Two problems for an account of ethnocentric hostility posed purely in terms of frustration–aggression therefore seem to be to specify *which* outgroup will be the target of aggression, and why the aggression is often a *collective* phenomenon.

Relative deprivation

Dollard *et al.*'s original formulation became increasingly untenable as evidence accumulated that, through social learning processes (e.g. Bandura 1977), aggression could easily arise independently of frustration, and that similarity could have independent effects of its own (Rokeach, Smith, and Evans 1960). In keeping with the general move away from psychodynamic explanation in social psychology (see Billig 1976), Berkowitz's (1962, 1965, 1972, 1974) reformulation of the determinants of aggression abandoned the Freudian assumptions made by Dollard *et al.* It was suggested that frustrations produce a *readiness* to aggress which is only expressed as overt aggression when the target can be safely attacked, is visible or distinctive, is 'strange', and is already disliked. Moreover, aggression is increased when learnt aggression cues (such as violent images and people, or weapons) are present. For example, subjects who have viewed slides of weapons are likely to deliver more severe electric shocks to a confederate who has insulted them than are subjects who viewed slides of neutral objects (Caprara *et al.* 1984). The actual presence of a weapon can also facilitate angry aggression (Berkowitz and Le Page 1967; Turner *et al.* 1977), a finding which provides a strong case for restricting the visibility of weapons worn by police in public settings.

Contrasting his account of aggression with more sociological explanations of *collective* conflict and violence, Berkowitz argued that, far from being rational or goal-seeking, riots demonstrate 'impulsive reactions' to environmental stimuli (Berkowitz 1972). Emotional arousal, produced by frustration or discomfort, fuels these impulses, as evident from the fact that riots seem to occur during particularly hot spells of weather (e.g. Baron and Ransberger 1978; Anderson and Anderson 1984). Naturally, there may be many forms of frustration, and one of these is economic and political subordination.

Berkowitz argued that people do not protest unless they have a strong sense of personal control over their situations (Berkowitz 1972; cf. Forward and Williams 1970). This may explain why American Indians struggled *less* against whites as white power became consolidated (Gurr 1970), and why better-educated Blacks were more likely to have rioted than poorly educated Blacks in Detroit and Newark (Caplan 1970). Another reason why it is the more privileged members of subordinate groups who often lead protest is that they regard themselves as being more similar to members of dominant groups, and hence perceive the injustice more acutely. The main thrust of Berkowitz's conclusions about the social conditions which give rise to collective violence is that, 'it is primarily when we look at objects we believe we have some chance of getting, because we regard ourselves as relatively similar to the person having those things, that we are frustrated at the inability to realize our hopes' (Berkowitz 1972: 88). Moreover, it is not so much intergroup inequalities which frustrate people as *intra*group inequalities. For example, Berkowitz (1972) interpreted Henry and Short's (1954) finding that homicide rates among Blacks decreased during the economic depression as being due to reduced intragroup differences in deprivation among Blacks. In effect, Berkowitz argued that the most powerful frustration is that brought about by a sense of relative deprivation.

The concept of relative deprivation (hereafter referred to as 'RD') was first used by Stouffer et al. (1949) in their study, *The American Soldier*, and later developed more formally by Davis (1959). It generally refers to feelings that, relative to certain other people, one is deprived of some desired object. One of the important early studies was conducted by Runciman, who found that many of his 1,500 subjects did not experience deprivation despite their objectively deprived situation (Runciman 1966). English manual workers felt more resentment if other manual workers' incomes exceeded their own, but were less concerned about the incomes of non-manual workers. It seems, therefore, that one reason why real injustices are not always reflected in direct political action is that people's subjective beliefs and social comparisons mediate between the two.

In his book *Why Men Rebel*, Gurr suggests that the main difference between the deprivations associated with marital strife and those leading to civil unrest is simply that the latter confront a *large number* of individuals simultaneously (Gurr 1970). Relying upon evidence such as media reports, he found that increases in civil unrest in 114 polities corresponded to increases in deprivation (measured by combining political and economic discrimination, separatism, dependence on foreign capital, religious cleavages, and poor educational opportunities). Gurr, however, ignored an important distinction made by Runciman between two types of RD (Runciman 1966; see Table 3.1 below). The first was termed 'egoistic' because it results from the individual's sense of deprivation relative to other similar individuals, while the second was termed 'fraternal' since it stemmed from comparisons between dissimilar individuals, and particularly between those from different groups. The available evidence strongly supports maintaining such a distinction, especially when viewed from a social identity perspective.

EGOISTIC RELATIVE DEPRIVATION

The 1970s witnessed a major initiative in research and theory concerning egoistic RD. Crosby's review of all of the available theories proposed an integrated model building upon earlier formulations (Crosby 1976), most of which assume that the sense of deprivation arises from social comparisons, and share Gurr's assumption that relative deprivation is 'a necessary precondition for civil strife of any kind' (Gurr 1970: 596). All except Crosby incorporate the assumption from frustration–aggression theory that the outcome of relative deprivation will be aggression, protest, and violence (Eckstein 1980).

Crosby's work (e.g. Cook, Crosby, and Hennigan 1977) reinforced a shift of emphasis from the objective social conditions which give rise to the mediating variable of relative deprivation, to the *subjective* psychological experience (a hypothetical construct) of relative deprivation. Many critics have pointed out that the objective and subjective are unlikely to correspond closely (Billig 1976; Crosby 1984; Muller 1980; Walker and Pettigrew 1984).

Due partly to its complexity, or 'overabundance of hypothesized preconditions' (Crosby 1984: 63) there have been only a few tests of Crosby's original model (Crosby 1976). One example is Alain's study of blue-collar and clerical workers, in which all of the preconditions contributed independently to feelings of egoistic RD (Alain 1985). In addition, Crosby's model accounted for more variance than those of Runciman, Gurr, or Davis (see also Bernstein and Crosby 1980). Based on her own field study of 345 employees in Massachusetts, which explored feelings of deprivation concerning division of labour within the home (Crosby 1982), Crosby opted for a simpler and more manageable model, concluding that most of the variance in RD is due simply to a discrepancy between feelings of *wanting* and *deserving* (Crosby 1984).

Unfortunately, the plethora of theories do not converge in specifying *which comparison* out of the many available (past–present, present–future, past–future, self–other, self–alter ego, etc.) will be most important, or when. In addition, they do not explain why these comparisons lead to wanting. Moreover, some regard social comparison as unnecessary (see Table 3.1). For example, Folger *et al.* (1983) propose that feelings of deprivation arise when people compare their actual state ('outcome') with one that is imaginable and desirable but not necessarily attainable (the 'referent cognition'). If, for example, it rains throughout your holiday, you may feel particularly annoyed when you consider that it is *usually* sunny at that time of year. Folger *et al.* found that subjects who had received no course credit for a task (low outcome) were more hostile towards the experimenter if they were subsequently told that they could have gained credits by participating in a second task (high-referent cognition) than when they were told that they could not (low referent). Folger *et al.* conclude that relative deprivation is purely an intrapersonal cognitive process which is not dependent on comparisons between people.

The idea that comparison between one cognition and another (more pleasing) cognition leads to dissatisfaction is not new (see Festinger 1957). However, to explain collective political violence using this notion would be highly reductionist (see Ch. 2 above), and overgeneralizes the emotional outcome of a cognitive process to large-scale effects in a social domain. It falls foul of the same problems as the original frustration–aggression formulation, namely failing to explain why any *particular* target should be selected for aggression. Essentially, there is no logical way to link collective political action with the consequences of an intrapersonal cognitive process.

Furthermore, theories dwelling on egoistic RD cannot explain why the frustration is not responded to by an increase in aggression towards *both* ingroup and outgroup members. Why are certain targets for aggression seen as more legitimate than others? For example, people may be less willing to aggress against police officers than others (Lange 1971). Clearly, there is an important social-cognitive component in reactions to frustration and deprivation (Billig 1976). We appraise the situation and the roles, status, and intentions of those who cause us frustration, and we already have beliefs and expectations about how we should respond to frustration in many circumstances (Linneweber *et al.* 1984). A key problem, then, is to specify the links between particular forms and sources of frustration or deprivation and the social behaviour which follows. It is this question which is partially resolved by theories of fraternal deprivation.

FRATERNAL RELATIVE DEPRIVATION

Runciman's model of fraternal RD encompasses two aspects: comparison with dissimilar individuals, and comparison between one's own group and other *groups* (Runciman 1966; see Table 3.1 below). The first of these (which is the less important) may involve both dissimilar ingroup and outgroup members. Martin argues that since people usually compare themselves with the outgroup members most similar to themselves (e.g. those doing the same job but for a different company), egoistic deprivation is more likely to occur than fraternal deprivation (Martin 1981). (However, her study confounded interpersonal with intergroup similarity.) Martin and Murray go on to

Table 3.1   Aspects of relative deprivation

Egoistic	Fraternal
Social comparisons with other individuals similar to self.	Social comparisons with other individuals dissimilar to self.
and/or	and/or
Within-self comparisons between actual and desired conditions.	Social comparisons between own and other groups.

conclude that 'the essence of the egoistic versus fraternal distinction is the degree of similarity of the referent, not whether the referent is explicitly an individual or a group' (Martin and Murray 1983: 195).

Contrary to Martin and Murray's view, research in the social identity tradition shows that interpersonal and intergroup comparisons can have markedly different consequences for self-evaluation, as we discuss below. It follows that it is the second aspect of Runciman's notion of fraternal RD (Runciman 1966) which has more relevance to large-scale social action, as was anticipated by Pettigrew (1967).

Vanneman and Pettigrew (1972) reported the results of twelve surveys conducted in the North American cities of Cleveland, Newark, Los Angeles, and Gary, following elections in which black candidates were standing for mayor. Among white voters, across all four cities, perceived deprivation relative to blacks was positively related to anti-black attitudes. Whites experiencing high racial fraternal RD were less willing to support or vote for black mayoral candidates, and more likely to blame 'subversive elements' (rather than racial discrimination) for riots than were those experiencing high egoistic RD. Vanneman and Pettigrew concluded that

> it seems obvious (then) that attitudes about structural change would involve group-to-group comparisons (fraternalist) and not individual-to-group comparisons (egoistic). And yet this point has been largely ignored or obscured by most of the researchers who have sought to link relative deprivation to movements for and against social change. There has been, in short, a consistent and erroneous individualistic bias throughout this literature.
>
> (Vanneman and Pettigrew 1972: 481)

While this bias exists in a great deal of more recent work (reviewed by Gurney and Tierney 1982; Walker and Pettigrew 1984), there is mounting supportive evidence for Vanneman and Pettigrew's view. For example Crosby (1982) found that subjects were more dissatisfied about the situation of women in general (fraternal RD) than about their own personal jobs or home lives (egoistic RD). Furthermore, for both men and women, measures of egoistic and fraternal RD were only weakly correlated. Likewise, Abèles revealed that measures of fraternal RD among blacks (*vis-à-vis* particular groups of whites) were always more positively related to militancy than were measures of egoistic RD (Abèles 1976).

Social comparisons which lead to feelings of deprivation and their behavioural consequences are not random but are made for particular social and historical reasons (see also Chs. 4 and 9). For example, in India the relatively recent decline in Muslims' status compared to Hindus, makes Muslims feel especially deprived. Tripathi and Srivastava found that feelings of fraternal deprivation among Muslims (in terms of job opportunities, support from the police, political freedom, etc.) were associated with more hostile attitudes towards Hindus (Tripathi and Srivastava 1981).

Similarly, Guimond and Dubé-Simard found that francophones from Montreal who felt more frustration and dissatisfaction when (fraternalistically) comparing salaries of francophones and anglophones in Quebec also held significantly more pro-Quebec Nationalist attitudes (Guimond and Dubé-Simard 1983). In contrast, egoistic RD was unrelated to such attitudes. Guimond and Dubé-Simard concur with the social identity perspective and with Walker and Pettigrew (1984) that intergroup comparisons are more likely to be responsible for nationalist attitudes than are interpersonal comparisons.

Taken together, the evidence concerning both frustration–aggression and RD shows that intergroup behaviour can only be explained with reference to the social context within which it occurs. The concept of fraternal deprivation allows us to escape from nominalist assumptions inherent in models such as Gurr's (1970). It also allows us to go beyond simple motivational models such as frustration–aggression, and to explore the more social bases of intergroup behaviour.

This returns us to a perennial question for social comparison theories: how can we predict which groups or individuals will be adopted for comparisons (Singer 1981)? Relative deprivation theorists (e.g. Muller 1980) have alluded to the role of culture in making certain comparisons normative and legitimate (e.g. comparisons between the economic positions of Protestants and Catholics are central in Northern Ireland but are less important in England). Another possibility is that there is a natural reciprocal pairing of groups such as black/white (Vanneman and Pettigrew 1972), although this idea cannot apply to some group comparisons (e.g. Britain–Argentina). The nature and choice of referents is one of the key remaining issues to be resolved by relative deprivation theory (Martin and Murray 1983).

Realistic conflict of interests

The most influential approach to provide an answer to the question of which group will compare with which others is the functional interdependence model, or realistic conflict theory, developed by Sherif (1962, see Ch. 5).

His theory was built upon the following premise: 'We cannot extrapolate from the properties of individuals to the characteristics of group situations' (ibid.: 8). Instead:

> '*intergroup relations* refer to relations between two or more groups and their respective members. Whenever individuals belonging to one group interact, collectively or individually, with another group or its members *in terms of their group identifications* we have an instance of intergroup behaviour.
>
> (ibid.: 5)

Sherif characterized groups and intergroup behaviour in terms of functional relationships. Members of groups have interdependent roles and statuses (there can be no leaders without followers, and the fate of one is tied up with the fate of all), and their attitudes and behaviour are bound by a set of norms or rules. The motives and interpersonal relationships of members *within* groups are not merely mirrored by those prevailing *between* groups. Instead, the presumed direction of causality can be reversed. Rather than individual frustrations, deprivation, or ideology leading to hostile behaviour towards outgroups, the relationship between the ingroup and outgroup could itself be the source of hostility and frustration. Indeed, while relations within a group may be harmonious and cordial, those same individuals may hold violent and bitter attitudes towards an outgroup. Sherif initiated a, now classic, programme of research in order to explore the genesis of intergroup relationships and the impact of functional interdependence between groups (summarized by Sherif 1966). The principal hypotheses were as follows. When a group forms it delineates itself (ingroup) from an outgroup. This categorical distinction then comes to embody value-laden content. Ingroup norms develop from interpersonal relationships within the group (see Ch. 8 below) which define the range and content of acceptable ingroup values, and the rewards or sanctions associated with adhering to these norms. Stereotypes are then applied to outgroups, the content of which depends on the actual or perceived relations between the groups in question. Specifically, if the groups are seen as being in competition, such that something which is good for one will be bad for the other, the stereotype of the outgroup is likely to be negative and derogatory.

Sherif set up his experiments at boys' summer camps attended by 11 and 12 year olds. In all of the studies the boys were unacquainted prior to arrival at the camp. They had been selected as being 'normal' in terms of intellectual, social, and physical attributes, and all had white, Protestant, middle-income backgrounds. The researchers were acting as camp organizers, and the boys were unaware that an experiment was in progress.

In the 1949 and 1953 experiments (Sherif 1951; Sherif, White, and Harvey 1955) the first stage allowed spontaneous friendships to develop among the boys. They all shared one large bunkhouse and could freely join in activities together. In the second stage ('group formation') the boys were divided into two groups, each living in separate cabins. The division was performed so that two out of three of each boy's best friends from the first stage were now in the other cabin. This intervention yielded a startling finding. When asked to indicate their best friends at the end of the second stage 90 per cent of those chosen were boys from their *own* cabin. These findings showed that it is possible for group formation to lead to interpersonal attraction (within the group) rather than the other way around (see Ch. 5 below).

In the 1954 experiment at Robbers Cave in Oklahoma (said to have been Jesse James' hideout) Sherif *et al.* (1961) simply began the study with two groups of boys who lived in separate cabins and independently engaged in activities such as cooking, camping out, carrying canoes over rough ground, and so on. Within each group different members quickly took on different responsibilities, and obvious leaders emerged. The groups developed their own codes, nicknames, and jargon, and defined their territory by naming various landmarks. They also kept their members in line by ridiculing those who did not adhere to group rules and norms. The groups also gave themselves names, such as (in the 1949 study) 'The Red Devils' and 'The Bull Dogs' or (at Robbers Cave) 'The Rattlers' and 'The Eagles'. Thus, in the group formation stage, each group evolved a clear set of norms and values to which all the members adhered.

The next stage was designed to see what would happen when the two groups came into contact, particularly when this contact involved competition for a prize. The two groups were pitted against one another in an organized tournament involving a variety of games such as baseball and a treasure hunt. The initial spirit of goodwill disappeared as the tournament progressed. The boys began to taunt and jeer at members of the other group, denouncing them as 'snakes' and 'stinkers'. By the end of the tournament the two groups virtually refused to talk to each other and began to launch secret raids and attacks on each other's cabin. In the Robbers Cave study the groups took part in a game where each had to collect as many (scattered) beans as possible in a set time. The beans supposedly collected by each person were displayed briefly on a screen, and the boys had to estimate how many there were. Although only thirty-five beans were actually shown each time, the boys overestimated the number collected by ingroup members and underestimated the number retrieved by outgroup members (cf. Blake and Mouton 1962). This stage demonstrated that, as a result of intergroup competition, an apparently amiable and well-adjusted collection of boys had been transformed. They now appeared 'wicked, disturbed, and vicious' (Sherif 1966: 85).

The conclusions to be drawn from this third stage in the studies (the 1953 study had to be terminated due to the extremity of intergroup antipathy!) were as follows. First, cultural, physical, and personality differences are not *necessary* for (and hence cannot be the only causes of) the emergence of intergroup conflict. Second, the existence of two groups in competition for a goal which only one can attain (competitively interdependent) is a *sufficient* condition for (and hence can be the sole cause of) intergroup hostility.

The final stage of the Robbers Cave experiment was designed to repair the relations between the groups and reduce intergroup conflict. One attempt to achieve this involved giving lectures on brotherly love and forgiveness at the Sunday services. Despite enjoying the services as a whole the boys seemed to have completely ignored the peaceful messages, and rapidly reverted to their preoccupation with beating or avoiding the outgroup. In the 1949 study, one successful means of ameliorating tensions between the two groups had been the introduction of a common enemy (a third competing group). However, as Sherif notes, this solution was undesirable since it simply meant a widening of intergroup conflict to a larger scale, 'and would not lead to a lasting change in attitudes between the two original groups (Sherif 1966).

At Robbers Cave two other methods were employed to create more friendly intergroup relations. First, the two groups were brought into *equal status contact*. As Williams (1947) and then Gordon Allport (1954) had argued, direct interpersonal contact between members of equal-status groups should lead to a reduction in intergroup prejudice as a result of the development of rewarding interpersonal relationships between members of the two groups (see Ch. 4 below; Miller and Brewer 1984; Hewstone and Brown 1986, for a recent overview of this hypothesis). However, Sherif hypothesized that contact would not be sufficient to reduce conflict. An additional requirement would be that the groups must meet, 'under conditions embodying goals that are compelling for the groups involved, but cannot be achieved by a single group through its own efforts and resources' (Sherif 1966: 88). Such goals are termed *superordinate goals*.

In the equal-status contact phase the two groups independently engaged in the same pleasant activities such as letting off fireworks, eating in one large dining hall, and watching films. However, on these occasions the opportunity was seized to berate and insult outgroup members. The common meals came to be called the 'garbage wars' – a reflection of the aggressive hurling of food, rubbish, and abuse between members of the two groups.

Finally, superordinate goals were introduced. One of these involved a 'crisis' in the form of a breakdown in the water supply. The two groups had to pool their information in order to ascertain the locus of the fault. A second superordinate goal was created when it was revealed that the camp authorities could not afford to pay for a film which both groups wanted to see. Only when *both* groups had contributed some money could either see the film. A third instance was provided when a food truck broke down during an outing to a lake. Only by jointly pulling on a rope (the same as was used for a tug-of-war in the tournament) could the boys get the truck started.

Individually, these episodes did not succeed in eradicating the intergroup hostility. However, the cumulative effect of participating in a series of co-operative acts did gradually attenuate the conflict. Indeed, by the time their stay at the camp was over, both groups elected to go home in one bus together rather than in separate buses. New friendships emerged which crossed the group boundaries.

Table 3.2   Sherif's functional interdependence model of group relations

		Interpersonal	*Intergroup*
Interdependent goal relations	Superordinate	Group formation	Intergroup harmony
	Competitively interdependent	Personal enmity	Intergroup conflict and intragroup solidarity

Sherif's experiments are an important landmark in social psychology since they provide an empirical demonstration of the discontinuity between individual and group processes. Table 3.2 depicts some of the consequences of different goal relations at the interpersonal and at the intergroup levels. The assumed primacy of personality and interpersonal relations in explanations of intergroup behaviour was neatly dispatched. Unfortunately, it remained unclear from Sherif's findings, what conditions are necessary and sufficient to create intergroup hostility. For example, Sherif showed that contact is not sufficient to reduce hostility, but implied that it may be necessary (since it is a prerequisite for acquiring superordinate goals). Conversely, he showed that seeking a superordinate goal with a co-operative group may be sufficient to reduce hostility, but not whether it was necessary. Even Sherif's results hint at the possibility that an explanation of intergroup behaviour couched purely in terms of goal relations in incomplete. In the 1949 and 1953 experiments, in which the groups were aware of one another's existence, but prior to intergroup competition, 'there were even signs of comparison between "we" and "they" . . . in each instance, the edge was given to one's own group' (Sherif 1966: 80). In addition, even after the superordinate goals stage of the Robbers Cave experiment, choice of outgroup members as friends had increased to around 30 per cent, but was still far below the choice of ingroup members (70 per cent) and ratings of the outgroup were still unfavourable, particularly among the members of winning groups.

Sherif's perspective seems to answer many of the problems we have identified with the authoritarian personality, frustration–aggression, and relative deprivation approaches. Hostile intergroup attitudes and behaviour are seen to arise as a function of an *intergroup* relationship, not interpersonal peculiarities. Conflict is generated by competition for real resources and not by an emotion of deprivation. Intergroup behaviour is a collective phenomenon and not a statistical aggregation of coincidentally similar individual acts.

There is consistent evidence that intergroup goal relations affect the cohesiveness (or mutual attraction among members) of groups. For example, Blake and Mouton showed that ingroup cohesiveness, accompanied by over-estimation of the quality of ingroup performance and trivializing of the outgroups' solution to problems were all increased when intergroup competition was introduced (Blake and Mouton 1961, 1962). However, as with Sherif's work, the question remains as to whether competition really is necessary to create intergroup conflict and whether co-operation really is sufficient to eradicate such conflict.

Rabbie and Horwitz found that interdependence of outcomes between groups was sufficient to create ingroup bias in ratings of the traits of members of the two groups, even when winning or losing was determined by the flip of a coin (Rabbie and Horwitz 1969). Rabbie and Wilkens found that subjects felt competitive even in a 'non-competition' condition (Rabbie and Wilkens 1971), and Ferguson and Kelley's subjects overevaluated ingroup products relative to those of outgroups in an explicitly non-competitive situation (Ferguson and Kelley 1964). This evidence has been interpreted as casting doubt on the idea that competition is a critical determinant of intergroup relations (Tajfel 1970; Tajfel and Turner 1979; Turner 1975).

It appears that intergroup relations usually involve competitiveness, but that this does not always result from incompatible goals. Even anticipated *cooperation* did not ameliorate ingroup bias in a study by Rabbie and De Brey (1971). Johnson and Johnson's research into attitudes towards handicapped individuals in schools has shown that, over a period of a few weeks, *actual* intergroup co-operation does seem to improve school performance, increase social interaction between groups (Johnson and Johnson 1982), increase acceptance of minority (e.g. handicapped) members within ingroups and outgroups (Johnson and Johnson 1984; Johnson et al. 1981) and weaken ingroup cohesiveness (Yager et al. 1985). However, these effects all seem to operate at an *interpersonal* level. For example, Hansell found that while co-operative goal structures do promote cross-sex and cross-race friendships within groups, they do not necessarily improve the *inter*group relations or stimulate cross-sex and cross-race ties between members of different groups (Hansell 1984).

One explanation for such findings is that intragroup interaction renders ingroup members more familiar and more attractive than outgroup members (but see Ch. 5 below). However, evidence has accumulated showing that membership of a group 'sometimes seems to cause intergroup differentiation even when there is neither cooperative interaction within nor competitive relations between groups' (Turner 1981b: 75; see also Brewer and Silver 1978; Doise *et al.* 1972). The question which realistic conflict theory leaves unanswered is: where does the competitiveness of intergroup relations come from? In the Sherifs' and Blake and Mouton's research, competitive or co-operative goal relations are imposed by the legitimate authority of the researchers. What processes mediate between 'objective' relationships between groups and ingroup biases?

Recall that research on relative deprivation has led to a focus on the subjective rather than objective criteria of felt deprivation. Similarly, it appears that subjective competitiveness is often a better predictor of ingroup favouritism than are objectively defined competitive goal relations. Brown has found that when school children are competing (own *versus* other school) for a prize they become more favourable toward their own school, as would be predicted by realistic conflict theory. However, even under co-operative conditions subjects still favour the ingroup, both when the relationship is anticipated (Brown 1984a, 1984b) or real (Brown and Abrams 1986). This indicates that objective relations affect the magnitude of ingroup favouritism but are not directly responsible for its presence. In Brown's experiments subjects' *feelings* of competitiveness were more predictive of ingroup favouritism than were the objective goal relations.

Minimal groups

We have seen that intergroup relations are frequently competitive, hostile, and antagonistic. Explanations in terms of personality, frustration, and egoistic deprivation all fail to account for the collective nature of intergroup relations. Explanations in terms of fraternal deprivation and goal relations dwell on the perception of differences of interests or attainments but neither appear to have identified the necessary or minimally sufficient conditions for intergroup conflict.

A resolution to this problem was provided when Tajfel and his colleagues devised the now classic 'minimal group' paradigm (Tajfel 1970). Since this paradigm is central to the social identity approach and has been employed in a large number of experiments (see Tajfel 1982b) we shall outline its basic characteristics. Subjects are brought together to participate in a study of 'decision-making'. Their first task is to make judgements or choose between two alternative options when presented with pairs of stimuli. For the second task they are divided into two groups, ostensibly on the basis of their individual judgements during the first task. Each subject is placed in a separate cubicle or room and is told to which of the two groups he or she belongs. Subjects are then provided with a booklet in which they are required to award points representing money to two other individuals, never to themselves, who are identified only by their group membership and by a code number. Subjects indicate how they wish to allocate the money to the two

Table 3.3 The minimal group paradigm

A distribution matrix

Ingroup member	7	8	9	10	11	12	13	14	15	16	17	18	19
Outgroup member	1	3	5	7	9	11	13	15	17	19	21	23	25

Distribution strategies monitored by minimal group matrices

Fairness (F):	equal distribution of points between groups.
Maximum joint profit (MJP):	maximize number of points obtained irrespective of which group receives most.
Maximum ingroup profit (MIP):	maximize number of points for ingroup.
Maximum difference (MD):	maximize the difference in favour of the ingroup in the number of points awarded.
Favouritism (FAV):	composite employment of MIP and MD.

---

individuals by selecting one of thirteen pairs of numbers which are presented in the form of a distribution matrix (Table 3.3). There are a number of pages in the booklet, each presenting a different matrix: some pair two individuals from the same group (both ingroup or both outgroup), while others pair an ingroup member with an outgroup member, as in the example in Table 3.3. The matrices are designed to reveal the distribution strategies being adopted by the subject. Tajfel and Turner describe this situation as follows:

> There is neither conflict of interest nor previously existing hostility between the 'groups'. No social interaction takes place between the subjects, nor is there any rational link between economic self-interest and the strategy of ingroup favouritism. Thus these groups are purely cognitive and can be referred to as *minimal*.
>
> (Tajfel and Turner 1979: 38–9)

The 'minimal group paradigm' (Turner 1978a; Turner, Brown, and Tajfel 1979) has yielded a consistent pattern of results (Tajfel 1982b). Subjects allocate more to ingroup than to outgroup members: they try to maximize ingroup profit. They are also competitive. Some of the matrices offer subjects the chance to allocate most to the ingroup when the outgroup gets even more (e.g. 19 to the ingroup and 25 to the outgroup) or, at the other extreme, to gain less for the ingroup but to ensure that the outgroup loses more (e.g. 7 to the ingroup and 1 to the outgroup). Whereas the former strategy maximizes both ingroup profit (MIP) and joint profit (MJP), the latter maximizes the difference (MD) between the groups, in favour of the ingroup. While displaying a degree of background fairness, subjects surprisingly usually go for MD rather than fairness, or the combined strategy of MJP + MIP. To put this another way, beating the outgroup is more important than sheer profit.

In the original experiments (Tajfel et al. 1971) the categorization was between those who underestimated or overestimated the number of dots on a screen, or between those who preferred paintings by Klee or by Kandinsky (in reality, the division of subjects into categories was random). This manipulation confounded the pure effects of categorization with the perception of intragroup similarity. Subjects may have assumed that others who made the same choices as themselves would also be more similar, hence more attractive, and hence should receive preferential treatment. However, Billig and Tajfel found even when the division into groups was explicitly random (based on the toss of a coin), with no interpersonal similarity, subjects expressed more ingroup favouritism than when similarity existed (based on painting preferences) but no categorization (recipients were referred to only by code numbers) (Billig and Tajfel 1973).

Turner has proposed that competition between groups may have two bases (Turner 1975). First, groups may engage in *objective competition,* as is the case in Sherif's studies. A battle over territory or bidding for a franchise, or even the arms race between the United States and the Soviet Union are all forms of objective competition (both sides have plenty to lose by lagging behind the other). However, when the aim is merely to alter the *relative* position of one's group irrespective of the objective gains or losses, this is called *social competition.* For example, the 'space race' (during the 1960s and 1970s) between the United States and the Soviet Union had as much to do with national pride and prestige as with material gain. (Also refer back to the Martin Luther King extract at the beginning of this chapter.) The finding that subjects in the minimal group paradigm express ingroup bias and opt for the maximum differentiation (MD) strategy, even when they are only awarding points, rather than actual money, suggests that they are engaging in social competition (Turner 1975).

There are several alternative explanations for social competition. For example, Gerard and Hoyt's perspective accounts for MD strategies in terms of demand characteristics and experimenter effects (Gerard and Hoyt 1974). However, such an explanation rests on the assumption that 'for some reasons . . . competitive behaviour between groups, at least in our culture, is extraordinarily easy to trigger off' (Tajfel and Turner 1979: 39). A series of studies has shown that minimal group discrimination is not produced by generic norms, contrary even to Tajfel's initial view (Tajfel 1970). Billig found that awareness of a norm of discrimination actually led to a reduction in discriminatory behaviour (Billig 1973), and Tajfel and Billig found that subjects who were unfamiliar with the setting, and might be expected to feel anxious and hence invoke social norms, also discriminated less (Tajfel and Billig 1974). More recently, St Claire and Turner asked observer subjects to predict the responses of real subjects in the minimal group paradigm (St Claire and Turner 1982). If there had existed a 'norm' of competitiveness the observer subjects should have been able to predict accurately the level of discrimination (cf. Semin and Manstead 1979). In fact, they predicted greater fairness than actually occurred. In addition, while fairness is perceived as the most socially desirable strategy, it has proven remarkably difficult to get subjects to follow explicitly co-operative norms (Hogg et al. 1986; Vickers, Abrams, and Hogg 1987) and recent research has confirmed that groups tend to be more competitive than individuals (Kormorita and Lapworth 1982). Although there has been considerable debate over the particular measures of favouritism, and the procedures in the minimal group paradigm (Aschenbrenner and Schaefer 1980; Bornstein et al. 1983; Branthwaite, Doyle, and Lightbown 1979; Turner 1980, 1983) it remains clear that simple normative explanations of minimal intergroup discrimination are inadequate. Even where norms of discrimination do exist we still need to know when and why people adhere to them. The answer may lie in the social psychological nature of group membership.

Social identity theory

What emerges from the minimal group studies is that social categorization – the discontinuous classification of individuals into two distinct groups – is sufficient to generate intergroup competition. From the social identity perspective (see Ch. 2 above) we would wish to argue that individuals in minimal group studies are categorizing *themselves* in terms of the social category provided by the experimenter, and that such a process of categorization (of self and others) accentuates intergroup differences on the only dimension available – the allocation of points. The accentuation of differences is biased in favour of the ingroup because individuals are deriving their social identity (in the relatively transient context of the experiment) from the social category which embraces the self. The involvement of self-definition activates a need to achieve or maintain a positive self-evaluation, and this can be accomplished by favouring the ingroup (and hence the self) over the outgroup, that is by engaging in ingroup-favouring social comparisons.

In order to unpack this explanation of the minimal-group effect and social competition in general, let us deal first with categorization. Is categorization alone sufficient? Is it really necessary to introduce the motivational assumption concerning self-esteem and positive social identity? In Chapter 4 we discuss the importance of categorization for perception of objects and people other than the self. In this chapter we shall confine ourselves to the effects of intergroup categorizations which incorporate the self.

Doise and Deschamps have argued that the cognitive process of social categorization produces differentiation between social groups (Doise 1978; Deschamps 1984). According to Doise, when a person cognitively differentiates between two objects by categorizing them differently on one dimension (e.g. behavioural), he or she will also tend to distinguish between them on other dimensions (evaluative and representative). Doise considers the behavioural dimension to be most critical. For example, when Britain recently engaged Argentina in the Falklands conflict (behavioural differentiation) all kinds of previously unexpressed hostile attitudes, beliefs, and evaluations about Argentinians emerged through the popular press. In Sherif's boys camp studies divergence or convergence of behaviour (towards incompatible and superordinate goals, respectively) produced corresponding shifts in attitudes between groups.

Doise and Weinberger found that when boys anticipated competing with girls they differentiated more between boys and girls and attributed more feminine characteristics to girls than when a co-operative encounter was anticipated (Doise and Weinberger 1973). Doise, Deschamps, and Meyer varied the salience of social categorization in order to demonstrate its impact on accentuation of intergroup differences and intragroup similarities (Doise, Deschamps, and Meyer 1978). Subjects were asked to describe traits (out of a list of twenty-four) of three girls and three boys whose photographs were presented. In the first condition subjects rated the three own-sex photographs and subsequently but without advance warning, those of the opposite sex. In the second (anticipation) condition the categorization was made more salient by telling subjects at the outset that they would be rating members of both sexes. In this latter condition subjects perceived less overlap between traits of boys and girls, but more overlap among boys and among girls. Doise's and other research shows that anything which increases the salience of social categorization leads to greater intergroup differentiation (e.g. Doise and Sinclair 1973). A division on one dimension (such as similarity, proximity, common fate, and social interaction) often is mirrored by intergroup differentiation on another.

But it is also true that the impact of a social categorization can be weakened. Deschamps and Doise found that when one categorization (e.g. male/female) becomes crossed or intersected by another (e.g. young/adult), the accentuation of differences in terms of traits between one (e.g. male vs female) tends to be balanced by accentuation of similarities within another (e.g. adult males and females) (Deschamps and Doise 1978). In another study Deschamps had boys and girls play pencil and paper games, in groups divided either in terms of sex (six boys vs six girls), or in terms of both sex and colour code (three red and three blue within each group of boys and girls) (Deschamps 1973). Simple categorization led to differential attributions of traits to the two groups, while crossed categorization did not. Deschamps concludes that 'crossed category membership can thus effectively neutralize the differentiation' (Deschamps 1984: 555). This phenomenon could be attributable to a conflict between incompatible structures or, more simply, to altered salience. When a person has to focus on two separate dimensions of categorization the amount of processing distinctly relevant to each is likely to be diminished (experiments in which salience of categories has been directly manipulated will also be discussed in Ch. 6 below).

This purely cognitive analysis of intergroup differentiation has difficulty in accounting adequately for variations in the *extremity* of differentiation and for the *ethnocentric* nature of that differentiation. Why does the ingroup attract more favourable evaluations than the outgroup (e.g. Doise and Dann 1976; van Knippenberg 1984)? A plausible answer to these questions is that because social categorizations are largely self-referent, locating oneself and others in the social world, this imbues social categories with different subjective values (cf. Tajfel 1959). Individuals have a vested interest in being associated with categories which are positive since these can confer positive self-evaluation and create feelings of self-worth or self-esteem. The social identity approach argues that it is this striving for positive self-esteem which, at the intergroup level, accounts for the ethnocentric character of intergroup differentiation and for variations in its extremity (see also Ch. 4 below).

So, from this perspective the explanation of social competition rests on two complementary processes: social categorization and social comparison. Turner argues that the categorization process creates an accentuation of similarities between self and other ingroup members, and among outgroup members, and a perceived exaggeration of the differences between groups (Turner 1981b; see Ch. 4 below for details). The social comparison process, due to its underlying motive to favour self through the medium of ingroup favouritism, selects the specific dimensions on which accentuation occurs. These will be dimensions on which the ingroup is more favourably placed than the outgroup. It is also responsible for amplifying the relative superiority or favourableness of the ingroup over the outgroup – or maximizing the evaluatively *positive distinctiveness* of the ingroup.

We are now in a position to explain the social competition which emerges from social categorization *per se* in minimal group studies. In the relatively abstract and empty context of these experiments, subjects construct meaning and order by employing the social categorizations provided by the experimenters to locate self with respect to others. The categorization process renders each group perceptually distinct from the other, as well as reducing the perceived variation between individuals within each group. Thus a distribution of individuals is transformed into two distinct groups. Social comparison on this basis occurs on the dimension of point (or money) allocation, as this is the only readily available dimension of intergroup comparison. The outcome is the maximization of intergroup differences in favour of the ingroup by adoption of the combined distribution strategies of MIP and MD. Positive distinctiveness is thus achieved. There is some evidence that such ingroup favouritism and intergroup discrimination in minimal group studies does indeed satisfy this self-esteem motive by causing increases in self-esteem (e.g. Hogg *et al.* 1986; Oakes and Turner 1980; Lemyre and Smith 1985; but cf. Crocker *et al.* 1987; see Ch. 10 below for further discussion of this issue).

THE SOCIAL CONTEXT OF INTERGROUP BEHAVIOUR

While minimal group studies may lay bare the operation of the raw processes of categorization and social comparison, they deal with groups which by definition and intention do not possess many of the qualities of social categories in the *real* world. Only rarely do we encounter a 'division of society into opposing groups, who have no material grounds for hostility but yet are expected to make a pretence of hostility' (Radcliffe-Brown describing the Haida of British Columbia, quoted in Mair 1972: 50). In reality there are frequently sharp status, power, and prestige differences between groups, which can be perceived to be legitimate, stable, and immutable to varying degrees. Groups can differ in numerical size, demographic distribution, access to channels of mass communication, and so on. Clearly, these factors must have some impact on the form and content of intergroup behaviour, and should therefore be theoretically incorporated to furnish an adequate explanation of intergroup behaviour. This is precisely what the social identity approach does in its *macro-social* emphasis (Tajfel and Tuner 1979; Taylor and McKirnan 1984): it treats categorization and social comparison as psychological processes which provide the parameters within which sociohistorical factors, or more accurately, subjective understandings of those factors, operate. While this macro-social analysis was introduced in Chapter 2, we shall now explore it in somewhat more detail (see also Chs. 4 and 9, where it is discussed in relation to stereotyping and language, respectively) (Fig. 3.1).

Tajfel distinguished between intergroup comparisons which occur in a fixed consensually legitimate, and stable framework and those which arise when there is dissensus – that is, between secure and insecure comparisons (Tajfel 1974). When groups agree about each other's status there is little pressure to alter the status quo. If at the end of the season a football team is at the bottom of its league, there can be little doubt that it deserves to be there. Members of such a team are unlikely to compare their team with those at the top of the league. In such a situation the players are faced with a potentially *negative* social identity, relative to those in the top teams. However, 'status' as conceived in social identity theory refers to subjectively perceived outcomes of intergroup comparison. It follows that the way in which people strive for or maintain positive social identity will be heavily influenced by their subjective perceptions of the nature of the relations between groups, and in particular how stable and legitimate (in sum, how secure) the outcomes of intergroup comparisons are.

Social mobility

People can possess a *social mobility* belief system, that intergroup boundaries are permeable, and that it is possible for people to move between groups. This belief system can then be a basis for attempts by individuals to leave their group ('exit') in search of one which provides a more satisfactory identity ('passing'). These mobility strategies are quite common. For example, a

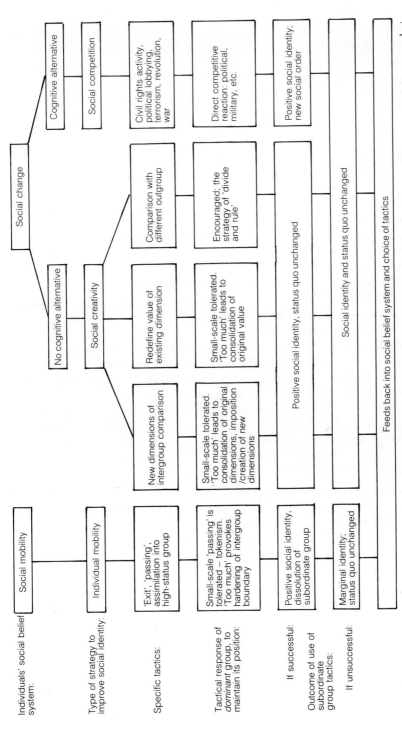

Figure 3.1 Outline of social identity model of large-scale intergroup relations: how members of *subordinate* groups may try to improve their self-image

player may transfer from one football team to another. Individuals seeking promotion may move to a new organization. It is also highly characteristic of women seeking traditionally male-occupied positions in organizations (Condor 1984; Crosby 1982). The strategy may improve one's personal position but it leaves the group's position unchanged. It therefore involves a degree of disidentification with the original group (Jahoda 1961; Milner 1981). Sometimes these transitions are harder to achieve in practice than in theory. Groups may exert pressure on their members in order to prevent them from leaving (as in the case of sanctions against the families of defectors). The difficulty is even greater when group membership is externally designated by attributes such as sex, skin colour, age, and so forth. However, mobility beliefs are well documented in such forms as the tendency for disadvantaged black children in the United States to identify with a white rather than a black doll (Fine and Bowers 1984). For people seeking to leave these groups, non-acceptance by a new group can lead to a sense of marginality (Breakwell 1979).

Generally, it may be to the advantage of high-status groups to foster social mobility belief systems (or 'false consciousness', in Marxist terms) among low-status groups as this inhibits the perception of conflict of interests and weakens the cohesiveness and ability to act collectively of those groups. The ethos of social mobility has a long history (Billig 1976), ranging from the Protestant work ethic (Kelvin 1984) to belief in a 'just world' (Lerner 1970) and the fundamental attribution error (Ross 1977). For example, in South Africa, the employment of blacks in the police force may encourage a perception that the position of blacks is not simply due to white oppression. This weakens the unity of blacks as a social group, and it strengthens the perceived legitimacy of the white regime.

Social change

In contrast to social mobility, people can possess a *social change* belief system, which rests on acceptance of the impermeability of intergroup boundaries and the relative impossibility of psychologically passing from a low- to a high-status group. Negative implications of group membership cannot be escaped simply by redefining oneself out of a group and into a dominant group. They can only be overcome by group strategies aimed at accomplishing a relatively positive re-evaluation of the ingroup. Tajfel and Turner outline two general classes of strategies which may be adopted: social creativity and social competition (Tajfel and Turner 1979).

Social creativity strategies occur when intergroup relations are subjectively perceived to be *secure* (legitimate and stable, if not necessarily desirable). New forms of intergroup comparison which can bolster ingroup identity may be sought. Tajfel and Turner suggest three possible strategies:

(1)   Groups may find *new dimensions* on which to compare themselves. Such

a strategy may succeed if the new dimension is also accepted as legitimate by the superior group (van Knippenberg 1984). So, for example, a traditional route for the achievement of positive gender identity is one in which boys and girls agree that each sex is 'better' than the other but as regards different qualities: boys are tougher, which is good, but girls are more understanding, which is also good (Abrams and Condor 1984; Abrams, Sparkes, and Hogg 1985; Condor 1986; see also Mummenday and Schreiber 1983).

(2) Group members may also *redefine the value* attached to various attributes. This is particularly effective if the attributes are central to or *criterial* of the group. For example, the United States heralds freedom as its first value, whereas the Soviet Union puts equality first. Both feel superior in terms of their most valued characteristics. In Chapter 9 we discuss the way ethnic groups which consider their language to be of crucial importance can bolster and enhance their social identity by accentuating their language – that is, by striving for positive ethnolinguistic distinctiveness. More transient groups may use other distinctive markers, such as clothing, as a vehicle for gaining positive distinctiveness. This has indeed been the case with punks.

(3) A strategy which is particularly potent is that of selecting *new outgroups* for intergroup comparisons. Here the objective is to compare your low-status group with other groups of equal or preferably lower status than your own rather than with the superior group, that is engaging in downward or lateral rather than upward comparisons. For example, German pupils of lower educational status in West Germany express more intergroup antipathy towards Italian and Turkish *Gastarbeiter* (guest workers) than do those of higher educational status (Schönbach *et al.* 1981; Wagner and Schönbach 1984). Lateral comparison may also be encouraged by the dominant group as it serves its interests – allows it to 'divide and rule'. For example, when the South African government extended voting rights to 'coloured' people in the early 1980s it also made that group a more salient comparison group for the unrepresented black majority. Also, it became possible for coloureds to regard themselves more favourably in relation to blacks; thus providing them with a sense of higher status than could be derived from comparisons with whites. In general, the most likely comparison groups are those which are most similar in terms of outlook and status. As a group becomes increasingly high in relative status its relevance as a comparison group may diminish (Brown and Abrams 1986), and the relative status and size of a group can drastically alter the amount of co-operative and competitive behaviour displayed (Espinoza and Garza 1985).

Social competition (i.e. direct competition between subordinate and dominant groups on dimensions consensually valued by both groups) arises when the comparison between groups is subjectively perceived to be *insecure*. When the legitimacy or stability of the status hierarchy is called into question, comparisons may be made with highly *dissimilar* groups, on the grounds that relative statuses can, or ought to be, changed. In democracies the legitimacy of power is agreed by consensus. Different parties continue to seek power, however, since the situation is inherently unstable – the electorate can change its mind! In totalitarian states the populace may perceive the power of the authorities as stable but not as legitimate. In both cases the critical feature is that there are *cognitive alternatives* to the existing state of affairs. For example, the Palestine Liberation Organization have no state of their own and are not recognized by the state of Israel. Yet the PLO continue to fight in the belief that they will achieve both wider international recognition and territory. They perceive their position as legitimate, if not stable. Naturally, social groups often disagree over the legitimacy of one another's claims. Examples of such disagreements abound in world politics. Britain and Argentina were in conflict concerning sovereignty of the Falkland/Malvinas Islands. Britain and Spain have had a history of disagreement about the status of Gibraltar. Often, formal constraints are drawn up in order to legitimize a particular arrangement (e.g. the European Economic Community regulations on fishing in the North Sea, or the contract to legitimize the transfer of power over Hong Kong from Britain to China).

Of course, insecure social comparisons influence both subordinate and dominant groups. When school children cease to regard the teacher as being in a position which commands respect, the teacher has to reassert his or her authority (Hargreaves 1967). Another powerful example of this comes from Northern Ireland. The majority Protestant community is committed to ensuring that Northern Ireland remains a part of the United Kingdom, while the minority Catholic community favours reunification with Eire (a move strongly favoured in some parts of Eire itself). Both groups regard the other's aims as illegitimate. Moreover, any signs of partiality on the part of the British authorities is met with strong protest. Recently, the so-called 'Anglo-Irish Accord' (an agreement that Britain and Eire should consult one another concerning policy for Northern Ireland) has incensed the Protestants and provoked widespread collective action. There are also more specific instances, such as when Catholics were allowed to march to commemorate the 1916 Easter Rising, but the Protestants were banned from holding their Apprentice Boys' March the following day. They reacted by organizing an immediate protest march of about 4,000 people, and later there was a massive riot (March 1986). The dynamics of these conflicts can only be fully understood in terms of the history of relations between Eire and England (see also Cairns 1982; Cairns and Mercer 1984). However, these examples illustrate how, once the legitimacy of status relations is challenged by a subordinate group, the superior group closes its ranks to defend its position.

Note also that although there are 'real' conflicts of interest in Northern Ireland, the group divisions which matter are along religious and cultural, as well as economic and national, lines. It is clear, therefore, that the battle is partly concerned with the maintenance of social identity (see Waddell and Cairns 1986).

EVIDENCE

Let us now examine some of the evidence for this macro-social aspect of the social identity approach (see also Ch. 9). Turner and Brown hypothesized that subordinate groups would seek positive distinctiveness increasingly as their status became more insecure (Turner and Brown 1978). Groups of Arts and Science Faculty students participated in a study which was supposedly about differences between Arts and Science students' reasoning skills. Status was manipulated by suggesting that one of these groups would produce a superior/inferior performance. Legitimacy was manipulated by stating that there was a reliable/unreliable empirical basis for this expected advantage. Stability was manipulated by informing subjects that the same pattern of results was very likely/unlikely in their own performances. When evaluating the two groups' performances high-status groups were more biased when their position was unstable but legitimate, while low-status groups were most biased when their position was both unstable and illegitimate. This pattern of results makes some sense. High-status groups seek to restore the stability of their 'rightful' status, while low-status groups only seek to raise their status when it seems both right and possible to do so. When high-status groups were in a position of both illegitimacy *and* instability, they stressed different dimensions of intergroup differences; they sought a different route to distinctiveness, which was not constrained by existing status positions.

In a task similar to that used by Turner and Brown, Turner manipulated the stability of Arts/Science differences along with the similarity of the outgroup (drawn from same *versus* different faculty as self) (Turner 1978b). Bias was strongest against similar (own faculty) outgroups, but especially when status was stable. In contrast, when outgroups were dissimilar (other faculty) bias was strongest when status was unstable.

In some circumstances, where status differences are accepted by both groups, there is no bias in evaluations. Van Knippenberg found that Dutch university students and polytechnic students agreed that the former had higher 'scientific' status (van Knippenberg 1978). Furthermore, the 'low status' polytechnic students perceived this difference to be even larger than did the 'high status' university students. Among the staff of such institutions in Britain there has been a gradual narrowing of the status gap, particularly in salary differentials. Bourhis and Hill found that university lecturers showed ingroup bias on consensually valued dimensions such as research quality, academic excellence, and prestige, and that polytechnic lecturers acknowledged their lower status on those dimensions, but emphasized their own superiority in terms of quality of teaching – an attribute not seen as particularly important by the university lecturers (Bourhis and Hill 1982). These findings illustrate the existence of social competition and are in accord with those found by Turner and Brown. The high-status group reacts to the stability of its position by expressing bias on consensually valued dimensions while rejecting the legitimacy of acquiring status on dimensions on which the low-status group is attempting to gain positive distinctiveness. Despite attempts to explain status/legitimacy effects in terms of equity (Caddick 1981, 1982), it seems that the maintenance of positive social identity is most likely to be at the heart of these findings (cf Ng 1982, 1984a; van Knippenberg 1984; van Knippenberg and Oers 1984).

Brown and Ross emphasized that it is important to examine the antecedents of status differences and of perceptions of illegitimacy (Brown and Ross 1982). Brown observed that due to a history of fluctuating (hence unstable) relative wage positions two out of three groups of engineering workers displayed ingroup bias when estimating 'appropriate' wages for each group (Brown 1978). In a similar vein, Vaughan observed that Maori children identified more with their ethnic group as urbanization proceeded (Vaughan 1978). He argued that this was partly due to the developing instability of status relations between the Pakeha and Maori groups.

Brown and Ross constructed an experimental situation to explore the impact of groups' evaluations of one another on their strategies for maintaining positive distinctiveness (Brown and Ross 1982). School children were explicitly randomly divided into two groups. Each completed a reasoning task, although one group had an easier version. Feedback to individual subjects about their group's performance (better or worse than the outgroup), was contrived to establish a status difference (but one with little legitimacy) after which subjects estimated the relative strengths of the two groups. The experimenters then provided further feedback, ostensibly the outgroup's evaluation of the ingroup's strengths. Three levels of threat were introduced. In the high-threat condition superior groups were told that the outgroup considered themselves to be equal in *all* aspects of intelligence, and inferior groups were told that the outgroup considered itself to be superior in *all* aspects of intelligence. These communications were threatening because they denied the possibility of competing for distinctiveness on any dimensions. In the moderate-threat condition the communication acknowledged ingroup status only on certain dimensions. In the low-threat condition the possibility of ingroup high status on all dimensions was acknowledged.

As predicted, ingroup bias was stronger among superior groups, although inferior groups accorded themselves higher status than the feedback indicated was appropriate. More importantly, liking for outgroup members decreased as the level of threat increased. In the high-threat condition the superior groups described the test as fairer than they had stated at an earlier stage, while the inferior groups described it as less fair. Hence the two groups were in conflict over the legitimacy of their relative statuses. Brewer and Kramer (1985) conclude that the evidence does support the view that *secure* high-status groups show less bias (e.g. Vleeming 1983) and that threats to their position promote attempts to gain increased positive differentiation (Amir *et al.* 1979).

Ng has examined the effects of a different kind of security on intergroup relations; namely security of power differences (Ng 1982, 1984a). He found that greater discrimination resulted when a group believed that it had complete control over the outgroup's rewards than when the outgroup could choose to engage with an alternative outgroup (Ng 1982). In this case secure power enables the superior group to exhibit more bias – the opposite from the consequences of secure status (Ng 1984b). Similarly, Sachdev and Bourhis found that intergroup discrimination is eliminated among members of low-power groups, but enhanced among members of high-power groups (Sachdev and Bourhis 1985). Ng has explained these effects in terms of intragroup and intergroup equity (Ng 1981, 1984a, 1984b; see also Abrams 1984, Caddick 1982, and Ch. 10 below). Surprisingly, much of the experimental work on intergroup relations has ignored the question of power. Given that the concept is central in sociological theory (Marx, Weber) this omission is all the more curious (Apfelbaum 1979). In fact, the 'power' has typically resided with the experimenter (Billig 1976; cf. Milgram 1974). Condor and Brown (1986) lament the fact that some research has employed real groups, such as males and females, to explore abstract hypotheses without first accounting for power and status differences between these groups (e.g. Doise, Deschamps, and Meyer. 1978). When these differences are deeply rooted in the structure of society it is unlikely that experimental manipulations will have sufficient impact to test such hypotheses. On the other hand, it is true that 'power' has now been recognized as an important feature of intergroup relations (Deschamps 1982; Ng 1982). We return to some of these issues in Chapter 10.

Conclusion

However influential individual differences may be in determining who *within* a group will exhibit more or less prejudiced behaviour, they cannot explain shifts of behaviour by the group as a whole. While the frustration–aggression dynamic may help us predict when individuals will *feel* like aggressing, and despite our awareness of certain limiting conditions (Berkowitz 1982), it cannot easily account for large *collections* of individuals selecting the same target of aggression. Both perspectives have problems explaining *collective* action since they do not provide any clues as to how frustration operates at the level of the group.

Relative deprivation theory introduces an important and fundamentally *social* element, namely that of social comparison. Perhaps the most interesting development has been the rediscovery and development of Runciman's notion of 'fraternal deprivation' (Runciman 1966). The finding that egoistic and fraternal deprivations lead to distinctly different reactions fits well with predictions derived from a social identity perspective. The evidence and theory converge in supporting the conclusion that variations in prejudice cannot be explained without reference to the nature of the relations between groups. The question remains of how perceptions of inequality are determined, and what consequences they have.

Sherif (e.g. 1966) also argues that intergroup behaviour must be explained in terms of the intergroup relationship rather than the characteristics of individuals, but still fails to account for the spontaneous competitiveness so characteristic of intergroup behaviour. It is in the formulation of social identity theory, starting with evidence from the minimal group paradigm, that the most persuasive explanation for intergroup behaviour in terms of *normal* psychological processes – categorization and social comparison – is found. This approach conceives of competitiveness as a consequence rather than a cause of group identification. In the concept of social identification Tajfel and Turner provide us with a process which places the group in the individual, thus dispensing with the paradox of why group behaviour is not always in the best interests of the individual (Tajfel and Turner 1979).

Social identity theory has extended its analysis of behaviour in minimal groups to provide an account of the *macro-social* relationships between groups which occupy different positions in the social status hierarchy. Social identity theory is one of the few which has confronted the impact of stability and legitimacy of intergroup relations head on. Most social psychological research has employed paradigms whereby the status quo is legitimized by the experimenter (Billig 1976). However, legitimacy has proven to be a vital determinant of intergroup behaviour when addressed by all of the other approaches mentioned in this chapter. The Freudian explanation of prejudice rests on the assumption that it is illegitimate to challenge authority figures (and hence a legitimate scapegoat is sought). Research on the frustration–aggression hypothesis has confirmed the importance of having a legitimate target for aggression. In the relative deprivation literature researchers have noted that only certain groups can be regarded as relevant (or legitimate) for comparison purposes.

Yet legitimacy is very much a product of social consensus and social perception. In the following chapter we explore the basis on which people are perceptually included or excluded from particular social categories. What cognitive processes enable or inhibit intergroup differentiation? How are these social perceptions structured, shared, and internalized by members of a social group? We now move on to discuss the question of stereotyping and the process of categorization.

Recommended reading

Social psychological approaches to intergroup behaviour are ·thoroughly reviewed by Brewer and Kramer (1985), Condor and Brown (1986), and Tajfel (1982b). The best overview of the authoritarian personality theory is still to be found in Roger Brown's (1965) text, while Billig (1976) provides a scholarly critique of psychodynamic explanations of intergroup relations. For an overview of aggression research go to Berkowitz (1982), and for relative deprivation read Crosby (1984) and Walker and Pettigrew (1984). Sherif (1966) summarizes his own research on realistic conflict in a concise and well-written book. Turner and Giles (1981) is perhaps the most accessible presentation of the social identity perspective in general on intergroup relations, while Tajfel and Turner (1979) is undoubtedly the best reference for the macro-social aspect.

4

From stereotyping to ideology

In the townships they call him the Beast. . . . If there is one man in South Africa who could be said to represent the philosophy of hard-line policing, it is Brigadier Swanepoel. The chief interrogator of the 1964 Rivonia trial – which put Nelson Mandela and others in gaol for life – and . . . best known as the officer who crushed the Soweto revolt which exploded 10 years ago today. He remembers June 16, 1976, with a sense of regret . . .:

> 'It's always difficult. It is not easy if you are in command and things get out of hand. You are trying everything to pacify the rioters and you see things are already completely out of control and it's not so easy to psyche yourself up to give the command to fire and say: "Right, pick off the leaders and shoot them". Talk was out of the question. You must realise that we were dealing with black people, we are dealing with a very emotional person. Whereas other racial groups would give you an opportunity to talk, with the blacks when they are out of control they are completely out of control. The only way you can get them under control is to use force – more force than they can take.'

(*The Guardian*, 16 June 1986)

Since the institution of slavery was so important to the economic development of America, it had a profound impact in shaping the social-political-legal structure of the nation. Land and slaves were the chief forms of private property. Property was wealth and the voice of wealth made the law and determined politics. In the service of this system, human beings were reduced to propertyless property. Black men, the creators of the wealth of the New World, were stripped of all human and civil rights. And this degradation was sanctioned and protected by institutions of government, all for one purpose: to produce commodities for sale at a profit, which in turn would be privately appropriated.

It seems to be a fact of life that human beings cannot continue to do wrong without eventually reaching out for some rationalization to clothe their acts in the garments of righteousness. And so, with the growth of slavery, men had to convince themselves that a system which was so economically profitable was morally justifiable. The attempt to give moral sanction to a profitable system gave birth to the doctrine of white supremacy.

Religion and the Bible were cited and distorted to support the status quo. . . . Logic was manipulated to give intellectual credence to the system of slavery. . . . Academicians eventually climbed on the bandwagon and gave their prestige to the myth of the superior race. Their contribution came through the so-called Teutonic Origins theory, a doctrine of white supremacy surrounded by the halo of academic respectability . . . . Even natural science, that discipline committed to the inductive method, creative appraisal and detached objectivity, was invoked and distorted to give credence to a political position. A whole school of racial ethnologists developed . . .

Soon the doctrine of white supremacy was embedded in every textbook and preached in practically every pulpit. It became a structural part of the culture. And men then embraced this philosophy, not as the rationalization of a lie, but as the expression of a final truth. In 1857 the system of slavery was given its ultimate legal support by the Supreme Court of the United States in the Dred Scott decision, which affirmed that the Negro had no rights that the white man was bound to respect.

(Martin Luther King Jnr, *Chaos or Community*, 1967)

These extracts capture some of the major issues dealt with in this chapter. The first illustrates the use of derogatory stereotypes and how the specific stereotype being employed (i.e. 'emotionality') fulfils a clear social function in explaining and justifying actions – in this case the use of force in controlling South African Blacks. The second extract takes the social function of stereotypes further: it describes the social processes through which intergroup practices are rationalized and explained and become ideologically legitimated. In this chapter we discuss the nature of stereotypes, how stereotypic perceptions arise, what functions they may fulfil for individuals, groups, and society, and how stereotypic content is related to the purpose of specific social collectivities.

Introduction

In constructing his scientific classification of living things in the late eighteen century, the great Swedish botanist and natural historian Linnaeus described 'the European' as 'fair, sanguine, brawny; covered with close vestments; governed by laws', and 'the African' as 'black, phlegmatic, relaxed; anoints himself with grease, governed by caprice' (quoted by Leach 1982: 83). These descriptions are stereotypes.

Stereotypes are generalizations about people based on category membership. They are beliefs that all members of a particular group have the same qualities, which circumscribe the group and differentiate it from other groups. A specific group member is assumed to be, or is treated as, essentially identical to other members of the group, and the group as a whole is thus perceived and treated as being homogenous. This homogenization can vary in its extremity and rigidity, and is more often than not heavily associated with evaluation. That is, there is a tendency to attach derogatory stereotypes to outgroups and favourable ones to ingroups. An important feature of stereotypes is that they are *shared*; that is, large sections of society will agree on what the stereotypes of particular groups are. So, for example, there is a wide consensus in some societies that the Irish are stupid, that Blacks are irresponsible, that women are emotional, and so forth, despite the existence of numerious exceptions (e.g. James Joyce, Martin Luther King, Margaret Thatcher).

Stereotyping is a fundamental and probably universal bias in perception which has important and far-reaching consequences for behaviour, ranging from relatively harmless assumptions about people to gross practices such as genocide. It is a central component of prejudice and intergroup relations, and its study is inextricable from the study of intergroup behaviour (see Ch. 3). Not surprisingly, social psychology has invested a great deal of energy in its explication. However, many traditional approaches tend to offer only a partial explanation because they focus largely upon one aspect of the phenomenon. A complete explanation must theoretically integrate an explanation of the individual psychological processes involved in producing the bias, the more social psychological processes which are responsible for the sharedness of stereotypes, and the social processes which assign different stereotypes to different groups and ensure their persistence over time as well as their resistance to change.

In this chapter we show how the social identity approach facilitates such an integrative analysis. We begin by briefly discussing the traditional descriptive approach to stereotypes – for psychodynamic approaches, specifically Dollard et al.'s frustration – aggression hypothesis (Dollard et al. 1939) and Adorno et al.'s authoritarian personality (Adorno et al. 1950; see the beginning of Ch. 3 above) – but dedicate the major portion of the chapter to the development, description, and extension of the social identity approach. We also discuss attribution, social explanation, social representation, and ideology in the context of a treatment of social processes involved in stereotyping. The end of the chapter offers a discussion of ways to reduce or eliminate prejudice, discrimination, and stereotyping, and a brief but critical exposition of the limitations of some contemporary social cognition treatments of stereotyping.

Descriptive approaches

Lippmann furnishes the first systematic social scientific treatment of the concept of 'stereotype' (Lippmann 1922). He believed that in order to function in an overwhelmingly complex social environment people construct a simplified 'picture' in their heads of that environment. This picture, which is effectively inserted between the person and the environment, Lippmann calls our 'quasi-environment'. Its content, which is at least partly culturally determined, constitutes stereotypes. In effect, stereotypes are viewed as simplified 'pictures' of the social world. Furthermore, they are considered to be undesirable because they are factually incorrect, are rigid and resistant to education, and are generated by a suboptimal reasoning process which represents the short-circuiting or bypassing of 'intelligence'.

Although Lippmann's analysis contains many of the principal themes which pervade much subsequent work on stereotyping, it is really Katz and Braly who provide the framework for early research (Katz and Braly 1933). They devised a procedure for eliciting people's stereotypes of specific social groups. People simply selected from a long list of adjectives all those they believed to 'be typical of' ethnic groups (in the United States) such as negroes, Jews, Irish, and Turks, and then indicated the five most characteristic of each group. Only these were subjected to analysis, to reveal that there is in general extensive agreement between people on what constitutes the stereotype of a particular social group; for example, Katz and Braly report that 75 per cent of their sample believed negroes to be lazy and 79 per cent that Jews are shrewd.

This procedure, and various modifications of it, spawned a great deal of research which was basically of a descriptive nature. Brigham reviews much of this work in some detail (Brigham 1971), and Tajfel summarizes some of the general findings (Tajfel 1978c): (1) People show an easy readiness to characterize vast human groups in terms of a few fairly crude common attributes, that is stereotypes; (2) such stereotypes possess a kind of inertia in that they are very slow to change, and such change when it does come is in response to social, political, or economic changes; (3) stereotypes are learnt at a very young age, even before the child has any clear knowledge about the group to which the stereotype refers (e.g. Milner 1981; Tajfel 1981a); (4) stereotypes become more pronounced and hostile when social tensions arise between groups; and (5) stereotypes do not present much of a problem when little hostility is involved (e.g. students' stereotypes of drama students as being 'theatrical'), but are harmful and extremely difficult to modify in a social climate of tension and conflict (e.g. stereotypes of trade unions in contemporary Britain).

The descriptive approach, particularly in its early days, was guided by the assumption that stereotypes are undesirable, and hence it invested a great deal of energy in addressing issues founded on this assumption. For example, the 'kernel of truth' controversy: is there a kernel of truth to a stereotype (are French males indeed more romantic than English males?) and if so, how much of a generalization is the stereotype? Since stereotypes are at best an unwarranted generalization and at worst a totally incorrect assumption, then are they due to reliance upon unintelligent, non-logical, inferior cognitive processes or upon perfectly adequate processing of information but information uncritically accepted from biased sources? Brigham concluded that these problems had not been satisfactorily resolved (Brigham 1971). In any case, such issues as the kernel-of-truth controversy are very difficult to resolve given the insurmountable problems attached to obtaining objective information on the *real* distribution of characteristic in a specific group. How can one speak of stereotypes as incorrect assumptions when there is no objective yardstick against which to compare their correctness?

Descriptive studies of stereotypes are indispensable in establishing what the stereotypes of a particular group are, what their evaluative connotations are, how strongly they are held, and what social consensus there is concerning such beliefs. We are here speaking of content or structure, that is the specific constellations of characteristics which are believed to attach to one target group rather than another. However, it is quite clear that to a great extent these are questions of cultural history to do with the economic, political, and social environment in which particular groups become stereotyped. The social psychological question concerns how the individual member of society embraces such stereotypes. The descriptive approach simply states that people hold stereotypes, and charts out such matters as the degree of consensus. However, because this approach remains descriptive, it does not directly address the underlying social psychological *process* responsible for stereotyping, that is the phenomenon of stereotyping *sui generis* and independent from the specific content.

While psychodynamic approaches to prejudice – for example, the frustration-aggression hypothesis (Dollard *et al.* 1939) and the authoritarian-personality approach (Adorno *et al.* 1950) – do focus upon psychological processes underlying stereotyping, they suffer from a number of limitations, including an absence of *social* analysis. These approaches and their limitations are discussed in the context of intergroup behaviour in Chapter 3.

In anticipation of the development of our argument we would propose that an adequate and truly social psychological explanation of stereotyping must be capable of interrelating the process of stereotyping with the specific content of a stereotype. We must be able to identify the psychological processes responsible for constructing Lippmann's 'quasi-environment' in its generic form, as well as have an understanding of the origins of its content and structure. Furthermore, we must interrelate all this with an understanding of the relationship between the 'quasi-environment', as a cognitive structural factor, and with what people actually *do* (i.e. their behaviour), as well as the dialectical relationship between cognitive structure as a *representation* of reality and the reality itself which simultaneously influences and is influenced by it. These notions should become clearer later on.

Categorization and stereotyping

The very first stirrings of the social identity perspective can perhaps be traced to the late 1950s when Tajfel developed his 'accentuation principle' (Tajfel 1957, 1959; Tajfel and Wilkes 1963; see also Tajfel 1981a) to address some issues which had emerged from the 'new look' approach to the study of perception (e.g. Bruner and Goodman 1947; see also Eiser and Stroebe 1972

An English student of Scandinavian languages is waiting in the departure lounge of an international airport. He hears that his flight has been delayed five hours and is desparate to while away the time in conversation with someone. There are only eight people in the immediate vicinity. They are a varied bunch: some smoking, others not; some clearly on holiday, others on business; some Japanese, and some Swedish; and all of different heights. The accentuation principle predicts how the student will perceive the height of these eight people. Let us now look at the effects of different *peripheral dimensions* on the *focal dimension* of height.

(1) *Uncorrelated peripheral dimension* of *smoking*: some are smoking (S) and others are not (N), but this bears no relation to how tall the person is perceived to be.

(2) *Correlated peripheral dimension* of type of traveller: all the shorter ones are tourists (T) and the taller ones on business (B).

(3) *Correlated peripheral dimension (imbued with subjective value)* of being able to while away the time in conversation: all the shorter ones are monolingual Japanese (J) and the taller ones monolingual Swedes (S). Recall that the student can speak Swedish as it is a Scandinavian language.

Figure 4.1 Perceptual accentuation: an illustration

and Eiser 1986 for discussion of this work). This 'principle' is illustrated in Figure 4.1.

Tajfel believed that judgements of physical stimuli (e.g. the size, weight, colour, temperature of objects) are not made in isolation of contextual variables. They do not occur in a vacuum. Rather, people recruit other relevant factors (called 'peripheral dimensions') in order to aid judgement of the stimulus (the 'focal dimension'). So, for example, if one is judging the relative size of coins of different values and one knows that the higher the value the larger the coin, then one might employ this knowledge to help make judgements of size. What we have here is a peripheral dimension or classification (coin value) which is correlated with the focal dimension (coin size). The presence of and reliance upon such a correlated peripheral dimension leads to what Tajfel calls an 'accentuation effect' (Tajfel 1957). So in this example there is an accentuation of differences in size between coins of different value. The larger coins (of higher value) are perceived to be larger than they really are, and the smaller ones (lower value) are perceived to be smaller than they really are (precisely this effect has been obtained experimentally by Bruner and Goodman 1947.) The accentuation effect serves the function of clearly distinguishing between stimuli and thus bringing into sharper 'focus' aspects of the environment which have special importance to the individual. It is obviously important to people to be able to distinguish between coins of different worth.

Tajfel was particularly interested in the special case of a continuously distributed focal dimension, such as height, and a correlated *dichotomous* peripheral dimension – effectively a binary classification or categorization, such as sex. He hypothesized that under these conditions there would be an accentuation of differences between stimuli in different categories or classes (men seen as taller, women as shorter than they really are) and an accentuation of similarities between stimuli within a class (differences between men and between women being seen as less than they really are) – that is, a perceptual accentuation of intercategory differences and intracategory similarities on the focal dimension. From Chapter 2 you will recall Tajfel and Wilkes' classic experiment testing these ideas, in which subjects significantly exaggerated the difference in line length between categories, and there was a non-significant tendency for intracategory similarities to be accentuated (Tajfel and Wilkes 1963; see also Tajfel 1981a). These effects did not occur when the lines were presented unlabelled, nor when the A/B labelling of lines was random (not systematically correlated with line length).

Doise reports a study in which the continuous focal dimension comprised tones increasing in frequency by steps of 120 cps, and the correlated peripheral dimension or classification the consonants *b*, *d* or *g* (Doise 1978: 133). As one progresses up the frequency scale the tones are spontaneously recognized as one of these consonants, with four or five 120 cps intervals within each consonant category. Subjects were presented with two tones (A and B) differing by 240 cps and a third tone (X) which was the same as A or as B. They had to indicate whether X was identical to A or to B. It was discovered that significantly more mistakes were made when A and B fell within than between consonant categories. This is interpreted as evidence for the perceptual homogenization of stimuli falling within a category – that is, the perceptual accentuation of intracategory similarities.

These two experiments uphold Tajfel's accentuation principle: the superimposition of a systematic classification of stimuli into two categories on a continuously distributed judgemental dimension results in the perceptual exaggeration of similarities within and differences between categories. That the effect is enhanced if the categorization has importance, relevance, or value to the subject, obtains support from a study by Marchand (1970, reported by Doise 1978: 135). Marchand conducted an adaptation of Tajfel and Wilkes' (1963) study in which the categorization was imbued with value by the simple expedient of assigning different numbers of points to each category and relating the task to a forthcoming game of darts (in which the objective was to win the most points). Under these conditions it is important for the subjects to be able to clearly distinguish between stimuli falling within different categories as the potential consequence is the number of points obtained. Marchand discovered that the accentuation effect was significantly enhanced by attaching value to the categorization.

Tajfel both believed and intended his accentuation principle to apply to the judgement of social stimuli (people) just as much as physical ones (e.g. Tajfel 1969a) (see Fig. 4.1). In both domains people recruit correlated peripheral dimensions to aid judgement on a focal dimension. So, for example, the task of judging the IQ of a range of people, some black and some white, might be affected by the 'knowledge' that black people have lower IQ than white people. The focal dimension is IQ, the supposedly (or rather subjectively believed to be) correlated categorization is black/white, and the consequence is accentuation – a tendency to perceive all the blacks as having lower IQ than all the whites. This is of course a stereotypic perception which is based on a cultural belief (the degree to which this approximates reality, i.e. whether there is a 'kernel of truth', is immaterial for our purposes) that a particular attribute (the focal dimension) is associated in greater measure with one than with another social category or group (the correlated peripheral dimension, classification, or categorization).

Evidence for the accentuation effect in the perception of people is plentiful. Razran had subjects rate each of thirty photographs of ethnically ambiguous females on an array of behavioural and personality dimensions (Razran 1950). Two months later the task was repeated but this time the photographs were presented with names of unambiguous ethnic origin (Scarno, d'Angelo, McGillicuddy, O'Brien, etc.). Stereotypic ratings emerged – photographs with names of similar ethnicity were perceived to be stereotypically similar and distinct from other ethnic groups. Secord obtained behavioural and personality trait and physiognomic negroness ratings of each of a series of photographs of negroes who varied systematically in degree of physiognomic negroness (Secord 1959; Secord, Bevan, and Katz 1956). The subset of these photographs which were spontaneously categorized by the (white) subjects as negro (i.e. subjects superimposed their own categorization) were perceived to be stereotypically identical. Furthermore, prejudiced subjects exhibited a more pronounced tendency to stereotype. Presumably for them the black/non-black categorization has more subjective importance, relevance, and value and is believed to be more strongly correlated with the relevant stereotypic dimensions.

Tajfel, Sheikh, and Gardner were concerned to conduct a more naturalistic study, one not employing photographs which might tend to encourage stereotypic perceptions (Tajfel, Sheikh, and Gardner 1964; see also Tajfel 1981a). Four carefully staged (but presented as spontaneous) interviews (two involving Canadian and two Indian interviewees) were conducted in front of a class of Canadian students whose task was to rate each of the four interviewees on a series of descriptive scales. The subjects were found to judge the two Indians as less different on stereotypical than on non-stereotypical dimensions, and likewise for the two Canadians. Doise, Deschamps, and Meyer conducted two studies to consolidate Tajfel, Sheikh, and Gardner's finding, but under conditions which rule out the possibility that the latter simply reflects true similarities and differences between the Indian and Canadian speakers (Doise, Deschamps, and Meyer 1978). These studies by Tajfel and Doise and colleagues clearly show how accentuation occurs only on dimensions with which the categorization is believed to be correlated, that is stereotypical dimensions.

Finally, there are a number of studies which demonstrate the accentuation effect in the judgement of attitudes (Doise 1978 and Eiser and Stroebe 1972 discuss these in detail). Attitude statements concerning a particular issue (e.g. nuclear weapons) can be ordered in a continuous distribution as regards the focal dimension of (say) favourability. The superimposition of a social categorization (say, member of the Campaign for Nuclear Disarmament/the army) as a correlated peripheral classification on this dimension produces the familiar accentuation effect – provided that the subject's position falls clearly within the range encompassed by one of the two social categories (McGarty and Penny 1986).

Categorization thus brings the world into sharper focus and creates a perceptual environment in which things are more black and white, less fuzzy and ambiguous. It imposes structure on the world and our experiences therein. It transforms William James' 'blooming, buzzing confusion' (James 1892) into a simplified, more manageable, and better-textured world within which it is easier to function adaptively. Categorization is a fundamental and universal process precisely because it satisfies a basic human need for cognitive parsimony (Allport 1954; Cantor, Mischel, and Schwartz 1982;

Doise 1978). In effect, categorization is the cognitive process responsible for the creation of Lippmann's quasi-environment (Lippmann 1922; see Billig 1985 for an alternative perspective).

Just as categorization causes accentuation effects in physical perception, so it does in social perception, where the effects are indistinguishable from stereotyping. Categorization can thus be considered to be the process underlying and responsible for stereotyping: in addition to the evidence already cited in support of this assertion, can be added more recent tests of the accentuation principle in the area of social perception (e.g. Taylor *et al.* 1978; see also Taylor 1981; Hamilton 1981).

It should be made quite clear that explaining stereotyping in terms of categorization is not reductionist: we are not attempting to explain social perception in terms of physical perception. On the contrary, we are proposing that categorization is a fundamental process which generates a unique form of perceptual distortion (i.e. accentuation) that imposes certain limits upon the way we perceive both physical *and* social objects. If pushed, we would take the stand that all perception is social to the extent that judgements, beliefs, and perceptions are overwhelmingly rooted in agreements between people on how to perceive the world. We pursue this in detail in Chapter 8, but see Moscovici (1976) and Hogg and Turner (1987a) for further discussion of this point.

There is, however, one important difference between the categorization of physical stimuli and 'social objects', namely that in the latter we ourselves are centrally implicated. We also are 'social objects' – people. Thus the relationship between self and the categories being used is an important factor which enters into the equation. It would indeed be perilous to disregard this consideration. For example, people tend to accentuate similarities between outgroup members more than between ingroup members (e.g. Park and Rothbart 1982; Wilder 1984). The next section is dedicated to the pursuit of this issue, in order to fill in the details of the categorization explanation of social stereotyping.

Social identity and stereotyping

Although categorization as an automatic cognitive process can explain stereotyping as a systematic perceptual bias, it cannot explain a number of other features of the phenomenon, namely that stereotypes of the ingroup tend to be evaluatively positive and those of the outgroup negative, that some people stereotype more extremely than others, and that the same individual will stereotype under some circumstances and not others. Similarly, categorization cannot address the origins of the specific dimensions employed to stereotype a particular group (see Ch. 3).

The social identity approach deals with these issues by theoretically linking stereotyping with group belongingness or social identity, through *self-*

categorization. Just as when we categorize others we place them in a box and accentuate their stereotypic similarities, so too when we categorize ourselves. Self-categorization is the cognitive process underlying social identification, group belongingness, psychological group formation, and so on (Turner *et al.* 1987; also see Chs. 2 and 5, this volume especially), and is also responsible for rendering behaviour and cognition stereotypic and normative. Self-categorization causes self-stereotyping, where stereotyping occurs on all and any dimensions which are believed to be correlated with the categorization, that is not only personality traits (the tacit focus of traditional research on stereotyping) but also behaviour, attitudes, beliefs, norms of conduct, emotional reactions, and physical appearance (Turner 1982). This is basically an extension of Tajfel's accentuation principle to the domain of *self*-categorization.

Precisely because stereotyping is associated with social identity and group membership through the common underlying process of categorization, it must inevitably be influenced by motivational factors involved in self-conceptualization and identity construction: specifically, a motive for positive self-regard or self-esteem which can be satisfied by accomplishing evaluatively positive intergroup distinctiveness in favour of the ingroup (but also see Ch. 10). It now becomes clear why ingroup stereotypes tend to be favourable and outgroup ones derogatory and unfavourable: self-categorization imbues the self with all the attributes of the group, and so it is important that such attributes are ones which reflect well on self. People (and societies) are motivated to try to achieve wide acceptance that ingroup/outgroup categorization is correlated with *only* those focal dimensions which reflect well on the ingroup. The ethnocentrism of stereotypic perceptions is difficult to explain in any other way.

Another consequence of the self-definitional and self-evaluative aspect of stereotyping is that the automatic accentuation effect which categorization produces is overlayed by a motivated attempt to amplify *even more* the ingroup/outgroup difference on those dimensions which evaluatively favour the ingroup. On heavily evaluative stereotypical dimensions intergroup differentiation will be doubly accentuated in order to maximize the ingroup's (and thus self's) relative evaluative superiority.

Social identity (group membership) is an important source of self-esteem, so it is not improbable to suppose that individuals with few evaluatively positive social identities or simply with a relatively threadbare repertoire of identities will invest a great deal of energy in their maintenance. They will cherish what identities they have, fiercely preserving their positive aspects *via-à-vis* outgroups, and engaging in pronounced ingroup/outgroup differentiation. They will indulge in prejudice: extreme and rigid stereotyping probably accompanied by overt behaviourial discrimination (see Tajfel 1969b for a discussion of the cognitive aspects of prejudice). Although prejudiced behaviour may occur because the individual has few positive social identities, it is important not to make the mistake of attributing this 'deficiency' to the individual as the final cause. The explanatory emphasis should rest on the sociohistorical conditions and social identity processes which provide restricted repertoires of positive social identities for certain segments of society. We shall discuss this further below.

The next point concerns immediate contextual influences on the way a given individual stereotypes. The immediate context largely determines which social categorization becomes subjectively salient or best fits the relevant perceived similarities and differences between people (Oakes 1987; Turner 1985). Different contexts cause people to categorize self and others in different ways and hence to generate different stereotypic perceptions, beliefs, and behaviours. However, as we discuss in Chapters 2 and 6, salience is not a purely cognitive phenomenon. Rather, individual actors in any given context actively try to 'negotiate' a salience which benefits self.

From the social identity perspective the crucial feature of stereotypes is that they are *shared*. They are not merely idiosyncratic generalizations which are coincidentally or by chance made by a number of people. (See Perkins' exclamation that 'Stereotypes are . . . prototypes of "shared cultural meanings". They are nothing if not social' [Perkins 1979: 141].) This sharedness is due to a *social* process of social influence which causes conformity to group norms, called *referent informational influence*. In turn, this process is underpinned by self-categorization which, as we have seen, renders self stereotypically identical to other ingroup members or to the individual's representation of the group's defining features, or prototype. Self-categorization thus generates social uniformity, intragroup consensus, or shared perceptions. In Chapter 8 we discuss in detail social influence processes in groups and conformity to group norms.

FUNCTIONS OF STEREOTYPING

Tajfel believes that stereotypes serve functions for both the individual and society (Table 4.1), and that it is very important to link theoretically these two classes of functions (Tajfel 1981b). He feels that only in so doing can we gain an integrative understanding of both the psychological form taken by stereotyping (intragroup homogenization, intergroup differentiation, etc.) and the form and content of specific stereotypes of specific groups in specific sociohistorical contexts.

INDIVIDUAL FUNCTIONS

Tajfel suggests that for individuals, stereotypes serve at least two functions: a cognitive and a value function. The former we have already discussed. It refers to the fact that as an accentuation effect, stereotyping brings the world into sharper focus. The latter refers to the way in which stereotypes, because they are above all evaluative, contribute to individuals' value systems. Let us pursue this value function a bit further.

Table 4.1   Individual and social functions of stereotyping

Individual functions	Social functions
(1) *Cognitive* (well-differentiated and sharply 'focused' world)	(1) *Social causality* (explanation of widespread and distressing social or physical events)
(2) *Value* (relatively positive self-evaluation)	(2) *Social justification* (rationalization or justification of treatment of social groups)
	(3) *Social differentiation* (accentuation and clarification of differences between social groups)

We have already seen how categorizations which are imbued with value and relevance to the individual enhance the accentuation effect and produce more rigid and extreme stereotyping. Neutral stereotypes are essentially those which have no strong positive or negative evaluative connotation, because they are associated with an intergroup categorization which has minimal subjective value or relevance to self; for example, 'Swedes are tall'. Stereotypes of this nature are easily remedied as the individual has little or no vested interest in distinguishing the category from other categories on this dimension. A few disconfirming instances would no doubt modify or abolish the belief that 'Swedes are tall'. However, where the category *is* value-laden and has direct and crucial relevance to one's own value system and conceptualization of self, there is a personal investment in preserving and accentuating intergroup distinctiveness. A disconfirming instance is extremely unlikely to have any impact on the stereotype. An obvious example would be the way in which men in western societies persist in accepting the traditional stereotype of women despite a massive number of disconfirming instances – successful (e.g. in business) women dangerously threaten the positive status of men and so successful women are seen as chance occurrences or strange quirks (see Deaux 1976).

A further consequence of the value function of stereotypes to the individual is that there is a vested interest in preserving the evaluative superiority of the ingroup at all costs. It is important that outgroup members are not accidentally included in the ingroup as this would gradually erode intergroup distinctiveness. As a result of this there is a tendency, when the categorization is imbued with a great deal of subjective value, to overexclude ambiguous individuals from the ingroup. Tajfel cites Bruner, Goodnow, and Austin's research on errors of overinclusion and overexclusion of ambiguous physical items in a category as supportive evidence (Bruner, Goodnow, and Austin 1956). He also draws attention to a number of historical examples of this phenomenon: the witchhunts of sixteenth– and seventeenth-century

Europe and the anti-Semitism of Nazi Germany are both instances in which errors of overexclusion reached the appalling extreme of mass murder and genocide. History is replete with such examples.

SOCIAL FUNCTIONS

Stereotypes also serve important functions for society. Tajfel nominates three such functions: social causality, social justification, and social differentiation (Tajfel 1981b).

Social causality refers to the search for an understanding of complex and usually distressing large-scale social (or non-social) events. A social explanation of such events involves the identification of a social group which is accused of being directly responsible and the elaboration and widely diffused promulgation of negative stereotypes which are relevant to the events being accounted for. This is the phenomenon of scapegoating. As examples, Tajfel cites the Nazis' use of the Jews as an explanation of the economic crisis experienced by Germany in the 1930s, and the use of Scots in Newcastle and Catholics in Oxford as scapegoats for the seventeenth-century plague in Britain. To this we might add the contemporary tendency of western industrial nations experiencing acute unemployment to blame immigrant groups for the crisis.

Social justification refers to the elaboration of a specific stereotype of a group in order to justify actions committed or planned against that group. Tajfel's example is the way that colonialist powers of the last century constructed derogatory stereotypes (dim-witted, simple, lazy, unable to look after themselves, etc.) of races that were being mercilessly exploited in the cause of imperialist expansion (e.g. British stereotypes of the Irish, and western stereotypes of African races; see also the Martin Luther King extract at the beginning of this chapter). The dehumanization of a group makes its exploitation seem justified, natural, and unproblematic.

Social differentiation refers to the tendency for ethnocentrism, in this case own-group-enhancing stereotypic differences, to be accentuated under conditions in which intergroup distinctiveness is perceived to be becoming eroded and insecure, or when social conditions are such that low status is perceived to be illegitimate and changeable. The conditions which trigger accentuated differentiation (repression or social change) and the different forms that these social strategies can take are discussed in Chapter 3 (see also Ch. 9; Tajfel and Turner 1979; Taylor and McKirnan 1984; van Knippenberg 1984).

The theoretical incorporation of social functions or macro-social aspects of stereotyping in the analysis of intergroup behaviour, not only adds historical substance but is necessary in order to make accurate predictions concerning specific instances of stereotyping: one needs to know the macro-social context in order to predict how individuals will behave in specific situations – for example, an experimental confrontation between groups. Hogg found, for example, that the behaviour of males and females under experimental conditions in which gender was highly salient, or very low in salience, could not have been accurately predicted without first considering the social functions of stereotypes of males and females for that population in that context (Hogg 1985a, 1987; Hogg and Turner 1987b; this work is described in Chs. 5 and 9 below). In general, a consideration of social functions and macro-social aspects of stereotyping and intergroup behaviour has been found to be useful in a number of areas, for example gender (Condor 1984; Huici 1984; Williams 1984; see Ch. 10 below), ethnolinguistic groups (Giles and Johnson 1981; see Ch. 9 below), and ethnic groups (Hogg, Abrams, and Patel 1987).

Attribution, social representation, and ideology

The analysis of social functions of stereotypes can perhaps be taken further if it is related to work on causal attribution and is located in the context of concepts such as social representation, ideology, and orthodoxy. Tajfel's social causality function deals with the way in which society identifies a specific social group as the direct cause of complex and distressing events in that particular society (Tajfel 1981b). This group attracts derogatory stereotypes and is often oppressed and persecuted. One explanation of why stereotyping serves a social causality function is provided by the attribution approach in social psychology (Harvey and Smith 1977; Heider 1958; Hewstone 1983; Jones and Davis 1965; Kelley 1967; Kelley and Michela 1980). This shares with the categorization approach the assumption that people have a basic need to simplify and impose order on the world. The attribution approach goes a step further in maintaining that there is a more fundamental underlying need to render the world predictable in order to be able to behave adaptively. Such predictability is cognitively represented by individuals as intuitive or naïve theories of the world which are arrived at by spontaneous and largely automatic cause- effect analyses of events. People are intuitive scientists engaged in the business of employing science-like but informal causal analyses in order to satisfy a fundamental need to understand the causal relationships between events, and thus render experiences, actions, and so forth, predictable and ultimately controllable.

Although the details of this approach tend perhaps to be overly concerned with the minutiae of the precise judgemental processes that people use to attribute causality, and the approach as a whole tends towards a concep-tualization of people as implausibly rational and coldly scientific creatures – see Nisbett and Ross's discussion of biases and errors which occur in making causal attributions (Nisbett and Ross 1980) – the basic assumption that people spontaneously seek causal explanations for events makes sense and has empirical support (e.g. Heider and Simmel 1944; Michotte 1963).

Traditional attribution approaches are, however, limited as regards the explanation of what causal attributions people make and when they make them. The emphasis is upon a distinction between causal attributions for people's behaviour to external environmental factors as opposed to internal dispositional or personality factors, while the entire perspective is one which focuses on the individual out of social context and fails to incorporate the impact of socially provided cultural knowledge (see Deschamps 1973–4, 1983; Eiser 1983; Hewstone 1983; Jaspars, Fincham, and Hewstone 1983; Semin 1980; Tajfel 1969b; for these and other criticisms of traditional attribution approaches). However, there is recent work, wedded in varying degrees to the social identity perspective, which suggests that in certain contexts and under certain conditions events or people's behaviours are attributed to group membership (social attributions) rather than individual personality or external factors (e.g. Deaux 1976; Taylor and Jaggi 1974; see also Hewstone 1983 and Jaspars, Fincham, and Hewstone, 1983).

The attribution perspective, particularly its 'social attribution' form accounts for the social causality function of stereotypes in terms of the motives of the individual 'attributor'. There is, however, also a social dynamic. Take for example the situation where distressing events with no ready explanation lead to social unrest within a society, providing fertile ground for minority pressure groups to engineer the attribution of blame to the dominant group. To circumvent this possibility and to consolidate their position of social advantage, the dominant group has a vested interest in disseminating as rapidly and widely as possible an immediate and completely plausible and acceptable (within the terms of reference of the wider society) causal explanation of its own. Hence a scapegoat (often the most potentially dangerous minority group) is found as a ready explanation, that diverts attention from the dominant group, ensures social cohesion, and averts social change (see also Ch. 7).

While the social attribution hypothesis has direct relevance for an understanding of the social causality function of stereotypes, its pertinence to an explanation of the social justification function is less immediate. In addition, it perhaps does not go quite far enough in breaking with traditional attribution theory, and thus remains tainted by some of the limitations of the latter (Hogg and Abrams 1985). Social stereotypes above all fulfil a 'social explanation' function which subsumes justification of actions as well as causal attribution for events and allocation of guilt, blame, and responsibility. The idea that stereotypes serve an overarching purpose of explanation resonates with concepts such as 'social representation' and 'ideology'.

Consider everyday commonsense understanding of, for example, evolutionary theory, relativity theory, Marxist economics, dietary and health preferences, AIDS, and of course psychoanalysis. These are all social representations (Moscovici's original formulation focused on the theory of psychoanalysis). Social representations (Farr and Moscovici 1984; Herzlich 1973; Moscovici 1961, 1981, 1982, 1983) are shared cognitive constructs that originate in everyday social interaction and furnish individuals with a commonsense understanding of their experiences in the world. They are

> a set of concepts, statements and explanations originating in daily life in the course of inter-individual communications, . . . [and are] the equivalent, in our society, of the myths and belief systems in traditional societies; they might even be said to be the contemporary version of commonsense.
>
> (Moscovici 1981: 181)

Although based on, and very similar to Durkheim's 'collective representa-tions', the two concepts differ in theoretical emphasis and in the level of consensuality or sharedness at which the representation is believed to operate. Durkheim was a sociologist wedded to a 'consensus' view of society as a relatively homogenous whole (see Ch. 2) and thus considered collective representations to be shared at the widest possible level, of society as a whole. His interest in how they were acquired by individuals went no further than recognizing them to be relatively static 'social facts' transmitted by socialization. Moscovici, on the other hand, prefers a conflict view of society in which there are numerous social collectivities each having its own consensual understandings, its own social representations. Furthermore, Moscovici dwells on the manner in which social representations are created and changed by social interaction – hence the substitution of 'social' for 'collective'.

Social representations are consensual understandings which emerge from the turmoil of everyday informal discussion and communication, in order to satisfy the individual's need to understand the world. As such, social representations transform the unfamiliar into the familiar and provide a framework for interpreting our experiences. They function in precisely the same way as Heider believed 'commonsense' or 'naïve' psychological theories do (Heider 1958). That is, they generate 'working hypotheses' on which are based expectations, anticipations, and predictions, and act as cognitive anchoring points against which events, occurrences, and experiences are compared. They are like Rosch's 'category prototypes' (the best, most representative embodiment of a category) against which are compared possible category members (Cantor and Mischel 1979; Rosch 1975, 1978).

Social representations have an enormous inertia in so far as experiences and perceptions are distorted to conform to the representation. If people are indeed naïve scientists, it is a science very unlike Popper's characterization in terms of 'conjecture and refutation' (Popper 1969). Rather, people try to *verify*, not refute, their hypotheses and conjectures, and by all accounts are highly successful at this. There is abundant evidence that preconceptions (Moscovici's 'social representations') distort reality in such a way as to preserve intact the preconception, and furthermore that they can even *create* a reality that fits (e.g. Lord, Ross, and Lepper 1979; Snyder 1981, 1984;

Snyder and Cantor 1979; Snyder and Swann 1978; Snyder, Tanke, and Berscheid 1977; see Moscovici's 1982 discussion).

Social representations appear to possess many properties in common with social stereotypes – both are shared, socially acquired, rigidly impervious to disconfirmation, employed to prejudge, and so on. Moscovici even relates them explicitly to category prototypes (Moscovici 1982; see our discussion of prototypes as stereotypes in Ch. 8 below). Like stereotypes they satisfy the individual's need for understanding (they furnish causal and justificatory explanations) and represent consensus and agreement (with relevant others) which facilitates communication and interaction and consolidates a view of reality.

The emergence of social representations involves an explicitly social process in which unfamiliar explanations of familiar phenomena are rendered familiar by being assimilated (distorted, simplified, etc.) through the course of everyday communication, and then enter into commonsense understanding. More precisely, small groups of 'qualified' individuals (specifically 'scientists' – in the broadest sense of the word) construct highly formalized, non-obvious, and unfamiliar explanations of familiar phenomena. Although these explanations can be, and are, taught through the medium of formal education, their dissemination is overwhelmingly through informal communication (conversations among friends in a coffee bar, etc.) This introduces systematic distortions in harmony with people's pre-existent commonsense understanding or framework of interpretation. Thus a social representation is formed and the formal scientific theory has entered into commonsense understanding in a simplified and distorted – one could say vulgarized and popularized – form. Jung illustrates the point very clearly when he writes, 'The hypothesis of a collective unconscious belongs to the class of ideas that people at first find strange but soon come to possess and use as familiar conceptions' (Jung 1972: 3).

There is, however, at least one serious limitation with the theory of social representations: it is extremely vague and imprecise (intentionally so, according to Moscovici 1982, 1983). For example, although it states that social representations are 'shared consensually by groups', it fails to define a group, doesn't identify a process relating consensuality to the group, and so forth. Potter and Litton discuss some of these ambiguities and recommend an analysis of the linguistic repertoires associated with different social representations (Potter and Litton 1985). However, this takes us little further – obviously different understandings of representations possess different 'terminologies', and the study of linguistic repertoires may elucidate the fine structure of such universes of discourse, but this approach seems to lift shared understandings out of their intergroup context, deny individuals any agency, err towards already descredited linguistic determinism (cf. Haugen 1977), and overlook the social identity dynamic underlying the origins of sharedness. A social identity analysis appears to fare much better as it can link the social functions served by social representations with individual motivational and cognitive processes. Social representations are internalized or acquired through the process of self-categorization associated with common group membership, or social identity. Contextual factors will determine identity salience (as discussed earlier) and thus the relevant level of common group membership which dictates the specific social representation which is engaged as a working hypothesis or internalized as a new frame of reference. The underlying dynamic is clearly associated with social identity.

The concept of social representations subsumes stereotypes and normative beliefs and thus highlights the latter's underlying function to furnish an understanding, explanation, or naïve commonsense theory to account for relevant events, experiences, or features of the environment. Social representations thus back onto the sociological concept of ideology (Larrain 1979) and potentially fall within the purview of hermeneutics (Bauman 1978).

It is beyond the scope of this book to pursue the 'sociological connection' in any detail, so only a very brief account will be given (for details see Bauman 1978; Billig 1976, 1982, 1984; Larrain 1979; Struhl 1981). Nevertheless, we feel it is important to make this connection as it completes our journey from cognitive process to social structure and clarifies the way that the concept of social identity is explicitly formulated to theoretically incorporate individual cognitive processes as well as societal dynamics in its explanation of stereotyping.

Consider the following extract from George Orwell's appendix to his *Nineteen-Eighty-Four*:

> Newspeak was the official language of Oceania and had been devised to meet the ideological needs of Ingsoc, or English Socialism. . . . The purpose of Newspeak was not only to provide a medium of expression for the world-view and mental habits proper to the devotees of Ingsoc, but to make all other modes of thought impossible. It was intended that when Newspeak had been adopted once and for all and Oldspeak forgotten, a heretical thought – that is, a thought diverging from the principles of Ingsoc – should be literally unthinkable, at least so far as thought is dependent on words. Its vocabulary was so constructed as to give exact and often very subtle expression to every meaning that a Party member could properly wish to express, while excluding all other meanings and also the possibility of arriving at them by indirect methods.
>
> (Orwell 1949: 305–6)

This extract captures many of the most important features of ideology. An ideology is a systematically interrelated set of beliefs and propositions whose primary function is explanation. Not only does it 'explain' but it also sets an agenda for *what* it is that one is, or should be, explaining – that is, it sets a problematic. Its terms of reference circumscribe one's thinking in such a way as to make it almost impossible to 'break out' of its mould and perceive things in a different way. Ideologies obscure contradictions, issues, and so forth that do not fall within their specific parameters. They are essentially 'schools of thought' which have the features of orthodoxy (see Deconchy 1984) in so far as they are narrowly circumscribed explanatory frameworks which inhibit the existence of cognitive alternatives.

So, for example, a capitalist ideology entails a very different way of viewing the world to a Marxist ideology. Each has an entirely different conceptual apparatus which is appropriate to its respective problematic. Fruitful interchanges between adherents of opposing ideologies is extremely difficult because of, among other things, the absence of a shared set of assumptions on what the phenomenon to be explained is, and the presence of starkly different universes of discourse (terminology, concepts, and so forth). Ideologies are essentially closed systems. They also define social groups in so far as they are correlated with, and thus presumably contingent in some way on, group membership – Muslims are defined by a different religious ideology from Catholics, and so on. An interesting discussion of the ways in which a social group ensures ideological conformity in its members is provided by Deconchy's analysis of the Catholic church (Deconchy 1984; religion is often considered to be the prototypical model of ideology – see Lefebvre 1968). He specifies an array of practical measures such as exclusively intragroup caucuses, and also terminological features of ideology itself.

In a stratified society, the dominant group attempts to impose its own ideology on others because in so doing it consolidates its position. The dominant ideology obscures issues which might otherwise cause subordinate groups to become acutely aware of their oppression and hence strive for social change. For example, the ideology of capitalism obscures the fact that for a capitalist system to flourish it must economically exploit a large segment of society; instead, it stresses the possibility of upward social mobility (see Ch. 3) by dint of entrepreneurial individual exertion. Another example is Hinduism: the caste system is justified and treated as immutable, and social improvement promised as a reward that accrues through rebirth into a higher social stratum. Finally, male dominance in many societies is ensured by a scientific ideology which justifies the subordinance of women in terms of innate biological differences.

Although the concept of ideology is clearly related to Moscovici's social representations (1961, 1981) and Tajfel and Turner's social belief structures (Tajfel and Turner 1979; especially see Chs. 2 and 3 above), it receives scant consideration in contemporary social psychology (but see Billig 1976, 1982, 1984). Instead, it remains within the confines of sociology and political science, where it has always been a topic of fierce controversy and debate (Bauman 1978; Larrain 1979) – one of the major issues being whether and in what sense ideology is false consciousness (not dissimilar to the social psychological issue mentioned earlier in this chapter, of whether there is a kernel of truth to a stereotype), and relatedly whether there can ever be an end to ideology (the existence of an impartial 'explanation' which does not serve the interests of one social group at the expense of others). Ideology is, however, seen to be a product of social conflict, and as such is deeply if not fundamentally rooted in an intergroup setting.

Let us now conclude this section by linking together some of the concepts that have been introduced in this and the previous section. The human need not only to categorize and explain the world but also to do this in a way which reflects favourably on self-perception, results in a heterogenous society containing many social groups which vie for relative dominance and recognition. The individual cognitive process of categorization is responsible for identification with a group, or psychological group formation, and also for an accentuation effect which manifests itself as stereotypic behaviour – that is, stereotypic in the broadest possible sense of consensual intragroup and differential intergroup beliefs, attitudes, values, attributions, conduct, and so on. The entire process is stamped to varying degrees with the need to favour the ingroup over other groups and to maintain or attain a position of relative social dominance (either with respect to society as a whole or with respect to specific relevant other groups). The particular normative actions and beliefs of different groups, and the stereotypes they hold of themselves and others is rooted in the dynamics of intergroup relations which form the basis of history. More specifically they are shaped or contextualized by broader social representations, or ideologies which develop to fulfil a fundamental need to be able to explain the nature of things. Large-scale and potentially complex events such as famine, war, plague, economic collapse, and so forth, engender their own self-interested social explanations or ideologies. These can be newly fashioned explanations, modifications of existing explanations, or unchanged explanations which have hitherto been suppressed or lain dormant.

The elimination of stereotyping and prejudice

The preceding analysis leads us to the rather gloomy conclusion that stereotyping cannot be eliminated. It is an inevitable product of a fundamental cognitive process which fulfils a basic human need for order and predictability. Furthermore, stereotypes are part of wider social explanations which again fulfil a human need to explain phenomena. Added to all this is a need for a relatively positive self-image which creates a vested interest in maintaining the stereotypic inferiority of relevant outgroups. So it would appear that stereotyping is an inevitable product of a constellation of fundamental human needs. (See Billig 1985 for a critical discussion and a different perspective.)

However, these needs should not be considered mechanical causes with a one-to-one relationship with behavioural outcome. Rather, they set the cognitive motivational limits of human behaviour within which there is a great deal of variability. Just as the human need for food means that eating is inevitable, there is still rich variation in what, how much, where, when, and how we eat. The question of the elimination of stereotyping should really be recast – clearly, the absolute elimination of stereotyping (or eating) is as impossible as it is harmful to the individual. Instead, we should ask how we can modify stereotypes so that they do not oppress; that is, how we can reduce the harmful or unacceptable extremes of derogatory stereotypes and discriminatory behaviour.

The state of affairs to be reformed is the all too common one in which one group in society is invested with all the apparatus of social control (police, armed forces, media, education, etc.) and thus possesses the power to enforce its own self-enchancing vision of social reality and promulgate negative stereotypes of minority rights groups. Furthermore, the dominant group also has the power to handicap materially subordinate groups by denying them economic and social equality, and thus create a reality which may not have existed previously. We have already referred above to the power of stereotypes alone to create in others behaviour which confirms the stereotype – for example, the work of Snyder and colleagues (Snyder 1981, 1984; discussed by Moscovici 1982) – so how much stronger this must be when associated with a precipitous power differential. Consider, for example, the plight of the Australian Aborigine: economically and educationally disadvantaged by the dominant white group over a long enough period to ensure a life-style which is degraded and impoverished to such an extent that the stereotype becomes an ugly reality (see Wilson 1982).

The reduction of prejudice is clearly a political issue, an issue to do with how minority groups can achieve radical social change (overthrow the *ancien régime* and construct a new social order which vanquishes overt oppression and discrimination), or how there can be a 'social-contract' (see Rousseau [1762] 1968) within which social reforms can be implemented to gradually attenuate extreme inequalities and rigid stereotypes. These issues are beyond the scope of this book, but it does seem clear that in order to reduce stereotyping and prejudice one must tackle the intergroup context – that is, reduce intergroup power differentials and disconfirm stereotypic differences which are most heavily evaluative, yet still preserve a degree of differentiation that furnishes groups with relatively positive social identity.

And how does one do this (within the terms of reference of a liberal-democratic social order which frowns on revolutionary change)? One popular belief is that interpersonal contact (e.g. between races) *per se* will achieve this. It is, however, more likely that it will not as it might simply confirm stereotypes, or might create a personal friendship between two individuals of different races which defines each individual out of his or her respective group and leaves group perceptions unaltered. If inter-racial contact does not disconfirm stereotypes (and how can it in the context of a prevalent ideology of racism?), then it leaves prejudice unaffected (see Hewstone and Brown 1986; Miller and Brewer 1984; Wilder 1986). Evidence for this abounds: as we saw in the discussion of Sherif's boys camp studies in Chapter 3, intergroup contact did not reduce discrimination unless there was a superordinate or shared goal which effectively furnished a superordinate common identity.

Other strategies include propaganda and education (see Tajfel 1973; Yinger and Simpson 1973; see also Ch. 3 above). However, although government-run exhortations which proscribe prejudice (usually with reference to an absolute or superordinate morality) may attenuate more extreme discriminatory practices, they are unlikely to make any significant impact unless accompanied by radical reforms aimed at reducing objective material and educational inequalities. For example, Kinder and Sears' theory of *symbolic racism* proposes that contemporary anti-black prejudice in the United States, far from having declined, merely finds its expression in rationalized and less immediately objectionable forms (Kinder and Sears 1981). These forms are often determined by a subjective perception of a conflict of racial group interests (see Bobo's 1983 analysis of whites' opposition to 'bussing'). Furthermore, it is difficult to see how education can have any significant cumulative effect if children are exposed outside of the classroom to a culture of prejudice (the media, parents' opinions, actual discrimination, and the objective fact of social inequality).

The essential point is that while prejudgement and social generalization are inevitable, prejudice and stereotyping are not. The latter can be reduced, but *only* by directly addressing their material and ideological bases. To the extent that a society comprises social collectivities which mediate relatively positive social identity yet do not possess exclusive and institutionalized material and ideological power over other groups, we have conditions under which no one group oppresses another. While this may be an admirable end-point or goal; its stability over time is of course an entirely different matter. The intrinsically competitive nature of intergroup relations sponsors forces for differentiation which militate against enduring stability and ensure a dynamic relationship or struggle between groups for social advantage.

Social cognition and stereotyping

Since the late 1970s the dominant approach in social psychology has undoubtedly been 'social cognition', represented by that literature concerned with the perceptual and mnemonic biases and errors that arise from the automatic functioning of cognitive processes (see Fiske and Taylor 1984; Landman and Manis 1983; Markus and Zajonc 1985; Nisbett and Ross 1980). This approach has much to say concerning person perception, and hence stereotyping (e.g. Hamilton 1981) and is closely related to certain aspects of the social identity perspective. However, there are marked differences. In this final section we shall merely outline (we cannot hope to do more in the space available) some of the principal features of the social cognition perspective in order to identify similarities to and differences from the social identity approach. Our principal aim is to try and identify what we consider to be some limitations of the social cognition approach as regards the explanation of stereotyping and prejudice, as well as group behaviour as a whole.

Social cognition treats people as 'cognitive misers' who employ an array of cognitive and judgemental processes which have heuristic value, in so far as they are perfectly adequate for everyday transactions with the world but fall short of optimal (science-like) standards for 'correct' judgement, perception, and information-processing in general. Reliance on these heuristics produces the systematic biases and errors which characterize human behaviour. With the aid of these processes people construct a simplified and manageable representation of the world and their experiences in it, and these representations in turn act as generalized preconceptions, theories, or hypotheses concerning the world. 'Human frailty' is viewed as the product of automatic cognitive processes and mnemonic structuring which actively construct a simplified and thus biased representation of the world.

The major emphasis in this tradition concerns the study of the minutiae of cognitive processes and mnemonic organization in person perception, and is thus heavily and intentionally based in cognitive psychology. It is often identifiable as *social* psychology only in so far as it studies the perception and judgement of *social* objects – people.

From this perspective social stereotypes are considered to be biases and errors. They are viewed as 'products of normal everyday cognitive processes of social categorization, social inference, and social judgement and so may be studied in terms of general principles of human cognitive activity' (Borgida Locksley, and Brekke 1981: 153). However, relatively little attention is actually paid to stereotyping. For example, Markus and Zajonc's 77-page review of social cognition dedicates only one paragraph (one-fifth of one page) to a discussion of stereotyping, (Markus and Zajonc 1985), while Hamilton's edited book is, to our knowledge, one of the very few complete treatments of cognitive processes and stereotyping from a social cognition perspective (Hamilton 1985).

While the term 'stereotype' is rarely used, it is clearly an element of cognitive or knowledge structure, and for this, social cognition has developed a rich conceptual vocabulary that includes inferential sets, hypotheses, theories, scripts, themes, frames, categories, prototypes, attitudes, and schemata. While there are differences between these concepts, recent developments seem to suggest that they are overwhelmed by similarities (Markus and Zajonc 1985: 149). 'Schema' is perhaps the most widely used term – it is a 'cognitive structure that represents organized knowledge about a given concept or type of stimulus' (Fiske and Taylor 1984: 140), and schemata are 'subjective "theories" about how the social world operates . . . [that] are derived from generalizing across one's experience with the social world' (Markus and Zajonc 1985: 145). A prototype is an 'abstract set of features commonly associated with members of a category, with each feature assigned a weight according to the degree of association with the category' (Cantor 1981: 27). A script is very similar to a schema but relates specifically to stereotyped sequences of events (e.g. eating out in a restaurant, making a purchase in a shop).

Once activated, a schema operates as a self-fulfilling prophecy; it distorts perception and memory to confirm it and can even create schema-congruent behaviour in the object of perception (see our mention earlier in this chapter of Snyder and colleagues' work). The object of perception can be oneself – a 'self-schema' (Markus 1977) – which is a 'familiar, affective, robust, complex, verbal self-portrait' (Fiske and Taylor 1984: 156) which is self-enhancing in so far as people would prefer to represent themselves in a positive rather than negative light. It should be noted that self-schemata are generally (but see Bem's 1981 discussion of gender-schema) treated as representations of self in terms of individuating personality traits (e.g. honest, extravert, sociable, hardworking) rather than group membership.

To deal with schemata of specific group memberships (what we would call social stereotypes), social cognition reserves the term 'role-schema'. Fiske and Taylor explicitly state that role-schemata account for stereotyping, as they contain stereotypic information concerning specific social roles (what we might term 'groups')' and have all the biasing qualities of schemata and knowledge structures in general.

Both the social cognition and social identity approaches treat stereotyping as a natural consequence of the automatic operation of cognitive processes, emphasize the functional value to the organism of simplified images of the social world, and thus endow stereotypes with cognitive inertia (resistance to modification in the light of disconfirmatory evidence, thus having the quality of a self-fulfilling prophecy). However, the approaches differ markedly in their understanding of the term 'social' in social psychology. For social cognition it simply means 'people', so judgement, perception, memory and so on, become social only to the extent that they concern people. There is no theoretical treatment of emergent properties of social interaction – such as *shared* perceptions, norms, and so on – or of group membership as a psychological state with specific and unique effects. For social identity the entire analysis rests precisely upon the theoretical analysis of group membership.

Recently, social cognition has come under attack for being asocial (e.g. Forgas 1981; Markus and Zajonc 1985; Moscovici 1982; Wyer and Srull 1984; also see Ch. 9 below), and it is so in a number of ways:

(1) Its model of human beings is asocial in that it views people as isolated

information-processing modules that are only social to the extent that certain sources of information are other people.

(2)   Its universe of discourse is quite alien to social psychology and is more akin to mainstream cognitive psychology. Although the adoption of cognitive psychological concepts and methods has undoubtedly contributed to greater experimental versatility and rigour, the cost has been the extirpation of the 'social' from social psychology.

(3)   It is asocial in its foci of concern. Instead of tackling the essential problems of social psychology such as aggression, competition, cooperation, conformity, communication, group processes, intersubjectivity, and so on, it dwells rather disappointingly on memory structure, judgemental heuristics, and so forth.

Markus and Zajonc even go so far as to conclude from their review that all that social cognition has achieved is a sophisticated methodology which has made it possible to finally confirm some of the more minor, and hitherto untested, assumptions of the 'new look' in cognitive psychology (Markus and Zajonc 1985: 196–7). The central tenet of the 'new look' (Bruner 1951, 1957) was that people construct hypotheses concerning the world and that these hypotheses function as preconceptions which distort perception. Markus and Zajonc are of the opinion that social cognition has made no significant *theoretical* advances on this earlier work. It is worth recalling at this juncture that the social identity perspective also has its roots in the new look (Tajfel's work in the 1950s on categorization, accentuation and stereotyping (see Eiser and Stroebe 1972) stemmed from issues addressed by Bruner), but has developed in a distinctly different direction to social cognition. As regards social cognition, Markus and Zajonc feel that the foremost issue is whether '*social* cognition is a process formally identical to other perceptual and cognitive processes – and whether it can therefore be studied by a straightforward application of cognitive science' (Markus and Zajonc 1985: 208); or whether different explanatory concepts must be introduced.

Our position is of course that other explanatory concepts *are* needed, specifically the concept of social identity which reflects a consideration of the social group as a psychological reality. By failing to do this, social cognition's treatment of stereotyping contains a number of related limitations (see Condor and Henwood 1986):

(1)   It fails to account for possibly the most important feature of stereotypes, that they are widely *shared, consensual* perceptions. There is no analysis of the parameters or function of consensuality, nor the process whereby consensuality may arise.

(2)   There is nothing on the dialectical relationship between individual and society, and thus no treatment of the macro-social determinants of

specific stereotypes and the role played by the individual in the acceptance or rejection of a specific social reality. The fact that social groups as elements in the broader intergroup context of a society as a whole create stereotypes for specific purposes is not incorporated in the social cognition perspective. Even the simple fact that stereotypes and social groups go together, and hence that group membership must be implicated theoretically to at least some extent, seems to have been overlooked.

(3)   In the absence of a theoretical link between macro-social dynamics and individual stereotyping behaviour, it is difficult to see how social cognition can deal with social change. If stereotyping is a normal product of automatic and presumably universal cognitive dynamics, then how can changes in stereotyping (content and evaluative connotation) be explained without at least some consideration of the actions of minority interest groups, and of individuals' (or group members') attempts to preserve or modify a specific status quo?

Conclusion

In this chapter we have presented the social identity analysis of social stereotyping (and prejudice). The automatic cognitive process of categorization fulfils a human need to simplify and 'bring into focus' the social world by accentuating differences between categories and similarities within categories on dimensions subjectively believed to be correlated with the categorization. Categorization of self is responsible for group belongingness and thus creates consensual group perceptions. Furthermore, people strive to maintain or acquire positive ingroup stereotypes in relation to other groups, as this reflects favourably on self-evaluation.

The social origins of stereotypes are traced to the wider intergroup context and the social explanatory and ideological needs of social groups as a whole in their struggle for relative superiority and dominance over other groups. Stereotypes are internalized by individual group members as self-definitions and as characterizations of other groups by the social influence process of referent informational influence which is predicated on the categorization process responsible for group belongingness.

This analysis is contrasted with other approaches whose limitations are adumbrated. Namely, the descriptive approach which fails to illuminate the *process* of stereotyping, and the social cognition approach which is distinctly asocial in its failure to theoretically address the normative, consensual, shared nature of stereotypes and the sociohistorical dimension of their origin.

We also discussed the thorny issue of how to eliminate prejudice and stereotyping, and concluded that since stereotyping fulfils fundamental human and societal functions, it cannot be eliminated. However, by tackling intergroup power differentials and corresponding derogatory stereotypes and repressive practices, the more repugnant and damaging features of extreme forms of prejudice can be eliminated.

Recommended reading

Ashmore and Del Boca (1981) provide a good general overview of stereotyping research and theory. Categorization and accentuation are covered well by Doise (1978) and Tajfel (1981a), while Eiser and Stroebe (1972) undoubtedly give the most detailed account. The social identity analysis of stereotyping is spelt out by Tajfel (1981b) and the social cognition approaches represented in books by Hamilton (1981) and Fiske and Taylor (1984).

5

Intragroup behaviour: processes within groups

The biggest job in getting any movement off the ground is to keep together the people who form it. This task requires more than a common aim: it demands a philosophy that wins and holds the people's allegiance.

Although the intense solidarity of the protest year has inevitably attenuated, there is still a feeling of closeness among the various classes and ages and religious denominations that was never present before. . . . There is a contagious spirit of friendliness and warmth; even the children seem to display a new sense of belonging.

These quotations come from Martin Luther King Jnr's autobiographical account of the historic events in Montgomery, Alabama, in 1955 and 1956 (*Stride Toward Freedom: The Montgomery Story*, 1958). Montgomery was the forerunner of the black civil rights movement of the next ten to fifteen years, in which Martin Luther King's role as figurehead and leader has entered into the annals of history: his magnificently rousing speeches and his single-minded adherence to the Gandhian principles of non-violent protest. In order to draw national attention to segregation and discrimination in Montgomery, the black community, led mainly by King, organized a boycott of Montgomery's buses (on which there was segregated seating). The battle was not easily won: the activities of the white community coupled with the inclemencies of winter weather took their toll. Yet the boycott persisted for a full year and accomplished its immediate goal: desegregation of the buses. King's account of the solidarity and cohesiveness of the black community, which was forged by the protest out of factional bickering and dispirited apathy captures many of the themes to be covered in this chapter.

It describes how solidarity and group cohesiveness is not just a matter of shared goals and aims but also something else which seems to keep people together, something which secures allegiance to the group rather than the individuals in the group. It also documents the waxing and waning of solidarity in response to the degree of salience of the group, its importance in and impact on everyday life. It also emphasizes how the closeness within the group transcends other non-salient social categorizations (such as sex, religious denomination, age, class), and how the liking felt by one group member for another is contagious and generalized within the group: how it is effectively a liking for all bounded by the parameters of the group.

Introduction

The preceding two chapters focused mainly upon relations between groups: Chapter 3 on intergroup behaviour and relations, and Chapter 4 on intergroup perceptions and representations. In the present chapter we change our emphasis and examine what goes on *within* groups: intragroup behaviour. This shift in emphasis recaptures the historical development of the social identity approach: it started out emphasizing *inter*group behaviour (e.g. Tajfel and Turner 1979) and gradually shifted to *intra*group behaviour (e.g. Turner 1982), while never forgetting that the two are theoretically inextricable.

The study of intragroup behaviour, often called 'small-group dynamics', has a long history in social psychology and constitutes one of the discipline's major fields. However, through approaching it in a different way from traditional theory, the social identity approach highlights limitations and offers theoretical integration. From our perspective, intragroup behaviour refers to interaction between two or more individuals that is governed by a common or shared social self-categorization or social identity. To explore this claim we shall focus on group cohesiveness, psychological group formation, and the relationship between identification and liking (attraction) in small groups, in the context of a more general documentation of small-group dynamics (e.g. communication networks and structures, leadership patterns, decision-making, group productivity, social facilitation, the impact of group norms). (See Hogg 1985b, 1987, for further details.)

Group dynamics

Group dynamics is that field which studies the behaviour of individuals in *small* groups, such as sports teams, decision-making groups, T-groups, friendship groups, work groups, and so forth. Some of the earliest work in this tradition concerned the power of group discussion to change the attitudes, beliefs, norms, and behaviour of group members (Coch and French 1948; Lewin 1943; Pennington, Harary, and Bass 1958; Radke and Klisurich 1947). It was with the study of group dynamics that experimental social psychology really blossomed. In 1945, under Kurt Lewin's directorship, the Research Centre for Group Dynamics was created, and attracted over the years a large number of social psychologists whose ideas have greatly influenced the complexion of contemporary social psychology, e.g. Lewin, Festinger, Schachter, Newcomb, Back, French (see Cartwright 1979; Marrow 1969; Festinger 1980).

Despite the promising emphasis upon theory, originally encouraged by

Lewin, pragmatics very soon prevailed. Even in the early days the paymaster was frequently the army, the government, or industry, who had some specific problem to be resolved, so not surprisingly the study of small-group dynamics rapidly sacrificed time-consuming theory construction for problem-solving and small-scale hypothesis testing (note the parallel with research into persuasive communication where the demands of the advertising industry have wrought the same effect – see Jaccard, 1981). Currently, 'small-group dynamics' is generally *not* mainstream experimental social psychology. It has its own journal (*Small Group Behaviour*), wherein one can witness the general emphasis upon problem-solving rather than theory development, and tends to be heavily influenced by psychodynamic analyses of psychotherapy groups (e.g. Kellerman 1981).

'Small-group dynamics' tends to address questions concerning the relationship between internal group structure and cohesiveness, and the efficiency or goal effectiveness of the group as a whole. So, for example, research has been done on formal communication networks and informal communication patterns in small groups in order to identify optimal arrangements for the achievement of different objectives, and on factors (e.g. the size of the group and its cohesiveness) which facilitate or hinder such arrangements. Leadership is another important area which constitutes part of a general analysis of the determinants and consequences of the internal structuring of groups: the way in which groups are internally differentiated by status, power, and prestige hierarchies containing different roles, cliques, subgroups, and so forth. Many small groups only exist in order to perform tasks or make decisions, so it comes as no surprise to discover that the study of the efficiency and productivity of small groups is perhaps the major focus of research in group dynamics (see also Ch. 6). The emphasis here is upon factors such as group size, group cohesiveness, group structure, communication structure, and leadership, and their effect upon productivity and decision-making. There is also an interest in the role of group norms (see also Ch. 8), as opposed to relatively mechanical features of group interaction, in dictating productivity levels and governing group decisions.

For specific and up-to-date details of findings in group dynamics see the references cited at the end of this chapter. Our interest is to identify and discuss some common themes underlying this research.

Group cohesiveness

TRADITIONAL PERSPECTIVES ON THE SOCIAL GROUP.

One factor which has a generally reliable effect on group behaviour is the cohesiveness of the group. In general it enhances group productivity (Schachter *et al.* 1951) and performance (Goodacre 1951), increases conformity to group norms (Festinger, Schachter, and Back 1950), improves morale and job satisfaction (Exline 1957; Gross 1954), facilitates intragroup communication (Knowles and Brickner 1981), reduces intragroup hostility and directs it toward an outgroup (Pepitone and Reichling 1955), and increases feelings of security and self-worth. There are, however, exceptions which we shall discuss below.

Group cohesiveness is the cornerstone concept in the analysis of small-group behaviour, and since its introduction in the 1940s and 1950s (French 1941; Lewin 1952) it has not noticeably relinquished this position (see Blumberg et al. 1983; Kellerman 1981). In its scientific experimental social psychological usage it is defined as 'the resultant of all the forces acting on the members to remain in the group' (Festinger 1950: 274) or the 'total field of forces which act on members to remain in the group' (Festinger, Schachter, and Back 1950: 164) and derives from the attractiveness of the group and its members and the extent to which the group mediates goals which are important for the members. The cohesiveness of the group as a whole is defined as the average magnitude of the forces acting on all the individual group members. The background to this analysis comprises Lewin's field theory approach to psychology (Lewin 1948, 1952). Very briefly, Lewin argued that behaviour is governed by the elements of psychological experience which are represented in our minds, and the evaluative relationships between these elements; all of which compose the 'life space'. This sets up a motivational network that guides behaviour. So, for Lewin, the group quality of cohesiveness, the way in which groups appear to vary along a dimension 'from a loose "mass" to a compact unit' (1948: 84), is reciprocally determined by the psychological representation in the individual's 'life space' of interindividual forces within the group.

Although the concept of group cohesiveness permits and recommends different operationalizations (Festinger, Schachter and Back 1950; Lewin 1952), it is usually optionalized both theoretically and empirically as attraction between group members: interpersonal attraction or liking. This tendency is clear both in early and more recent work (e.g. Back 1951; Berkowitz 1954; Downing 1958; Newcomb 1953; Pepitone and Reichling 1955; Schachter et al. 1951; versus Knowles and Brickner 1981; Nixon 1976; Wolf 1979). It is well documented that for all practical purposes the term 'cohesiveness' is used to refer only to interpersonal attraction (Cartwright 1968; Hogg 1985b, 1987; Lott and Lott 1965; McGrath and Kravitz 1982; Turner 1984; Zander 1979). Interpersonal liking becomes 'the "cement" binding together group members' (Schachter et al. 1951: 229) and hence the sine qua non of psychological group formation or group belongingness: 'without at least a minimal attraction of members to each other a group cannot exist at all' (Bonner 1959: 66; see also Shaw 1981). This rapid restriction of the concept of group cohesiveness has been accompanied by an equally rapid and complete abandonment of its background in Lewinian field theory. What remains is the belief that mutual liking transforms a collection of individuals into a group.

This idea of group cohesiveness embraces a distinctive model of the social group, which we can call the 'social cohesion' model (Hogg 1985b, 1987; Turner 1982, 1984). It likens the group to a molecule in which individual atoms are people and inter-atomic forces are interpersonal attraction (e.g. Kellerman 1981). (In turn, this represents a manifestation of the wider, well-documented tendency in social science to adopt physical or biological metaphors as models of social processes, as documented by Pepitone 1981.) The social cohesion model attributes the emergence of 'inter-atomic' forces of interpersonal attraction to the multitude of factors which are known to determine liking, including co-operative interdependence to achieve shared goals, attitude similarity, physical proximity, common fate, shared threat/a common enemy, being liked or approved of by the other, attractive personality traits, and success on group tasks (Lott and Lott 1965). It is taken for granted that one is attracted to or likes people who are 'rewarding' and that a 'reward' is some action, attitude or attribute of oneself or another that satisfies a need (desire, drive, motive, etc.). Thus it follows that a collection of people come together to form a group, spontaneously or deliberately, to the degree that they have needs capable of mutual satisfaction and in this sense are *dependent* upon one another.

Turner, Hogg, Oakes, Reicher, and Wetherell have identified the fundamental hypothesis as being the belief that people who depend upon each other (which need not be an exclusive dependence) to satisfy one or more of their needs, and who achieve or expect to achieve satisfactions from their association, develop feelings of mutual attraction and hence become a group (Turner *et al.* 1987). There is wide acceptance of the gestalt assumption that the 'wholeness' of the group, despite what may be very different 'parts' (i.e. members), reflects the interdependence of those 'parts'. The differences that exist between theorists are largely to do with how explicit an emphasis is placed on interdependence, what antecedents or aspects of interdependence are stressed, and whether or not interpersonal attraction is credited explicitly with a direct role. To substantiate these points let us briefly review a selection of important treatments of the group (see Hogg 1987).

In general, theories tend to fall into one of two camps: those stressing explicit interindividual interdependence (e.g. Lewin, Sherif, Deutsch), and those stressing interindividual similarity (e.g. Festinger, Heider), respectively, as the basis of attraction. Lewin believed that the 'essence of a group is not the similarity or dissimilarity of its members, but their interdependence. A group can be characterized as a "dynamical whole"' (Lewin 1948: 84). Cohesiveness (as mutual forces of attraction within the group) is also considered to be a fundamental quality of the group (e.g. see Lewin 1952: 162), and so interdependence and cohesiveness co-vary and relate to need satisfaction. Need satisfaction is the motive for interdependence, and the more complete the latter, the greater the need satisfaction and the greater the group's cohesiveness.

The Sherifs consider co-operative interdependence in the pursuit of shared goals that cannot be achieved by an individual alone to result in the establishment of a well-defined group structure (i.e. role relations and shared rules of conduct), and it is this that distinguishes a group from a mere aggregate of individuals (Sherif 1967; Sherif and Sherif 1969; see also Ch. 3 above). However, psychologically speaking, the crucial process is repeated positive interindividual interaction: group formation proceeds 'from interaction among unrelated individuals to the stabilization of role-status relations and norms' (Sherif and Sherif 1969: 132). Mutual need satisfation through co-operative interaction imbues group members with positive valence and so makes the group attractive and encourages members to remain within it. Although Sherif believes there is more to group formation than the development of spontaneous personal friendships (Sherif 1967), his theory, nevertheless, rests upon the implicit idea that individual members become attractive (and the group therefore cohesive) to the degree that they contribute through interindividual interaction to the attainment of one's goals.

Deutsch's analysis is extremely similar, except with the emphasis on goals rather than activity (Deutsch 1949, 1973). Goals which can only be achieved through the co-operation of individuals are 'promotively interdependent', and an individual 'will acquire positive valence . . . (become attractive) if . . . seen to be promotively related to need satisfaction' (Deutsch 1949: 138); that is, an individual will 'accept, like or reward' (ibid: 138) another's actions which achieve promotively interdependent goals, and this in turn will generalize to liking for the actor (see ibid: 146). It is clear that the promotive interdependence of individuals is believed to create attraction between them through need satisfaction. It is also clear, therefore, that interpersonal attraction is at the heart of the group as a psychological entity, since the psychological group comprises individuals who 'perceive themselves as pursuing promotively interdependent goals' and whose cohesiveness is determined by 'the strength of goals perceived to be promotively interdependent and . . . the degree of perceived interdependence' (ibid: 150). The basic message is that interpersonal attraction is the psychological force responsible for group belongingness and that its emergence can be traced to mutual need satisfaction through co-operation for promotively interdependent goals.

There is an ambiguity in the Lewinian and the Sherifs' approaches to interdependence and interpersonal attraction that is well reflected in the views of Cartwright and Zander (1968). On the one hand, the stress on the group as a dynamic system of interdependent members strongly implies that there are properties of the group as a whole, such as cohesiveness, which cannot be reduced to mere interpersonal attraction, but on the other hand there is a theoretical failure to explain how attraction to the *group* could be generated by any process that does not ultimately boil down to inter*personal* attraction. Thus Cartwright and Zander adhere to the interdependence theory of the group, are explicit in their recognition of the role of cohesiveness, and seek to restrain the tendency to identify it solely with interpersonal attraction, but despite an extremely detailed treatment, there is no definite indication of what alternative process is being suggested.

Interdependence and attraction also lie at the heart of social exchange, reinforcement, and equity approaches to the group. Social exchange approaches (Homans 1961; Kelley and Thibaut 1978; Secord and Backman 1964; Thibaut and Kelley 1959) emphasize the cost–benefit aspects of social relations. They reduce interaction to the transaction of rewards and costs and simply state that interaction continues to the extent that rewards outweigh costs. Cohesiveness is considered to be the essential quality of groups and its magnitude 'will be greater to the degree that rewards are experienced in belonging to the group' (Thibaut and Kelley 1959: 114). However, since the unit of analysis is typically the dyad, cohesiveness in practice is interpersonal attraction based on interpersonal rewards. This link between cohesiveness and mutual interpersonal attraction is made quite explicit by Secord and Backman (1964).

Reinforcement approaches are even more explicit (Lott 1961; Lott and Lott 1961, 1965). Interaction which mediates goal achievement or is rewarding in some way is reinforcing and hence results in interpersonal attraction. Cohesiveness is then defined as 'that group quality which is inferred from the number and strength of mutual positive attitudes among the members of a group' (Lott 1961: 279).

Equity theory (Berkowitz and Walster 1976) defines the group in terms of 'equitable' (i.e. fair, just, etc.) interdependence between individuals: the perception of inequity creates pressures for its reinstatement or for the termination of interdependence, in which case the group has disbanded. It is assumed that equitable interdependence creates interpersonal attraction which functions to produce group cohesiveness.

In contrast to the treatments discussed so far, Festinger and Heider provide examples of theories which stress the role of pre-existing similarities in attitudes and values between people in attraction and group formation. Festinger's social comparison theory (Festinger 1950, 1954; Festinger, Schachter, and Back 1950; Suls and Miller 1977; see also Ch. 8 below) argues that people affiliate with others in order to validate their opinions, attitudes, and beliefs. If physical, non-social means of validation are unavailable, we rely on comparison with relatively similar others. The agreement of others, that is their *similarity* to us in attitudes and so on, gives us confidence in the correctness of our views and so satisfies a basic need to evaluate ourselves and know that we are correct. Since similar others are rewarding in that they satisfy informational needs, we are attracted to them and affiliate with them. This idea has become a cornerstone of research on interpersonal attraction (e.g. Byrne's 1971 'attraction paradigm'). Festinger is explicit that we compare with other individuals, not groups, and that mutual interpersonal attraction reflecting shared attitudes is the basis of group formation. (The theory has been extended by Schachter 1959 to include emotions.)

Heider's theory rests upon the principle of cognitive balance, which postulates a need within the organism for balance between different cognitions (Heider 1958). He argues that positive sentiment relations (i.e. liking for others) and positive unit relations (a sense of togetherness, oneness, being linked, being the same) between individuals tend to go together. Interpersonal attraction and being in the same group are therefore inextricably linked. Heider's theory is somewhat different from the others in that attraction to similar others is seen to flow from a basic need for cognitive consistency, and there is an implication that group membership need not merely reflect interpersonal attraction but could also directly produce it. Newcomb, however, in his application of cognitive-balance concepts argues that liking is more likely to lead to positive unit relations than *vice versa*; that is, people we like are soon seen to be members of the same groups as ourselves (Newcomb 1968).

Finally, social impact theory (Latané 1981; Latané and Nida 1980) specifies factors in a group which determine its impact on potential group members – that is, increase conformity, group belongingness, and cohesiveness – and nominates (1) group size – the larger the number of physically present others the greater the group's impact; (2) immediacy – the closer the others are in space and time the greater the impact; and (3) strength of source – characteristics of the group and its members that are attractive to potential members (see Chs. 6 and 7 below for further details). The first two factors seem to relate to social interaction and the last to interpersonal attraction; implicitly, therefore, the theory appears to be based on an interpersonal interdependence model of the group.

In this section it has been shown how interpersonal attraction lies at the core of a wide array of superficially diverse conceptualizations of the social group (see the top half of Fig. 5.1). Current definitions of the social group (as can be seen in most contemporary social psychology texts) employ an admixture of components drawn from these theories. The group is essentially a numerically small face-to-face collection of individuals interacting to perform a task or fulfil shared goals. The members like each other and have role relations with respect to each other which emerge from intragroup structural divisions developed in the fulfilment of the group's purpose. A product of continued interaction is a sense of identity as group members. However, the fundamental process responsible for the psychological formation of the group and the degree of cohesiveness of the group in all these approaches is interpersonal attraction.

THEORETICAL AND EMPIRICAL LIMITATIONS
Theoretical limitations of the concept of group cohesiveness arise from the

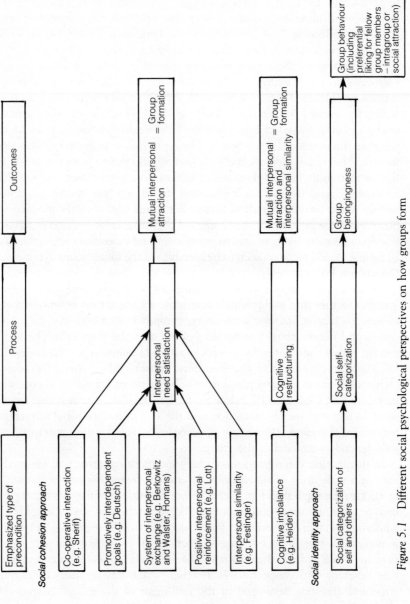

Figure 5.1   Different social psychological perspectives on how groups form

type of theory that it has come to represent. The reduction of what was intended as a group quality to an interpersonal process of attraction, and the determinants of group formation to the antecedents of interpersonal relations, denies the concept of group cohesiveness any independent theoretical status separate from that of interpersonal attraction (cf. Albert 1953; Eisman 1959) – a phenomenon already well researched in its own right (e.g. Huston 1974; Berscheid and Walster 1978). Furthermore, the adoption of and tendency to reify the 'molecule' metaphor (e.g. Kellerman 1981) of the relationship between individual and group has tended to obscure the point that, people in groups, unlike atoms in molecules, can contain psychologically the whole within themselves; that is, they can cognitively represent the group to themselves and act in terms of that cognitive representation.

The disappearance of the group as a theoretically distinct entity is nicely enunciated in Steiner's anguished cry, 'Whatever happened to the group in social psychology?' (Steiner 1974) and his later 'Whatever happened to the touted revival of the group?' (Steiner 1983; see also Smith and White 1983; Steiner 1986), and is attributed to pragmatic and ideological considerations by Cartwright (1979), Festinger (1980), Pepitone (1981), and Triandis (1977). (Also, see Ch. 2 above for documentation of the broader critique of individualism and reductionism in social psychology.) Not surprisingly, sociologically oriented social psychologists (e.g. Heine 1971) register disbelief that experimental social psychology has boiled down the complexity, variety, and historical significance of social groups to individuals' liking for each other.

Holding clearly in mind the metatheoretical critique, some more specific theoretical weaknesses can be identified. Aherence to a 'molecule' model has encouraged the use of sociometric choice (Moreno 1934) as the predominant method for charting who likes whom within a group in order to arrive at the cohesiveness of the group as a whole. This method has limitations (Golembiewski 1962), of which perhaps the most relevant is that it is largely unidimensional (Cohen 1981; Hare 1962; but see Jennings 1947); that is, it fails to allow for a qualitative distinction between sociometric choice as an indicator of friendship and as an indicator of attraction between group members (Hagstrom and Selvin 1965; Scott 1965). The same objection can be levelled at the use of Bales' 'interaction process analysis' method to study communication patterns in small groups (Bales 1950). This method stresses the *quantity* of communication directed by one person to another in terms of categories based on task management functions and the valence of socio-emotional reactions, but makes no allowance for any qualitative distinction between intragroup and interpersonal relations.

A second problem is that it is not possible to select one unique conceptual definition of cohesiveness for the purpose of operationalization. The concept encompasses a multitude of different sources of attraction (to the prestige of the group, its task, members' traits, etc.) and lends itself to a number of valid operationalizations which research has revealed not to be significantly correlated (Bovard 1951; Eisman 1959; Jackson 1959; Ramuz-Nienhuis and van Bergen 1960). Since a group which is cohesive by one definition may not be by another, no one operationalization covers all aspects of group cohesiveness, and interpersonal attraction is at best an incomplete or partial explanation (cf. Gross and Martin 1952).

Third is the issue of motives or motivation in group formation: why join a group? The frequently encountered sentiment that joining a group entails sacrifice of individual freedom (e.g. Gergen and Gergen 1981) suggests that groups suppress individuality and that individuality is superior, antithetical, and ontogenitically prior to group behaviour (see Ch. 7 below). If this is so, why do people join groups? As we have seen, the usual answer is in order to satisfy needs which range from specific goals to supposedly fundamental drives for affiliation (Watson and Johnson 1972), reinforcement, identity (Knowles 1982), and the validation of beliefs. The first point to make is that these needs in themselves represent 'reasons' for, rather than 'causes' of, group membership (see Buss's 1978 distinction between reasons and causes), and it is interpersonal attraction which is the *causal* process. Second, while individuals' needs, aims, goals, attitudes, beliefs, and so on may act as motives for affiliation, there is an important sense in which they must also be considered as determined by one's group membership (e.g. Christians have similar beliefs because they are Christians, as well as being Christians because they have similar beliefs). Emphasizing such factors as belief/attitude similarity or shared goals as bases of group belongingness simply begs the question of the origin of those beliefs, attitudes, and goals, and hence the origin of such similarities in the first place. In so far as group memberships determine similarities between people then they also determine interindividual bonds and variations in cohesiveness and are not merely an effect of purely individual motives and needs.

The fourth and perhaps most serious problem with cohesiveness as interpersonal attraction is that of group size. The concept was originally explicitly derived and intended to address numerically small face-to-face predominantly task-oriented groups, and hence any attempts to make generalized statements about its relevance to larger-scale groups is unwarranted. Although most researchers restrict the concept's applicability accordingly, others are less cautious and give the impression that interpersonal attraction is experimental social psychology's explanation of the group, independent of size.

Defining the group in terms of number generates problems in specifying precisely the parameters of *small*-group dynamics and hence cohesiveness. For example, Shaw, although convinced that less than ten individuals is a small group and more than thirty is a large group, is driven to maintain that a cohesive 25-person group is a small group whereas a non-cohesive fifteen-person group is not a small group (Shaw 1977, 1981). So, for 'small' we should read 'cohesive', and we are left with no independent criterion of the range of applicability of the social cohesion model!

The sensible solution to this dilemma is to accept that mutual face-to-face interaction between individuals (a phenomenon which is by definition restricted by number, as well as time and place) entails behaviours perhaps uniquely dependent on such conditions, but also to recognize that there may be some other process independent of interpersonal attraction which is responsible for group behaviour *specifically*. Interpersonal attraction may have relevance for the analysis of small-group phenomena, but it is plainly inadequate as an explanation of a large audience, crowd, nation, or any other group for that matter in which interpersonal interaction between all members is not possible.

That cohesiveness as interpersonal attraction merely redescribes inter*personal* relations within groups which are small enough to allow mutual interindividual interaction, rather than addresses truly intra*group* phenomena, is suggested by the way group size (within the small-group purview) reduces the cohesiveness of the group as a whole. As the group gets larger, structural divisions emerge to create subgroups and friendship cliques, which although internally cohesive tend to lower overall or average cohesiveness (Gerard and Hoyt 1974; Kinney 1953; Porter and Lawler 1968). Increasing size dictates structural subdivisions and supposedly weakens cohesiveness because it makes personal relations between all group members increasingly difficult. But, increasing group size is also reputed to magnify the impact of the group on the individual and strengthen adherence to group norms, according to Latané's social impact theory (Latané 1981). Cohesiveness cannot easily explain this paradox, that as the group gets larger and its cohesiveness decreases, the impact of social norms can become stronger and the group thus becomes more 'groupy'. Cohesiveness as inter*personal* attraction does not appear to be isomorphic with group belongingness.

A fifth difficulty also stems from attempts to distinguish between small and large groups. A common distinction is between groups on the one hand and 'categories' and 'roles' on the other, where 'category' typically refers to large-scale affiliations such as nationality, sex, or religion, and 'role' to an individual's position in a group such as leader, gossip, joker, and so on. However, role is also employed to refer to position within the small group based on large-scale group membership (e.g. sex, ethnicity, class, education). The implication is that small-group dynamics deals with the impingement of large-scale category memberships and intergroup relations on the functioning of small, *ad hoc* collections of individuals in face-to-face relations by reference (usually theoretically unelaborated) to the concept of behavioural role. The social cohesion model, therefore, is reduced to juggling with two largely separate and unintegrated sets of concepts, where the social identity approach would invoke cross-cutting social self-categories predicated upon the same underlying identity process.

Despite the theoretical limitations we have discussed, the group-cohesiveness concept has survived relatively unscathed, no doubt because on the whole it has proved useful. In general, research reveals that interpersonal liking in small groups enhances productivity, efficiency, adherence to group norms, the friendliness of the group atmosphere, and so forth (see beginning of this chapter). However, there are instances when this empirical relationship fails, and it is these which question the validity of the social cohesion perspective (see Hogg 1987; Lott and Lott 1965). For example, it appears that many factors which usually create liking (e.g. proximity, attitude similarity, co-operation) do not elevate cohesiveness if there is an emotionally charged or salient intercategory boundary (e.g. class, ethnicity) between the interactants, and only succeed in elevating cohesiveness within the confines of an already well-established common category membership (e.g. Brewer and Silver 1978; Brown and Turner 1981; Byrne and Wong 1962; Doise et al. 1972; Gundlach 1956; Kandel 1978; Sole, Marton, and Hornstein 1975).

Another example is failed groups. Groups which experience failure presumably do not mediate rewards for their members and consequently should experience reduced cohesiveness. However, everyday experience teaches us that losing, being defeated, or failing as a group may not only leave cohesiveness unaffected but can even greatly elevate it. This tallies well with historical documentation of national, ethnic, or military groups through the ages which emerge from defeat or deprivation with heightened solidarity (see Herodotus' account of classical Greek history). There are also a number of experimental demonstrations of this point. Turner, Hogg, Turner and Smith allowed individuals to choose to join a relatively abstract laboratory group for a task in which they had to find synonyms (Turner et al. 1984). Their performance was evaluated, and they were subsequently informed that they had succeeded or failed (under conditions in which the failure could not be denied, attributed to the activities of an outgroup, or explained away in some other way). Members of groups which had failed expressed greater cohesiveness (attraction to the group, its members, and activities; behavioural ingroup favouritism and preference; identification with the group; and other measures of group behaviour) than did those who had joined a group which succeeded. Along slightly different lines, but still focusing on groups which should not mediate interpersonal attraction, Turner, Sachdev, and Hogg found that unpopular groups (that is, groups which were consensually disliked in the experimental context) manifested greater cohesiveness (monitored similarly to above) than did popular groups (Turner, Sachdev, and Hogg 1983).

Social anthropology provides rich examples of social groups which do not seem to depend on interpersonal attraction for their existence, maintenance, or solidarity. For example, Ruth Benedict's ethnography of the Dobu of

N.W. Melanesia describes them as a social unit which abides by shared norms and engages in collective rituals, yet is not characterized by interpersonal attraction (Benedict 1935: 94–119). Liking is, instead, a strategic weapon which is employed to exact revenge on adversaries in a cut-throat world of dog-eat-dog.

Perhaps the most telling disconfirmation of the cohesiveness thesis comes from minimal group studies (see Ch. 3) which reliably and repeatedly obtain group behaviour in the absence of all the traditional determinants of interpersonal attraction (see Tajfel 1982b: 24). The only necessary precondition seems to be the explicit categorization of an individual as a group member (e.g. Billig and Tajfel 1973). Those minimal group studies which explicitly contrast social categorization with interpersonal attraction *per se* (Hogg and Turner 1985a, 1985b; see also Hogg 1985b, 1987) reveal, in keeping with other minimal-group studies, that categorization *per se* is sufficient for group behaviour. However, they also reveal that attraction can under certain conditions be associated with group formation and group behaviour. We shall pursue this further below when discussing the social identity approach to intragroup attraction.

The theoretical problems and empirical limitations documented in this section seriously undermine the social cohesion perspective on group formation, group cohesiveness, and group processes in general, and strongly suggest that a social identity analysis may be more profitable.

Social identity

The social identity approach can quite easily explain the empirical findings mentioned above, by focusing on group behaviour as a product of self-categorization and thus disentangling cohesiveness (as group belongingness) from interpersonal attraction. It can also help to resolve some of the theoretical problems of the cohesiveness model. For example, the simple expedient of redefining the social group in cognitive terms, as an internalized cognitive representation of the group, unshackles theorizing from seductive aspects of interpersonal interaction and transcends problems attendant on a numerical definition of the social group.

The two approaches – social cohesion and social identity – can be clearly differentiated over the issue of group belongingness, or psychological group formation (see Fig. 5.1). For the social cohesion model a given collection of individuals (they must be few in number and engage in mutual interaction) becomes a group to the extent that it expresses an array of group behaviours (co-ordinated interaction, adherence to norms, cohesiveness, and so forth). The boundary of the group is set by those individuals physically present, and the specific features which uniquely define this group in contrast to other groups is determined by the relevant unique qualities of the group members. Large-scale category-congruent behaviour – that is, behavioural content which derives from 'groups' whose parameters lie far beyond that of the specific small group – is generally labelled 'role' and excluded from the cohesiveness equation or is treated as a cause of liking due to interpersonal attitude or goal similarity. Psychological group formation, the process whereby the *individual* becomes psychologically 'attached' to the group, is accomplished by the development of bonds of mutual attraction between the individual and all other group members.

For the social identity approach, a collection of individuals (and here there is absolutely no theoretical restriction on number) becomes a group to the extent that it exhibits group behaviour. The content of the behaviour may be defined by unique qualities of those present and the unique purposes and goals of the aggregate, but it may also be determined by qualities of a far greater number of people than those present, for example a religion, race, or sex. *Psychological* group formation is accomplished by self-categorization in terms of the relevant category (small *ad hoc* face-to-face short-lived experimental group, or large-scale widely dispersed trans-generational social category).

In Chapter 3 we discussed how social categorization and social identifica-tion are related in the generation of intergroup behaviour, and in Chapter 4 how self-categorization produces stereotypic perception and treatment of ourselves and others. For the remainder of this chapter we focus on the relationship between self-categorization and intragroup attraction (cohesive-ness), and later make some suggestions concerning the way in which the social identity approach can contribute to a reinterpretation of two specific phenomena falling within the rubric of small-group dynamics – 'groupthink' and leadership.

But first, what evidence is there that the *process* of self-categorization is responsible for psychological group formation? While it is strongly *implied* by minimal-group findings, there are a couple of recent experiments which furnish perhaps slightly more direct evidence (Hogg 1985a, 1987; Hogg and Turner 1987b). Under conditions of experimentally elevated gender salience males and females categorized and defined themselves more strongly in terms of their own sex, and expressed accentuated sex-stereotypic behaviours and perceptions. The fact that accentuation effects emerged along with identification and situation-specific gender-contingent behaviours tends to suggest that the underlying process is self-categorization (see Ch. 4 for a discussion of why accentuation effects can be considered such strong evidence for the operation of a categorization process).

SOCIAL IDENTIFICATION AND INTRAGROUP ATTRACTION

From the social cohesion perspective, group belongingness, and interpersonal attraction are one and the same thing, so it is impossible to talk of a relationship between them. However, the social identity approach, in separating the two phenomena, does enable us to address this issue. Group belongingness as self-categorization can generate intragroup attraction, that is liking between individuals who are members of the same group, in a number of different ways (see Hogg 1985b, 1987; Hogg and Turner 1985a, 1985b; Turner 1982, 1984). First, self-categorization may allow the development of conditions under which the traditional determinants of interpersonal attraction operate. For example, it may increase social and verbal interaction, physical proximity, co-operation, and perceptions of belief similarity: all of which are antecedents of interpersonal attraction. Or cues to self-categorization (e.g. extreme belief similarity – we have very similar beliefs therefore we must be members of the same category) function entirely independently as determinants of interpersonal attraction. In both these cases group belongingness and interpersonal attraction are correlated via the mediation of mutual variables, and intragroup attraction is effectively inter*personal* attraction among group members.

There are, however, two ways in which the categorization *process* itself may more directly generate attraction. First, categorization of self and other as members of the same category renders self and other stereotypically identical (see Ch. 4); that is, self and other become stereotypically interchangeable as regards cognitive and affective reactions. One likes, is attracted to, and positively evaluates co-members of the group precisely because in general one likes and positively evaluates oneself, that is one has generally positive self esteem (e.g. Abramson and Alloy 1981; Martin, Abramson, and Alloy 1984). Second; ingroup stereotypes tend to be evaluatively positive for the very reason that self-categorization confers such characteristics on self and they thus contribute to self-esteem (in Ch. 3 we discussed the lengths to which groups go in striving to fashion and maintain positive social identity). So self-categorization imbues other group members with stereotypically positively evaluated characteristics and renders them stereotypically attractive. Outgroup members are of course rendered stereotypically unattractive and are thus disliked.

This form of interindividual attraction which is grounded in group membership and is generated by the process of self-categorization responsible for psychological group belongingness, can be termed *social attraction*. It is true intra*group* attraction. It can be theoretically distinguished from *personal attraction*, which is interindividual attraction based upon idiosyncratic preferences and firmly rooted in close personal relationships (see Hogg 1985b, 1987; Hogg and Turner 1985a, 1985b).

Our distinction between social and personal attraction resonates with related distinctions made in the social identity literature between social and personal identity, social and personal behaviour, and social change and social mobility belief structures (Tajfel and Turner 1979). The difference between social and personal attraction is essentially at the level of generative process, so both forms of attraction are subjectively experienced as an interindividual attitude with cognitive, conative, and affective (or evaluative) components (following the most widely accepted conceptualization of attraction; see Duck 1977a). The difference is that while the object of personal attraction is a unique idiosyncratic individual person, that of social attraction is completely interchangeable. It is attraction to an ingroup stereotype and hence to any and all individuals who are perceived to be stereotypic or prototypic of the group.

The distinction can also be approached within an attribution framework (Harvey and Smith 1977; see end of Ch. 4 above). Social attraction is attraction which is subjectively causally attributed to shared (in the case of liking) or disjunctive (disliking) category membership, while personal attraction is attributed to idiosyncratic characteristics of the other and the relationship. This analysis draws upon evidence that people make attributions to group memberships (social attributions) or individuality (personal attributions) (Deschamps 1983; Hewstone 1983; Taylor and Jaggi 1974) rather than the more traditional distinction between internal and external (Kelley 1967) or dispositional and situational (Jones and Nisbett 1972) attributions. As yet there has been no research done into social *versus* personal attributions for liking (see Regan 1976; Harvey and Weary 1984).

Having seen how group belongingness can generate intragroup attraction through the self-categorization process, we can now perhaps turn this analysis on its head to address the traditional empirical finding that cohesiveness as interpersonal attraction often *does* appear to produce 'groupiness'. Just as similarity generally leads to attraction (Byrne 1971; Griffitt 1974), attraction can enhance or exaggerate perceptions of interpersonal similarity (e.g. Backman and Secord 1962; Fiedler, Warrington, and Blaisdell 1952; Kipnis 1961): we tend to feel similar to those whom we like. However, under conditions of minimal interpersonal information, for example when the relationship between self and other has had little time to develop, this similarity is unlikely to be in terms of very *personal* constructs of self and other (cf. Duck 1973a, 1977b), rather it will be in terms of more general similarities shared with large numbers of other people: the similarity is not so much personal as social. Interpersonal attraction can perhaps under these circumstances act as a cognitive criterion for common category membership and hence produce psychological belongingness through self-categorization. Where there is more individuating information, usually as a consequence of a developed (enduring) interpersonal relationship, the effects of attraction are less likely to be cognitive assumptions of common category membership, and group behaviour is less likely to occur.

Basically, interindividual liking can lead to group belongingness but only under conditions which inhibit personal attraction and allow social attraction. These conditions arise under all circumstances where the relationship between two or more individuals contains limited individuating interpersonal information; that is, first encounters between strangers, early stages of developing relationships, and above all social psychology experiments. So, it is not unreasonable to conjecture that anomalous findings concerning the relationship between attraction and group behaviour in the 'small groups' literature (see Lott and Lott 1965) may be attributable to methodological and/or demographic features of the relevant studies which have generated personal rather than social attraction. Most experiments tend to involve social attraction, because they deal in short-lived groups, first encounters, homogenous subject samples (as regards age, education, race, etc.), and so forth, and hence obtain the traditional positive relationship between cohesiveness (as interpersonal attraction) and group behaviour. But some, no doubt, involve personal attraction and hence do *not* obtain the traditional cohesiveness/group behaviour relationship. A meticulous review of the relevant studies would tell us if this is true. For example, Tyerman and Spencer tried to replicate Sherif's (e.g. 1966) boys' camp studies (see Ch. 3 above) but failed, unlike Sherif, to break up pre-existent friendships and create intergroup antagonism (Tyerman and Spencer 1983). This may be because the boys all belonged to the same scout troop, and friendships were based on social attraction, so intergroup antipathy in the context of the experimentally created divisions was simply not possible as it was imposed on a powerful shared identity.

The social attraction hypothesis does have some support from a minimal group study by Hogg and Turner, in which social and personal attraction were experimentally varied (Hogg and Turner 1985b). Anonymous ingroup members were individually described in terms of generally likable or generally dislikable personality profiles (the personal attraction variable). Each profile was entirely idiosyncratic, or there was one positive or one negative component characteristic which was common to all members (the social attraction variable). Subjects expressed group behaviours only when the group was *socially* likable (shared an evaluatively positive trait). Idiosyncratic personal likableness had no effect on group behaviour but simply influenced interpersonal perceptions. Clearly, negative social attraction is grounds for a cognitive assumption of self–other category disjunction: a point which of course applies to our entire analysis of social attraction. It is positive social attraction, social liking, which is associated with group belongingness.

The social attraction hypothesis invites a reappraisal of the nature of attraction phenomena. It suggests that attraction between individuals does not merely vary quantitatively, but also qualitatively depending on the nature of the relationship between individuals. Relationships based on common or disjunctive category memberships generate, through self-categorization, social attraction, while relationships rooted in idiosyncratic personal relationships generate personal attraction through belief similarity or complementarity, social support, likableness, and so on. As relationships develop they become more idiosyncratic and personal, and thus attraction shifts towards personal attraction. Affective reactions in first encounters, official encounters, and the early stages of relationships are more likely to be at the level of social attraction. In general, as the nature of the relationship between two individuals shifts back and forth between social and personal, the generative base of the ensuing affective reaction also changes, and so someone can be liked as a friend but disliked as an outgroup member, or liked as a fellow ingrouper but disliked as a person. A familiar example might be a long-standing close friend whose political affiliations are very different to one's own.

It is, however, important to bear in mind, as with all features of group behaviour, that groups develop norms to govern their intragroup and intergroup transactions, and that therefore attraction phenomena will also be affected by such norms. The expression of intergroup social dislike and intragroup social liking is inevitably bound to be affected by norms, norms which may for example inhibit overt expression of intergroup dislike (cf. LaPiere 1934) or intragroup liking (e.g. male 'machismo' which censures displays of affection between males). It is not in the spirit of the social identity approach to explain phenomena by recourse purely to cognitive generative processes: the explanation must integrate social factors. A particularly interesting focus for further research is sex: here we have traditionally very close personal relationships between the sexes contrasted against a highly salient intergroup division (see Ch. 10).

To complete this section, we identify areas of contact between the social attraction hypothesis and literature on interpersonal attraction and personal relationships. Although much of this literature tends to assume that 'the phenomena of attraction are undifferentiated (except in degree)' (Newcomb 1960: 104), that is, 'may be described in terms of sign (plus or minus) and intensity' (Newcomb 1961: 6; see reviews by Marlowe and Gergen 1969, and McCarthy 1976, 1981), there are those who feel that 'most of us . . . are intuitively aware of differences in the ways we feel attracted to different persons' (Newcomb 1960: 104), and that 'the differences among such phenomena as the comradeship felt by members of a team, the respect held for a powerful leader, sexual attraction for a person of the opposite sex, a mother's devotion for a child, and the gratitude of a person relieved of distress far outweigh the similarities' (Marlowe and Gergen 1969: 622). The multidimensional nature of interpersonal attraction is further reflected in the existence of descriptive typologies of different forms of attraction (e.g. Blau 1962; Rubin 1973; Triandis 1977; see also Huston 1974).

More specifically, Newcomb has discovered that interindividual attraction has a different form in more, as opposed to less, cohesive groups: it is based in admiration and value support in the former and in perceived reciprocation in the latter (Newcomb 1960). A similar difference is documented by Segal, who urges a theoretical separation of 'interpersonal affect based on pair relationships from feelings of respect based on individual behaviour seen as benefiting the group' (Segal 1979: 260), and furnishes evidence that friendship is mutually reciprocated affect while respect and liking are more unidirectional and group based. Again, along similar lines, Hare has criticized the use of sociometric choice to chart liking within groups on the grounds that it fails to distinguish between liking based on interpersonal factors and liking based on group membership (Hare 1962). Finally, Andreyeva and Gozman suggest that ingroup liking and outgroup antipathy may arise due to the positive and negative valence of ingroup and outgroup stereotypes, respectively (Andreyeva and Gozman 1981), however no distinction is made between this form of affect, which resembles social attraction, and a more personal form resembling personal attraction.

There is also some suggestion that certain antecedents of attraction may generate liking via the mediation of a process rooted in group membership. Attitude and belief similarity have long been known to lead to attraction (Byrne 1971; Griffitt 1974), however Duck has recently argued that it is not attitude or belief similarity *per se* but rather the fact that they function as reliable cues to much deeper construct similarities, where constructs are people's theories of the world (Kelly 1955, 1970), that links these factors to attraction (Duck 1973a, 1973b, 1977b, 1977c). Construct similarity facilitates social intercourse and action and generates attraction. Presumably to the extent that constructs are socially elaborated, shared, and rooted in category membership, there is the possibility of a link here with the concept of social attraction. Two other points relating to similarity/attraction are (1) that people are attracted to similar others only if the similarity is in terms of positive, socially desirable, likable characteristics (Ajzen 1974), and (2) that personality similarity is not a reliable determinant of liking (see Lott and Lott 1965). This again suggests that similarity may be related to attraction by means of its role as an indicator of shared positive social identity.

Recent trends in research into personal relationships (see Mikula 1984) are interesting, in particular their emphasis upon the way that true personal relationships (and concomitant attraction) develop out of attraction phenomena based in more general and less idiosyncratic or personal relationships between individuals. Huston and Levinger draw this distinction from a review of a very large quantity of research into attraction and interpersonal relationships (Huston and Levinger 1978).

Of this tradition perhaps Duck's work has most relevance for the distinction between social and personal attraction (Duck 1973a, 1977a, 1977b, 1977c). Duck writes:

> One clear difference between liking relations is that some are long term (with a past history of complex interdependency, shared experience and so forth) and some are short term (spontaneously evoked liking towards a perfect stranger). The central question in the study of acquaintance is precisely the psychological relationship between these two types of liking.
>
> (Duck 1977a: 15)

Duck believes that,

> at the most early points of an encounter the two people in an interaction are
> stimulus *objects* for each other rather than stimulus *persons*. It is not until later that
> their personalities emerge for one another and they become people rather than
> things or role occupants or stereotypes.
>
> (ibid: 96)

For Duck, liking in relationships is based upon construct similarity (see above) where close personal relationships 'provide opportunities to test the most subjective (and otherwise untestable) constructs: namely, those about other people's personality' (1977c: 386). Although Duck speaks of simple attraction and friendship, short-term and long-term relationships, and degrees of 'depth' or idiosyncracy of personal constructs, the similarity to social and personal attraction, social and personal relationships, and social and personal identity is striking. Duck does not, however, employ the self-categorization process as an explanation of liking generated in what he refers to as short-term relationships, or what we would perhaps prefer to call intragroup relationships.

Some further extensions

By reconceptualizing the basis of group behaviour the social identity approach potentially has something to say about all phenomena traditionally considered within the rubric of small-group dynamics. Here we shall illustrate how this may be done, by considering two traditional small group phenomena which will not be dealt with elsewhere: leadership (see also Ch. 8) and 'groupthink'.

The term 'groupthink' was coined by Janis to characterize a small-group decision-making phenomenon which produces markedly poor decisions that can have disastrous consequences (Janis 1971, 1972). Janis attributed the Bay of Pigs Fiasco, escalation of US involvement in Vietnam and Korea, and US unpreparedness for the bombing of Pearl Harbour to groupthink in presidential decision-making groups. The analysis states that in highly cohesive small groups 'we-ness' overrides critical thinking because group meetings are friendly, amiable affairs during which complete concurrence, even on critical issues, is preferred to conflictual give and take of ideas, which would spoil the group's cozy atmosphere. Individuals suppress their own doubts or have them suppressed by self-appointed mind-guards, and the group becomes· turned in on itself and oblivious to external problems, alternative modes· of thought, and so forth. This state of affairs arises because highly cohesive groups comprise close friends, and there are among friends strong pressures for consensus (Dion, Miller, and Magnan 1971; Festinger, Pepitone, and Newcomb 1952; Wyer 1966), the breaking of which constitutes a violation of friendship (Brandstätter 1978; Schuler and Peltzer 1978).

Groupthink, which is considered a *pitfall* of highly cohesive groups on the assumption that cohesiveness should in general improve group functioning, is analysed purely in terms of interpersonal attraction: mutual attraction between group members or attraction only for the group leader (Flowers 1977; Raven 1974). This analysis falls prey to all the limitations of group cohesiveness discussed in this chapter, in particular that groupthink is ultimately and explicitly attributed to friendship not intragroup or group-based liking. Yet groupthink is *also* attributed to unidirectional and non-reciprocated attraction to the leader, a circumstance which is likely to attentuate the *overall* cohesiveness of the group (in terms of patterns of mutual sociometric choice). We cannot have it both ways.

An alternative way to treat groupthink avoids value proclamations to do with both the decisions made and the group process resulting in those decisions, by considering it simply as conformity to group norms exhibited by a group of individuals who strongly identify not only with the decision-making group *per se* but also (in Janis's examples) the wider political ideology represented by the group. (In Ch. 8 we discuss how groups, through discussion, can conform to a group position which is more extreme than that of the average of the individual members, that is upon an extremitized or polarized group norm.) Many of the features of groupthink – for example, the restricted choice of alternatives to discuss, the lack of consideration of majority views, and the avoidance of expert opinion or selection of 'tame' experts who validate the group's position – all fit neatly into Deconchy's discussion of orthodoxy and ideology (Deconchy 1984; see Ch. 4 above). Escalation of American involvement in Vietnam, for example, is explicable in terms of presidential committees making decisions in line with an anti-Communist ideology that, in keeping with ideology *sui generis*, furnishes a restricted or narrowly circumscribed world-view. Although personality dynamics undoubtably play a part in the relevant committee meetings, this part is played out within the confines of a social identity dynamic revolving around adherence to a shared ideology which may become extremitized, or more narrowly orthodox, during the discussion.

Finally, we turn briefly to leadership, which is traditionally a central topic of group dynamics (e.g. Bass 1981; Fiedler 1971; Hollander 1985). The classical view of leadership as an in-born quality – the 'great man' theory of leadership – currently enjoys little support. It has largely been replaced by the view that leadership represents an interaction between individual qualities and contextual demands. The leader is the individual who best embodies the context-relevant norms of the group and is able to ensure optimal group functioning to fulfil these norms. In recognition of this demanding task, the leader is rewarded by the group with power, which paradoxically enables divergence from the very norms which projected him/her into the position of leadership in the first place: the leader thus acquires what Hollander calls 'idiosyncrasy credits' (Hollander 1958). The array of functions of the group leader (see Kretch, Crutchfield, and Ballachey 1962; Lord 1977) comprises defining the group's goals, formulating policy and means of goal achievement, maintaining group harmony and solidarity by arbitrating intragroup differences, acting as a scapegoat for group failures, representing the group in intergroup encounters, and standing as a symbol of identification.

This analysis is firmly grounded in the group cohesiveness model. The leader is such by virtue of fulfilling the role of mediating group cohesiveness through the satisfaction of shared goals and the maximization of harmonious intragroup interaction. Interpersonal transaction perspectives, which are based in equity theory (cf. Berkowitz and Walster, 1976), consider leadership power to be the way in which group members reward the leader for facilitating the satisfaction of their needs. However, the recognition of the 'norm embodying' and 'symbol of identification' functions of the leader directly suggests that there is more to leadership than mediation of liking. 'Identification' is here employed in a strictly Freudian sense (Freud 1922; Scheidlinger 1952) to refer to the 'followers'' internalization of the leader's qualities because the leader functions as a 'father figure' to the group.

In the language of· social identity, the leader can be considered the *prototype* or most stereotypical member of the group, the individual who is the best exemplar of all the group's characteristics and thus best represents the group, or *is* the group. Self-categorization in terms of the social identity represented by the group results in self-description in terms of the prototype and concomitant social attraction among all group members, including the leader. Being the most prototypical member of the group paradoxically permits the leader to diverge most radically from the views, behaviour, and so on, of the group as a whole. This paradox emerges because the group as a whole looks to the leader to define the nature of the group and thereby extends consensually legitimated power to the leader to impose his/her preferred *modus operandum*: 'Ultimately a genuine leader is not a searcher for consensus but a molder of consensus' (Martin Luther King, *Chaos or Community*, 1967). (See Ch. 8 below for a more extensive discussion of leadership and social influence in the group.) In small decision-making groups or laboratory experimental groups, this process may not go very far, but consider the dynamics of presidential committees which are characterized by groupthink! In terms of larger-scale social phenomena – for example, Hitler and Nazism, Ayatollah Khomeni and Muslim fundamentalism, Bhagwan Shree Rajneesh and the 'Orange people', the Reverend Jim Jones and the Jonestown massacre (see Ch. 7) – we can clearly see how leadership is linked to dominant power élites who are in a position to impose a version of reality, an ideology, upon those who look to them, and yet how the dominant groups enjoy a degree of individual freedom and idiosyncrasy not enjoyed by their followers.

Conclusion

In this chapter we have shown how the social identity approach can overcome an array of theoretical and empirical limitations of the traditional social cohesion or interdependence approach to small-group dynamics. In particular, we have addressed the role of interpersonal attraction in group behaviour and group belongingness, and introduced a theoretical distinction between two forms of attraction: social attraction (attraction between group members) and personal attraction (attraction based on close personal relationships). We have also suggested how this distinction appears to have relevance for both current conceptualizations in the study of personal relationships and findings in the literature on interpersonal attraction. Finally, we sketched out some applications to related areas, and in Chapter 8 we show how group polarization (a tendency for small face-to-face discussion groups to make more extreme decisions than individuals) can be reinterpreted from a social identity perspective. In the meantime, Chapters 6 and 7 are devoted to a discussion of the impact of the group upon the individual in the group.

Recommended reading

For a general coverage of research and theory in small-group dynamics we suggest Blumberg et al. (1983), Crosbie (1975), Kellerman (1981), Lott and Lott (1965), and Paulus (1983). Lott and Lott are especially explicit about cohesiveness as interpersonal attraction. The interpersonal relationships literature that we refer to is nicely covered by Duck and Gilmour (1981). Perhaps a slightly more detailed description of the social identity analysis of the relationship between attraction and group formation can be found in Hogg (1987).

6

Social presence and social performance

The mass meeting is . . . necessary for the reason that in it the individual, who at first, while becoming a supporter of a young movement, feels lonely and easily succumbs to the fear of being alone, for the first time gets the picture of a larger community, which in most people has a strengthening, encouraging effect. The same man, within a company or a battalion, surrounded by all his comrades, would set out on an attack with a lighter heart than if left entirely on his own. . . . The community of the great demonstration not only strengthens the individual, it also unites and helps to create an ésprit de corps. The man who is exposed to grave tribulations, as the first advocate of a new doctrine in his factory or workshop, absolutely needs that strengthening which lies in the conviction of being a member and fighter in a great comprehensive body. And he obtains an impression of this body for the first time in the mass demonstration. When from his little workshop or big factory, in which he feels very small, he steps for the first time into a mass meeting and has thousands and thousands of people of the same opinions around him, when, as a seeker, he is swept away by three or four thousand others into the mighty effect of suggestive intoxication and enthusiasm, when the visible success and agreement of thousands confirm to him the rightness of the new doctrine and for the first time arouse doubt in the truth of his previous conviction – then he himself has succumbed to the magic influence of what we designate 'mass suggestion'. The will, the longing, and also the power of thousands are accumulated in every individual. The man who enters such a meeting doubting and wavering leaves it inwardly reinforced: he has become a link in the community.

(Adolf Hitler, *Mein Kampf*, 1925)

Unflinchingly driven by this creed, Adolf Hitler has entered the history of this century, not only for the appalling atrocities committed by the Nazis but also for the awesome effectiveness of his oratory in completely mesmerizing and bringing under his spell the tens of thousands who attended the rallies held in Nuremberg during the 1930s. At these events separate individuals were seemingly completely transformed into a single body with one will. In this chapter we discuss the impact on the individual of being in the physical presence of others. The extract above touches on a number of themes which will be explored – for example, the way in which the presence of others can facilitate certain behaviours; the contagiousness of actions and ideas in the presence of others; the loss of self-awareness and individuality (the de-individuation) of people in the presence of others; the apparent self-presentation and impression management aspect of behaviour in the presence of others.

Introduction

As we saw in Chapter 5, in a very real sense groups exist within individuals. For sociologists this comes as no surprise. Yet the thrust of social psychological theory has, from the beginning, been to regard groups as some kind of social clothing, which may be used to insulate against the environment, to facilitate certain activities, and to signal things about an individual's attitudes. A person may wear a suit one day, and jeans another; a uniform while at work, but not at home. Although there may be a degree of choice in what to wear, the properties of certain kinds of clothing constrain behaviour (such as whale-bone girdles used to, or skin-tight jeans may do). However, whatever clothes they wear, people remain basically the same. Social psychologists have generally asked what impact the group has *on* the individual; to examine the actions of the 'individual in a group's clothing'! The present chapter traces the development of such questions from 1897 to the present day. We begin by examining theories of social facilitation and social impact, before moving on to look at the broader issues of self-awareness and self-presentation. Our discussion of bargaining and negotiation high-lights the social nature of the presence and performance of self and others. The problem we raise is that at every point where a social identity analysis would seem a useful path to follow, researchers have side-stepped and taken the track of individualism. The explanation of group behaviour is seen as residing in the impact of individuals on individuals. The implications of the social identity approach are explored and developed as the chapter progresses.

It is hard to imagine a social psychology which did not take account of the fact that people spend much of their time with one another (Robinson, Converse, and Szalai 1972). Even when alone, a considerable proportion of one's time might be consumed by preparing for social behaviour, such as imagining how a friend might respond to a request, selecting gifts at Christmas, taking tests, attending interviews, and so on. Thus, even when alone, one may psychologically be surrounded by others. We have elected to call this the *social presence* of others as, whether real or imagined, it has implications for social behaviour. In this chapter we shall examine the quantity and quality of the effects of what we term social presence.

Social presence

In 1954 Gordon Allport remarked, 'the first experimental problem – and indeed the only problem for the first three decades of experimental research – was formulated as follows: What changes in an individual's normal solitary performance occur when other people are present?' (Allport 1954: 46). Of course, it is this question which changes psychology into social psychology. Does waiting for a bus in a queue feel different from waiting alone? Does a person drive in a different way when a passenger is in the car? Do people work more or less efficiently when they are all engaged in the same activity together than when they are isolated?

The first social psychological study in this area was conducted by Triplett, who, on examining the records of bicycle race times, observed a now familiar phenomenon. Cyclists who were competing in the same race managed faster times than did those with a pace-maker, and both of these were faster than cyclists who raced alone, against the clock (Triplett 1898). Triplett pursued the idea that it was the *presence* of others which improved performance. He gathered together a group of children and sat them down to reel in lines on a fishing rod. When the children reeled in one another's presence they did so more quickly than when alone.

SOCIAL FACILITATION

These effects on performance have come to be known as 'social facilitation' effects. One remarkable feature of the research which followed Triplett's is that much of it has used animal rather than human subjects. Consequently, the theory which eventually emerged is distinctly asocial and reductionist. The research is summarized excellently by both Zajonc and Cottrell, who distinguish between two kinds of study (Zajonc 1965; Cottrell 1972). Studies of *co-action* compare solitary individuals with individuals in groups all performing the same task, while *audience* studies compare the performance of solitary individuals under either private or public circumstances. Most of the animal experiments use the co-action paradigm, as well as a delightful and exotic array of species. However, the behaviour under observation has usually been one which is habitual and which is not necessarily *social* in nature. The activities range from excavations by ants, to eating by chickens, armadillos, and even oppossums! In all cases, the presence of others of the animal's own species (called 'compresence') resulted in 'more' of the behaviour under observation. Of only slightly greater relevance to the human context, it seems that sexual indulgence is similarly contagious: rat-couples copulated more often and more rapidly in the presence of other rat-couples than when left in private. On the other hand, co-action can also impair performance, particularly on tasks which involve learning (e.g. among greenfinches, parakeets, and cockroaches).

Floyd Allport asked human subjects to engage in a variety of tasks either alone or in groups around a table (Allport 1920). Performance was improved on some tasks but impaired on others as a result of co-action. Studies using passive audiences also seemed to yield mixed results. For example, Bergum and Lehr found that National Guard trainees were more vigilant when a Lieutenant was observing (Bergum and Lehr 1963), but Pessin found that subjects were worse at learning nonsense syllables in the presence of an audience than when alone (Pessin 1933).

The apparent contradictions in empirical evidence led Zajonc to depict social facilitation research as having reached an impasse, and to suggest a resolution in terms of Hull–Spence drive theory (Fig. 6.1). A stimulus evokes *habits*, each of which has a given strength. As drive increases it becomes more likely that a *dominant* habit in the hierarchy will be produced as a response, and that subordinate ones will be inhibited. Zajonc argued that the 'mere' presence of conspecifics is an innate releaser of drive, and hence encourages the emission of dominant responses. What this means is that given a lot of practice, or a well-ingrained habit, compresence will enhance the appropriate response. Conversely, if one is still only learning a task or acquiring a skill, inappropriate responses will be dominant, and in the presence of others will obliterate correct but subordinate ones. An everyday example of this process is learning to drive a car. While a skilled and practised driver may be more careful and accurate when carrying passengers, a novice may be more erratic with passengers, than when alone.

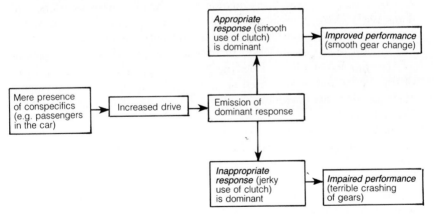

Figure 6.1 Zajonc's drive theory of social facilitation: applied to the task of changing gear in a car

Zajonc was so confident in his theory that he, rather flippantly, recommended that the student should

> study all alone in an isolated cubicle, and . . . arrange to take his examinations in the company of many other students, on stage, and in the presence of a large audience. The results of his examination would be beyond his wildest

expectations, provided, of course, he had learned his material quite thoroughly.

(Zajonc 1965: 274)

On closer inspection however, the whole edifice of social facilitation theory seems to rest on very shaky foundations. One of the main problems stems from the supposed parsimony of the theory. Zajonc contends that 'mere' presence is an *innate* source of drive which applies to all species, and hence yields similar effects in each. Are the suppositions supported?

A debate ensued, with Cottrell arguing that audience presence results in 'evaluation apprehension' (anticipation of negative or positive outcomes) and that this is a *learnt* source of drive (Cottrell 1972). Thus performance is affected less when the potential audience is blindfolded (Cottrell *et al.* 1968) or non-evaluative (Henchy and Glass 1968). However, in line with Zajonc, Markus found that the mere presence of a laboratory technician improved and impaired the speed at which subjects dressed in familiar and unfamiliar clothes respectively (Markus 1979).

In 1977 Geen and Gange concluded that twelve years of research at least supported a drive explanation of these effects. Despite Zajonc's claim that mere presence increases drive because drive represents a state of readiness in the face of the inherent 'unpredictability' of people (Zajonc 1980), and Sanders' account of drive as resulting from distraction and attentional conflict caused by the presence of other people (Sanders 1981), recent reviews reveal that the effects themselves are highly unreliable (Bond and Titus 1983). While Guerin and Innes' (1982) review only found ten studies supporting Zajonc's model, they retain an explanation in terms of uncertainty and arousal (e.g. Guerin 1983, 1986) – a concept different from but not unrelated to that of drive (see Berlyne 1979). They emphasize the social bases of this arousal but do not dwell on the fact that there is little convincing evidence that the presence of others necessarily does increase arousal (Kushner 1981).

The key problems centre on the concept of drive. It is unclear what 'drive' is and how it can be measured. Glaser argues that it is merely a mathematical construct (Glaser 1982). If this is the case, social psychologists may have been, as it were, in search of a unicorn. Moreover, even if drive *does* exist, it may not be sensible to divide behaviour into response hierarchies. Of course, well-learnt dominant habitual responses can be created experimentally, but public behaviour is rarely so easily quantifiable. It is also difficult to specify what constitutes a 'response' in the first place. Imagine you are listening to a recital of a piano concerto. Is a 'response' the movement of each finger on the keyboard, the configuration of notes played at any one time, a bar of music, a phrase, or a complete movement? Would you judge the performance by the number of notes correctly played, or would you attend more to the *way* they were played?

Drive theories of social facilitation are essentially reductionist. Their perspective is quite consistent with Davies' view that 'Much of human emotional life is organically rooted and phylogenetically based on perhaps billions of years of vertebrate evolution' (Davies 1980: 68). Indeed, Davies applauds the fact that 'Psychologists not of the stimulus–response persuasion seem to have abandoned their own knee-jerk reaction of refusing to consider that there are indeed organic components of behaviour' (ibid: 68). More pointedly, Davies quotes MacKenzie's view that 'any statement that is true in biology . . . is also true in sociology' (MacKenzie 1978: 92).

Even the more social applications stemming from Cottrell's version – for example Wine's treatment of dispositional differences in test anxiety (Wine 1971, 1980) – explain performance in terms of two factors: task difficulty, and intra-individual capacity. What is missing is any appreciation of the fact that most 'presence' is social in nature. This has implications for the content, and not just the level of performance. It follows that most performance is also social – serving functions for interpersonal relationships, self-definition, communication, and so on. Efforts to recognize this have only gone a little way towards 'socializing' performance research. We shall consider three of these areas: social impact, self-awareness, and self-presentation.

SOCIAL IMPACT

Social impact, according to Latané and Nida is the 'changes in physiological states and subjective feelings, motives and emotions, cognitions and beliefs, values and behaviour that occur in an individual human or animal as a result of the real, implied or imagined presence or actions of other individuals' (Latané and Nida 1980: 5). They propose three principles of social impact. First, it is a multiplicative function of the *strength* (e.g. status, power, importance, etc.), *immediacy* (physical and temporal proximity), and *number* of sources (observers, etc.) present in the environment of a particular target (performer, actor, etc.). Second, the relative impact of each additional person decreases (the difference between one and two observers being more important than that between 99 and 100). Third, when a target person is a part of a group or collection of other targets, the impact of observers is divided among targets and is therefore reduced. Just as the impact of source shows smaller increments as their number increase, so the effects of division of impact show smaller decrements as the number of targets increase. Latané and Nida are explicit, and even proud, that the theory is based in laws of physics, engineering, and economics. They do not appear to question whether this kind of theorizing is appropriate to human social life. In particular, they see no discontinuity between different-sized collections of individuals. (See Ch. 5 above for further critique of social impact theory.)

Latané's model has attracted some support. For example, individuals who were asked to clap or cheer produced more noise when they believed they were alone than in groups, and more when their own performance was separately identifiable than when it was not (Latané, Williams, and Harkins

1979; Williams, Harkins, and Latané 1981). Such evidence encourages a belief that groups create 'social loafing' in their members, and thus supports an anti-collective stance. At best, behaviour within groups is lazy (Jackson and Williams 1985). At worst, social loafing is 'a kind of social disease [that has] negative consequences for individuals, social institutions, and societies' (Latané et al. 1979: 831). Moreover, observation by groups creates unpleasant tension (Jackson and Latané 1981). Unfortunately, there is a tendency to confuse an observable phenomenon (reduced output) with a causal process (social impact). Thus the reduction in quality of the Beatles' songs when Lennon and McCartney co-authored as opposed to writing separately can be described as a function of social impact (Jackson and Padgett 1982), but one might also wish to argue that they wrote for different audiences and that a criterion of chart ratings and sales figures is hardly indicative of song quality. Other extensions of social impact theory appear in Chapters 7 and 8.

While on the one hand the presence of others can facilitate performance, on the other co-action can impair it. Paulus attempts to reconcile these findings into a single cognitive-motivational model of group task performance (Paulus 1983). This model begins by distinguishing between complex and simple tasks and then delineating the impact of effort, arousal (conceptualized as similar to drive), and task-irrelevant processing. Groups can confer positive or negative consequences for individual performance (e.g. in intragroup co-operation or competition respectively), and the magnitude of consequence increases with group size.

The model specifies that when increasing group size makes it more likely that there will be positive social consequences (e.g. approval) this leads to increased individual effort and facilitated performance. When negative consequences are decreased, task-irrelevant processing, effort, and arousal are reduced and performance is facilitated only on complex tasks.

The utility of such a model is somewhat limited. We have noted our reservations concerning the concept of drive and response hierarchies. A more serious problem concerns the way in which 'group' is conceptualized. From a social identity perspective it is meaningless to talk of 'social consequences', 'task difficulty', and group size unless we have a clear conceptualization of the individual's relation to the group. The nature of the group may specify what tasks are to be done, and for what ends. Also, the power of numbers can change dramatically if the source of influence can be categorized as an outgroup (cf. Abrams et al. 1986; Mullen 1983, 1984).

SELF-AWARENESS

One of the most important developments in theories of social performance was Duval and Wicklund's theory of objective self-awareness (Duval and Wicklund 1972). They argued that performance facilitation resulted not from drive but from a self-evaluative process which is brought about by self-focused attention. Without undoing the nuts and bolts of the theory it can be said that self-awareness often brings to light a discrepancy between one's actual state or achievements and one's desired state or aspirations. Such discrepancies are unpleasant and so one attempts to avoid them either by avoiding self-awareness or by reducing the discrepancy.

When attention is directed towards the self (by 'reflective' stimuli such as mirrors, audiences, cameras, etc.) performance on simple tasks tends to be improved (Wicklund and Duval, 1971), although different kinds of self-focusing stimuli do have slightly different effects (Abrams and Manstead 1981). The reasons for this are pretty obvious: observing oneself in a mirror may make one aware of facial blemishes, but not anxious about them. Those same blemishes might generate great embarrassment if they are visible to a potentially critical audience!

The self-attention account of the effects of social presence adds two important dimensions to previous models. It introduces the self-concept as a key variable and it extends to content domains, which are far more interesting (and social) than task performance. By demonstrating that similar effects *can* result from the presence of an audience, or a mirror/camera, and so on, self-awareness theorists have shown that 'presence' is primarily a social psychological rather than a physical variable (cf. Carver and Scheier 1978). One of the basic findings has been that self-attention clarifies awareness of salient aspects of oneself (Wicklund 1980). Thus presence of a mirror intensifies reactions to pleasant or unpleasant pictures (Scheier and Carver 1977), elevates angry aggression (Scheier 1976), improves discrimination between different tasting stimuli (Gibbons *et al.* 1979), and improves self-report validity (Pryor *et al.* 1977). Not only does self-awareness make affect more prominent, but also personally held attitudes (Scheier and Carver 1980), morals (Gibbons 1978), and self-attributions (Duval and Hensley 1976). It therefore appears that while social facilitation phenomena can be subsumed by self-attention theory (Carver and Scheier 1981a, 1981b; Hormuth 1982; Wicklund 1980), the latter extends to a far more interesting range of social phenomena.

There are three variants of self-attention theory, each with a different emphasis. Carver has developed a cybernetic model in which self-focus constitutes a 'test' of whether behaviour matches a standard (Carver 1979). Depending on one's expectation of success one will either try harder or withdraw from a task when self-focused. Carver's contribution has been considerable and is distinctively cognitive.

Buss and Scheier have pursued a different line (Buss 1980; Scheier 1980; Fenigstein, Scheier and Buss 1975). Social psychology abounds with distinctions between different aspects of the self (see Burns 1979; Gergen 1971, 1982b; Higgins, Klein, and Strauman 1984), and self-awareness theorists have adopted the familiar distinction between private and public aspects of self. Private aspects are covert and non-observable (feelings, attitudes, etc.), while public aspects are overt and may be scrutinized by others (appearance, clothing, conversation, etc.). Different stimuli may direct attention to different aspects of the self, but it also appears that there are dispositional differences in private and public self-awareness (termed 'self-consciousness'). According to Scheier and Carver, people who are high in *private* self-consciousness 'are presumed to be particularly attentive to their thoughts, feelings, attitudes and other private aspects', while those high in *public* self-consciousness 'are especially cognisant of how they are viewed by others' (Scheier and Carver 1981: 193). The public/private distinction has been very influential in self-awareness research, and has partly determined the way in which group influence on individuals has been conceptualized. Later we discuss the implications of this model of the structure of self for explanations of group behaviour.

The most social version of self-awareness theory is that proposed by Wicklund (1980, 1982), who draws on William James and Tomatsu Shibutani for inspiration. It is also in Wicklund's writing that we find the clearest statement of the relationship between groups and individuals. He views society as being the social group which frames people's lives, and argues that self-awareness arises when individuals find themselves to be different (Duval 1976) or where routine is disrupted. Furthermore, dynamic aspects of the self 'such as emotions or strong motivational states generally take precedence over more static aspects of self (values, logical thinking)' (Wicklund 1982: 218). It follows also that social pressures will only be influential in the absence of strong internal affect. This kind of argument – one which recurs throughout self-awareness theories – rests on the assumption that the individual is a more potent force than the group, and that the two are psychologically discrete. (Of course, this view is in stark contrast to the social identity perspective which puts society within the individual.) In Chapter 7 we describe the way this has been done in de-individuation theory. However, here the same point can be made with reference to the way private and public self-focus have been used to account for social influence.

Social performance

Scheier and Carver argue that a private or public aspect of self will 'influence the person's behaviour *only* if that self-aspect is taken, at least temporarily, as the object of the person's own attention' (Scheier and Carver 1981: 192). When the public self receives attention, it seems that the individual attempts to gain social acceptance by complying or conforming to a group norm. For example, the presence of the video camera increases endorsement of positive reference group attitudes (Wicklund and Duval 1971) and reliance on normative information when making psycholphysical judgements (Duval 1976). It also makes people more anxious to surpass normative ('social') standards of performance than to match their own personal aspirations (Diener and Srull 1979). Moreover, an evaluative audience promotes adherence to what subjects believe to be social norms for delivering punishment, while a mirror (producing private self-attention) promotes adherence to personal attitudes even when they contradict social norms (Froming, Walker, and Lopyan 1982). Both situationally and dispositionally determined private self-attention inhibit attitude change while public self-attention promotes attitude change following counter-attitudinal behaviour (Scheier 1980).

These findings lead us inevitably to a position where conformity is explained in terms of self-presentation, and 'socially desirable' responding (a theme which is explained fully in Ch. 8). For example, Froming and Carver obtained a negative correlation between private self-consciousness and compliance to the responses of three (bogus) subjects on a judgemental task (Fromer and Carver 1981). The correlation between public self-consciousness and compliance was positive. Carver and Humphries found that among Cuban Americans (for whom Cuba represents a negative reference group), hostility to statements made by the Castro regime was greatest among those who were also high in public self-consciousness (Carver and Humphries 1981). Conversely, private self-focus inhibits conformity to pressure from other individuals. Wicklund prefers to avoid the public/private distinction but insists that 'a highly salient, free behavioural commitment carries more weight for the self-aware individual than does external group pressure' (Wicklund 1980: 204). Indeed, the main utility of self-awareness for a group is that it makes individuals more 'accurate and honest in self-descriptions . . . more predictable by the group' (ibid.); in other words, it facilitates the group's capacity to control the individual. We return to self-awareness theory in Chapter 7. For the moment we shall pursue the idea that the impact of groups on individuals is primarily a self-presentational phenomenon.

SELF-PRESENTATION

Bond has proposed that social facilitation effects are often a result of the self-presentational concerns of the actor (Bond 1982). That is, performers aim to project an image of competence in the presence of others. Anticipation of success or failure (depending on task complexity) leads to performance facilitation or impairment, respectively. In his review, Borden argued that the variable of social psychological importance is the perceived nature of the *audience* (see Borden 1980; see also Hollingsworth 1935; Paivio 1965). For example, the presence of a male audience leads to more aggression than a female audience (Borden 1975). However, Borden only touched on the possibility that the audience might affect the content of behaviour. He noted that increasing the numbers within an audience only has an effect if each person is seen as contributing some new evaluative implication (see also

Wilder's 1977 similar argument as regards conformity; see Ch. 8 below). Hence, an audience of one male is no different from an audience of two, since the evaluative implications are identical. The parallels with principles of social categorization derived from a social identity perspective are obvious. If the audience can be categorized, its impact derives from the characteristics stereotypically associated with the category rather than from the specific characteristics of the constituent members. Seen in this light, social presence has its effect on social performance by virtue of the way that the psychological 'audience' is categorized in relation to oneself.

Despite this, research on social presence has almost entirely dwelt on task, skill, and group *size* as bases for predicting the magnitude of output in social performance (Mullen 1984). The 'socialness' of the performance is typically explained in terms of the private or public self-concerns of the actor. For example, Greenberg has shown that private self-attention encourages distribution of rewards on the basis of *equity* (an 'internal' standard), while public self-attention encourages *equality* (thereby creating a favourable impression) even at cost to self (Greenberg 1983a, 1983b). In a group setting it appears that individuals claim credit for success and not for failure of group performance, when their claims are private, but not when other group members will see these claims. Under such 'public' conditions subjects also claim relatively less credit for success compared with the credit they give to other group members (Miller and Schlenker 1985). The explanation given is that people engage in self-effacing impression management in groups.

Such data are readily reinterpreted as social identity effects. Naturally, to the extent that group behaviour is public and therefore communicative, it reinforces consensual self-categorization as *group* members. Under such public conditions the members will perceive greater intragroup similarity and hence will cease to distinguish their own contributions from those of other group members. In a nutshell, the usual supposition that behaviour in groups reflects impression management and not the 'true' self is unwarranted. At this point we take a short digression into the area of self-presentation theories, since, if we are to question a self-presentation explanation of group influence, we should at least identify the protagonists!

Self-presentation theories stemmed from Goffman's insightful descriptive work which depicted social life as a series of performances, an unfolding drama (Goffman 1959). Important in this model was the assumption that people are well acquainted with the roles and expectations associated with each context, and that the smooth running of society relies upon the fact that participants observe the rules of social conduct specified for their roles. Patients would be shocked if their doctor started divulging his or her *own* medical history to them! An interviewer would be surprised if an interviewee for a job started asking why the interviewer wanted to work with the company. According to Goffman, the need to keep the interaction flowing is primary, and participants engage in all kinds of manoeuvres to maintain one another's roles.

The social psychological adoption of Goffman's ideas has involved a shift of emphasis. Rather than focusing on *presentation* and interaction, theories have been concerned with the *self* and motivation. Hence, Jones views ingratiation as a tactic which people use to influence the attributions others make about them (Jones 1964). Thus people may tailor their expressions of attitudes to match those of their audience (Newtson and Czerlinsky 1974). Those who have done poorly on one task may try to exaggerate their competence on another (Schneider 1969).

What we have here is a model in which social performance is a scheming, tactical ploy, designed to deceive others and to gain power over them (Jones and Pittman 1982). It is as if themes from fiction (e.g. the film *The Sting*, Ben Johnson's play *Volpone*, or the story of *Red Riding Hood*) have been taken as the only possible way of thinking about self-presentation. In such a world, people engage in 'self-handicapping' strategies, such as deliberately getting drunk the night before exams in order to avoid the *possibility* that failure is blamed on lack of ability (Jones and Berglas 1978, Smith, Snyder, and Perkins 1983). They bask in the 'reflected glory' of others by associating with them selectively – *our* team did well/*they* lost (Cialdini *et al.* 1976), and feign helplessness or sickness when it will elicit supportive responses (Baumeister, Cooper, and Skib 1979; Rosenhan 1973).

The purposes behind such strategies may be twofold. One is to influence the audience's view of oneself and the other is to service one's own self-esteem. Self-esteem may be directly implicated, such as where favourable evaluations from others make one feel good (Jones *et al.* 1981). Alternatively, it may be indirectly implicated as it is simply a question of creating a *generally* socially desirable public image, irrespective of audience (Baumeister 1982). So the impact of the group is to draw out the full range of subtle skills and tricks which individuals can use to do well for themselves.

PRIVATE AND PUBLIC BEHAVIOUR

The shift of emphasis from the social nature of social performance to the personal basis of self-presentation returns us to the private/public distinction. The task of the research becomes one of unmasking the actor, revealing a true inner self, getting round his or her defences, and so on. To this end, ingenious devices have been employed, such as the 'bogus pipeline' method in which subjects are hooked up to a bogus lie detector in order to deter them from being dishonest (Jones and Sigall 1971). While it is acknowledged that self-presentation might *create* changes in the self-image (rather like Woody Allen's character 'Zelig', who took on the whole personality and appearance of those he was with), this is more often regarded as an outcome than as an integral part of self-presentation (Jones, Gergen, and Davis 1962; Jones *et al.* 1981). Considerable effort has gone into developing taxonomies of self-presentational strategies, tactics, and styles (Arkin 1981; Jones and

Pittman 1982; Schlenker 1985; Tedeschi and Norman 1985; Tedeschi and Reiss 1981). The theorizing has become decreasingly social and increasingly individualized. The ultimate expression of this transition is found in Snyder's self-monitoring scale (Snyder 1974, 1979). Self-monitoring is an individual differences construct which refers to the ability and propensity of individuals to orient their behaviour to their audience, even to the extent that they will conform *or* be independent, whichever is more desirable (Snyder and Monson 1975).

What we are given by such approaches is a model which places the self in contrast to society. Any kind of public behaviour can be interpreted in self-presentational terms so long as the audience and the actor are treated as separate entities. Schlenker is exceptional in attempting to integrate the two (Schlenker 1984, 1985) – the self can be its own audience: 'the important distinction is not whether behaviour is public or private, but what context (audience and situation) is salient to the actor at the time' (Schlenker 1985: 82). But even Schlenker's approach restricts us to an individualistic level of explanation. Attitude change, expression of attraction to others, and so on, can only be seen as personal weakness (if real) or personal cynicism (if self-presentational).

Social identity and the social performer

The missing dimension, of course, is that of group identification and self-categorization. As we saw in Chapter 3, intergroup differentiation results from social categorization even when subjects' behaviour is not individually identifiable. Other research (e.g. Turner *et al.* 1984) shows that, far from basking in reflected glory, group members feel stronger identification following group failure than following success. In Chapter 8 we show how, when the presence of others arises in the context of a *group*, real shifts of opinion can occur. We describe this process not in terms of collective self-presentation (each group member wishing to *appear* to surpass the others; see Orive 1984) but in terms of collective self-identification (wishing to *be* as one's group membership specifies). For example, the behaviour, appearance, and allegiance of British football supporters at a soccer match can be alarmingly fierce. The function of wearing team colours, chanting slogans, and slow hand-clapping the opposing team is not merely to intimidate the rival supporters. It also creates a feeling of solidarity and self-definition. Support for the home team is more than an act, it is a part of identification with that team and/or what it represents. Judgements about the fairness of referees' decisions, the quality of each team's performance, and the 'dirtiness' of tactics used may all favour one's own team during the match, but be far less 'biased' when one ponders on the outcome in private. It strains credibility to argue that such bias is merely a self-presentational tactic. Instead, we can argue that it reflects a salient social identification (Turner 1982) and the associated perceptual and evaluative biases that follow from the self-stereotyping process (see Chs. 4 and 8). Rather than explaining the variability of social behaviour in terms of self-presentational tactics, the social identity perspective accounts for it in terms of changes in *self-definition*.

We are not arguing that self-presentation does not occur, but that apparently inconsistent social performances may result from switches between personal and social identity. Individual differences in self-presentational aptitude may lead to variations in the skill with which people can present their different identifications, but this variation is likely to be less significant than is often assumed. Group contexts often expose amazing *uniformity* in behaviour across individuals (see Ch. 7). The gross effects (such as wearing one's team colours) tend to be in terms of the *content* of action (i.e. wearing *versus* not wearing those colours), while individual differences may relate more to the extremity of action (some don the full garb while others elect only to wear a badge or scarf).

A social identity perspective is important for understanding social presence and social performance since so much of social behaviour does involve interaction with members of different social categories or groups. In schools most interaction is constrained by the fact that there are 'teachers' and 'pupils'. At work people transact with others from different sections of the workforce (e.g. warehouse and sales workers, or sales and accounts). In both of these contexts there is evidence that group identification constrains and guides behaviour (Brown and Williams 1984; Emler 1984). Similarly, unemployed individuals continually engage in communications with state bureaucracy. In short, when we deal with others we often do so as *representatives* of some social category, group, or role. The impact of the presence of others is rarely 'merely' neutral. It embodies both meaning and purpose (Strauss 1977; Goffman 1959).

BARGAINING AND NEGOTIATION

These considerations lead us to look briefly at another area of research into social presence, that of bargaining and negotiation. The intriguing problem for negotiators, particularly those working in industrial relations, is that they are charged with the responsibility of working for their own side but have to do so by interacting with the other side. If this interaction is to flow smoothly at all, it is essential that there is a minimum of personal animosity between negotiators. Stephenson has elucidated the theoretical significance of this potential clash between interpersonal and intergroup constraints (Stephenson 1981, 1984). Most bargaining research has been oriented towards producing 'successful' outcomes (satisfying to both parties), just as the group influence research has dwelt on task performance. It has generally been assumed that superordinate goals and co-operation hold the key to success. And yet the outcome has implications both for the negotiators' interpersonal relationships and for the parties they represent. Stephenson argues that most interpersonal bargaining research is individualistic:

> Individuals' relative concern with agreement or with success (from whatever source their concerns come), in relation to the perceived trustworthiness of their opponent, will determine choice of strategy, and consequently, the chances of achieving satisfactory outcomes. The bargainers are haggling over the terms of *interpersonal* exchange.
>
> (Stephenson 1981: 176)

He cites reviews of gaming and negotiation research, all of which countenance no problem in extrapolating from interpersonal to collective bargaining (e.g. Klimoski 1978; Pruitt and Kimmel 1977) other than to consider role constraints of representatives as a *hindrance* to successful outcomes (e.g. Druckman 1978). Indeed, some researchers have argued that the representative role, and public presentation of each side's position, are detrimental to success, and that more rational solutions will be obtained where negotiators can operate away from the spotlight (McGrath 1966; Rogers 1969). Stephenson follows Douglas (1957) in recognizing the absurdity of such a view:

> The unfettered negotiation group of course, is supposed to emerge with the appropriate solutions, the implication being that negotiations best take place *independently* of relations between groups. In truth, of course, negotiations are a *consequence* of intergroup relations, and have no independent validity.
>
> (Stephenson 1981: 180)

Another feature of collective bargaining which makes it especially interesting is that it tends to be conducted over a period of time, and series of encounters. The social presence of the participants is not a 'one-off' chance event, it is part of a developing relationship. Stephenson and his colleagues argue that skilful negotiators may deliberately create engagements with their counterparts in ways that increase or decrease the personal presence of the two parties. It seems that when negotiations are conducted in an intergroup mode the side with the objectively stronger case tends to win (Morley and Stephenson 1970). Conversely, a side with a weak case stands a better chance of success if the negotiations have a more interpersonal basis. Factors which increase intimacy and individualization (such as one-to-one, face-to-face meetings) tend to promote interpersonal reciprocity or equity between negotiators. When negotiations take place over the telephone, interpersonal considerations fade and the intergroup mode dominates (Rutter 1985; Rutter and Robinson 1981). When they are conducted face-to-face the interpersonal significance of behaviour emerges. Therefore, far from being disintegrative, biased, irrational, or intransigent, intergroup negotiations tend to be task-oriented, rational, and thorough. Stephenson and Tysoe directly manipulated the interpersonal/intergroup orientation of the negotiators and found results which clearly supported this view (Stephenson and Tysoe 1982).

Shifts of emphasis from intergroup to interpersonal negotiating seem to follow a pattern in the course of negotiations. In general the sides take a clear intergroup stance at the outset, but then once their positions have been established the discussions become more open and less entrenched. When naive judges are asked to identify the side of negotiators from a transcript of the negotiations, they are more accurate for earlier stages of the negotiations. In other words, the negotiators tend to arrive at compromise by an integration of their purposes and positions (Douglas 1962; Morley and Stephenson 1977). In some negotiations it becomes necessary to call in arbitrators who, according to Webb, take on responsibility for the interpersonal phase of negotiations (Webb 1982). That is, the two sides take up distinctive group positions (claims for money, resources, holidays, conditions, etc.) and then the arbitrator deals with each in the more interpersonal mode necessary for resolving the conflict. The arbitrator's role is to paper over the cracks, highlight areas of agreement, and obtain the consent of each party to his or her judgement.

Stephenson's work has shown forcefully that the difference between individual and group behaviour is one of quality and not just one of degree. We cannot extrapolate directly from one form of behaviour to the other. Even such seemingly 'basic' processes as memory operate differently when recollection is a group task (Stephenson, Brandstätter, and Wagner 1983; Stephenson et al. 1986). Collaborative group recall tends to be more concrete and less interpretive than individual recall. It also engenders a greater feeling of confidence (irrespective of right or wrong) (see the discussion of 'groupthink' in Ch. 5). Furthermore, this effect is not obtained when individuals recall in co-action with, but confidentially from, the other group members. In other words, creating a *group* product is not the same as each individual producing a product separately and simultaneously. In the case of recall, as with the creation of a social norm (Sherif 1936) or polarization (Wetherell, Turner, and Hogg 1986; see Ch. 8 below) the group judgement persists when the constituent members are asked to give their own view at a later time, and once out of the group. Such phenomena can best be explained in terms of social identification: an inseparability of the group and the self.

THE SOCIAL NATURE OF PERFORMANCE

In this chapter we have described how the social performance literature is dominated by a fallacy: that the study of *mere* presence can tell us something about *social* presence. Similarly, the study of 'task' performance does not necessarily help us account for social performance. A preoccupation with how well people perform has obscured the more fundamental questions of *what* the performance is, who it is by, and who it is for. We have not used the social facilitation theorists as straw men here, but have tried to show that the tradition of social performance theories has, historically, a bias towards intra-individual explanations without due regard to the social bases of behaviour. Compare, for example, self-awareness and self-presentation theories in social psychology with those of their sociological ancestors: Cooley, Mead and Goffman.

The 'self' is a core concept in both sociology and social psychology. In both disciplines theorists have distinguished between the existence and the awareness of self (e.g. James 1890; Mead 1934), although a plethora of distinctions between different aspects of the self is now available (Burns 1979). However, while social psychologists have placed increasing emphasis on the structure and content of self (Higgins, Klein, and Strauman 1984; Markus 1977; Markus and Nurius 1984), sociologists have placed more weight on self as a *process*. Thus Cooley in introducing the notion of the 'looking-glass self' stressed that

> the thing that moves us to pride or shame is not the mere mechanical reflection of ourselves, but an imputed sentiment, the imagined effect of this reflection on another's mind . . . the character and weight of that other . . . makes all the difference with our feeling.
>
> (Cooley 1902: 380)

It was, however, Mead who stated more explicitly that 'the self, as that which can be an object to itself, is essentially a social structure, and it arises in social experience . . . it is impossible to conceive of a self arising outside of social experience' (Mead 1934: 384). These two quotes embody the foundations of our critique of the social performance literature. If the self is a social structure, the physical presence of others is not such a crucial variable as has been assumed. Rather, it is social presence (the nature of the audience whether in mind or reality) which has its effects on social performance. We would go further than Wicklund, who argues that the social world provides standards or end-points towards which people are directed when self-aware (Wicklund 1980, 1982). From a social identity approach, the social world provides potential self-definitions with associated beliefs, feelings, and motives.

We doubt the utility of the idea that compresence creates generalized drive – along with attempts to divine general cross-specific laws about the effects of compresence. The concept of drive may be relatively meaningless. If the presence of others is an energizing factor, what happens when the 'dominant' response is one of inaction (the student who always falls asleep in lectures)? Surely a more plausible line to take is that the presence of others embodies a particular meaning (threat, support, embarrassment, pride, observability, uniformity, etc.) which is interpreted with respect to one's self-image (role, group membership, etc.), and it is this which provides a motivation to act in a chosen way. These social motivations are much more tangible and conceptually useful than the concept of drive. For direct evidence of such social motivation we can return to the minimal group experiments (see Ch. 3). Most of these are conducted with subjects together in one room but seated separately, with confidentiality guaranteed. Subjects know their own category, but do not know to which category the others belong. The 'mere' presence of anonymous individuals should have a simple uniform effect (drive/self-awareness is increased, dominant response is emitted). Yet it is due to the social nature of that presence that subjects make a cognitive distinction between ingroup and outgroup members. There is no 'dominant' response (cf. Billig 1973). Instead, subjects choose to behave differently towards ingroup and outgroup members.

In the following chapter we develop this idea. Specifically, we show how theories of social presence which rely on interpersonal 'social' impact, and those which call upon a state of self-awareness, have contributed to conventional explanations of *collective* behaviour.

Conclusion

By way of a review and preface to the next chapter let us consider again the metatheory which has housed the traditional approaches to social presence and social performance. At the outset of this chapter we used the analogy of group as a set of clothes. Social presence theories subscribe to such an analogy in implicitly separating the individual from his or her group. Thus we have 'alone' *versus* 'audience' conditions, one individual's *versus* individuals' performance, privately held *versus* publicly stated attitudes, and resistance to *versus* compliance with interpersonal pressures. Finally, there may exist the real *versus* the presented self. The clothing of others' presence is somehow held responsible for hiding the vulnerable nakedness beneath. In other words, social presence has been conceived of as *external* constraint on individual behaviour. It is tempting to accept this metatheory since nothing can be more clear-cut than the physical presence or absence of others. Yet the mixture of empirical evidence and the theoretical ambiguities of that position lead us to argue that social presence is a psychological and not a physical phenomenon. As such it falls neatly into a social identity perspective, which treats the individual's perception of the social categorical alignment of those who are socially present as a critical variable.

With regard to social performance, our conclusions are similar. Traditional social psychology has been misguided in its preoccupation with the magnitude or outcome of social performance – for example, Milgram's documentation of how severe an electric shock will be delivered to a learner by teachers under different degrees of pressure from others (Milgram 1974). Experimental studies rarely present subjects with a choice (other than in a very simple manner) about *what* to perform, to whom, and when. The research on bargaining and negotiation, as well as earlier research on reference groups (Newcomb 1947) and sociological research into deviance (Becker 1963) and rules (Goffman 1959) show the importance of looking at the *kind* of behaviour, not just how well it is performed. The social identity approach incorporates an explicit statement that the nature of behaviour changes when different self-images become salient (e.g. Brown and Turner 1981).

In the following chapter, we develop this idea in order to argue for a discontinuity between interindividual and collective behaviour. Specifically, we show how theories which have explained collective behaviour in terms of social impact and self-awareness have obscured the psychological basis on which any collective behaviour could arise.

Recommended reading

For general reviews of social facilitation, social impact, and self-awareness approaches the best single source is a book edited by Paulus (1983). Guerin (1986) provides the most thorough review of the social facilitation literature, while Scheier and Carver (1981) deal with the private/public distinction made by self-awareness theory. Self-presentation approaches are covered by Schlenker (1985) and Snyder (1979), and Stephenson (1984) discusses negotiation and bargaining from an intergroup perspective. As yet, the social identity approach to these issues has not been presented elsewhere as an integrated overview.

7

Collective behaviour

[his] remark was lost in the din of the shouting and gesticulating mob . . . The women had come into sight, nearly a thousand of them, dishevelled after their tramp, in rags through which could be seen their naked flesh worn out with bearing children doomed to starvation. Some of them had babies in their arms and raised them aloft and waved them like flags of grief and vengeance. Others, younger, with chests thrown out like warriors, were brandishing sticks, whilst the old crones made a horrible sight as they yelled so hard that the strings in their skinny necks looked ready to snap. The men brought up the rear: two thousand raving madmen, pit-boys, colliers, repairers in a solid phalanx moving in a single block, so closely packed together that neither their faded trousers nor their ragged jerseys could be picked out from the uniform earth-coloured mass. All that could be seen was their blazing eyes and the black holes of their mouths singing the *Marseillaise*, the verses of which merged into a confused roar, accompanied by the clatter of clogs on the hard ground. Above their heads an axe rose straight up amidst the bristling crowbars, a single axe, the banner of the mob, and it stood out against the clear sky like the blade of the guillotine. . . . indeed, rage, hunger, and two months of suffering, and then this wild stampede through the pits, had lengthened the placid features of the Montsou miners into something resembling the jaws of wild beasts. The last rays of the setting sun bathed the plain in blood, and the road seemed like a river of blood as men and women, bespattered like butchers in a slaughterhouse, galloped on and on.

(Emile Zola, *Germinal*, 1885)

This powerfully evocative and classic description, from the pen of one of the greatest of all literary commentators on the crowd, not only encompasses the entire range of collective behaviour, but describes the same historical events which early crowd theorists (e.g. Gustav Le Bon) employed as their prototype. Zola's style of description set the mould for what many social psychologists, even to the present day, consider to be the problematic of collective behaviour. The extract illustrates many of the themes to be discussed in this chapter: the uniformity and solidarity of the crowd; its unanimity and the poignancy of its symbols; the animal nature of crowd action; its madness, as well as its logic and its wider intergroup context (poverty, oppression, etc.).

Introduction

Demonstrations, sit-ins, strikes, and riots are all examples of collective behaviour. They come about when people collaborate in order to achieve some objective. That collaboration may not be planned or well organized, but it is goal-directed and often involves large numbers of people. In Chapters 5 and 6 we examined the way that groups form, and the consequences of being in a group for individual behaviour. This chapter takes us on a step, to see how large collections of individuals who are together at the same place at the same time manage to behave in unison *as* groups.

We explore two themes in the social psychology of collective behaviour. The first, which stems from the ideas of Gustave Le Bon ([1896]1908) assumes that the behaviour of crowds can be explained by extrapolating from processes which are deeply rooted and exist within its individual members (albeit at an unconscious level). We have already described (in Ch. 3) Berkowitz's and Gurr's extension of frustration–aggression theory to the level of collective behaviour. These theorists share with Le Bon and others a belief that any differences which exist between collective and individual behaviour can be explained as resulting from the *physical* existence of the crowd. The throng, multitude, or horde (terms commonly used by Victorian crowd theorists) unlocks or liberates latent impulses which already reside within its individual members, but which are normally securely contained, under the control of rational thought. Modern social psychology has continued to endorse this view in the form of de-individuation theory (Zimbardo 1970).

The second perspective, which is most obvious in the theorizing of Marx ([1844]1963), Durkheim ([1893]1933), and also partly in that of Mead (1934) and Berger and Luckmann (1967), embraces a conception of collective behaviour which demands its own level of explanation. In the context of social psychology this is embodied in the social identity approach. Rather than depicting collective behaviour as a manifestation of latent impulses, it is considered to result from altered self-conception. Rationality is not so much suspended as changed.

The major part of this chapter is dedicated to critical discussion of traditional explanations of collective behaviour. This provides the proper context for introducing and assessing the contribution made by the social identity approach – which occupies the later part of the chapter.

Early theories of the crowd

Le Bon's classic account of the crowd drew from his medical and anthropological background and combined elements of hypnosis and evolutionary theories (Le Bon 1908, 1913). His special concern that French society in the Third and Fourth Republics was in danger of collapse and decay, and that the existence of ruling élites and social stratification were essential for the development of an economically strong and stable society, underpinned much of his 'sustained attack upon collective protest' (Reicher 1987: 174). His observations of the French Revolution of 1848 and the Paris Commune of 1871 made him anxious and determined that the political élite must be equipped to control the masses.

Basic to his account of crowd behaviour was a view of the crowd as primitive, base, and ghastly. The intention was to discredit the rebellious activities of the working classes, and particularly of socialist thought. It is ironic that, despite the lack of originality of his ideas (see Reicher and Potter 1985), and the fact that he was shunned by the academic establishment for being unscientific, Le Bon remains one of the few theorists who is still widely read today. However, even in his own time, his florid and exciting writing had massive influence on more accepted academics such as Tarde (1901). Le Bon's influence later spread to political leaders such as Mussolini, who openly praised and was well-versed in his ideas.

According to Le Bon the crowd submerges the rationality and self-consciousness of its members. What replaces these faculties is a 'collective mind' in which 'the sentiments and ideas of all the persons in the gathering take one and the same direction, and their conscious personality vanishes' (Le Bon 1908: 23–4). While some theorists have suggested that this collective mind may occasionally contain virtuous, noble, and altruistic aspects (McDougall 1921), Le Bon claimed that it only possessed 'ancestral savagery' which was born of a 'racial unconscious'. This racial unconscious emerged when the pure line, or racial heritage of a crowd was contaminated by racial assimilation. The racial unconscious held the basic instincts of the primal horde, devoid of reason or culture. The danger, then, of collectivities was that this racial unconscious would surface and take over.

The characteristics of crowd behaviour were considered to result from three essential features of crowds: first, the *anonymity* of crowd members instilled a 'sentiment of invincible power' and lack of personal responsibility. Second, the *contagion* of ideas and feelings among the crowd allowed rapid and unpredictable shifts in behaviour. Third, and most important, the *suggestibility* of crowds enabled them to hold ideas, and behave in ways, which were completely at odds with the normal predispositions of the individual members. It is through 'suggestion' – a process akin to hypnosis – that contagion occurs. The sinister aspect of this phenomenon was that the suggestion operated at the level of the racial unconscious. This 'fact' was the basis of Le Bon's 'law of the mental unity of crowds', which explained at once the primitive nature and the homogeneity of crowd behaviour.

Other theorists explored the processes responsible for the suggestibility of crowds. Tarde believed that social life was based on imitation, which in turn depended on physical contiguity and hence found its most extreme manifestation in crowds (Tarde 1901). Trotter likened crowds to animal herds wherein the actions of the 'lead' individual transmit themselves to others by suggestion (Trotter 1919). The power of suggestibility is determined by the extent to which the suggestion appears to emerge from and reflect the herd view or instinct. It was McDougall, in his book *The Group Mind*, who developed this theme to its logical conclusion (McDougall 1921). For McDougall it was the constitutional or racial similarity of members of a crowd which determined the rapidity with which a suggestion took hold. He regarded emotions as being inherently contagious, and 'each instinct . . . capable of being excited in one individual by the expressions of the same emotion in another' (ibid.: 25).

The contagion view of crowd behaviour also finds expression in the more explicitly 'medical' analogy presented by Penrose (1951). He asserts that 'an unhealthy mental process may be concealed under the façade of almost any kind of crowd behaviour' (ibid.: 5). Noting the 'close analogy between the epidemiology of infectious diseases carried by bacteria or viruses and the dissemination of ideas in communities' (ibid.: 13), Penrose proceeds to explain crazes, panics, religious conversion, voting patterns, and even war using this medical model. The infection of a community by an idea arises from 'an abnormal mental condition in one of their number, while its spread is limited by the geographical and social isolation, and the racial and occupational homogeneity of the group. Susceptibility is a function of 'ignorance'. Ignorance, in turn, may have two causes: on some occasions 'the intellect can be so outraged that it ceases to function ., . . [while on others it] . . . may be determined partly by in-born factors, both chemical and structural' (ibid.: 31).

While this theme, of the group as a releaser of disorganized and rampant impulses, has not gone unchallenged by sociologists or political theorists (e.g. Marx 1963; Rudé 1964; Tilly 1978), the individualistic nature of the level of analysis has always appealed to psychologists (see Nye 1975 for a history of Le Bon's ideas). One of the first and most influential to incorporate Le Bon's view was Freud, whose *Group Psychology and the Analysis of the Ego* endorsed at least the view that crowds 'unlocked' the unconscious (Freud 1922). Freud's contribution was to develop a theory of the role of leaders as providing a focus for the group's actions. The leader of a crowd supplanted the super-ego in each individual, and hence had power over the masses.

This power originates in the 'primal horde' (or original human group at the dawn of social existence, in which rebellion against the primal father allowed the establishment of an equitable new form of society). Since the need for leadership remains, and takes many forms, including religion and totemism, leaders take on the mantle of the primal father. They provide the 'group ideal' which replaces the ego-ideal (super-ego). Freud, then, casts the leader in the role of hypnotist.

Ulman and Abse have used Freudian theory to account for the Jonestown massacre, in which followers of the self-appointed 'Reverend' Jim Jones ultimately were persuaded to participate in an act of mass suicide (Ulman and

Abse 1983). Ulman and Abse set out with the premise that 'unconscious dynamics' were at work between Reverend Jim Jones and members of his 'People's Temple'. Such groups, and their leaders can be described as charismatic (Tucker 1970; Weber 1958). The leaders are typically narcissistic (a result of their traumatic childhoods), possessing both charm and poise and enormous self-assurance. The group members, in taking on the leader's ideals make 'profound alterations in the central self' (Ulman and Abse 1983: 644). Secondary identifications and associations with other group members foster the development of the 'group self' (Strozier 1982). There then occurs a collective regression:

> The individual group member not only seeks to be like the leader, but in addition, gradually takes over the more primitive and archaic layers of the leader's super-ego . . . a regression because the individual member is repeating an unconscious psychic process already completed during childhood and adolescence.
>
> (Ulman and Abse 1983: 649)

Ultimately this regression may become pathological.

Although the evidence is drawn from non-objective sources, it does seem that Jim Jones's own life was a story of paranoia and delusion. Convinced from an early age that he deserved a place in history, he quickly enticed others into his vision of the world as a dangerous and threatening place. He would interrogate those followers who began to fall out of line and would intimidate and punish them. He was obsessed with the idea of mass suicide as a means of escaping from enemy forces or global catastrophe. By the time that Jones had taken his followers from California to Guyana, the People's Temple was well established.

Members of the Temple were subjected to physical, sexual, and emotional humiliation by Jones, yet there was surprisingly little resistance to his authoritarian and autocratic regime. Increasingly, he was able to replace his followers' individuality with his own way of thinking and his own will. (This resembles the phenomenon of 'brainwashing' which we discuss in Ch. 8.) Ulman and Abse believe that the Jonestown massacre was as much due to the 'collective madness of his followers' (ibid.: 655) as of Jones himself. They are convinced that it was psychological, rather than economic or educational, vulnerability which made members easy prey for Jones. The followers were typically weak-willed, insecure, and in search of a father figure.

The most sinister aspects of the Temple became increasingly dominant as Jones began to stage 'white nights'. On these occasions, according to Deborah Blakey (1979) (one of the inner circle of the Temple):

> The entire population of Jonestown would be awakened by blaring sirens. Designated persons approximately fifty in number would arm themselves with rifles, move from cabin to cabin, and make certain that all members were

responding. A mass meeting would ensue. Frequently during these crises, we would
be told that the jungle was swarming with mercenaries and that death could be
expected at any minute . . . [During one 'white night' we] were informed that our
situation had become hopeless and that the only course of action open to us was a
mass suicide for the glory of socialism. We were told that we would be tortured by
mercenaries – were we taken alive. Everyone, including the children was told to
line up. As we passed through the lines we were given a small glass of red liquid to
drink. We were told that the liquid contained poison and that we would die within
45 minutes. We all did as we were told.

(Quoted from Ulman and Abse 1983: 653)

These quotes are dramatic and powerful, just the kind of evidence which
was used by Le Bon, and other early twentieth-century crowd theorists.
Ulman and Abse's analysis of group psychology holds the same kind of
intuitive appeal. Yet when the veneer of scientific theorizing is stripped away
there are the familiar problems of all Freudian analyses of collective action
(see Ch. 3 above). Moreover, owing to the inaccessibility of the proposed
unconscious processes, they are impossible to verify. Second, accounts which
rest on the vulnerability of a meekly suggestible crowd to a powerfully
hypnotic leader do not explain how it is that other individuals, who may
have psychological constitutions similar to those of members of collectivities,
do *not* end up either as craven followers or charismatic leaders. For example,
Rejai and Phillips actually found that revolutionary leaders were as likely to
have had tranquil as unsettled childhoods (Rejai and Phillips 1979). There
was no distinctive pattern of socialization which had influenced all of the
thirty-two leaders they studied. Oedipal conflict appeared to be the least
explanatory psychological characteristic (Rejai 1980). As we shall see, many
of the assumptions made by Ulman and Abse's analysis resurface in a slightly
different form under the rubric of de-individuation theory.

De-individuation

How have the ideas of Le Bon, and his followers been imported into social
psychological theory and laboratory experimentation on mass behaviour?
Initially, the concept of de-individuation (Fromm 1941) was based on the
idea of a loss of, or lack of 'individuation' – which Jung defined as 'a process of
differentiation, having for its goal the development of the individual
personality' (Jung 1946: 561; quoted from Dipboye 1977). Thus de-
individuation is thought to be akin to a loss of personal identity.

One of the most often cited, and one of the first, studies was conducted by
Festinger, Pepitone, and Newcomb (1952). They asked subjects in small
groups to discuss their feelings about their parents, and found that the less
subjects viewed each other as individuals, and the less identifiable they were,
the more rash and daring were their contributions to the discussion. An
attempt to replicate this finding by Cannavale, Scarr, and Pepitone was

successful with male subjects, but not females (Cannavale, Scarr, and Pepitone 1970).

A subsequent study by Singer, Brush, and Lublin (1965) showed that non-identifiable individuals (dressed up in laboratory coats) used more obscene language when discussing erotic literature than did identifiable individuals. Singer *et al.* attributed this to reduced feelings of self-consciousness and distinctiveness under conditions of de-individuation. In 1970 Zimbardo published a spirited warning of the dangers of de-individuation. In one of his experiments groups of subjects who were required to dress up in baggy overalls and hoods (reminiscent of the Ku Klux Klan) subsequently delivered electric shocks of significantly greater duration to a (confederate) learner than did those subjects who wore conventional dress. Zimbardo argued that these effects were a result of de-individuation, whose antecedents were anonymity, large group size, diffusion of responsibility, and the presence of co-acting others. These factors alter the individual's subjective world: self-consciousness is reduced, resulting in 'a weakening of controls based on guilt, shame, fear and commitment' (Zimbardo 1970: 259).

Dipboye concluded, from his review of de-individuation research (Dipboye 1977), that lack of identifiability and the wearing of non-descript uniforms leads to a greater propensity to aggress towards an individual victim (e.g. Donnerstein *et al.* 1972). However, some evidence (e.g. Diener 1976) casts doubt on the generality of this effect. Even in one of Zimbardo's studies, using Belgian soldiers, subjects were *less* aggressive when anonymous, and dressed in baggy clothes and hoods, than when identifiable but dressed in uniform. Dipboye concluded that 'the inhibiting effects of anonymity seem more likely to occur in an established group or a group of acquaintances, since an individual is more likely to seek support from such a group than from a group of strangers' (Dipboye 1977: 1060). Diener has suggested that, sometimes, dressing up in peculiar clothes might make one feel more silly and self-conscious, rather than less (Diener 1980).

Up until the mid-1970s de-individuation theory seemed to lack precision and clarity. For example, which of Zimbardo's antecedent variables were necessary, and which sufficient? What role did group size, group membership, physical proximity, and so on, play? To what extent was diffusion of responsibility a consequence or a cause of de-individuation? Diener addressed many of these questions in his research, and formulated the following 'definition' of de-individuation: 'A de-individuated person is prevented by situational factors present in a group from becoming self-aware. De-individuated persons are blocked from awareness of themselves as separate individuals and from monitoring their own behaviour' (ibid.: 210).

He regards the psychological state of the group member as being on a continuum from 'extreme self-awareness to a total prevention of it'. Focusing attention on the group, perceiving it as a whole unit, engaging in physical activity, and a 'high conscious processing load' all prevent self-awareness.

This means that individuals do not monitor themselves or retrieve norms and standards from long-term memory; they do not reinforce themselves, and they do not plan or think about their actions. Consequently, they are rendered susceptible to immediate stimuli, motivations, and emotions:

> People who are deindividuated have lost their self-awareness and their personal identity in a group situation. . . . Thus prevented from self-attention . . . they become more reactive to immediate stimuli and emotions and are unresponsive to norms and to the long term consequences of their behaviour.
>
> (ibid.)

This view embodies most of the current perspectives on group behaviour. For example, Carver and Scheier's self-awareness theory assumes that de-individuation results from a shift of self-regulation at a conscious, relatively abstract level to a lower one (Carver and Scheier 1981a, 1981b). Wicklund's self-awareness theory makes the same assumptions:

> To the extent that individuals collect in deindividuated units, thus transforming the unit of analysis from 'I' to 'we', the potential of each individual member for the discomfort of self-focus is thereby reduced . . . [thus] lowered control *via* values and personal standards . . . a condition just opposite to self-awareness will arise – that of deindividuation – which entails the relaxing of standards and morals.
>
> (Wicklund 1982: 226)

(See Ch. 6 above for further discussion of self-awareness.)

There is, then, general agreement concerning the psychological *effects* associated with de-individuation, but not so much about how de-individuation is brought about. It is usually assumed that it does arise in groups, but not that it results from anonymity (Diener gives the example of a masked bank robber who, although anonymous, is highly conspicuous, and hence self-aware). Diener, Lusk, DeFour, and Flax found that subjects felt more self-aware in smaller groups, and when there were more observers (Diener *et al.* 1980), and Diener, Fraser, Beaman, and Kelem found that anonymous children playing trick-or-treat at Halloween stole more sweets from a bowl when among a group of other children than when alone (Diener *et al.* 1976). It seems, then, that anonymity reduces the threat of punishment but is not sufficient to reduce self-awareness. Lack of individual observability is also required. Indeed, Diener argues that the hood-and-robes type manipulation used by Zimbardo makes subjects feel self-aware and adhere more closely to the implicit requirements of the experiment (i.e. aggression, anti-Semitism; cf. Carver 1974).

Diener has tried to demonstrate that lack of self-awareness is a sufficient condition for de-individuation (Diener 1979). Groups of eight (of whom six were confederates) engaged in group activities for half an hour, after which some subjects were made self-aware by wearing name tags, being referred to by name, filling in personal questionnaires, and reading out personal information to one another. In addition, the real subjects wore overalls, but the confederates did not. A second set of subjects found themselves in groups where all participants wore overalls, had to rate jokes, and had to press a pedal rhythmically (a manipulation designed to direct their attention outwards). In the third, de-individuation condition the confederates created a warm atmosphere, touched the subjects, and all sang and swayed together in unison. Following these sessions subjects were asked to select from a list of forty activities (twenty safe and twenty 'disinhibited', or risky) those they would like to engage in. The de-individuated subjects reported feeling less self-conscious, acting more spontaneously and feeling more positive towards the group compared to subjects in the other conditions. They also chose to engage in more disinhibited behaviours. In general, subjects who were less self-aware also felt less wary of evaluation, a stronger sense of group unity, and preferred more disinhibited behaviour. Together with the considerable evidence that self-awareness promotes behavioural adherence to specific standards, Diener felt confident that 'the deindividuated person has lost the self in the group' (Diener 1980: 230).

A key question which must be asked of these theories is *why* one allows oneself to become a part of the group, and why, once in the group, one succumbs to its influence. There seems to be little consensus on these points (see Ch. 5). For example, Fromm believed that excessive individuality led to feelings of isolation which motivated a 'return to the group' (Fromm 1941). Similarly, Wicklund has suggested that groups provide a 'happy escape' from self-awareness (Wicklund 1982). At the other extreme, Dipboye and Fromkin identify one major source of the extremity of crowd behaviour as 'a retaliation against the source of deindividuation and a reaffirmation of identity rather than a loss of self-control resulting from the freedom of anonymity' (Dipboye 1977: 1058; see Fromkin 1972). However, that view makes it difficult to explain why crowd members tend to exaggerate their behaviour in the same direction as one another. If individuality was the aim, then individuals should resist the group and crowd behaviour should assume an almost random character. Why, if a person is seeking to re-establish individuality, should a person demonstrate excessive affiliation with the group?

In the early 1980s it became clear that the standard practice of equating de-individuation with lack of self-awareness was seriously flawed. One problem was that behaviour in groups does tend to be consistent with some kind of group norm. Another was that some forms of self-attention appeared to promote, rather than inhibit, behaviour which conformed to group standards (e.g. Carver and Humphries 1981; Diener and Srull 1979; Diener and Wallbom 1976; Froming and Carver 1981; Wicklund and Duval 1971). A response to these problems was to distinguish between public and private self-attention. Lack of private self-attention was a basis for de-individuation, while the amount of public self-attention simply determined the course of action taken by a group member. Consensus on this point developed with such rapidity that it is almost as if a group mind had directed the pen of the various different theorists (see Prentice-Dunn and Rogers 1982; Greenwald 1982; Scheier and Carver 1981; Carver and Scheier 1981a) (Fig. 7.1).

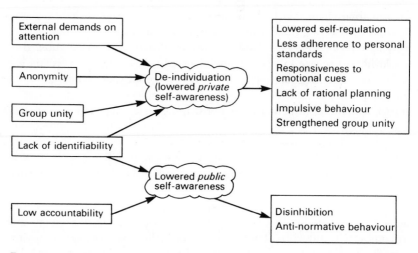

Figure 7.1   Self-awareness model of de-individuation

For example, Prentice-Dunn and Rogers argue that there are two kinds of cues in group settings: attentional cues pull the person's attention away from the self and towards the group, whereas accountability cues increase concern with social standards and conformity (Prentice-Dunn and Rogers 1982). In their experiment, groups of subjects were asked to deliver electric shocks to a (confederate) learner. When subjects were made to feel more accountable (anticipating a later meeting with their victim) *or* when they were self-attentive (as opposed to listening to some music) they delivered less shock. When they were unaccountable they were less aware of their public self, and when they attended to music they were less aware of their private self (see Ch. 6 above for details of the public/private distinction). Prentice-Dunn and Rogers concluded that 'one category of group aggression results from a group member's active calculations that his or her attacks on another person will not be subject to scrutiny or possible retaliation . . . [the other] . . . may result from decreased cognitive mediation of behaviour' (ibid.: 512).

This quote captures the general assumption, whose origins can be traced to Le Bon's work, that group behaviour is unreasoning, destructive, uncontrolled, or at best Machiavellian. Some findings do not fit well with this model. For example, Nadler, Goldberg, and Jaffe found that lack of self-attention can lead to more *pro-social* behaviour (Nadler, Goldberg, and Jaffe 1982). In addition, there is no reason why lack of control should lead to *any* particular behaviour. Also, some de-individuation studies are methodologically flawed in that they explicitly instruct subjects to focus outward or inward. Thus strong demand characteristics may have influenced responses. Two important questions to ask of existing theories are (1) is the self lost in the group? and (2) does lack of private self-awareness lead to loss of self-control? (Recall that de-individuation theories claim that the self is lost because of an absence of private self-awareness.)

LOSS OF IDENTITY AS AN EXPLANATION FOR GROUP BEHAVIOUR

De-individuation researchers have concentrated on explaining the phenomenon of crowd violence rather than the general processes underlying crowd behaviour. For example, Haney, Banks, and Zimbardo replicated the phenomenon of group-mediated aggression amongst subjects who were playing the role of guards in a simulated prison (Haney, Banks, and Zimbardo 1973). However, disinhibited behaviour, and particularly aggression, may only be one possible outcome (rather than an integral part) of immersion in a group. Those playing the role of prisoners in the above study did not become aggressive. In fact, although there were definite changes in the behaviour and thoughts of those participating in the simulation, it was more the acquisition of a new role rather than a loss of identity which was responsible. Subjects were able to play these roles precisely because they were meaningful, not because they were devoid of meaning.

Maslach, in a rather pointless confusion of terms, has suggested that group behaviour may result from 'collective individuation' – a process whereby 'one loses oneself in the group and in doing so gains a new self, a new identity rooted in the group' (Maslach 1974: 234). The group is positively reinforcing in such circumstances. (This view corresponds directly to the group cohesiveness model of group formation and group belongingness, which we discussed in Ch. 5.) Her instrumental model of group affiliation suggests that people try to individuate themselves when they might receive rewards and de-individuate themselves when punishment is likely. Moreover, there are thought to be reliable individual differences in the willingness to be individuated which may explain why not all members of a group behave in an identical fashion (Maslach, Stapp, and Santee 1985). One major limitation of Maslach's ideas is that they do not tell us under what conditions collective individuation can occur, simply one form that it might take. Furthermore, we are no closer to understanding how group behaviour is controlled or regulated.

The importance of (private) self-awareness in the de-individuation process is unquestionable. After all, the *definition* of de-individuation is a loss of self-awareness (Diener 1980; Scheier and Carver 1981; Prentice-Dunn and Rogers 1982; Singer *et al.* 1965; Zimbardo 1970). However, while it seems undeniable that immersion in a group does alter self-perceptions and identity, there is no evidence that it necessarily entails a *loss* of identity.

Recently, research has focused on the effects of differing group size on self-attention (Mullen 1983, 1984; Latané and Nida 1981). One of the more promising lines is that developed by Mullen, who suggests that group members become more self-attentive, and thus more concerned to adhere to particular standards, as the relative size of their subgroup decreases. The smaller group attracts attention because it is perceived as 'figure' against the 'ground' of a larger group. Hence those in a larger group become less self-aware while those in the smaller group become more self-aware. Using a formula called the 'Other–Total' (O–T) ratio, it is possible to predict how self-aware the members of a particular group will be. This ratio is derived by dividing the total number of people in the alternative subgroup by the number of people in both groups combined. Thus, if there were eight people in the other subgroup and four in the subject's subgroup the O–T ratio would be $8/12 = 0.75$. If there was only the subject alone and eight others the O–T ratio would be $8/9 = 0.89$. Mullen's analysis of several studies of social impact and de-individuation (including Diener *et al.* 1980) showed that the O–T ratio reliably predicted the levels of subjects' self-attention. In a direct experimental test, Mullen found that as the number of others in a group increased (where self is own subgroup and all others are defined as other subgroup) subjects made more self-referent completions on the Exner Self-Focus Completion Blank (an index of amount of self-awareness) (Mullen 1983; see Exner 1973).

Mullen's analysis of twelve conformity studies, such as those conducted by Asch (1951), revealed the relevance of this effect for group processes. Conformity was reliably predicted by the O–T ratio. The more conspicuous was the individual, and the larger the number of confederates, the more he or she conformed. Similar findings were obtained for pro-social behaviour, social loafing, and anti-social behaviour. The effects even extend to making members of religious congregations more willing to participate when there are relatively more ministers present (Mullen 1984). Mullen's explanation for de-individuation effects is particularly interesting. He suggests that the victim of aggression (e.g. in Zimbardo-type studies) is the other subgroup, while the aggressors are the subject's own subgroup. Hence, with attention focused on the smaller group (i.e. the victim) the subjects are non-self-aware.

The extension of de-individuation and O–T ratio accounts of group behaviour to explain crowd behaviour is, however, problematic at both the empirical and theoretical levels. Both sets of problems derive from the assumption that the process underlying the apparent disinhibition of behaviour in groups is loss of self-awareness. At an empirical level, de-individuation can promote pro-social behaviour as well as anti-social behaviour (Johnson and Downing 1979). Second, *public* self-awareness intensifies conformity to group norms even in typically de-individuating conditions (Orive 1984). Third, it is not clear that the conditions which de-individuate a subject in the laboratory (anonymity and lack of identifiability) are the same as those which arise in a crowd.

At a theoretical level, there is no reason why lack of self-regulation should intensify *any* kind of behaviour; rather, the actions of individuals should be unrelated to those of others in the group. Second, there is no theoretical basis for determining, *a priori*, what constitutes normative, anti-normative, regulated, or unregulated behaviour (see Ch. 8). Third, and most importantly, these approaches share with other numerical analyses of group effects (e.g. social impact theory) the problem of defining what constitutes a group (see Ch. 5). While there can be little doubt that the numerical distinctiveness of a group can be an important determinant of the salience of that group (Taylor 1981; Wilder 1984), there is still a missing dimension (see Oakes 1987). In Wicklund's terms, the critical question is how the unit of analysis gets transformed from 'I' to 'we', and how behaviour is regulated when it does (Wicklund 1982). The remainder of this chapter turns to the contribution of theories which explain the actions of individuals in terms of group processes. The first of these, which dwells on normative processes within the crowd, goes some way to resolving the problems outlined above. The second, social identity theory, provides the vital link between the self and the group. Both are distinct from de-individuation-type theories in accounting for collective behaviour and group processes without resorting to notions of collective regression or loss of self.

Collective action as normative behaviour

One of the most important steps in the psychology of collective behaviour was taken by Turner and Killian in formulating their 'emergent norm theory' (Turner and Killian 1957; summarized by R.H. Turner 1974). Following the ideas of reference group theorists and researchers such as Sherif and Asch, they proposed that collective behaviour is a form of group behaviour. They argued that the crowd is merely an extreme form of group (where other kinds of collectivities, such as institutional gatherings and social movements, fall more in the middle of a continuum with formal organizations at the other extreme). Thus they broke with traditional crowd theories in stressing the continuity between crowd and other group behaviours (but see Freud 1922). What was distinctive about the crowd was that it had no tradition. The problem to be explained, therefore, was how the crowd was controlled from within. What is it that makes a funeral in South Africa become the setting for a violent clash between blacks and the police? How can soccer supporters co-ordinate a mass wave of hands as was seen frequently during the 1986 World Cup Final? What is the basis of the organization of the crowd?

Part of the value of Turner and Killian's work is precisely that it *asked* this kind of question. Rather than assuming that crowd behaviour was abnormal, or resulting from hidden forces, they assumed that some group process generated order and purpose in the crowd. R.H. Turner (1974) distinguishes between contagion theories (which explain collective action in terms of a rapid spread of ideas, unaffected by rational cognitive processes, e.g. Le Bon 1908; McDougall 1921; Tarde 1901; Trotter 1919), and convergence theories (which explain collective action as resulting from the simultaneous expression of similar response tendencies among individuals through processes such as social facilitation, e.g. Allport 1924; Cantril 1941; Dollard *et al.* 1939; Gurr 1970). The essence of the convergence explanation is embodied in Floyd Allport's statement that, 'The individual in the crowd behaves exactly as he would behave alone, *only more so*' (Allport 1924: 295; see also Chs. 3 and 6 above).

R.H. Turner points out some serious limitations of these two approaches. Contagion theories dwell on relatively extreme instances of crowd action, accounts of which are difficult to verify, and are frequently biased by the observer's ideology. In addition, such theories do not explain shifts in collective behaviour, nor how such behaviour is organized. Convergence theories share these shortcomings, but also cannot explain which of many possible responses will be magnified by the crowd. That is, they explain the intensity, but not the direction of behaviour.

The emergent-norm approach is different in that it explains the pattern of differential expression in the crowd as resulting from a social norm. Because the crowd lacks formal organization (it may have no specific goal, no obvious leaders, and no well defined boundary to membership) 'the norm must be specific to the situation to some degree – hence emergent norm' (Turner 1974: 390). The uniformity of the crowd is an illusion (to both members and observers), created by the fact that certain individuals engage in distinctive action, and hence attract more attention. These acts imply a norm, and consequently there is a pressure *against* non-conformity – non-normative intentions, and inappropriate emotions are suppressed. The relative *inaction* of other crowd members implies consent and support. For example, jollity is suppressed at funerals, misery is suppressed at carnivals. The process of norm formation involves communication among crowd members who create rules, definitions of the situation, and justifications for their intended actions (such as when a lynch mob comes to believe that they will not obtain 'justice' from the official judiciary, and that their victim is definitely guilty). The emergence of a norm also provides the *limits* of crowd emotion and behaviour, which accounts for the fact that there is no ever-increasing spiral of contagion (although these limits may not correspond to those adopted in the wider culture).

The actual means of control, according to R.H. Turner, is the maintenance of an individual's identity within the crowd. Thus, 'control of the crowd is greatest among persons who are known to one another, rather than among anonymous persons' (Turner 1974: 392). The norms are established and take hold through processes such as rumour. Consider, for example, the stock markets. Here it is rumour which has perhaps the strongest influence upon decisions to buy or sell shares, and it is rumour which is clearly responsible for the dramatic swings which are so common. This suggests that share transactions tend to reflect a collective rather than individual perception of market trends. Thus rumour is a collective decision-making process which occurs when a collective definition of a situation is required in order to co-ordinate actions of its members, to establish the direction of the group's actions, and provide meaning for those actions.

Emergent-norm theory represented a tremendous shift from earlier formulations. It allowed social scientists to think of collective behaviour as a normal social process, bound by rules and norms, and possessing internal coherence. Yet ultimately the cohesion of the group and its uniformity are an 'illusion', a consequence of surveillance by other group members. The assumptions of emergent-norm theory also find their expression in social psychological models of group cohesiveness, conformity, social influence, and polarization (see Chs. 5 and 8). The individual crowd member only accepts and is constrained by a group frame of reference when accountable to other group members. The underlying motivation is clearly a desire for social reinforcement and approval, and a fear of social rejection and disapproval. Thus, influence is purely *normative*. In contrast, the social identity approach allows the lines between group and crowd psychology to be drawn more closely by conceiving of group formation as a psychological rather than a physical phenomenon.

Social identification and collective behaviour

Both Diener and Reicher criticize emergent-norm theory (Diener 1980; Reicher 1982). Diener argues that since a norm-regulated crowd would have to be a self-aware crowd, and since being in a group decreases self-awareness, the whole formulation is flawed. A recent comparison of emergent-norm and de-individuation theories supports Diener's view: subjects were more aggressive when anonymous than when indentifiable, irrespective of whether a norm of leniency or aggressiveness had been established by a confederate (Mann, Newton, and Innes 1982). However, the fact that anonymity can elevate aggressiveness and may decrease adherence to norms, does not mean that group behaviour is not regulated by norms.

Reicher criticizes emergent-norm theory for being unable to explain the unity of crowd action (as opposed to its being composed of disparate subgroups), and for its dependence on identifiability. Taken together with Diener's criticisms, it is clear that what is required is an explanation of crowd action which does involve norms but does not depend on accountability and identifiability. Reicher shows how social identity theory provides such an explanation.

If the crowd is defined as a social group – one that 'differs only as a matter of degree' (Reicher 1982: 69) from other groups – it follows that the same processes of social categorization and identification will determine crowd action (Fig. 7.2). The homogeneity of behaviour within the crowd results from its members acting in terms of a *common* social identification. A process of 'referent informational influence' (Turner 1982) takes place, whereby all the members of a group learn the norms and criterial attributes necessary for group membership. For a full discussion of the process of referent informational influence see Chapter 8 below. What is important here is (as in the emergent-norm process) that crowd members, in identifying with the crowd, infer not just what is normal for an ideal and typical group member but also what the *limits* of group behaviour are. Because the group is defined more widely than the immediate crowd – it is a psychological entity – the norms are not necessarily those provided by those who are physically present. Let us take a simple example: a football supporter quickly learns which behaviours will be recognized as demonstrating support for the home team – the wearing of particular coloured scarves, hats, and banners, singing certain chants and slogans, even occupation of a particular location in a stadium. In order to show support for the team the supporter must take on these characteristics. Moreover, the attributes for group membership set limits in the sense that chanting must not support the opposing team, should not take place outside of the group context, and so on.

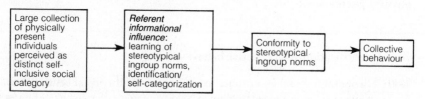

Figure 7.2   Collective behaviour through social identification

Two important questions arise in explaining crowd behaviour in terms of social categorization, identification, and referent informational influence. First, how does the categorization occur, and second, how does each individual divine the rules and norms of the group? The first problem is often resolved *a priori* by referring to the reason for the crowd's existence. Football supporters are there together because there is a match to see. Demonstrators gather to show opposition to a specific issue or group. Often the situation is marked by the presence of opposing or distinctive groups (such as police and students), which forms a basis for social categorization. These factors also encourage identification with one's group and open the way for referent informational influence to take place. The actual norms of the group are inferred from the action of its members (Reicher 1987). However, certain individuals are seen as prototypical, or exemplary, members of the group (such as known community or political leaders, or those who best fit one's stereotype of group characteristics), and it is they who will exert most influence in providing norms for other group members (see also our discussion of leadership in Ch. 5). Reicher argues:

> It is fair to assert that, in the case of an individual in a crowd, group salience is extremely high. Therefore, the act of identification with the crowd will lead to an instantaneous assimilation of its criterial attributes . . . to the extent that any new idea, emotion or behaviour becomes a criterial attribute of the crowd, it too will be assimilated.
>
> (Reicher 1982: 72)

This argument is similar in many ways to those behind emergent-norm theory. There are similar emphases on the group level of analysis, the observation of certain other group members, and the establishment of norms in the crowd. There are also superficial similarities to de-individuation theories, such as the diminished salience of personal identity in the crowd, and the lack of individual responsibility. Elements of convergence and contagion are also involved, in that the members of a crowd act in terms of the same norms, and appear to do so almost in unison. However, the social identity approach differs from all four positions in stressing that control of the crowd occurs via a *new* identity – social identity as a crowd member. The norms, as with emergent-norm theory, are partly evident from the cultural backdrop to, and the ideological and political reasons for, the crowd's existence, and partly from the situationally constructed norms. Control then comes from within the individual rather than by surveillance and overt pressure from others. Identity determines the course of action taken. When one identifies with the crowd, one adheres to crowd norms because those norms are taken on as one's own.

There is now mounting evidence for the greater parsimony of the social identity approach. Social identity theory proposes that group behaviour will occur irrespective of anonymity and identifiability when social identity is salient. In order to test this proposition Reicher conducted a series of experiments concerning the way in which salience of social identity influences the expression of attitudes. First, Reicher showed that when social identity was made salient, subjects were more likely to endorse attitudes to vivisection, which they believed were typical for ingroup members, than when it was not (even when subjects were dressed in baggy overalls and hoods, as in Zimbardo's de-individuation studies) (Reicher 1984a). Social science students expressed more anti-, and science students expressed more pro-vivisection attitudes when their faculty affiliation was used to divide them into groups than when they were mixed together in an unlabelled group. In another experiment the salience of social identity was increased by referring to subjects as 'social science students', or decreased by referring to them by personal code numbers (Reicher 1987). Subjects watched a video tape concerning the pros and cons of punishing sexual offenders and were informed of the modal opinions of various groups (they were led to believe that social science students strongly favoured punishment). After listening to a recording of a (bogus) previous subject expressing his opinions, subjects expressed their own views. When social identity was salient they were more pro-punishment and were uninfluenced by the bogus answers. When it was not salient they were influenced by the bogus subject's attitudes. These results show that 'the conditions associated with crowds make social identity salient and that under these conditions behaviour both conforms to and is limited by the ingroup stereotype' (Reicher 1987: 191). They also illustrate the point that when social identity is salient, individuals are resistant to interpersonal influence.

A further question is whether the self becomes obliterated by the group, as de-individuation theorists suppose (e.g. Diener 1980), since Reicher's data do show that personal views become submerged in some form. It is also possible that group members are merely engaging in self-presentational tactics, designed to please the experimeter or other group members (Froming and Carver 1981; Orive 1984). Both of these interpretations beg the question of why group norms are adhered to, and why subjects would want to present themselves in a particular way. Turner has described subjects in de-individuation experiments as being 'depersonalized' because their *personal identity* is no longer salient (Turner 1981b). Instead, social identity is salient. Since social identity is an aspect of the self-concept this is the core of the argument against a de-individuation account of crowd behaviour (Reicher 1987).

Abrams explored some of these questions using the minimal group paradigm (Abrams 1985). Recall (from Ch. 3) that in this paradigm there are no explicit group norms, no interpersonal communication, and no personal accountability. Group membership is completely anonymous. Compared to subjects in the standard categorization condition, subjects who attended more to their group membership were most biased in favour of their ingroup, and were most consistent in the way they allocated points to the two groups, whereas those who were distracted from their group membership were least biased and least consistent. These findings supported a social identity interpretation, that when attention is paid to intergroup boundaries self-definition as a group member plays a greater part in the regulation of behaviour. A more telling blow to de-individuation theory was that subjects felt more identified with their group when group membership was salient, and that this was magnified by *private* self-awareness. In another experiment subjects who were highly privately self-aware were also most concerned to maintain positive distinctiveness for the ingroup (Abrams and Brown 1986).

Finally, when pupils of two schools were asked to evaluate one another, ingroup bias was highest among those who felt strongly identified with the school and who were privately self-aware (Abrams 1983). These results show clearly that, far from being deregulated, group behaviour is highly regulated in terms of the self-concept.

Taken together, the evidence from these studies by Reicher and by Abrams falls strongly on the side of a social identity analysis of group behaviour. Abrams has suggested that it is possible to resolve the differences between social identity and de-individuation theories (Abrams 1983, 1984; Abrams and Brown 1986). De-individuation theorists posit a *loss* of identity in the group, social identity theorists posit a *switch* of identity in the group (from personal to social). Put simply, Abrams suggests that the continuum of self-regulation to de-individuation is independent of the continuum from personal to social identity. This means that in some group contexts the individual may be consumed by attending to what other members of the group are doing, and may not be considering his or her own actions at all (the typical de-individuation situation), while in others, the group exerts a high degree of control over the individual via his or her feelings of identification with that group (the typical social identity situation). When personal identity is salient the same considerations apply – the individual may or may not regulate behaviour in terms of the self-concept. The distinction between social identity and de-individuation approaches is depicted in Figure 7.3.

The bulk of research on self-awareness and the group ignores the relevance of social identity and therefore ends up contrasting regulation and non-regulation in terms of personal identity. Researchers who have equated immersion in a group solely with a loss of personal identity have blinded themselves to the possibility of observing the group level of *self*-regulation.

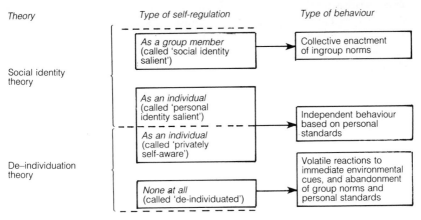

Figure 7.3 Contrasts of social identity and de-individuation theories of crowd behaviour

SOCIAL IDENTITY IN THE CROWD

Perhaps the most vivid way of demonstrating this process in real life is to use an example of the kind of crowd behaviour which is typically explained using the assumptions of contagion, convergence, and de-individuation type theories. Reicher has applied a social identity analysis to an actual riot – which took place in England in the St Pauls district of Bristol in the spring of 1980 (Reicher 1984b; Reicher and Potter 1985). Reicher obtained statements from police and fire officials, along with recordings of relevant TV, radio, and newspaper commentaries. He also interviewed a number of adults and children from St Pauls, and six participants in the riots.

The riot was precipitated by the entrance into the Black and White Cafe of two plain clothes policemen, intending to mount a raid for illegal drink and drugs. More officers, with dogs, who had been waiting outside in police vans then entered the cafe and removed stocks of beer from the cellars. Although there was no outright objection at this stage, there was a general feeling that the police were overstepping the limits of legitimate action. Because these events occurred as children were going home from school there were many observers of the police action, and news of it spread rapidly throughout the community.

Next, it seems that three police officers were seen manhandling or chasing a black youth outside the cafe, and this (or some similar incident) was followed by an attack on the three officers, who were pelted with bricks. Although an influx of more police restored calm, when they tried to take the crates of beer away, their van was obstructed and overturned. Some officers remained trapped inside the cafe. Soon, between thirty and forty police officers had regrouped behind a local pub and marched to the cafe to relieve their colleagues. However they came under attack and had to defend themselves by making forays into the crowd, using truncheons and milk crates to disperse them. A police car was overturned and set alight. While the car was towed away, one of the crowd hurled a stone at the police, and this was immediately followed by a hail of stones from others in the crowd. An attempt by the police to regroup and march into St Pauls from a different direction was also met with a barrage of missiles.

All of these events took place when the streets were full of people – at a time when most would have been returning home from work. As the riot progressed there was a pitched battle between police and the crowd, and a concerted attack on two police cars that caused them to flee from the area at high speed. Remarkably, 'throughout this time traffic was flowing through the area, people were coming home, some were shopping, many were watching' (Reicher 1984b: 9). More significant still, is that the crowd members only chased the police up to the perimeter of the St Pauls area, and did not generally stray beyond these bounds even when the police had withdrawn.

Reicher is at pains to point out how orderly the 'riot' actually was. The crowd helped to keep traffic moving, prevented damage to domestic property, and were careful to regulate which commercial properties were attacked. The explanation for these limits (in terms of who should be attacked, and within what boundaries) of crowd action is that the crowd shared a common social identification. They perceived the police as representatives of an oppressive and illegitimate authority. According to one participant, 'it was just an assumption by everyone in the crowd – get [the police] out' (white male, age 17). After the riots, crowd members reported having felt confident, joyful, and invigorated. Another participant summed up the feeling: 'we feel great, we feel confident, it was a victory' (black male). Although the media coverage of the riot depicted it as a race-riot, both blacks and whites participated. It was the community of St Pauls rather than any particular ethnic group, that was protesting.

When authority is considered as an outgroup, the problem of explaining crowd action changes radically (Tilly, Tilly, and Tilly 1975). Instead of having to explain the sudden emergence of 'contagious' impulses (which happen to resist the prevailing social order) the task is to explain how an *ad hoc* gathering of people are able to become so quickly organized as to take a single direction. How do the norms of the crowd become defined? Since we have already illustrated the answer to this question (they are defined by the relationship to an outgroup, and by inductive inference from the behaviour of other group members) what remains is to demonstrate the importance of being a member of the crowd for understanding its actions. Reicher and Potter (1985) analysed Reicher's (1984b) transcripts and distinguished between the accounts given by outsiders (non-participants, observers, etc.) and insiders (members of the crowd). While outsiders perceived the crowd as formless and rampant ('hundreds of people running down the street smashing glass and damaging cars' – a local publican, quoted in *The Guardian*, 3 April 1980), insiders perceived the whole event as a conflict with the police. The police themselves, although acting very much as a group, explained the behaviour of the rioters using a 'group mind' kind of account. The local Chief Constable stated, 'it was like a powder keg and the spark came along and touched it off and people started to behave irresponsibly and unreasonably' (BBC Radio Bristol, 3 April 1980). In the more extensive rioting that followed in the summer of 1984 at Toxteth, the analogy of a tinder-box was used by almost all the major news media, as well as by the Home Secretary, in order to explain the rioting. The importance of what kind of explanation is adopted becomes clear when one observes the way that authority reacts to rioting. In England in the early 1980s the response was to improve policing and alter the laws to limit congregation in large numbers – it being assumed that people's wicked impulses will get the better of them as soon as they form a crowd. Precisely the same justification lies behind the imposition of South Africa's state of emergency in 1985. However, in the case of South Africa it is quite clear that black insurgency is a part of a collective protest.

Conclusion

In this chapter we have presented different approaches to the psychology of collective behaviour. One branch of theory stems from the ideas of Le Bon, Tarde, and McDougall and has been developed into more specific de-individuation approaches in social psychology. Another, through the ideas of Freud, finds expression in the psychology of revolutionary leaders and mass insanity. A third, more recent approach stems from early social psychological approaches to the group – Sherif, Asch, Newcomb – to provide a theory stressing the normative and organized nature of crowds. The fourth, and theoretically most exciting, is the social identity approach. This allows us to explain the order and purpose of the crowd in terms of the common identity of its members without resorting to the earlier lack-of-consciousness or distorted-psyche approaches. However, this analysis is based on the hypothesis that conformity to group norms really is based on conformity to one's self-definition rather than to interpersonal pressure. It is this issue – the nature of referent informational influence – which we pursue in the next chapter.

Recommended reading

R.H. Turner's (1974) chapter provides an excellent overview of contagion and convergence approaches to the analysis of collective behaviour, and summary of emergent-norm theory. The analysis of the Jonestown massacre by Ulman and Abse (1983) gives some flavour of psychodynamic accounts. The best source for de-individuation theory is still Diener's (1980) chapter, while Reicher (1982, 1987) covers the social identity approach.

8

Conformity and social influence

It is in William Golding's classic 1954 novel *Lord of the Flies* that some of the more subtle aspects of conformity are illustrated. A group of British schoolboys are marooned on a tropical island during a fictional nuclear war. There are no adults present, and the book documents the rapid decay of 'civilized' standards of conduct, the attempts by some of the boys to ensure conformity to these standards, and the ultimate degeneration of the group into warring factions and savagery. One of the boys, Maurice, kicks sand in the eye of a younger child:

> Percival began to whimper with an eyeful of sand and Maurice hurried away. In his other life Maurice had received chastisement for filling a younger eye with sand. Now, though there was no parent to let fall a heavy hand, Maurice still felt the unease of wrong-doing. At the back of his mind formed the uncertain outlines of an excuse. He muttered something about a swim and broke into a trot.

And again, later:

> Roger stooped, picked up a stone, aimed, and threw it at Henry – threw it to miss. The stone . . . bounced five yards to Henry's right and fell in the water. Roger gathered a handful of stones and began to throw them. Yet there was a space around Henry, perhaps six yards in diameter, into which he dare not throw. Here, invisible yet strong, was the taboo of the old life. Round the squatting child was the protection of parents and school and policemen and the law. Roger's arm was conditioned by a civilization that knew nothing of him and was in ruins.

These extracts capture some of the major points which this chapter pursues namely that what one conforms to is a group or cultural norm, an agreed way of acting, and that such norms are binding to the extent that one considers oneself to belong to the group or culture which is defined by the norm. Furthermore, the social influence process associated with such conformity does not necessitate surveillance by the group or its representatives or agents. Of course, conformity also includes the very obvious uniformities of conduct and belief represented by, for example, teenage fashions, 'dark suited businessmen in the city', and Nazi rallies of the 1930s.

Introduction

There is a sense in which social psychology can be considered to be little other than the study of social influence (Latané 1981): 'an attempt to understand and explain how the thought, feeling, and behaviour of individuals are influenced by the actual, imagined, or implied presence of others' (Allport 1968: 3; see Ch. 2 above for discussion of definitions of social psychology). Defined in this way, social influence becomes the process lying at the heart of social science since it is responsible for all that part of human behaviour which is not directly determined by biology. Given the breadth of the phenomenon it is perhaps not surprising to discover that social psychology has no *general* theory of social influence. Rather, there is a large number of specific short-range propositions or empirical relationships which are wedded to clearly circumscribed sub-areas of the discipline, with their own problematics, universes of discourse, and empirical paradigms.

For example, all the following areas and topics in social psychology can be considered to deal relatively directly with social influence processes or to address social influence phenomena: mere presence, social facilitation, and audience effects (Zajonc 1965; see Ch. 6 above); compliance with requests (Cialdini *et al.* 1978); obedience to authority or of commands (Milgram 1974); conformity to group norms (Kiesler and Kiesler 1969); attitude change (Triandis 1971); persuasive communication (Roloff and Miller 1980); mass communication (Roberts and Bachen 1981); minority influence and social change (Moscovici 1976); brainwashing (Barlow 1981; Lifton 1961); leadership (Bass 1981; Fiedler 1971); risky shift, and group polarization (Myers and Lamm 1976); hypnosis (Barber 1973; Hilgard 1973; Kihlstrom 1985); hysterical contagion (Smith, Colligan, and Hurrell 1978); crowd behaviour (R.H. Turner 1974; see Ch. 7 above).

Since our interest is in a social indentity approach, which is principally concerned with groups, we restrict our coverage to a consideration of the influence process associated with groups; that is, how the individual is influenced by the group – *conformity*. We begin by discussing what is meant by conformity, and in what ways it differs from other influence phenomena. The adoption of a theoretical as opposed to empirical definition extends the concept's applicability beyond its traditional domain and cuts across many of the sub-areas listed above. The traditional classics of the social psychology of conformity are discussed, issues confronted, and limitations highlighted, in preparation for a discussion of the contribution made by the social identity approach. The remainder of the chapter focuses the social identity approach to conformity on a selection of phenomena to which it has relevance.

Conformity as normative behaviour

The distinctive feature of conformity is that it involves norms. For sociology, norms are the emergent phenomena of human association. They are Durkheim's 'social facts' and largely the data of social anthropological descriptions of culture (e.g. Radcliffe-Brown 1952). Norms are the set of expectations concerning the appropriate and accepted playing out of roles in society (e.g. Goffman 1959), where the contents of roles are themselves norms. Norms also embody the socially acceptable modes of action to achieve society's goals.

Norms can be concretized, through legislation, as the laws and rules of society, or more often they are so pervasive and so saturate society that they are 'taken-for-granted' and are invisible. They are the 'hidden agenda' of everyday interaction, the background to our behaviour, the context within which things happen (Garfinkel 1967).

Norms are responsible for uniformities of social behaviour. They arise to govern and ensure smooth and predictable social interaction and thus enable society to exist as a cohesive and stable entity. They suppress strife and conflict by furnishing consensus and agreement on an acceptable *modus operandum* for social life. Norms, as 'social facts', are transmitted to individual members of society through socialization enforced, to varying degrees, by agents of social control (e.g. parents, teachers, police) who have the power to ensure normative (socialized) behaviour.

This perspective on norms derives from a 'consensus' view of society as a relatively homogenous whole (see Ch. 2). If, in contrast, we adopt a 'conflict' view of society as a heterogenous collection of different groups of different sizes which stand in power and status relations to each other (again see Ch. 2), then we can posit that different norms attach to different groups. Norms now become the set of expectations concerning the attitudes, beliefs, and behaviour of a particular group of people. They are the social uniformities within groups which also distinguish between groups. They are the stereotypic perceptions, beliefs, and modes of conduct associated with a group; later we shall discuss the relationship between norms and stereotypes (also see Ch. 4).

Norms thus *describe* and *evaluate* the typical behaviour of a typical member of a particular group or social category. They also *prescribe*. That is, above all norms constrain behaviour by dictating that as a member of a particular group you *ought* to behave in a particular circumscribed manner. Norms fulfil a crucial function for the individual. They simplify, render predictable, and regulate social interaction. Without them social life would be unbearably complex and stressful: the individual would collapse beneath the tremendous cognitive overload involved in interaction.

The central question for social psychology concerns how, through what process, and under what conditions the individual embodies the norms of a group. For sociology this is the issue of socialization (but referring to society as a whole), while for social psychology it is *conformity*. This characterization differs in at least one important respect from social psychology's most widely adopted definition of conformity as 'a change in behaviour or belief toward a group as a result of real or imagined group pressure' (Kiesler and Kiesler 1969: 2), in that it stresses the shared and prescriptive (i.e. normative) nature of behaviour to which the individual conforms. In other words, conformity is distinctly an *intra*group phenomenon whose analysis must reside in a systematic theoretical treatment of the nature of the social group. We shall build upon this reasoning below when describing the social identity approach to conformity.

Although norms occupy an important position in sociological enquiry, this is not so obvious in social psychology, where the concept, when invoked, is rarely employed in a capacity other than that of common parlance. In experimental social psychology, the consideration of norms is largely restricted to the early work of Sherif (1936), Asch's conformity research (Asch 1952), and more recent writings by Rommetveit (1969) and Moscovici (1976). Later, it should become clear that social representations (Farr and Moscovici 1984; Moscovici 1961), social stereotypes and social belief structures (Tajfel 1981b; Tajfel and Turner 1979), orthodoxy (Deconchy 1984), and ideology all have relevance to the concept of norm, as does the entire framework of the self-categorization theory of group behaviour (Hogg and Turner 1987a; Turner 1985; Turner *et al.* 1987; Wetherell, Turner, and Hogg 1986).

Before proceeding it should be emphasized that conformity can broadly be distinguished from other social influence phenomena in that the behavioural content is normative: it represents a group which it differentiates from other groups and thus contains information about social rather than personal identity. Nevertheless, the very nature of norms is such that most behaviour concerns information about group membership and identity, and hence that most social influence phenomena contain an element of conformity. For example, compliance with a request to select a book to read (hardly conformity in any sense other than conformity to a generic norm for compliance with requests), may contain an element of conformity to *group* norms as revealed by the specific *choice* of book. Similarly, while voting may be compliance with a law (in some countries) that compels voting, voting *choice* reflects political norms.

Traditional conformity research and theory

The first experimental social psychological examination of the concept of norm was conducted by Sherif (1935, 1936), who, following Durkheim, believed that norms are an emergent property of social interaction which fulfils the function of ordering, simplifying, and regulating interaction. Furthermore, norms, once created, continue to exist and influence interaction in the group even when the original members of the group are no longer present. To examine these fundamental properties of norms Sherif employed the autokinetic ('self-moving') effect: a static pinpoint of light in the dark appears to move, because there is no reference point against which to anchor it. Subjects individually viewed the light over a number of trials and estimated how much they thought it moved, until they had established their own stable range of judgements. Subjects were then brought together into two- or three-person groups to make the same judgements of movement. In the group the judgements rapidly coverged on the mean of the group, which Sherif considered to be the group norm.

Sherif conducted variations on this paradigm to reveal that convergence on the mean (norm formation) occurs much more rapidly and more completely if there is no period of individual judgements preceding the group judgements. If subjects are tested individually after the group phase there is a slight tendency to revert to individual judgemental ranges: the finding that divergence from the norm is so small indicates the power of the norm to constrain judgement even when independent of the group. If the group phase involves only one subject paired with an experimental confederate who has been instructed to stick to a predetermined range and not to converge towards the mean, then it is the *bona fide* subject who does all the moving and the confederate's judgemental range becomes the group norm. This tends to suggest that norm formation, or conformity, does not have to be a mechanical convergence on the mean of a set of judgements, but can be influenced more by some members of the group than others (an important point which will be taken up again below).

Further research employing the autokinetic effect has revealed that judgemental norms, once established, can still have an effect on individual judgement more than a year later (Rohrer et al. 1954), and also that the group norm exacts rapid conformity even when all the original group members have been replaced (Jacobs and Campbell 1961; MacNeil and Sherif 1976). MacNeil and Sherif conducted a study to show that the persistence and power of influence of a norm depends on its arbitrariness (MacNeil and Sherif 1976). In the experimental condition the original group contained one subject who was confronted by three confederates who made either a moderately extreme or highly extreme judgement of movement, while in the control condition there were no confederates, just four subjects. The initial group norm was thus extreme, moderate, or normal. MacNeil and Sherif discovered that over successive generations of the group (for each generation one confederate, or subject, was replaced by a new subject) the more extreme (arbitrary) norms gradually regressed to the normal norm.

The autokinetic studies reveal:

1. A steady norm is an emergent product of social interaction.
2. It is not an arbitrary product, but is constrained by reality in so far as it is rooted in perceptions of the physical and social world.
3. It is a quality of the group rather than the individuals in the group.
4. It exacts conformity from those who join the group.

5. It has an enduring effect upon group members even when they are no longer in the physical presence of the group.
6. The precise complexion of the norm does not have to be the statistical mean of individual judgements – some individuals have greater influence than others, or conversely some individuals are influenced more than others.

While these findings concern physical perceptual norms, there is no good reason to expect the conclusions not to be relevant to less physical norms, such as those concerning aesthetic appreciation (we discuss the putative distinction between physical and social reality in some detail below). For example, Newcomb documented how girls from a conservative background who attended Bennington College were rapidly influenced by the liberal political norms of that college. (Newcomb 1943). He found that 'conservative' juniors who were members of sororities with liberal seniors rapidly conformed to the more liberal norms. The effect persisted after they left the college, and was still present more than twenty years later (Newcomb et al. 1967). Siegel and Siegel did a simple control to show that people from a liberal background are equally influenced, under similar conditions, by politically conservative norms (Siegel and Siegel 1957).

By the 1950s the research emphasis had shifted from norms to conformity, specifically to the examination of interpersonal influence in the group or rather how the group (as a numerical majority) exacts conformity from the individual (as a minority or lone deviate). One strand of this research is represented by work at the Research Center for Group Dynamics into informal communication in groups (e.g. Festinger 1950; but see Ch. 5 above and 9 below), and the other by the Asch conformity paradigm (Asch 1952, 1956; Crutchfield 1955; Deutsch and Gerard 1955).

The original Asch studies involved a group of seven to nine people sitting in a semi-circle taking it in turn to declare which of three simultaneously presented stimulus lines was the same length as a standard comparison line (Asch 1952, 1956). Only the last person to respond was a true naïve subject, all the others, unbeknown to the subject, were confederates of the experimenter. There was a number of separate trials, of which a proportion had been designated as critical trials. On these, the confederates gave a unanimous erroneous judgement. Asch was interested in how the subjects would respond to this group pressure, particularly since the task was in reality totally unambiguous – subjects performing on their own were always correct. The results revealed that subjects registered incredulity and gave signs of distress and anxiety. Only 25 per cent managed to resist the group pressure throughout, 33 per cent conformed on half or more of the focal trials, and 5 per cent conformed on all of them. All in all subjects yielded on about 33 per cent of trials. Asch reasoned that since the stimuli were unambiguous (unlike Sherif's autokinetic studies) subjects could not be using the others' judgements as information about the correct response, rather they were conforming in order not to appear different or in order to avoid censure and rejection by the other members of the group.

Deutsch and Gerard reasoned that if the task was unambiguous (i.e. the Asch rather than Sherif situation) *and* the subjects gave their judgements under conditions of complete privacy and anonymity in which the group could not identify them, then there should be no conformity; after all, there is an objectively correct answer and no means of being punished or reinforced for diverging from it (Deutsch and Gerard 1955). In order to test this idea Deutsch and Gerard modified the Asch paradigm so that all members of the group were isolated in cubicles and communicated via a complex apparatus involving switches and light bulbs. Not surprisingly, conformity was reduced. However, it did not by any means disappear: subjects conformed to the erroneous majority on over 20 per cent of trials. Clearly, people do conform for social approval reasons, but how do we explain the residual conformity left when neither informational nor social approval motives are present? Deutsch and Gerard suggest that people simply have a fundamental propensity to take other people's opinions into account and that this ineradicable feature of human nature is responsible.

The fact that some people conform more than others in conformity experiments (e.g. 5 per cent of Asch's subjects conformed all the time, while 20 per cent never conformed) has resulted in a great deal of research committed to establishing the existence of a conformist syndrome, or conformist personality. 'Conformists' appear to have low self-esteem (DeCharms and Rosenbaum 1957; Rosenberg and Abelson 1960; Stang 1972), a high need for social support or social approval (Crowne and Liverant 1963; McGhee and Teevan 1967; Strickland and Crowne 1962; see Costanzo 1970 for a review), a need for self-control, low IQ, high anxiety, feelings of self-blame and insecurity in the group, feelings of inferiority (Crutchfield 1955), feelings of relative low status in the group (Raven and French 1958; Stang 1972), and a generally authoritarian personality (Elms and Milgram 1966). There are, however, negative findings (e.g. Barron 1953; Barocas and Gorlow 1967), and evidence that those who conform in some situations do not do so in others (e.g. Vaughan 1964). It is now felt to be more parsimonious to seek an explanation of why some people conform and why some remain independent, in terms of qualities of the group, the situation, the task, and the individual's relationship to the group rather than in terms of personality (see McGuire's 1968 review). After all, we all conform sometimes, so the question becomes when, why, to what, and to whom? This is entirely consistent with more recent conceptualizations of the relationship between the person and the situation, in which so-called stable personality syndromes are treated as products of stable situational factors rather than internally programmed 'gyroscopes' (e.g. Marlowe and Gergen 1969; Mischel 1968, 1969; Mischel and Peake 1983).

A similar logic has been invoked to argue that the greater conformity of females than males revealed by research (and readily accepted due to its consistency with supposedly 'commonsense' assumptions) is largely due to the conformity tasks employed (ones in which males have greater expertise and hence are more ambiguous to females) or other ancillary factors independent of the sex of the subject (e.g. Eagly 1978; Sistrunk and McDavid 1971).

As regards characteristics of the group which exact greater conformity, there is evidence that attractive groups are more potent (e.g. Deutsch and Gerard 1955), probably due to the fact that they may act as reference groups (e.g. the Bennington study, Newcomb 1943). There is also evidence that conformity increases linearly with the numerical size of the majority in some situations (e.g. Mann 1977), but in others reaches its full strength with a majority of 3 to 5 and then levels off (e.g. Asch 1952; Stang 1976). Wilder provides convincing evidence that it is not the *absolute* number of individuals in the group which is important but the number of discriminably independent social entities or groupings (Wilder 1977). In general, the effect on conformity of increasing number appears to be a function of the task being employed (Shaw 1981). Finally, Mullen shows how the presence of independent subgroups can create conformity by affecting subjects' self-awareness (whether one's attention is focused externally on the group or internally on oneself) (Mullen 1983; see Ch. 7 above).

One of the most exhaustively researched features of the group is its unanimity (Allen 1975). Conformity is drastically reduced by the presence of social support for non-conformity (Allen 1965; Edmonds 1964; Hardy 1957), by the presence of a dissenter or dissenters, and even by the presence of a deviate who cannot decide on what response to give (Shaw, Rothschild, and Strickland 1957). The earlier in the response sequence that the support, dissent, or deviation occurs, the more potent is its effect (Morris and Miller 1957). Allen and Wilder suggest that this is so because of the function it fulfils in allowing the recognition of a cognitive alternative to the majority position (Allen and Wilder 1980). In general, it is thought that support, dissent, deviation, and so forth have their effect in reducing conformity because they break the majority's consensus (Allen 1975). Unanimity and consensus are potent forces for conformity.

On what sort of tasks and in what sort of situations do we tend to conform? Research suggests that greater conformity occurs on ambiguous tasks and for ambiguous stimuli (i.e. where there is a sense of subjective uncertainty) (Asch 1952; Blake, Helson, and Mouton 1956), when responses or judgements are given publicly rather than privately (Deutsch and Gerard 1955), when the task is directly relevant to the group's existence and function, when the task explicitly involves giving the 'correct answer' rather than a 'personal preference', and when group cohesiveness and responding as a group are stressed (Thibaut and Kelley 1959).

Hogg and Turner suggest that these findings allow the detection of at least three major sources of influence on conformity (Hogg and Turner 1987a).

First, the *normative clarity* and *relevance* of the group – that is, the extent to which the behaviour of the group conveys a distinct and reliable group norm which distinguishes it from other groups. Factors contributing to this are the intragroup homogeneity, consensuality, unanimity, or stereotypicality of the group's behaviour, and the degree to which this behaviour is directly relevant to the group's existence. The second source of conformity resides in the individual's *relationship to the group*, which determines whether the group is 'chosen' as a source of influence to respond to. This is affected by factors such as group attractiveness, which may render it a relevant reference group for the individual. The third influence stems from the individual's *relationship to the stimulus*. Being in a situation where one would tend to expect a degree of agreement with others concerning the stimulus, or how to behave, and yet encountering disagreement, creates a feeling of subjective uncertainty about the objective validity or appropriateness of one's perceptions, judgements, opinions, or behaviours. The greater the subjective uncertainty, the greater the pressure to conform.

NORMATIVE AND INFORMATIONAL INFLUENCES

Theoretical treatments of conformity contain a number of conceptual distinctions (Table 8.1), of which some of the more important are between public compliance and private acceptance (Kiesler and Kiesler 1969), normative and informational influence (Deutsch and Gerard 1955; also see Jones and Gerard 1967), group locomotion and social reality testing

Table 8.1   Some descriptions of social influence: classification of terminology in terms of two processes

Theorists	Two distinct terminologies	
Deutsch and Gerard (1955) Kelley (1952)	Normative influence	Informational influence
Kiesler and Kiesler (1969)	Public compliance	Private acceptance
Kelman (1958, 1961)	Compliance, identification	Internalization
Festinger (1950, 1954)	Group locomotion	Social reality testing, social comparisons
French and Raven (1959) Raven and Kruglanski (1970)	Coercive power, reward power	Expert power, informational power
Jellison and Arkin (1977) Sanders and Baron (1977)	Cultural values	—
Burnstein and Vinokur (1977) Vinokur and Burnstein (1974)	—	Persuasive arguments

(Festinger 1950), different sources of social power to exact conformity (French and Raven 1959; Raven and Kruglanski 1970), different conformity phenomena arising from different 'reasons' for conforming (Jahoda 1959; Kelman 1958, 1961), and different sources of independence and resistance to influence. To this can be added 'cultural values' (Jellison and Arkin 1977; Sanders and Baron 1977) and 'persuasive arguments' (Burnstein and Vinokur 1977; Vinokur and Burnstein 1974) explanations of group polarization (we discuss this later in the chapter). Hogg and Turner argue that these issues can be integrated and simplified to arrive at a relatively straightforward distinction between two forms of social influence which together share the burden of explanation: *normative* and *informational influence* (Hogg and Turner 1987a, adopting the terminology of Deutsch and Gerard 1955, but see also Jones and Gerard 1967). It is this distinction which we shall discuss here.

Normative influence (Deutsch and Gerard 1955; Kelley 1952) results from the individual's need for social approval and acceptance. It creates conformity which is merely *public compliance* with, rather than *private acceptance* (Kiesler and Kiesler 1969) or *internalization* (Kelman 1958, 1961) of, the group's attitudes, beliefs, opinions, or behaviours. It is not associated with true internal change. The individual 'goes along with' the group for instrumental reasons such as attainment of group goals (called *group locomotion* by Festinger 1950) or avoidance of punishment, censure or rejection for deviation, or in order to cultivate social approval and acceptance. Normative influence arises under conditions in which the group (or individual) is perceived to have coercive power (i.e. the power to criticize, derogate, threaten, punish, or enforce laws and regulations for which there are penalties attached for non-compliance), or reward power (the power to reinforce compliance or administer affection, praise and material rewards) (French and Raven 1959; Raven and Kruglanski 1970). Thus an important precondition for effective normative influence is the perception of surveillance by the group. This can also be seen in Latané and Wolf's explanation of social influence in terms of 'social impact' (Latané and Wolf 1981; see also Chs. 5 and 6 above for description and critical comments).

Hogg and Turner (1987a) suggest that normative influence may also underpin the *referent power* (Raven and Kruglanski 1970) of a group – that is, its power to exact conformity on the basis of being a relevant reference group for the individual. Since reference groups are implicitly defined in terms of emotional attachment on the basis of liking and admiration (see Kelley 1952) it is quite likely that pressures for uniformity within such groups are based on a desire for approval, acceptance, and so forth. This analysis probably still holds despite Kelman's use of the term *identification* to classify the conformity process underlying referent power (Kelman 1958, 1961). Kelman considers reference groups to comprise significant reference others who are people to whom one is attracted, and with whom one therefore wishes to maintain a relationship. Thus conformity via referent power is actually a relationship maintenance process.

Informational influence (Asch 1952; Deutsch and Gerard 1955; Kelley 1952), on the other hand, results from the individual's need to be correct. It is 'true influence' in that it results in private acceptance or internalization of beliefs, attitudes, and behaviours. The power of informational influence resides in the perceived expertise or expert power (i.e. possession of knowledge that others repeatedly need to draw upon), or the informational power (possession of a specific piece of information that is needed) of others (French and Raven 1959; Raven and Kruglanski 1970). The precondition for effective informational influence is subjective uncertainty, or lack of confidence in the objective validity of one's beliefs, opinions, and so forth, which cannot be directly resolved by objective tests against physical reality. Under these conditions social comparisons (Festinger 1954) or social reality tests (Festinger 1950) are made.

While normative and informational influence are theoretically distinct processes, in most circumstances they operate together to create conformity. We should note, however, there are those who propose a deep psychological need for individual freedom and independence, which activates a psychological arousal state (reactance) aimed at resisting influence attempts which are perceived to threaten individual freedom of thought and action (Brehm 1966). In a similar vein there are those who argue that independence also stems from a desire to be identifiably unique, which varies in strength from individual to individual (Maslach 1974; Snyder and Fromkin 1980) and can override the usual desire to 'blend in' in order to avoid the unpleasant sensation of objective self-awareness (Duval and Wicklund 1972). Finally, Singer, Brush, and Lublin suggest that de-individuation (anonymity and lack of identifiability) provides the individual with the freedom to be independent and not conform (Singer, Brush, and Lublin 1965; see Ch. 7 above).

Limitations of traditional approaches to conformity

One important limitation of the two-process model of conformity is that conformity can still occur when *neither* process would be expected to operate. Witness Deutsch and Gerard's finding that people still conform at the rate of more than 20 per cent when they are neither under surveillance by the group (responses were private and anonymous) nor confronted by an ambiguous stimulus requiring social validation (Deutsch and Gerard 1955). *Post hoc* explanations of this 'residual' conformity in terms of a universal tendency for people to take others' views into account (e.g. Deutsch and Gerard) are inadequate since they fail to explain why, having taken account of others' views, we should necessarily conform to them. Also, all conformity research rarely obtains 100 per cent conformity – so where is this *universal* tendency? The fundamental question of conformity is left unanswered.

The 'dependency bias' of much conformity research fails to deal adequately with the question of independence and non-conformity (Hollander and Willis 1967; Wrightsman 1977). Attempts to tackle this problem in terms of static personality characteristics have largely been rejected on both empirical and theoretical grounds in preference for a more situational analysis (see above). More recent treatments of independence are also limited in their explanatory scope. For example, although reactance theory may explain why some people under some circumstances may resist overt pressure to conform, it fails to account for independence in the absence of such overt pressure, and these circumstances presumably account for the greater part of the phenomena of independence and non-conformity. Furthermore, it betrays a tendency to generalize and reify what might well be a specific cultural or subcultural value for unique individuality and individual freedom (see the social anthropological evidence that the Zuñi Indians of New Mexico place inordinately less value on individual freedom than does wider American culture – Benedict, 1935). The postulation of a desire to be unique which sponsors independence fares little better. If, as is hypothesized, it is a personality trait which varies in strength from individual to individual, then the explanation contains the same errors as other personality explanations (see, for example, the self-consciousness explanation discussed in Ch. 6). Also, evidence reveals that it is not a desire to be merely unique but rather to be uniquely better (Myers, Wojcicki, and Aardema 1977). This at least suggests that independence from or non-conformity to one group may actually represent differentiation from the group on specific dimensions which place the deviate in another consensually more highly valued group.

The reference group approach (e.g. Hyman and Singer 1968; Singer 1981) attributes independence and non-conformity to circumstances in which the source of influence is not a relevant reference group for the individual. The group is, however, ultimately defined in terms of interpersonal interdependence and mutual attraction, which is a conceptualization that suffers from a number of theoretical and empirical limitations (e.g. Hogg 1987; see also Ch. 5 above). Furthermore, since the social influence process associated with reference groups appears to be normative influence (see discussion above), the approach deals with compliance not conformity, and suffers from all the limitations of the two-process model.

By emphasizing normative and informational *dependency*, the traditional approach not only underemphasizes independence and non-conformity but also social change. In particular, it overlooks the phenomenon of minority influence, where a numerical minority confronts the dominant consensus and actively solicits conformity to its own position from members of the majority (Moscovici 1976). It paints a very static picture of society in which mass opinion cannot be changed because the process of social influence is one which involves conformity of individuals and minorities to the numerical majority. It is consistent with de Tocqueville's portrayal of (mid-nineteenth-century American) democracy as the 'tyranny of the majority' (see Brogan 1973), and it seems to be grounded in what we referred to in Chapter 2 as a 'consensus' rather than a 'conflict' model of society.

A general and very fundamental shortcoming of the two-process approach to conformity is that it displaces the study of norms to the sidelines. By focusing on interpersonal influence in the group, it renders very difficult the study of norms, given our view that they are an emergent property of groups which, although they may be transmitted by interpersonal interaction, transcend individuality. No theoretical link is made between conformity and normative behaviour or group belongingness. And yet norms, as prescriptive consensuses, are heavily implicated in conformity: factors which enhance conformity (e.g. the unanimity of the majority, the criteriality of the behaviour to the group's existence, that the group need only contain sufficient members for a clear consensus to be perceived) all contribute to the normative clarity of the group's behaviour, and to the prescriptive relevance of the behaviour to the individual. The anaysis of conformity as adherence to norms, or as normative behaviour, cannot simply be conjured out of a collection of separate interpersonal processes.

Recently, however, norms have once again been brought centre-stage, initially by Moscovici and Faucheux, who reinterpret the Asch paradigm as an exercise in *minority* influence rather than conformity of an individual to a majority (Moscovici and Faucheux 1972). They remind us that no experiment occurs in a social vacuum divorced from the effect of the subjects' extra-experimental real-life experiences (Tajfel 1972c). The subjects in the Asch paradigm are not faced by an erroneous *majority* but rather by an erroneous *minority* which makes judgements of line length that are starkly at variance with the judgements people reliably make in the *real* world. The experimental group norm is at odds with the real-world norm brought to the experiment by the subjects, and the explanation of conformity must rest upon an examination of why some subjects choose the experimental group norm to determine their behaviour rather than the real-world norm. Moscovici and Faucheux have essentially stood the Asch paradigm on its head and reminded us, in Cooley's words, that 'the one who seems to be out of step with the procession is really keeping time to another music' (Cooley 1902: 301). What was considered to be a paradigm to examine how a majority extracts conformity from an individual as a majority of one, now becomes an examination of how a minority manages to make an individual abandon the majority viewpoint and conform to the minority. (We discuss minority influence below.)

To pursue our emphasis on conformity as normative behaviour let us return to informational influence. You will recall that, unlike normative influence, informational influence is *true* influence because it induces *private acceptance* of a viewpoint, opinion, belief and so on, not merely behavioural compliance. Subjective uncertainty concerning the nature of objective reality motivates one to seek further information to validate or confirm perceptions, and to the extent that there are no reliable and readily available non-social physical means of testing perceptions, one turns to others' views and opinions as a source of information (Festinger 1954). Social comparisons make one dependent on specific others as a source of information and lead one to accept their views and opinions as valid evidence about objective reality: conformity occurs (see Hogg and Turner 1987a; Turner 1985; Ch. 5 above).

There is a problem with this approach to social influence, which resides in the distinction drawn between physical and social reality. The point, made by Moscovici, is that even beliefs about physical reality are largely socially constructed and validated and that physical reality-testing rests upon a cultural consensus no less than social reality-testing (Moscovici 1976; Moscovici and Faucheux 1972):

> It is true, of course, that technical instruments (including one's senses) permit an individual to make decisions about the environment by himself; but even these instruments conceal a consensus, since the mode of action of a tool or the appropriateness of a measuring device must be agreed upon by all if the result of such operations is to carry any information.
>
> (Moscovici 1976: 70)

Although physical reality is 'out there', how we perceive it and how we validate our perceptions is a matter of consensus, and the 'evidence of our senses' is thus to a large extent mediated by the conventions (e.g. scientific) of our culture. If physical reality-testing (the use of measuring devices, sight, sound, etc.) does indeed differ from social reality-testing ('asking' other people), it is probably simply that in the former the role of consensus is indirect, implicit, 'taken-for-granted', hidden (see Tajfel 1972a; see also 'hidden agendas' in Garfinkel 1967).

This analysis has some very interesting ramifications. For example, subjective uncertainty need not be related to the objective ambiguity of a stimulus. In fact, knowledge that a stimulus is truly ambiguous should, paradoxically, destroy any sense of subjective uncertainty. After all, if one *knows* that reality is inherently unstructured, then why should anyone else's opinions and perceptions be more valid or 'correct' than one's own? The power of consensus to reduce uncertainty resides precisely in its implication that others have disambiguated reality: that they have valid knowledge. To support this, we can cite Sperling's finding that if subjects in an autokinetic study (cf. Sherif 1935) are explicitly told that the effect is an optical illusion, then the usual judgemental convergence does not occur (Sperling 1946). Similarly, subjective uncertainty can arise when the stimulus is totally non-ambiguous. Post-experimental interviews reported by Asch reveal quite clearly that the subjects, who were viewing lines of totally unambiguous length, reported experiencing uncomfortable feelings of doubt and uncertainty (70 per cent reported this explicitly), which was more acute for those who conformed (Asch 1952). Subjective uncertainty is fundamentally a social product, an effect of disagreement and social conflict: we feel uncertain when there is disagreement with those with whom we expect to agree (see Hogg and Turner 1987a; Moscovici 1976; Turner 1985).

The general implication to be drawn from this discussion is that Festinger's distinction between physical and social reality testing is untenable and that all one's beliefs rest directly or indirectly upon social consensus for their subjective validity. While the agreement of others confers certainty, so disagreement, social conflict, or dissensus produce uncertainty. However, it is only disagreement with others with whom one expects to agree which has this effect – that is, with others who are categorized as identical to self as regards the attributes relevant to making a sound judgement of the specific stimulus being judged (e.g. normal eyesight for Asch's lines, compatible musical acuity for judging a new piece of music). Consequently, disagreement may not lead to subjective uncertainty and concomitant conformity, specifically if it can be attributed to salient differences between self and others. For example, a common reaction of Asch's subjects is to search for dissimilarities which might explain the disagreement. Allen suggests that if the majority has been presented as, for example, visually abnormal or handicapped in some relevant way, then both uncertainty and conformity would have been markedly reduced. (Allen 1975: 30). Also, if disagreement is expected, then again there is no uncertainty. This is presumably what occurred in the Sherif paradigm when subjects were told that the stimulus was an illusion: others are not expected to react in the same way as oneself (Alexander, Zucker, and Brody 1970; Sperling 1946).

The preceding arguments suggest that the categorization of self and others as identical, in the context of a stimulus situation which is perceived to be shared or identical, is a precondition for effective social influence. This is because in such a situation shared category membership leads people to expect to agree about the nature of the stimulus, and to believe on the basis of such agreement that their response is correct: that is, the objectively appropriate one. Any such achieved consensus will tend to be prescriptive, and is therefore a social norm. Disagreement within the confines of common category membership arouses an uncomfortable feeling of subjective uncertainty which is remedied by adherence, or conformity, to the perceived group norm. As such, the explanation of conformity should be sought in processes associated with group belongingness or psychological group formation.

Social identity and conformity

From the social identity perspective the contours of social categories or groups are furnished precisely by their respective norms, which serve to describe and prescribe those attributes which characterize one group and differentiate it from other groups. The contents of group behaviour (the distinct and above all shared beliefs, attitudes, behaviours, appearances, and so forth) are the norms of the group, and thus group behaviour is synonymous with normative behaviour. Psychological group belongingness is inextricably linked with stereotypical social uniformities in behaviour, attitudes, perceptions, and so on, and thus with expression of or conformity to ingroup norms. No distinction is made between physical and social reality testing.

REFERENT INFORMATIONAL INFLUENCE

Intragroup consensus, agreement and uniformity are generated by a distinct form of social influence responsible for conformity to group norms, called *referent informational influence* (Hogg and Turner 1987a; Turner 1982, 1985). This process occurs in three stages; first, people categorize and define themselves as members of a distinct social category or assign themselves a social identity; second, they form or learn the stereotypic norms of that category; and third, they assign these norms to themselves and thus their behaviour becomes more normative as their category membership becomes salient (Fig. 8.1).

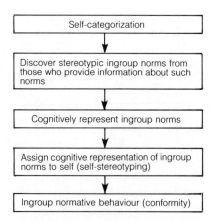

Figure 8.1   Conformity through referent informational influence

The underlying process is one of self-categorization (Turner 1985; Turner *et al.* 1987). As we saw in Chapter 4, self-categorization accentuates self-ingroup similarities and self-outgroup differences on all dimensions (attitudinal, behavioural, emotional, affective, etc.) stereotypically associated with the intergroup categorization. In Chapter 5 we discussed how self-categorization also places one's self in the cognitive representation of a social category and is thus responsible for psychological group belongingness. In this way, group belongingness and normative behaviour, or conformity to group norms, are inextricable products of a cognitive process of categorization which generates a perceptual distortion (accentuation) responsible for stereotyping.

In equating stereotypes and norms we are (following Turner 1982; see Ch. 4 above) departing somewhat from the usual usage of the term 'stereotype', although Sherif quite automatically assumes the term norm to include stereotypes (Sherif 1936). Traditionally, stereotypes seem to differ from norms in that they are primarily descriptive not prescriptive features of groups, and they refer to a more restricted range of behaviours than do norms (e.g. Brigham 1971; Katz and Braly 1933). However, these differences may reflect different universes of discourse in which the terms are employed rather than fundamental qualitative differences in their respective referents. This point may also have relevance for other apparently separate provinces of inquiry. For example, ideologies (Larrain 1979; Billig 1982, 1984), orthodoxies (Deconchy 1984), social belief structures (Tajfel and Turner 1979), and social representations (Farr and Moscovici 1984; Moscovici 1961) all share an underlying commonality which places them squarely in the province of the study of norms: they all deal with socially patterned social phenomena that define the contours of social groups.

Social consensus or agreement, then, is an intrinsic property of the social group, and disagreement or dissensus is unexpected and creates pressures for conformity, or the recognition of disjunctive category membership in order to explain disagreements. Consensus both resolves subjective uncertainty and confers objective validity upon opinions, perceptions, and conduct because it permits external attributions to be made: if you find that a large number of 'similar' people to you agree that a certain movie is good, you are likely to attribute this shared response to the movie. It is an intrinsically good movie. If there is disagreement, you are not so sure whether your response is due to the movie or to some idiosyncracy of yours: the movie may not really possess the property of 'goodness'. This idea comes from attribution theory (Kelley 1967) but is implicit in both Asch (1952) and Festinger (1950).

One interesting implication of referent informational influence theory concerns who influences whom in a group and, more generally, precisely to what it is one conforms. While we may use others' behaviour to construct an image of the normative or stereotypic characteristics of the group, it is this cognitive *representation* to which we conform, not necessarily the overt behaviour of others. After all, self-categorization, which generates normative behaviour, is a *cognitive* process that can only act upon cognitive content. Although within a group there will usually be a great deal of agreement between group members on what constitutes the normative or stereotypic tendency of the group (after all, social stereotypes and norms are *shared* representations – see Tajfel 1981b; see also Ch. 4 above), there may be circumstances in which such agreement is markedly reduced; that is, there will be pronounced disagreement between individual group members or subgroups. This might be true of times of social change when groups are actively involved in the re-negotiation of their defining characteristics and norms (see Tajfel and Turner 1979; see also Ch. 3 above) – for example, ethnolinguistic minority rights groups such as French speakers in Quebec (see Giles, Bourhis, and Taylor 1977; see also Ch. 9 below). Another set of circumstances might encompass novel situations for which the ingroup has no initial norms of behaviour (see Ch. 7 above).

While pronounced intragroup normative disagreement is likely to be rare, the preceding paragraph does suggest that total agreement is probably even less likely. It is probably more accurate to speak of the normative tendency of a group: the group embraces a relatively wide range of behaviours within which there is a clear normative tendency that identifies an individual or subgroup as best representing, expressing or embodying this tendency. By definition, this individual or subgroup is most 'informative' (i.e. has greatest power to exact conformity) as it conveys the relevant or appropriate ingroup norm, and thus confirms the valid, correct, appropriate behaviour. Turner (1985; Turner et al. 1987) employs Rosch's (e.g. Mervis and Rosch 1981) term 'prototype' to refer to the individual or subgroup which best represents the normative tendency of the group. What we have now is a far cry from the traditional conformity model; instead of static unidirectional submission of the individual to the behavioural dictates of the majority, we have a dynamic intragroup 'negotiation' of prototypicality or normativeness which invests different positions within the group with greater power to induce conformity. Clearly conformity need not entail convergence on the behavioural *mean* of the ingroup: if the prototype is displaced from the mean for some reason or other, then conformity will manifest itself as convergence on this displaced mean (we shall discuss this phenomenon below).

Referent informational influence accounts for conformity as private acceptance or true change as a consequence of social identification through self-categorization. There are, however, other reactions to group influence, and it is quite important to be able to distinguish between them (Table 8.2); for example, Stricker, Messick, and Jackson show that conformity, anti-conformity, and independence are three very different phenomena (Stricker, Messick, and Jackson 1970). Hogg and Turner suggest that in order to classify different responses to group pressure, at least two orthogonal dimensions are needed: the context of group influence (whether the group has or is perceived to have the power to coerce, through sanctions, punishments or rewards), and the individual's psychological relationship to the group (identification, non-identification, or active disidentification and rejection of the group) (Hogg and Turner 1987a). They argue that (extreme) coercion under any circumstances results in behavioural compliance: coercion exerted by a group with which one identifies is likely to cause disidentification and hence transform conformity into compliance. In the absence of coercion, people conform to a group with which they identify, remain independent from one with which they simply do not identify, and express anti- or counter-conformity if the group is one from which they actively wish to dissociate themselves. Other slightly different models are proposed by Jahoda (1959) and Kelman (1958, 1961).

Table 8.2   Determinants and reactions to group influences*

| | | Relationship between individual and group† | | |
		Identification	Non-identification	Disidentification
Context of group influence†	No coercion	Conformity	Independence	Anti-conformity/counter-conformity
	Coercion	Compliance	Compliancè	Compliance

Notes:
*Table adapted from Hogg and Turner (1987a).
†It is important to remember that these are *dimensions*, not sets of discrete categories.

Referent informational influence differs from normative and informational influence in a number of ways (see Hogg and Turner 1987a; Turner 1982). Normative influence occurs through social communication or group pressure from (usually attractive) people who have the power to reward conformity and punish deviation. Surveillance by the group increases conformity. Informational influence operates through social comparisons made with similar others who provide information about physical or social reality. Ambiguity or complexity surrounding physical or social reality increases conformity. Under both normative and informational influence one conforms to the observable behaviour of others. In contrast, referent informational influence operates through self-categorization (identification). Interpersonal communication and comparison have a role in establishing the appropriate ingroup norm, but are not the vehicle or process of influence. One is influenced by those who provide information about criterial ingroup norms; they need not be attractive nor similar, and although usually ingroup members they do not have to be, they could be persuasive outgroup members (e.g. the mass media). Conformity is increased by identity salience; because the more salient the identity, the greater the expectation of agreement between common category members, and hence the greater the pressure for conformity when perceived or actual disagreement is encountered. Finally, one does not conform to observable behaviour, but to one's cognitive representation of the appropriate ingroup norm, and thus behaviour may become more normative (conformist) at the same time as it diverges from the behaviour of other group members.

EVIDENCE, APPLICATION, AND SIGNIFICANCE
Referent informational influence theory has oblique support from a number

of sources (see Hogg and Turner 1987a; Turner 1982: 32). There are studies which show that when a person's social identity is salient, others' goals and needs can become motives for one's own behaviour (Hornstein 1972, 1976; Horwitz 1953), and that conformity to group norms increases without direct influence from others (e.g. Charters and Newcomb 1952; Doise 1969; Shomer and Centers 1970; Skinner and Stephenson 1981; White 1977). There are also several studies which show that people express different norms in different contexts as a function of which group membership is salient at the time, such as Minard's study of racial attitudes and normative behaviour above and below ground in a racially heterogenous coal mining community in West Virginia (Minard 1952; Ch. 3 above).

Other oblique support for referent informational influence can be recruited from evidence that people, once placed in a certain role or assigned a specific identity, can and do adopt with ease those behaviours stereotypically associated with the role or identity. A striking example of this is furnished by Zimbardo's classic simulated prison experiment (Zimbardo 1975; see Banuazizi and Movahedi 1975; see also Ch. 7 above). Finally, there are the findings of traditional conformity research which we summarized earlier as revealing 'normative clarity', the psychological relationship between the individual and the group, and subjective uncertainty to be the three major categories of variables which influence conformity.

DIRECT TESTS

Referent informational influence theory has been directly tested by Hogg and Turner (1987a). They report four experiments employing Crutchfield's adaptation of the Asch paradigm, in which participants are isolated in booths and only communicate *via* the experimenter in making their judgements of stimuli (Crutchfield 1955). This method allowed the experimental manipulation of a number of variables to do with the relationship between individual and group, the response distribution of the group, and the degree of privacy and anonymity of the individual. It was found that under conditions of private responding (i.e. no normative influence) a non-unanimous erroneous majority which includes a correct response on each trial (i.e. no informational influence) attracts greater conformity from individuals who are either explicitly or implicitly categorized as fellow group members than those who are not categorized. It was also found that although the normative clarity and ingroup relevance of the majority's behaviour enhance conformity, the effect is further accentuated when subjects respond privately, and thus is unlikely to be mediated by normative influence. It seems then that conformity may represent private acceptance, because it is not dependent on surveillance. Finally, it was found that conformity is not to the majority *per se* but to that subgroup which is the subject's explicit or implicit ingroup by the criterion of spontaneous agreement.

Additional support comes from a couple of experiments by Abrams,

Wetherell, Cochrane, Hogg, and Turner employing Sherif's autokinetic paradigm and Asch's conformity paradigm (Abrams *et al.* 1986). In the autokinetic experiment confederates were conformed to only when they were *not* explicitly categorized as members of a different group from the subjects: when categorized their influence was ineffectual, and subjects established and conformed to their own distinctive ingroup norm. In the Asch study, subjects who gave their judgements publicly in front of the confederates displayed almost no conformity when the confederates were designated as outgroup members, but well above usual levels when the confederates were designated as ingroup members. These results are only explicable in terms of referent informational influence. In both studies the level of surveillance was constant between conditions (very low in the autokinetic study, and very high in the Asch study), therefore there is no differential normative influence; and in both studies the actual informational content was the same across all conditions, therefore there was no differential informational influence.

Taken together, these data, in punctuating the role of group belongingness in conformity, tend to favour referent informational influence. That it is self-categorization that underlies normative behaviour has some support from a pair of related experiments which monitor behavioural change as a consequence of gender self-categorization. Males and females were found to adopt context relevant own-sex stereotypic behaviour (Hogg and Turner 1987b) and corresponding speech-style changes (Hogg 1985a) as a result of self-categorization.

GROUP POLARIZATION

Further support for referent informational influence is furnished by its systematic theoretical application to the phenomenon of group polarization (Abrams *et al.* 1986; Wetherell 1987; Wetherell *et al.* 1986). Group polarization, the tendency for groups to make decisions which are more extreme than individuals in the direction initially favoured by the group (Myers and Lamm 1976; Moscovici and Zavalloni 1969), has traditionally not been considered a conformity phenomenon because individuals do not converge on the average position of the group. Traditional explanations largely fall into two camps (see Table 8.1). Those stressing the motivational consequence of comparison with others on socially desirable (culturally valued) dimensions argue that people are aware of the socially desirable position on an issue, and in the presence of others express it in order to obtain social approval (e.g. Jellison and Arkin 1977; Sanders and Baron 1977). Those emphasizing the impact of novel and persuasive information raised by discussion (persuasive arguments) argue that through discussion a collection of individuals who already tend one way on an issue are exposed to an expanded pool of arguments supporting their position, which further entrenches group members in their views (Burnstein and Vinokur 1977;

Vinokur and Burnstein 1974). Although both approaches enjoy some empirical support, they fail to provide an analysis which is linked *theoretically* to an explanation of the social group as a qualitively distinct process, and as such underemphasize the fact that polarization involves not only a unidirectional post-discussion shift in responses but also *convergence* and homogenization. The post-discussion opinions of individual group members are not only polarized but also more homogenous, less diverse, than they were before discussion.

The social identity analysis of group polarization (Turner 1985; Wetherell 1987; Wetherell *et al.* 1986) argues that it is a conformity phenomenon mediated by referent informational influence. The argument builds on the notion of prototype discussed above. Conformity is essentially behaving in the manner of the individual who is perceived to be the most prototypical member of the group, the individual who is considered to best exemplify the norms of the group. If we consider a small *ad hoc* group of individuals giving their opinions on some issue (see Figure 8.2 for concrete example), then it is reasonable to suppose that the norm may be the average and therefore that the most prototypical member is the one holding the opinion which falls nearest the middle of the distribution of ingroup opinions. Conformity will manifest itself as convergence on the mean. However, it is equally likely that the prototype or norm‟ may not fall in the middle of the range; it may be displaced from the mean or average of the real distribution of opinions. This is because one crucial function of norms and stereotypes is to differentiate between groups, and differentiation is achieved by accentuating intergroup differences (cf. Tajfel and Wilkes 1963; see also Ch. 4 above). If our hypothetical group were to meet in the physical or cognitive presence of another group holding a set of different opinions on the same issue, then differentiation would be satisfied by displacement of the ingroup norm away from the outgroup norm. The ingroup norm is thus polarized; the most prototypical ingroup member is not the one who espouses the average or mean ingroup position, but the one who is more extreme than the mean in a direction away from the outgroup. In other words, conformity manifests itself as polarization.

This analysis does not require there to be an *explicit* outgroup. The opinions held by the ingroup members are only a sample of the wider range of opinions that could be held: they are a subset of all possible opinions that the individual can subjectively conceive that other people might hold. Those opinions not held by the ingroup *could* potentially be held by an outgroup, and thus there is an implicit outgroup from which to be differentiated. If the individual's conceivable range of opinions on the issue is called the *subjective frame of reference*, then it can be argued that whether the ingroup norm is polarized or not is dependent on the position of the ingroup distribution within the subjective frame of reference. Specifically, if the mean of the ingroup distribution is displaced from the middle of the subjective frame of

Picture a collection of individuals at a restaurant. They have this initial distribution of attitudes towards eating meat.

Through discussion their attitudes converge on the average position of the group.

They overhear a conversation at an adjacent table which clearly labels the occupants as strict vegetarians. Their opinions now converge not on the average, but on a position polarized away from that of the vegetarians.

The vegetarians leave, only to be replaced by a group of Texas cattle men. Our original group of individuals now polarize towards a more anti-meat eating attitude.

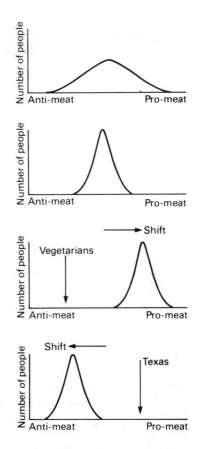

Figure 8.2   Group polarization: an example

reference (i.e. the ingroup is relatively extreme in relation to the range of positions that people *could* hold), then the group norm will be polarized, that is displaced beyond the ingroup mean in the same direction as the group mean is displaced from the middle of the frame of reference, and hence away from the positions that other people might hold. So, as a simple illustration, conformity for socialist, conservative, and liberal groups would manifest itself respectively as polarization to the Left, polarization to the Right, and convergence on the mean!

While it is quite likely that in the absence of an explicit outgroup the *salient* subjective frame of reference is simply the response scale provided by the experimenter (e.g. a 1-to-9 attitude scale) or tacitly carried in our own heads, it is equally likely that when an outgroup is present then the salient subjective frame of reference encompasses only ingroup and outgroup positions. Basically, the salient subjective frame of reference only contains contextually relevant positions, which of course represent only relevant comparison others.

There are now several studies which support the social identity analysis of polarization (see Abrams *et al.* 1986; Hogg and Turner 1987a, 1987c; Mackie 1986; Wetherell 1987; Wetherell *et al.* 1986). The general paradigm is one in which people give their opinions or judgements on a number of issues (which have or do not have clearly socially desirable positions), then participate in or listen to a spontaneous or experimentally controlled group discussion, arrive at a group consensus (or group position), and finally give their own private opinion for a second time. The results show that (1) the position of the prototype is determined by the position of the ingroup with respect to the subjective frame of reference; (2) polarization requires identification with the group; and (3) when it does occur polarization represents convergence on a polarized prototype of the group position. Thus, for example, when a distribution of opinions is divided into two discrete categories, individuals' judgements converge on the more extreme positions characteristic of their own category, rather than on the average of either their own category or the distribution as a whole. Furthermore, that polarization can occur in the absence of any novel information and on items which do not have a socially desirable position tends to question the validity of traditional approaches.

MINORITY INFLUENCE

Referent informational influence has significance for a number of areas in social psychology. For example, the phenomenon of minority influence. Traditional treatments of conformity contain what has been termed a 'conformity bias' (Moscovici 1976; Moscovici and Faucheux 1972). That is, they tend to focus on how the majority modifies the individual's behaviour, thus inducing conformity, to the exclusion of serious consideration of the effect that the individual may have on the majority. And yet there is evidence that the individual, as a deviate from majority consensus, does have influence: his or her intransigence can cause the majority to modify its views and adopt behaviours aimed at reducing deviance (e.g. Schachter 1951). Moscovici, Mugny, and colleagues (e.g. Moscovici 1976; Moscovici and Mugny 1983; Mugny 1982) consider those who seem to resist or be impervious to majority influence (deviates, dissenters, independents) to constitute a minority, and that social change potentially lies in their hands. The analysis is principally aimed at active minorities: small groups of individuals (e.g. social movements, innovative artistic or scientific schools) who actively seek to change the dominant normative structure or ideology that represents the status quo.

Since minorities (by definition) rarely have at their disposal the material resources (e.g. control of the media, the military, the educational system) to impose their own version of reality, this channel of influence, which is the mainstay of majority influence, is closed to them. Nor can minorities rely on an attractive and widely appealing positive social image to attract adherents. Minorities are typically vilified and derogated as embodying all that is undesirable from the perspective of majority culture. Moscovici and colleagues attribute the power of minorities to their behavioural style, and in particular, to their consistency over time (diachronic, or repetitive) and consistency between individuals (synchronic, or consensual).

The role of consistency is well established by early research using the Asch paradigm (see Allen 1965, 1975; see also this chapter above). These studies show that a consistent majority is more powerful in inducing conformity than an inconsistent one, and a consistent deviate (or deviates) is more powerful than an inconsistent one in inducing independence from or non-conformity to the majority. Moscovici and colleagues have conducted a number of studies employing a similar paradigm which specifically focus on the behavioural consistency of a numerical *minority* (see Moscovici and Mugny 1983). On the whole the results uphold the hypothesis that greater consistency accentuates the influence of the minority. More recent initiatives address specific issues to do with optimal levels of consistency (too much may be perceived as dogmatic rigidity and thus discredit the minority), and the optimal magnitude of apparent minority-majority normative or ideological difference (e.g. Mugny 1982).

Minority consistency is considered to have impact because it introduces the possibility of an alternative to the taken-for-granted, unquestioned, consensual majority perspective. Suddenly people can discern cracks in the façade of majority consensus. New issues, problems, and questions arise which demand attention. The status quo is no longer passively accepted as an immutable and stable entity which is the sole legitimate arbiter of the nature of things. People are free to change their beliefs, views, customs, and so forth. And where do they turn? One direction is to the active minority. It (by definition and design) furnishes a conceptually coherent and elegantly simple resolution of the very issues which, due to its activities, now plague the public consciousness. In the language of 'ideology' (e.g. Billig 1982; Larrain 1979; see Ch. 4 above), active minorities seek to replace the dominant ideology with a new one. Consistency allows them more easily to achieve this, as it not only facilitates an unequivocally distinct statement of the new problematic but also the presentation of a clear alternative 'explanation' appropriate to the new problematic: that is, a new ideology (see Deconchy's discussion of orthodoxy: how it is maintained and how it can be changed – Deconchy 1984).

Moscovici's analysis of social influence, in the context of minority influence (Moscovici 1976), is compatible with that offered by the social identity approach, and indeed stems from the same critique of traditional perspectives in social psychology. Both argue that conformity must be distinguished from mere compliance; that all group members are potential sources of influence; that influence processes are related to the production and resolution of social conflicts and are directed towards social change as much as social control; and that mutual influence is best conceptualized as a form of social negotiation of disagreements rather than a submission to superior authority or power. Hogg and Turner suggest that Moscovici's analysis differs from that of the social identity approach mainly as regards the role attributed to the process of identification and self-categorization (Hogg and Turner 1985a). Recently, however, researchers in the minority influence tradition (especially Mugny 1982) have related their ideas to the social identity perspective.

It is immediately apparent that minority groups, just like majority groups, furnish an identity with its distinctive norms of belief and conduct. Therefore the process of minority influence, irrespective of what factors may facilitate it and how they may differ from those relevant to the majority group, is very likely to be one of referent informational influence. Although consistency as a behavioural style may initially loosen the grip of majority identity for relatively informational reasons (i.e. radical new ideology), it is identification with the minority that ensures the adhesion of its norms to individual 'fugitives' from the majority. A referent informational analysis has clear relevance here particularly in so far as Moscovici and colleagues' analysis sometimes betrays a tendency to resurrect, albeit in a slightly different guise, the traditional distinction between normative and informational influence (and attendant distinctions). Majority groups exact conformity through normative influence (they have the material power to administer rewards and punishments, impose sanctions, mobilize surveillance, etc.), while minority groups do so by informational influence (they provide an alternative and more 'truthful' version of reality, one which appears more convincing and better able to resolve contradictions, etc.).

OTHER APPLICATIONS

There is a number of other areas where the social identity approach to conformity can and has been extended. We shall briefly mention a few of these. At the end of Chapter 5 we discussed leadership (e.g. Bass 1981; Fiedler 1971; Hollander 1985), showing how current interactionist or transactionalist approaches tend ultimately to explain leadership in terms of interpersonal reinforcement. The group member who is most able to ensure that the group, and hence its members, efficiently achieves its goals is effectively most responsible for members' rewards, and therefore they, the members, in turn reward this individual with power and unilateral respect, admiration, and liking – that is, leadership. This analysis recasts leadership, which is characteristically a group phenomenon, as an interpersonal phenomenon and so stumbles on many of the problems discussed in Chapter 5 concerning the social cohesion, or interpersonal interdependence, model of group processes.

A social identity or self-categorization analysis would be very different. Leadership is all about how some people in a group have disproportionate power to influence others. It is a question of social influence in groups and therefore a question of conformity. The most prototypical member of a group is the group 'leader', the person who embodies the defining characteristics of the group. Under conditions of heightened group salience it is this individual's behaviour that is recreated (conformed to) by all the other members of the group. Furthermore, this individual becomes socially or stereotypically attractive (see Ch. 5) – the target of unilateral respect, trust, and liking expressed by the followers – precisely because he or she embodies the group stereotype. The individual occupying the prototypical group position is by definition looked to by the rest of the group as the arbiter of intragroup disagreements over what is and what is not normative, and so acquires consensually legitimated power to define or redefine the nature of the group.

This analysis can explain a variety of types of leaderships, ranging from 'leaders of fashion', such as Twiggy or Madonna, to autocratic leaders of nations, such as Hitler or Ghengis Khan. The 'fashion' example is in many ways an exact illustration of our social identity analysis; here, the 'leader' is very much simply the person who just happens at the time to fit the stereotypic image. The 'autocrat' example only differs perhaps in so far as the leader has secured the material trappings of monolithic power (authority over the agents of ideological control and physical coercion), and group identity is extremely salient, pervasive, and enduring.

In Chapter 5 we discussed 'groupthink', that is the tendency for highly cohesive decision-making groups to make disastrous decisions, such as that resulting in the Bay of Pigs Fiasco (Janis 1971, 1972). Traditional explanations tend to focus on extreme interpersonal attraction between members of the decision-making groups as being responsible for a deficit in decision-making capabilities which results in the 'poor' decision. This analysis has already been criticized in Chapter 5. From a social identity perspective it is possible to explain groupthink as a group polarization phenomenon. Groupthink describes highly cohesive decision-making groups where the social identity represented by the group is extremely salient, and hence where conditions are ripe for extreme conformity. Where the relevant norm is already extreme in contrast to the rest of the population, which seems to be the case in all the examples Janis provides (e.g. US congressional committees which contain strongly anti-communist members), then group discussion will polarize the norm and result in group polarization. It may not be the decision that is poor but that the consequences of putting that decision into action (e.g. escalating US involvement in Vietnam and Korea) which are disastrous. An interesting postscript to this is that groupthink and risky-shift may actually be different ways of describing the same thing: decision-making groups which are not timid, cautious, and conservative in their decisions.

Central to referent informational influence theory is the tenet that behaviour conveys information about group membership, and so through conforming, not conforming, or counter- or anti-conforming, identity may be communicated. It would not be surprising then to expect that conformity within highly valued ingroups may even acquire a competitive aspect: individual group members competing to be the most prototypical group member, the one who best embodies the qualities of the group and thus attracts the maximum kudos of membership in the group. This is the familiar 'first among equals' syndrome: actors at a party all attempting to be more thespian than each other. Experimental evidence for this phenomenon is provided by Codol, who dubs it the PIP (*primus inter pares*) effect (Codol 1975). Codol's analysis is not in terms of referent informational influence, but such an analysis is clearly invited.

Another application is in the analysis of collective behaviour (see Ch. 7), where the social identity perspective has been employed to resolve a number of limitations of traditional approaches. Referent informational influence is considered to be the social influence process responsible for crowd behaviour (Reicher 1987), and direct tests tend to support this view (e.g. Abrams 1985; Reicher 1987).

Finally, a phenomenon which seems particularly ripe for a referent informational influence analysis is 'brainwashing' (e.g. Barlow 1981; Lifton 1961; Schein, Schneier, and Barker 1961), which offers a strikingly vivid illustration of the link .between identity and normative behaviour. Brain-washing involves 'psychological death', in which one's former identity is stripped away through techniques involving isolation from the usual support necessary for achieving and maintaining social identity; followed by 'ideological rebirth', where a new identity is constructed around a clear and unambiguous set of new beliefs and practices. The crucial feature of brainwashing is that in order to effect complete and true behavioural and attitudinal change it is identity which must be tackled, thus the underlying process of influence is quite possibly referent informational influence. (For an example of brainwashing, see the description of the Jonestown massacre in Ch. 7.)

Conclusion

Social influence lies at the heart of social behaviour, and conformity at the heart of the social group as something qualitatively separate from individuality. In this chapter we have discussed conformity. We have distinguished it from other forms of social influence on a theoretical basis: it is an intragroup, rather than interpersonal, phenomenon which manifests itself as normative behaviour. Our discussion of norms and conformity research and theory culminated in the adumbration of a number of limitations. These limitations were considered largely to stem from a reductionist tendency coupled with advocation of a two-process dependency model of social influence which has progressively eclipsed the crucial role of norms and group belongingness in conformity. The social identity approach reinstates norms and identifies referent informational influence as the social influence process associated with conformity to group norms. Referent informational influence generates conformity via the self-categorization process responsible for identification with the group. Extending this basic hypothesis, norms and stereotypes are treated as being conceptually identical, and related to prototypes and prototypicality. Empirical support for referent informational influence was presented, and the wider significance of the concept considered. We discussed some direct tests of the theory, and also dealt with group polarization, minority influence, and more briefly leadership, 'groupthink', the PIP effect, crowd behaviour, and 'brainwashing'. In the next chapter we move on to explore the principal medium by which social influence occurs: communication via language and speech.

Recommended reading

Kiesler and Kiesler (1969) and Wheeler et al. (1978) provide readable descriptions of much of the traditional work on norms and conformity, while Myers and Lamm (1976) cover group polarization, and Moscovici (1976) and Moscovici and Mugny (1983) minority influence. Referent informational influence theory and the social identity approach to conformity phenomena are best summarized in Hogg and Turner (1987a).

9

Language, speech, and communication

An English gentleman – deer stalker tweed jacket and all – climbs out of his Range Rover in a quiet village in the heart of Wales. He is lost. He is also weary. He has driven all the way from London to attend a weekend champagne and caviar party at the country retreat of some of his urbane friends from the city. Above all, he is irritated: he is lost because some inconsiderate vandal had painted out all the road signs. He enters a small store to ask directions of the proprietor, who is just finishing a phone conversation. In purest Oxford English he asks, 'I say, my good man, would you be so kind as to tell me the way to Aberystwyth'. The middle-aged shopkeeper smiles congenially and answers politely. But in Welsh! He has clearly understood the question (after all, he was just speaking English on the phone), and is quite obviously giving directions. The English gentleman tries again – accentuating the clarity of his Oxford accent. After all, he thinks, perhaps the shopkeeper didn't really understand – rural folk like the Welsh are perhaps a little 'slow'. The shopkeeper again replies in Welsh – perhaps with a discernible accentuation of the Welshness of the reply.

Although anecdotal, this example illustrates something which happens, to varying degrees, almost all the time: we cater our style of speech, or the way we say something, to the context of the communication. We simplify our grammar, use only short words, and speak slowly and ponderously when addressing foreigners and children. We refine our language and speak very precisely and fluently when being interviewed for a job, and also perhaps when trying to distance ourselves from someone we don't like or who belongs to a social group with which we don't wish to be associated. We are apt to slacken our grammar and introduce slang and expletives when joshing with our peers. There are numerous examples.

We can change our speech style to improve comprehension, but often, as in our example above, we don't – rather it is done to convey information about what sort of person we are, about our identity. To make sense of the example above we need to consider language as a symbol of identity – we need to understand something about the status of the Welsh in British society, about the Welsh language revival, and about the intergroup relations between our English gentleman and our Welsh shopkeeper. In this chapter we address these and other related issues.

Introduction

When people are together they spend much of their time transmitting or receiving information via speech. Information is also continually being communicated by body posture, facial gestures, dress, and other non-verbal channels. Even when alone, communication occupies our time; for example driving a car involves communication via traffic lights, car indicators, and so forth. We are constantly bombarded with speech (radio, TV, films, plays) and written language (advertising hoardings, books, labels on products). We even think or represent the world in terms of language. In fact it is almost impossible to single out periods of human activity which do not, at least to some extent, involve language, speech, or communication. The very fact that language, speech, and communication require, as the *sine qua non* of their existence, a framework of *shared* meanings, renders them doubly social. Without speech and language social influence would be unbelievably restricted, and without communication it would not exist at all. We would be like Leibniz's 'windowless monads', isolated and utterly alone.

Just as social influence lies at the heart of social psychology (see Ch. 8) so must language, speech, and communication. In this chapter we discuss social psychology's contribution to the study of these phenomena. The dominant emphasis is on the contribution of the social identity approach which has, over the last ten years, been directly responsible for revolutionizing the field and carving out virtually its own distinctive subdiscipline of the social psychology of language. By restricting ourselves to social psychology conceived as a relatively experimental science (see Ch. 2), we shall not discuss less experimentally oriented social psychological treatments of language, for example Harré's ethogenic approach (1979, 1983; also see Potter, Stringer, and Wetherell 1984). However, since virtually all explanations of human behaviour, by necessity, have something to say in this domain, we will find ourselves being perhaps more eclectic than elsewhere in this book.

Language, speech, and communication in social psychology

Although better known for creating the first experimental psychology laboratory in Leipzig in 1879, Wundt also had some important things to say concerning social psychology. He felt that social psychology's proper concern should be the study of collective mental phenomena, which owe their creation not to individuals in isolation but in interaction. Culture, intuitive everyday working hypotheses about the world, and above all language are such socially created phenomena. Thus Wundt's social psychology, his

Völkerpsychologie (1916), considered the study of language to be of fundamental importance (see Farr 1980). The challenge was not taken up, or rather it was ignored by a social psychology increasingly wedded to Floyd Allport's notorious dictum that the individual must be the ultimate and only unit of psychological analysis (Allport 1924; see Ch. 2). The demise of language in social psychology was facilitated by Wundt's distinction between 'Volk' (folk, culture) and 'individual' – a distinction which shadowed that between sociology and psychology and left no room for social psychology. Language fell in the *Volk* camp and thus became the province of sociology, social anthropology, and other disciplines concerned with culture. Furthermore, Wundt's *Völkerpsychologie* was distorted in ideologically predictable ways by Nazi social psychologists of the 1930s to produce a characteristically fascist social psychology of national character and race, which of course discredited, by association, Wundt's original ideas (see the account by Farr 1980).

Wundt considered language to be a collective mental phenomenon in the sense of Durkheim's social facts or 'collective representations'. It is but a short step to conclude that language is normative behaviour which may be at least partially amenable to a social identity analysis of social norms. In Chapter 8 we linked 'social facts' to normative behaviour via Sherif's research on the emergence of and adherence to norms (Sherif 1936). We shall take this up later in the chapter.

George Herbert Mead and the symbolic interactionist school assign to language a pivotal position in social behaviour (Mead 1934, 1938; see Meltzer, Petras, and Reynolds 1975; Stryker 1981). Social interaction is overwhelmingly symbolic in that behaviour is replete with consensually understood meanings, it is not merely meaningless action. Interaction between people is thus largely a 'conversation of gestures' and verbal behaviour is the richest medium of such symbolic interaction. Mead even maintains that the emergence of the self is dependent on the existence of language, because language as speech has the unique quality that the speaker is simultaneously the active subject, the 'I', as well as the audience, the passive object, the 'me'. Through speech one becomes an object to oneself and thus emerges a concept of oneself: the self. Symbolic interactionism has until recently had rather little impact on mainstream experimental social psychology (but see Chs. 6 and 7). Its influence is instead more to be seen in sociology (e.g. Goffman 1968) and in recent developments in the study of the child's acquisition of language (e.g. Lock 1978, 1980).

Social psychology in general skirts around language, affords it no distinctive status, and instead focuses upon communication exclusively as information transmission. For example, research into rumour and gossip examines the way in which the particular message or information is distorted and changed as it passes from person to person (Allport and Postman 1947; Rosnow 1980). Research into group dynamics considers that 'communication lies at the heart of the group interaction process' (Shaw 1964: 111), yet in focusing upon communication structures which render the group more productive or better able to achieve its goals (see Shaw 1964) it dwells upon who speaks how much to whom as it relates to group cohesiveness, group size and the group's purpose (see Ch. 5 for critical discussion of this work). Information transmission and processing, not language, is the emphasis of research into group polarization (see Ch. 8; see also Wetherell 1987), groupthink (see Ch. 5; see also Janis 1971, 1972), persuasive communication (Eagly and Himmelfarb 1978), attitude change – the list is virtually endless. Finally, language is explicitly excluded from a large and important part of social psychology, namely the study of non-verbal behaviour (Argyle 1975; Birdwhistle 1974; Mehrabian 1971; Scherer and Ekman 1982; Wieman and Harrison 1983).

Although there have been those who provide or advocate a social psychological consideration of language, they are so few in number as to have made until recently little impact (for example Brown 1965; Carswell and Rommetveit 1972; Ervin-Tripp 1969; Moscovici 1967, 1972; Robinson 1972).

While the social psychology of the 1940s and early 1950s may have failed to consider language, its focus on group dynamics at least permitted consideration of communication. Since then, however, even communication has been increasingly dispatched to the sidelines as social psychology underwent repeated 'paradigm' changes. In the 1960s there was cognitive consistency – the study of attitude and behavioural changes motivated by inconsistent cognitions (Abelson et al. 1968). Then in the 1970s attribution theory occupied centre-stage with its characterization of people as intuitive scientists constantly seeking causal explanations for events in order to impose order on the world (e.g. Harvey and Smith 1977; see Ch. 4 above). In the late 1970s attribution lost favour and was displaced by social cognition with its ultra-cognitive and ultra-individualistic focus on cognitive processes, judgemental heuristics, social memory, and so forth (Fiske and Taylor 1984; Landman and Manis 1983; Nisbett and Ross 1980; see Ch. 4 above).

Social cognition has always had as its critics those who feel that it is so reductionist, as to be only passingly *social* psychology at all (e.g. Forgas 1981; Markus and Zajonc 1985; Moscovici 1982; Tajfel 1981b; Turner and Oakes 1986; see Ch. 4 above for details). Early objections were largely European in origin: predicated upon the wider critique of individualistic reductionism discussed in Chapter 2, which has functioned as the critical context of the social identity approach. Recently, however, voices of dissent within the social cognition camp itself have multiplied and increasingly include some of its erstwhile doyens (see Wyer and Srull 1984). One suggested remedy for the ails of social cognition involves the study of language and communication (Higgins 1981; Higgins, Fondacaro, and McCann 1981; Kraut and Higgins 1984).

Kraut and Higgins believe that the 'study of social cognition is only marginally social [because] the emphasis is on the asocial determinants of cognitions about social phenomena' (Kraut and Higgins 1984: 87), and that a shift of emphasis onto communication would benefit both social cognition and the study of language and communication. Communication and language are considered to be social because (1) they occur between people; (2) they are predominantly about people (e.g. rumour and gossip); and (3) they are overwhelmingly consensual rule governed social products of a language community. They are cognitive because the production and reception of information involves cognitive activity and social knowledge. Higgins identifies the principal limitation of traditional social psychological treatments of verbal communication as being their failure to deal adequately with its distinctively normative and rule governed nature (Higgins 1981).

Higgins and colleagues advocate a 'communication game' approach which emphasizes that language and communication involve following the 'rules of the game' (see Burke 1962; Garfinkel 1967; Goffman 1959; Lyman and Scott 1970; Wittgenstein 1953). These rules, which are considered to be generic rules of conversation, include conveying the truth, optimizing the quantity of information conveyed, adapting the message to the listener and the context, being clear and concise, paying attention to the speaker, providing feedback, and so forth (Clark and Clark 1977; Higgins 1981; Rommetveit 1974). Conversations follow a script (Schank and Abelson 1977) which furnishes a basic structure: a structure which is dependent on context, topic, interactants, goals, purposes, and so forth.

Higgins documents some consequences of the existence of these rules for social cognition and person perception (Higgins 1981). For example, there is evidence that catering one's message to features of the listener can, over a period of time, result in the speaker subscribing to the modified message rather than the original belief (Higgins, McCann, and Fondacaro 1982; Higgins and Rholes 1978). Here we have an elegant empirical vindication of Newcomb, Turner, and Converse's warning that 'although it is easy to think of . . . public expressions as superficial and "expedient", they may have . . . real attitudinal effects' (Newcomb, Turner, and Converse 1965: 108–9). This is also relevant to our discussion of compliance and cognitive change in Chapter 8: public verbal expression of ingroup normative beliefs may have real attitudinal effects.

Higgins and colleagues' analysis is principally concerned with the syntax of interpersonal communication through the channel of verbal behaviour, and the consequences for person perception, and social cognition generally, of the existence of such syntax. Although passing reference is made to the way that language and speech style may convey group membership information, the effect that this may have on the communication process is not explored. By focusing on generic norms of communication the endeavour is undoubtedly an advance on much traditional social psychology of communication, but it is an advance largely within the confines of an interpersonal social psychology which is not equipped to deal with the social group as a theoretically distinct entity. As such, much of language is left unexplained. After all, as Wundt recognized some time ago, language is above all a vehicle of culture, a symbol of identity. For example, can the richness of verbal communication between a black and a white South African be adequately dealt with without at least some consideration of the nature of the intergroup relations between the different social categories to which they belong?

The problem which has faced social psychologists is that language lies beyond the explanatory reach of the conceptual apparatus of individualistic social psychology. Language is an emergent property of interaction which transcends individuality and has properties of collective mental phenomena such as intersubjectivity and normativeness. These are precisely the properties of human behaviour with which traditional individualistic social psychology encounters most difficulties (see Ch. 8 on norms, Ch. 5 on the group as a 'nominal fallacy', Ch. 7 on the crowd and collective behaviour, and of course Ch. 2 on the general critique of individualism). The need for, and failure of, the development of a social psychology of language has been documented and discussed by Miller (1951) and, more recently, wedded to the critique of individualism, by Moscovici (1967, 1972) and Rommetveit (1967, 1974) (also see Markova 1978).

A further reason for language being social psychology's 'blindspot' is not unique to social psychology: it may be common to us all. As we go about our taken-for-granted daily lives, the world is largely treated as being as it appears. We do not see its overwhelmingly symbolic nature. We are so immersed in our lives that the environment as a socially constructed system of symbols is reified. In Garfinkel's terminology, it becomes the unproblematic background to our lives which generally attracts little or no attention (Garfinkel 1967). Language is the dominant component of this background since it is overwhelmingly through language that this symbolic aspect is represented and conveyed. This can do little but further obscure language from the gaze of an individualistic social psychology.

Language, then, is exiled from the province of social psychology. It surfaces instead in other areas of psychology and in other disciplines. We now discuss some of these in order to set the scene for our discussion of the recent emergence of a social psychology of language.

Language, speech, and communication outside social psychology

Traditional psychological approaches to the study of language and communication owe their complexion very much to the work of Noam Chomsky and his structural linguistic perspective (Chomsky 1957; see Greene 1972).

The emphasis is upon the hierarchical structure of language and the generative rules that dictate acceptable grammatical strings which convey meaning, that is the rules which govern for a specific language community, the combination of phonemes, morphemes, words, clauses, sentences, and larger units of discourse, and how all this is wielded to convey meaning (see Bolinger 1975 for an overview of linguistics). The psychological approach is also interested in explaining how the rules of grammar and semantics (meaning) are combined with features of intonation (rising pitch, stress, etc.) and with paralinguistic ('ums', 'ahs', pauses, etc.) and kinesic ('body language') factors in order to communicate information. However, the perspective is distinctly individualistic in that, as Moscovici puts it, 'a sort of soliloquy for several voices is substituted for true dialogue' (Moscovici 1967: 227). There is little serious examination of role playing, intersubjectivity, and the psychological impact of the social context. Instead, these factors are considered non-problematic. Chomsky attributes universal features of language to the innate possession of shared fundamental grammatical rules which underpin all languages – the great diversity of spoken languages in the world is merely cultural icing on the innate cake of language (see Rommetveit 1967).

Further problems are created by Chomsky's distinction between linguistic competence and linguistic performance, and de Saussure's distinction beween *langue* (language) and *parole* (speech) (de Saussure 1955; see Moscovici 1967). Language and linguistic competence relate to the structure of language and the rules for correct language usage and are thus the province of linguistics. Speech and performance, on the other hand, refer to what actually occurs in interaction – the less than perfectly grammatical or fluent day-to-day usage of language in context by members of a speech community. This is the province of social psychology. But how can social psychology sensibly deal with speech as contextualized intersubjectivity if, as Floyd Allport warns us, the individual is and must always be the ultimate unit of analysis? As we have seen in the previous section, traditional social psychology finds this difficult.

It is in developmental psychology that we encounter perhaps the most systematic demonstrations of the inadequacy of an asocial Chomskyan approach to language. Explanations of how children learn to speak that focus purely on the acquisition of grammatical or linguistic competence (e.g. holophrastic and telegraphic speech, and 'pivot-open' grammar – see Bloom 1970; Brown 1965) fail to account for the fact that meaning cannot be adequately deduced *in vacuo*. Grammatically identical utterances can have strikingly different meanings in different contexts (e.g. Bloom 1970). Meaning is not exclusively contained, as Chomsky would have us believe, in the deep structure of language (see Rommetveit 1974). Furthermore, the assumption of innate deep structural linguistic universals is unwarranted. Recent advances in the study of language acquistion focus on the function of language as a means of communication and regulation of social interaction (see earlier mention of symbolic interactionism, see also Ch. 2). This perspective, which is explicitly social, has enjoyed some success in showing how the fulfilment of universal social interactional needs through co-ordinated social behaviour, creates in the pre-linguistic child cognitive co-ordination and a syntax of action which contain all the basic grammatical structures that the child needs in order actively to acquire language with the assistance of adult caretakers' guidance (see Dunn 1984; Lock 1978, 1980; Robinson 1984; Romaine 1984). This approach at once obviates the need for innatist or *a priori* concepts to explain language acquisition, and recommends examination of social interaction and social context.

The study of language in its social context is epitomized by sociolinguistics (see recent review of sociolinguistics by Hudson 1980; also see Fishman 1972). Sociolinguistics, as a distinct field, emerged in the mid-1960s in conscious reaction to what was considered to be the asocial nature of linguistics and psycholinguistics. It deals with the social organization of language behaviour in its social context, and as such focuses upon such things as language usage, attitudes to language, and overt behaviour towards language and language users. The approach is principally descriptive in dealing with language varieties (different languages or different social, occupational, regional, or stylistic clusters of phonological, lexical, and grammatical co-occurrences) and linguistic repertoires in multilingual societies. It addresses questions to do with, for example, the social conditions responsible for the emergence, maintenance, and disappearance of bilingual-ism, or the factors which determine who uses which language variety when, where, and for what purpose.

These are clearly social psychological issues, and yet, although socioling-uistics is distinctly multi-disciplinary in its approach, the principal input is from sociology and social anthropology. Social psychology is noticeably absent (e.g. see Fishman 1968), though there are some notable exceptions (e.g. Argyle 1975; Brown 1965; Gardner and Lambert 1972; Lambert 1967). However, the mid-1970s witnessed an increasing dissatisfaction with sociolinguistics (see Scotton and Ury 1977), which provided fertile ground for social psychology to make its contribution.

It was felt (for details see Giles, Robinson, and Smith 1980a; Smith, Giles, and Hewstone 1980) (1) that traditional sociolinguistics is too taxonomic and descriptive, and insufficiently explanatory and predictive; (2) that it focuses upon the linguistic correlates of convenient contextual (e.g. formality) and socio-demographic (e.g. class, sex, race) variables without due consideration of the subjective or phenomenological importance of such variables to the individual (i.e. it omits the language user and attendant motivations, subjective perceptions, self-definitions, and so forth from the equation); and (3) that it is too socially deterministic in emphasizing the social structural determinants of language use to the exclusion of serious consideration of the potential role of language use in redefining and creating social reality.

In short, sociolinguistics is characterized as being in the business of describing the objective socio-demographic and contextual correlates of language use. It is descriptive, static, and undirectional. Giles and colleagues consider these to be shortcomings which can only be remedied by focusing upon the individual language user's attitudes, motivations, intentions, identities, and so forth as the crucial factors which mediate between objective, social, and contextual variables on the one hand, and the individual's language behaviour on the other. What is sought is explanation which captures the dynamic tension that exists between language and society. Social psychology is ideally suited to this task. For an example of the practical application of this recommendation, see Hogg, Joyce, and Abrams' treatment of the language situation in the German-speaking part of Switzerland, where the population is bilingual – speaking Swiss German in informal contexts and High German in formal ones (there is a functional differentiation of the two language varieties, which resembles 'diglossia') (Hogg, Joyce, and Abrams 1984).

Although some sociolinguists have moved in this direction (e.g. Labov 1970; Sankoff 1972; Scotton 1980), credit for concerted action goes primarily to Giles and his growing circle of colleagues. Since the mid-1970s there has been a colossal amount of activity which clearly indicates that a new (the) social psychology of language has arrived. There is now a large number of books in the area (e.g. Giles, Robinson, and Smith 1980b; St Clair and Giles 1980; Scherer and Giles 1979; Giles and St Clair 1979; Giles and Powesland 1975; Giles 1977; Giles and Saint-Jacques 1979; also see Smith 1983; Robinson 1983).

The remainder of this chapter is dedicated to a discussion of this 'new look' in the social psychology of language. Although activity in this area has not generally fed back into mainstream social psychology (see Smith 1983), it owes its unique contribution to sociolinguistics to social psychological theorizing, specifically and overwhelmingly the social identity perspective. Furthermore, the critical framework within which the approach flourishes is one which consciously eschews individualism and is identical with that which frames the social identity perspective. The breadth of scope of this new social look at language behaviour is documented by Hogg and Abrams (1985) and Smith (1983), among others.

Social psychology of language

SOCIAL MARKERS IN SPEECH AND LANGUAGE

A recurring theme of the discussion so far is that speech and language communicate information in at least two ways. First, and this is the focus of traditional social psychological treatments, they convey referential information via message content – what is said. Second, they contain social markers (Scherer and Giles 1979); that is, language varieties and speech styles contain information concerning the speakers' personality, social status, age, mood, social group membership, and so forth. It is this function of speech and language which occupies the attention of the 'new' social psychology of language.

The basic premise is that we all have a repertoire of speech styles (Hymes 1967) upon which to draw in dealing with, for example, different situations (e.g. formal debate *vs* informal seminar), different audiences (child *vs* adult), and different mood states (irritated *vs* calm). Much of the time speech style modifications are completely automatic and unreflexive, and even when we are aware of them it can be very difficult indeed to gain control over them (e.g. trying to sound calm when in fact we feel angry). At other times we can consciously adopt a particular speech style to deal with a particular situation or listener. An individual's repertoire can include different varieties of the same language or even an array of different languages. The crucial feature of the repertoire is that it contains speech and language varieties which fulfil a social function in conveying information about who is speaking, who is listening, and the context in which the speech occurs. Thus the *sine qua non* of social markers in speech and language is the existence of a framework of shared meanings. Since *how* we speak can convey so much information, it is not surprising that, where possible, people consciously modify speech style to achieve self-presentational or impression management goals (see also Ch. 6).

Let us now ground this general description in research into social markers in speech. Developmental psychology furnishes abundant evidence that adults the world over employ a distinct and characteristic speech style (called 'motherese') when addressing young children (see Elliot 1981); a similar speech style is also employed when addressing foreigners ('foreigner talk' – see Clyne 1981; Corder 1981: 107–14), and mentally retarded individuals. Even very young children have been shown to cater their speech to the listener's age (Helfrich 1979). In general, it has been shown that young children have a much richer speech repertoire than hitherto thought (see review by Shatz 1983), and that their communicative competence is therefore more advanced than the mere content and grammar of their speech betrays.

Although there has been research into the way in which personality, emotion, and psychopathology are expressed via, and inferred from, speech (Scherer 1980), the overwhelming bulk of research concerns the way in which speech and language contain markers of social category membership – in particular, social class, ethnicity, and sex (Smith 1983). Social class is marked by the complexity and elaborateness of language usage. Bernstein characterized middle-class speech as adopting an 'elaborated' code, while working-class speech employs a 'restricted' code, and went on to show how working-class speech *per se* is somehow responsible for educational disadvantage (Bernstein 1971). This position is consistent with a traditional view that the working classes are somehow less skilful communicators (e.g. Alvy 1973).

More recent approaches are critical of this 'deficit' view of working-class speech and tend to emphasize that speech style differences do not reflect differences in communicative skills but rather the different functions that they fulfil (e.g. see Edwards 1979, 1985; Higgins 1976; Labov 1970; Rosen 1972; Trudgill 1975). Working-class speech style is perfectly suited to the communicative function that it has arisen to satisfy. School is, however, a middle-class institution which employs middle-class speech and thus creates an alien atmosphere for the use of working-class speech. The educational disadvantage which seems to emerge, is however, not due to speech *per se*, but rather due to middle-class reactions to speech (Edwards 1979). The dominant middle-class social group (e.g. teachers) negatively evaluates working-class speech (see Giles and Powesland 1975), derogatively stereotypes those who employ it, and downgrades and has lower expectations of their performance. This renders educational achievement extremely difficult for working-class children and typically results in educational disadvantage. Basically, to understand the educational effects of speech style, an intergroup perspective which focuses on status and power differences between social classes is needed. It is typically at school that children are first and very powerfully exposed to this intergroup context.

LANGUAGE AND ETHNICITY

We shall now turn in more detail to a discussion of ethnicity markers in speech and language. It is here that the social identity perspective has been most explicitly employed (see Giles 1978; Giles, Bourhis, and Taylor 1977; and especially Giles and Johnson 1981). Little reflection is needed to conclude that virtually all contemporary nations are multicultural; that is, they contain two or more social groups which can be distinguished to varying degrees in terms of culture, where culture includes the entire array of normative practices which distinguish between and characterize groups. Language is frequently a highly salient feature of such cultural differences and can become the most potent symbol of ethnic identity. (For this to be the case though, not all members of the ethnic group need be able to speak it; rather, it is readily available and acts as a symbol of ethnic identity.) Some examples of intranational ethnolinguistic diversity would be French and English in Canada; Quechua and Spanish in Peru; Welsh and English in Wales; Tamil and Sinhala in Sri Lanka.

A basic feature of most multicultural societies is that the language of the dominant group is the *lingua franca* of the nation (e.g. English in Wales), and it is to the subordinate ethnolinguistic group's advantage to be able to speak it. Failure to do so can carry heavy social and economic penalties. Furthermore, the subordinate group's language is often considered to be a low prestige variety, and as such attracts ridicule, abrasive humour, and ethnophaulisms (derogatory ethnic labels) from the dominant group. A useful and popular method for studying such evaluative reactions to language was introduced by Lambert, Hodgson, Gardner and Fillenbaum, called the 'matched-guise' technique (Lambert *et al.* 1960; see Edwards 1985; Ryan, Hewstone, and Giles 1984). Subjects evaluate, on a number of dimensions, a tape-recorded speaker's personality after hearing him or her read the same passage in each of two or more language varieties. Their judgements are considered to represent stereotypical reactions to the given language varieties, as the speaker is, for all 'guises', the same person, and the subjects are unaware of this. In general it is found that an ingroup language variety is upgraded on 'solidarity' dimensions (e.g. trust, liking), while an outgroup variety is upgraded on 'status' dimensions (e.g. competence, intelligence) if it is the standard dominant variety, but downgraded if it is a regional, ethnic, or lower class variety.

Given the evaluative connotations of language a central issue here concerns the conditions under which a subordinate ethnic group loses its language, maintains it, or promotes or resurrects it, and what is the reaction of the dominant group. To deal with this Giles, Bourhis and Taylor have coined the term *ethnolinguistic vitality* (Giles, Bourhis, and Taylor 1977; see Giles 1978). It refers to the degree to which an ethnolinguistic group acts as a collective entity and thrives as a distinct social group, and it is dependent on the specific socio-structural complexion of the intergroup context. Three major socio-structural influences are *status*, *demography*, and *institutional support* as set out below. If an ethnolinguistic group has economic control over its destiny, consensually high self-esteem, pride in its past, and a respected language of international repute, then it can be considered to have high status. This confers vitality which secures its survival as a distinct entity with a future. Demography refers to the sheer number and distribution of group members. Large numbers concentrated in an ancestral homeland, favourable ingroup-outgroup numerical proportions, low emigration and high birth rates, and a low incidence of mixed ingroup–outgroup marriages, are all demographic factors which favour enhanced vitality. Finally, the degree of institutional support refers to the representation that the language enjoys in the institutions (e.g. government, church, school, media) of the nation or territory. Institutional support enhances vitality.

Giles suggests vitality configurations for a number of ethnolinguistic groups (Giles 1978). For example, Anglo-American enjoys high status, demography, and institutional support, and thus has overall high vitality, whereas Albanian-Greek is low on all counts. Welsh enjoys medium status and demography, and medium to low institutional support, and so has relatively medium overall vitality, while French Canadian is slightly better off, as, although its status is slightly lower, it enjoys high demography and medium institutional support.

Giles and colleagues (especially see Giles and Johnson 1981) employ the social identity perspective to conceptualize the way in which these objective

Status variables
- Economic control of destiny
- Consensually high self-esteem
- Pride in the group's past
- Respected language of international repute

Demographic variables
- Large numbers concentrated in ancestral homeland
- Favourable ingroup–outgroup numerical proportion
- Low emigration rate
- High birth rate
- Low incidence of mixed ingroup–outgroup marriage

Institutional support variables
- Good representation of language in national or territorial institutions (government, media, schools, universities, church, etc.)

socio-structural factors relate to actual language use. The analysis adopts Tajfel and Turner's macro-social analysis of the role of social belief structures, self-esteem, and social identity in mediating between social structure and individual behaviour (Tajfel and Turner 1979; see Chs. 2 and 3 above for detailed treatment of this). Ball, Giles, and Hewstone label this analysis of language *enthnolinguistic identity theory* (Ball, Giles, and Hewstone 1984).

Ethnolinguistic groups, like other large-scale social categories, strive for an evaluatively positive social identity that enhances the self-esteem of its members. How they, the members of the group, do this depends on their social belief structures – beliefs about the nature of intragroup relations. These beliefs may or may not be accurate representations of the *real* nature of intergroup relations.

A belief in *social mobility* stems from an assumption that intergroup boundaries are permeable and easily crossed. Unfavourable social identity can be resolved by upward mobility: simply passing into and becoming a member of the dominant group. This is an individualistic strategy which is linguistically reflected in the adoption of what is subjectively believed to be the dominant group's language. Ethnolinguistic speech markers are attenuated and individuals speak the dominant group's language, for example the ultra-precise Oxford English attempted by Eliza in Shaw's *Pygmalion*. This is linguistic assimilation. It can result in language erosion, language death, or more accurately 'language suicide'. This can be facilitated by 'lexical transference', where the original language increasingly employs dominant outgroup terminology for concepts which are irrelevant to or not contained in the original ethnolinguistic culture. The ingroup language gradually becomes redundant, withers away, and perishes.

If, however, ethnicity is an important anchoring point for an individual's identity, then the loss of the ethnic language as a salient ethnic marker can result in feelings of anomie and low self-esteem coupled with a sense of betrayal in speaking the dominant group's language (Lambert 1979). This undesirable consequence of assimilation can be further accentuated by the ingroup's reaction, which may involve stigmatization of those who readily assimilate. Furthermore, the dominant group may become concerned by too successful assimilation that threatens its own position of dominance, and may adopt a strategy of upward divergence. This entails a continuous redefinition of what constitutes its language and thus renders linguistic assimilation very difficult. The dominant group's language becomes an ever-shifting target that the ethnic ingroup must constantly try to locate.

On the other hand, a *social change* belief structure does not create these problems. Individuals recognize that intergroup barriers are impermeable and that upward mobility is realistically impossible. Unfavourable social identity can only be remedied by group strategies aimed at changing the ethnolinguistic group's evaluation (social creativity) or changing the status quo itself which is responsible for the ingroup's low prestige (social competition). *Social creativity* strategies do not alter the objective status hierarchy or differential, yet do enhance positive social identity. Social creativity strategies include (1) diverting social comparisons from the dominant outgroup to other subordinate groups (e.g. Indians in the UK making comparisons with West Indians rather than Anglo Saxons), or to ingroup members (i.e. intragroup comparisons); (2) changing the consensual evaluation of the ingroup's characteristics, including its language; (3) changing the dimension of intergroup comparison, for example the resurrection of an ethnic language which is considered prestigious by both in and outgroup – such as for example, Hebrew in Israel (Fellman 1974) and Punjabi in Pakistan (Pandit 1978).

Social competition occurs when the status quo is seen to be illegitimate, unstable, and hence changeable. Cognitive alternatives emerge and intergroup comparisons become active. Under these conditions ethnic language revivals emerge as politicized or revolutionary phenomena of which there are numerous examples: Quebec, Wales, Belgium, the Basque region of Spain. Ethnic revival in one place can help awaken it elsewhere in a different inter-ethnic context, in so far as subordinate ethnic groups learn from the experiences of other such groups. Under conditions of social competition, language accentuation and divergence, in the service of psycholinguistic distinctiveness (Giles, Bourhis, and Taylor 1977), will arise along with ethnic pride. These are the seeds of conflict and possible ethnolinguistic and social change. The dominant group's reaction will include derogation of the ethnic language, abrasive humour, oppressive policies, and other measures aimed at preserving their position of dominance.

While factors such as status, demography, and institutional support may affect the objective enthnolinguistic vitality of a language, Giles and Johnson are careful to recognize that it is *perceived* vitality (or subjective vitality –

Bourhis, Giles, and Rosenthal 1981) which counts in determining whether ethnolinguistic features are accentuated (Giles and Johnson 1981). That is, vitality has its impact on language use in the same way as do other socio-structural factors, via subjective perceptions of, or beliefs concerning the nature of things, rather than the objective reality of things. Just as the dominant group may wish to foster a social mobility belief structure in order to prevent social change, it may also wish to construct the appearance of low vitality for a subordinate group. The reality may of course be that vitality is high and social mobility impossible. An example of ideological obfuscation of social reality along these lines might be the case of men's vested interest in preserving 'women's' speech (e.g. Kramarae 1981).

One further consideration in predicting whether social conditions favour ethnolinguistic revival concerns the individual's repertoire of social identities. Clearly, a restricted repertoire or one in which ethnicity figures very highly (for whatever reason) is more likely to be associated with ethnic revival and accentuated ethnic speech usage.

Giles and Johnson argue that ethnolinguistic identity theory is an advance on other approaches to the explanation of language and ethnicity, because it constitutes an integrated theory linking social structure to individual language behaviour in such a way as to be able to account for the great diversity of interethnic scenarios throughout the world (Giles and Johnson 1981; see Giles' 1978 taxonomy). Furthermore, it can explain the use of different language strategies by different groups, and can account for intragroup heterogeneity as regards language usage. Support for the theory resides in its ability to explain these phenomena (e.g. Giles and Saint-Jacques 1979).

However, Edwards has suggested that while the concept of 'vitality' and the broader use of Tajfel and Turner's macro-social analysis is indispensable to a proper social psychology of language (Edwards 1985; see Tajfel and Turner 1979), the approach would benefit from a more developed sociohistorical perspective on ethnolinguistic vitality (see also Clyne 1985; Husband and Saifullah Khan 1982). Although Edwards concedes that 'the theories of intergroup relations and social identity (Tajfel) and speech accommodation (Giles) probably represent the most comprehensive approach available within social psychology, to the presentation and manipulation of language and identity', he questions 'whether or not the theories advance our understanding of the processes discussed or simply restate or formalise, from a particular perspective, existing knowledge', and concludes that he feels that 'the answer, as is usually the case within social psychology, is the latter' (Edwards 1985: 155).

SPEECH ACCOMMODATION

Thus far we have largely restricted our discussion of the social psychology of language to the identity function served by language, and to the dynamics of large-scale intergroup relations between ethnolinguistic categories. However, it is people not categories which speak, and they speak to one another. A great deal of speech, as communication, occurs between individuals who are engaged in face-to-face interaction. A well-established feature of such interaction is that one or both of the interactants may modify his/her language or speech style (see our earlier discussion of 'motherese', this ch.; also see Bourhis 1979; Giles and Powesland 1975). Traditional sociolinguistic explanations of this phenomenon tend to focus upon static situational norms and rules of language use (see Bourhis and Genesee 1980), while more recent approaches incorporate a consideration of individual motivational factors. This more dynamic social psychological approach is called *speech accommodation theory* (Giles 1984; Thakerar, Giles, and Cheshire 1982; Beebe and Giles 1984; see also Giles 1978) (Table 9.1).

Table 9.1   Classification of type of speech style shift as a function of status, inter-individual social oreintation, and social belief system

	Subjectively salient interindividual orientation		
	Interpersonal	*Intergroup*	
Relative status of interlocutors		*Social mobility (no cognitive alternatives)*	*Social Change (cognitive alternatives)*
High	Downward convergence	Upward divergence	Upward divergence
Low	Upward convergence	Upward convergence	Downward divergence

Language or speech style changes in social interaction are characterized by unilateral or bilateral divergence or convergence which occurs in order to satisfy motivations rooted in similarity-attraction (Byrne 1969) and the need for positive social identity. Although accommodation can occur simply to facilitate communication (e.g. 'motherese', or speaking French to a monolingual French speaker) it can also reflect an identity dynamic or the need for social approval, which operates within the normative constraints imposed by the specific context of the interaction (see Ball *et al.* 1984 for an explanation of situational normative constraints on accommodation).

Generally speaking, convergence evokes positive reactions in the recipient (Bourhis, Giles, and Lambert 1975; Giles and Smith 1979), particularly if the behaviour can be attributed to the converger's intention rather than to contextual pressures (Simard, Taylor, and Giles 1976), and thus satisfies a need for approval or liking. Clearly, the greater the individual's need for social approval, the greater the convergence (Natalé 1975 provides evidence). However, the magnitude of this need is not necessarily a static personality attribute. It is more often a function of the relative status and prestige of the interactants, with the low-prestige speaker converging (upwards) more than the high-prestige speaker converges (downwards). Divergence indicates an absence of need for approval, or a desire for interpersonal dissociation.

If the interaction occurs in the context of an intergroup orientation, then accommodation fulfils an identity function. Under these conditions what occurs can only be predicted from a consideration of the social relations between the groups involved. Divergence achieves psycholinguistic distinctiveness, and this emerges in the context of a social-change belief structure which encompasses the existence of cognitive alternatives, while convergence is a social-mobility strategy that represents the existence of a social-mobility belief structure and the absence of cognitive alternatives.

Experimental evidence is consistent with this reasoning. Bourhis and Giles predicted that in the context of the contemporary Welsh-language revival in Wales, Welsh adults should possess a social-change belief structure and that consequently they should express 'downward divergence' (an accentuation of their Welsh accent) in the presence of a higher-status RP English ('received pronounciation' – standard, non-regional English) speaker (Bourhis and Giles 1977). The hypothesis was confirmed: after hearing an RP speaker, Welsh adults accentuated their Welsh accents (as rated by independent and naïve judges) over pre-experimentally established individual base rates. A similar paradigm was used by Bourhis, Giles, Leyens, and Tajfel to obtain a parallel finding among Flemish speakers in Belgium, where there is analogous language revival (vis-à-vis French speakers in Belgium) (Bourhis et al. 1979). In contrast, Hogg has experimentally obtained 'upward convergence' by British female students who spoke in a more male and less female stereotypic manner when engaging in debate with male students (Hogg 1985a). The intergroup context was one in which females might be expected to have a social-mobility belief structure.

An interesting ramification of speech accommodation in an intergroup context is evidence that what people converge on or diverge from is a *stereotype* of the ingroup or outgroup language rather than the language itself (Hogg 1985a; Thakerar, Giles, and Cheshire 1982). This indicates that the process underlying accommodation in a group context is conformity to language or speech style norms through self-categorization (see Ch. 8).

SECOND-LANGUAGE ACQUISITION

Speech accommodation and ethnolinguistic identity theories have exciting consequences for the study of second-language acquisition. Specifically, regarding the achievement of native-like (rather than formal classroom) proficiency in the language of the dominant group, under conditions of ethnolinguistic competition stemming from high perceived vitality and a social-change belief structure containing clear cognitive alternatives. The fact that these conditions are precisely those which favour psycholinguistic distinctiveness and downward divergence, suggests that the attainment of native-like proficiency may be severely compromised.

Research into second-language acquisition treats motivation to learn rather than 'aptitude' as the crucial variable (Clément 1980; Gardner 1979, 1981, 1982). This motivation is a product of features of the social context and social milieu in which second-language learning occurs. Although this approach explicity recognizes that acquiring native-like proficiency in a second language is very different to most other learning tasks because it involves adopting an alien cultural perspective and is therefore a question of identity (Gardner 1979), it tends not to explore the intergroup context (Ball, Giles, and Hewstone 1984; Giles and Byrne 1982). Second-language acquisition usually occurs in just such a context: where one ethnic group is learning the language of another ethnic group (di Pietro 1978). It is possible that positive ingroup feelings may hinder achievement of native-like proficiency in an outgroup language (Lambert 1974; Taylor, Meynard, and Rheault 1977).

Giles and Byrne employ ethnolinguistic identity theory and speech accommodation principles to develop an intergroup model of second-language acquisition (Giles and Byrne 1982; see also Ball, Giles, and Hewstone 1984) (Figure 9.1). The specific focus is upon native-like mastery of the language of a dominant ethnic collectivity. They hypothesize that native-like proficiency is unlikely if there is strong identification with an ingroup for whom language is a central feature, if there are few other groups or only lower-status groups with which to identify, if subjective ethnolinguistic vitality is high, and if a social change belief structure which sponsors social competition prevails. Under these conditions native-like proficiency would be 'subtractive' to a sense of ethnic identity; it would attract ingroup hostility attached to accusations of ethnic betrayal; and it would create

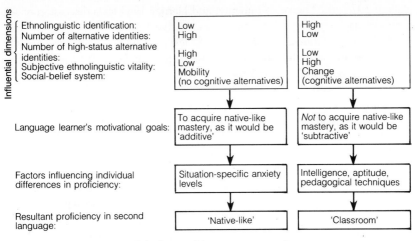

Figure 9.1   Intergroup model of second-language acquisition

feelings of fear of assimilation (Clément 1980). Only class-room proficiency would be acquired, and individual differences here would reflect intelligence, aptitude, and pedagogical (goodness of teaching techniques) differences.

Under conditions not embodying high subjective vitality, strong ingroup identification, social-change belief structures, and so forth, native-like proficiency would be acquired. Here it is 'additive' in so far as it furthers integration and facilitates access to social and material rewards (Gardner 1979). Individual differences are less likely to reflect factors such as intelligence but rather anxiety levels contingent on specific situations of second-language usage. The terms 'additive' and 'subtractive' are borrowed from Lambert (1974), but have a different meaning from that originally intended by Lambert.

Here we have described two extreme forms of intergroup context and related them to second-language learning. Clearly, most societies fall somewhere between these two ideal types, and so Ball, Giles, and Hewstone have applied the model to these 'intermediate' conditions with the aim of furnishing a more finely honed predictive model, which could perhaps be used by educational policy makers (Ball, Giles, and Hewstone 1984; cf. Hogg and Abrams 1985). For our purpose, however, the important point is that second-language acquisition, as an intergroup phenomenon, is readily amenable to a social identity analysis.

SEX AND LANGUAGE

Earlier in this section it was mentioned that the social psychology of language dwells mainly upon social markers of category membership in speech and language, and that the majority of research concerns ethnicity and sex. We have discussed ethnicity and now shall briefly mention sex in order to reveal the relevance of the social identity perspective here (also see Ch. 10). (See Lakoff 1975 and Thorne, Kramarae, and Henley 1983 for a discussion of sex and language from a sociolinguistic perspective.)

Although sex differences in speech are less pronounced than stereotypes of masculine and feminine speech would lead us to believe, they nevertheless function as potent social markers of sex (Kramer 1977; Mulac, Incontro, and James 1985; Smith 1985). They are not, however, exclusively static markers of biological sex, rather they can be exaggerated or attenuated as a function of the sex-role orientation of the speaker (Giles, Smith, Browne, Whiteman, and Williams 1980; Giles, Smith, Ford, Condor, and Thakerar 1980; Smith 1979, 1980, 1985). That is, the degree of masculinity or femininity of male and female speech is, at least to a degree, a function of how traditionally masculine or feminine the individual perceives him or herself to be. In other words, speech style is a property of gender identity, just as language may be an attribute of ethnic identity. Furthermore, it appears that the subjective situational salience of gender to the speaker has effects on speech style, and that therefore speech style is a normative property of gender which is generated by self-categorization (Hogg 1985a). Speech accommodation theory permits the clear prediction that in an intersex encounter in which gender is salient, females should manifest upward speech style convergence while males show speech style maintenance. This prediction, which is predicated on the nature of the social relations between men and women, was indeed upheld in the study by Hogg described above (Hogg 1985a; see Kramarae 1981; Williams and Giles 1978).

Conclusion

Proceeding from a discussion of the essentially social nature of communication, speech, and language, we have attempted to show that although the phenomena are fundamental to social psychology, traditional approaches have typically excluded language and only deal with communication as information transmission. This omission is traced to metatheoretical trends in traditional social psychology.

Language is, however, an important focus of other disciplines and sub-disciplines. We discussed limitations of psychological approaches to language on the grounds that they tend to focus on the individual and pay insufficient attention to the fact that speech and language are means of communication which are inextricable from the communicative context and the relationship between the interlocutors. In focusing upon the communicative function of language, recent developmental psychological approaches to the acquisition of language go some way towards transcending this limitation. It is sociolinguistics, however, which epitomizes the study of language behaviour in its social context. Yet sociolinguistics has come under attack on the grounds that its approach is largely descriptive and unidirectional because it lacks a social psychological component to deal with the dialectical mediation of motivations, beliefs, and identity between social structure and individual language behaviour.

The 'new' social psychology of language has recently arisen to address this lacuna. The endeavour adheres to the metatheoretical critique of individualism, and overwhelmingly employs the social identity perspective. Emphasis is placed on the fact that speech and language contain category-membership information, and that therefore intergroup relations and subjective perceptions of such relations are dynamically related to language behaviour through the mediation of social identity mechanisms. Ethnolinguistic identity theory (Giles and Johnson 1981) focuses the social identity perspective on language and ethnic group relations, while speech accommodation theory (Giles 1984) focuses more upon speech and language shifts in social encounters, and how this is affected by individual motivations, including those linked to social identity and intergroup relations. Finally, we discussed how the social identity approach to the social psychology of language allows the development of an intergroup model of second-language acquisition (Giles and Byrne

1982) and an exploration of the relationship between sex and language (Smith 1985).

This chapter has been dedicated to a discussion mainly of speech and language, and thus may appear to clearly separate these phenomena from the focal phenomena of other chapters. We would wish to argue that the separation is principally a matter of independent universes of discourse, and that strong links with other phenomena emerge from the social identity perspective applied to this field. Specifically, speech style and language are attributes of social identity. They can be stereotypical or criterial of social groups, and thus language behaviour has a strong component of normative behaviour, as discussed in Chapter 8. Speech style and language can be added to the list of attributes, behaviours, beliefs, appearances, feelings, and so on, which differentiate between and define groups. They are all group norms or social stereotypes.

Recommended reading

Moscovici (1967) and Kraut and Higgins (1984) offer slightly different critical comments on traditional social psychological approaches to language, speech, and communication. Sociolinguistics is clearly introduced by Hudson (1980), and the topic of social markers in speech is well covered in a book edited by Scherer and Giles (1979). General coverage of topics in the 'new' social psychology of language can be found in Giles and Street (1985), Robinson (1983), and Giles and St Clair (1979), while more specific references to ethnolinguistic identity theory and speech accommodation theory are to be found in Giles and Johnson (1981) and Giles (1984) respectively. Smith (1985) offers a very scholarly discussion of sex and language.

10

Conclusions

It's good for a girl to be educated but not to be educated too much. After marriage, she may do courses as a hobby. If her family is very liberal, she may work, perhaps in a primary school, just for a year or two; or in a women's hospital. She may work anywhere, really, where she knows that she will not, on her daily journey, or in the course of events, come across a man. There's a whole sealed-off floor at the Ministry of Planning, where women economists sit at their desks and communicate with their male colleagues by telephone. . . . It is apartheid: stringent, absolute. The cafés are segregated, the buses. Allah has laid a duty on both men and women to seek knowledge but . . . Education is an ornament. It makes one a better mother. The girls have a chilling saying: 'We will hang our certificates in the kitchen.'

Saudi women believe their sisters in the West have been the victims of a confidence trick. They believe that men have lured them, with promises of freedom, from the security of their homes and made them slaves in offices and factories. Their proper domain has been taken away from them and with it the respect and protection to which their sex entitles them. Their honour has been sold; their bodies are common property. Liberation, say the Saudi women, is a creed for fools.

There is no crime in Saudi Arabia, the newspapers say. There is no corruption. All women are chaste. All families are happy. . . . Patrols walk the shopping malls, vigilantes armed with canes; they are the delegates of the Committee for the Propagation of Virtue and the Elimination of Vice. . . . There are no crimes but there are punishments. A woman is stoned to death. Amputations are carried out, after Friday prayers.

(*Good Weekend*, 20 March 1987)

This extract is from a short essay (awarded the inaugural Shiva Naipul prize) by Hilary Mantel entitled 'Last Morning in Al Hamra' describing some of her experiences in Saudi Arabia. The extract contains many of the themes we have discussed in this book, in the context of intergroup relations between the sexes. There is intergroup differentiation and discrimination to the extreme of segregation; complete power and dominance rests with the male, who can mete out savagely inhuman punishments which are legitimate in the eyes of the state; there is ideological control through censorship and promulgation of lies; and there is acquiescence on the part of women who justify their position in the language of the dominant ideology, and condemn their 'liberated sisters' in the west. In this chapter we briefly overview the social identity approach and then suggest ways in which it can be and has been used to analyse intergroup relations between the sexes.

Introduction

This book is about intergroup relations and group processes, and more fundamentally the causes, consequences, and generative processes of group belongingness. We advocate the social identity approach, and so it is also primarily an exposition of this approach. In this final chapter we draw together the various themes, issues, and theoretical advances which characterize the approach. We began by providing an overview of the metatheory which houses the social identity perspective, stressing the importance of developing non-reductionist theories and explanations in social psychology. The emphasis is on the fusing of cognitive and social (sometimes societal) processes in accounting for the relationship between individual psychological functioning and the social nature of identity, behaviour, and cognition. Its application is broad: behaviour both within and between groups is explicable largely in terms of the social identifications of their individual members. This simple transition (from regarding the group as external to regarding it as part of the self-concept) allows a reinterpretation of many of the phenomena which are familiar to social psychologists but which have previously been explained as purely intrapersonal or interpersonal effects. The interrelationships between a diverse range of hitherto uninte-grated topics, from discrimination, prejudice, stereotyping, attraction, groupthink, social facilitation and self-presentation to conformity, collective behaviour, language and communication, can be understood within the framework of the social identity perspective.

Our aim in this chapter is to summarize very briefly the social identity analysis of the individual in society, and to explore and raise further issues which arise from it, by focusing upon a specific intergroup context: the relations between the sexes. There are already a number of excellent and detailed such treatments (listed in 'Recommended Reading'), and ours draws from these. However, ours is narrative (e.g. it is very sparsely referenced) and is only intended to fulfil the function of illustration, to show how the themes from each chapter in this book interweave and combine to contribute to the overall scenario. (A similar exercise is possible with other intergroup contexts.) From this illustration a number of issues and questions are raised, which we summarize as providing important directions for the social identity approach. The chapter concludes with a summary of its success in achieving its metatheoretical goals, and with our enthusiasm for the future.

Theory

The theory of social identity rests on an assumption that categorization is the process by which people order, and render predictable, information about the world in which they live. This process of categorization operates on objects, other people, and oneself, and consequently people are seen as belonging to the same or different categories as oneself. Partly because the categorization involves a simplification and clarification of perception, and partly because there is a motivation to positively value the self, differentiation between one's own and other category members is often extreme, and biased in favour of the ingroup. These factors account for the existence of social competion and for the rigid and derogatory stereotypes held of outgroups.

The inclusion of self in the categorization process is crucial. It is the fact that one's self is categorized as being stereotypically the same as other ingroup members which creates social attraction – attraction to others *because* they are ingroupers, regardless of their personal characteristics. Self-definition as a group member serves to orient the individual to others in a particular way. For example, the manner in which the self is presented depends upon whether the audience, which does not necessarily have to be physically present in large numbers or even at all, is composed of ingroup or outgroup members. The group is a *psychological* entity, which can find its form in collective social behaviour, where collective action is co-ordinated by the common social identity of the actors. Self-categorization allows group members to find meaning and order by specifying norms or stereotypically 'ideal' attributes which apply to self as a group member. In the process of referent informational influence, people use their knowledge of group memberships in order to determine to which of the myriad of possible norms they should conform. This knowledge is spread and altered through behaviour, and mainly through the medium of language, whereby individuals may communicate to which groups they belong (or aspire to belong), and from which they distance themselves.

Within the constraints of relatively 'objective' power and status relations between groups, individuals may subjectively perceive particular relationships in one of two general ways, each having different implications for the maintenance of a positive social identity. The subjective social-belief system of social mobility regards group boundaries as permeable, and movement between groups as being possible for individuals. The subjective social-belief system of social change regards group boundaries as impermeable, and alterations of the relationship between groups as being beyond the scope of individuals and as residing in the ability of groups to stake their claims. On the one hand, this may involve direct social competition over consensually·valued resources, while on the other, it may involve social creativity to find new ways of improving the group's position. For subordinate groups social competition involves risky engagement with the dominant group, while social creativity does not challenge the status quo.

Application to relations between the sexes

It is uncontroversial to say that the recent history of relations between the sexes in western civilization has been a history of oppression (e.g. Millett 1969). Men have held economic power over women for centuries, and today men have higher-status occupations, take greater responsibility for organizational and political decisions, are represented as more prestigious in the mass media, and are taken to have the ideal characteristics of the individual in society. The roles traditionally assigned to each sex place males as breadwinners, competitors, providers, achievers, and women as dependants, supporters, consumers, and emotional responders (e.g. see Archer and Lloyd 1982; Deaux 1985). These traditional role relationships and their implications have been challenged by women, in forms such as women's suffrage (in the nineteenth century), the womens' liberation movement, and feminism (in the twentieth century). Despite these organized social movements, and historical conditions which forced society to place women in 'men's' roles (e.g. during the Second World War women were employed to run services and produce armaments), it is true to say that the fundamental structure of society has not changed dramatically.

THE INTERGROUP DIMENSION

Against this background characterization of the 'objective' structure of society, and the 'natural' consignment of men and women to masculine and feminine roles, there occurs a process of social identification. If there were no power, status, and prestige differences between the sexes, we would expect direct competition in terms of the valued attributes of individuals in general. However, the relative subordinacy of women means that, for them, only the belief structure of social change, and only the perception that intergroup differences are insecure, allows social competition to take place. This is the endorsement of a radical sex-role ideology and the path of feminism. In contrast, when intergroup differences are seen as secure, women may engage in social-creativity strategies, ranging from exaggeration of existing differences on valued feminine dimensions, to finding new dimensions of 'femininity', to finding alternative groups against which to compare themselves (American women, French women, Muslim women, Jewish women, feminists, etc.). Thus social-change beliefs may contribute both to the maintenance and to the alteration of the status quo, but both depend on the perception of the relationship at an intergroup level and on self-categorization and identification with one's own category. We can therefore refer to this as 'sex-identification' because it involves a perception of oneself in terms of attributes which are common to others in one's own sex-category, and distinct from the attributes of others in the alternative category.

At the other extreme are those individuals who possess a social-mobility belief structure. Under these circumstances, women assume personal responsibility for their position in society and thus may be successful in a male domain, without perceiving this in sex-competitive terms. They explain the differences between the sexes as a matter of preference (innate or otherwise), and regard the boundaries as merely symbolic. Self is enhanced by competing on equal terms with other individuals regardless of sex, and by psychologically 'passing' into a male world. This ideology of individualism, of course, maintains the status quo to the extent that the two worlds remain unchanged. Moreover, it allows members of the dominant group to attribute their own position to their personal characteristics ('The reason I am the boss and she is the secretary is that I am the only one around here who can really make decisions', etc.).

The dominant group also responds positively to many social-creativity strategies, especially when these reinforce attributes which consign the subordinate group even more to its existing position. Men may overtly admire women for their physical beauty, for their ability to care, cook, have babies, and so on ('Long blonde hair attracts me, but there is no ideal woman. I like a girl who is good-looking and basically nice' – Pat Cash, quoted in *Cosmopolitan*, February 1986: 59). Men also are overtly scornful of subgroups of women who challenge the status quo (e.g. lesbians), or who depart from the norms of stereotypical femininity (e.g. 'tomboys', body-builders), thus nominating alternative outgroups for traditional women. Social-creativity strategies are incorporated into the existing social arrangement if they leave the groups equal but different, and so long as the difference favours the dominant group in terms of prestige and power.

When the security of relations appears threatened and the status quo is challenged by the subordinate group, this can be met with either acceptance or resistance by the dominant group. Resistance is likely when women appear to be becoming 'too' mobile: legislation is introduced which reinforces the man's responsibility for household income (e.g. the British practice of treating husband and wife as a unit for taxation and social security purposes), or which reduces the support for women with children to pursue a career (e.g. restricted crèche facilities, coupled with an imbalance between maternity and paternity leave). When they are becoming 'too' competitive, traditional values are re-emphasized (a return to family values), or creativity strategies are suggested ('women should take advantage of their capacity to care'). Acceptance by the dominant group may take different forms too. On the one hand, when women become increasingly successful in traditionally male professions (e.g. clerical work) the gates are opened and women become actively recruited. On the other hand, this is often coupled with an evaluative downgrading of the job (office assistant, typist), and men deserting it for those of higher status (accountant, sales manager, word-processing programmer). Even the open endorsement and acceptance of women's pursuit of male jobs may actually be the patronizing and magnanimous gesturing of secure dominant-group members.

One important medium through which the status quo is maintained is, of course, language and communication. Language crystallizes the stereotypes whose function is to reify the categorical distinction between males and females. Communication, through language, conveys the content of stereotypes, embodies the manner in which they are used, and is the process which enables the stereotyping to become shared. Describing women in terms of their beauty, supportiveness, dependency, and so on, reinforces the perception that women differ from men on these dimensions. This allows the justification of a status quo, which is founded upon the now assumed reality (or 'naturalness') of these differences (Huici 1984). Language, or at least speech, is also used in a more dynamic way to reinforce or undermine categorical differences. One means by which people have sought to reduce the association between males and power has been to directly alter the language used to describe individuals (chairperson, humanity, he or she, instead of the 'generic' terms chairman, mankind, and he). More subtle variations in the paralinguistic aspects of speech also contribute to stereotyping. For example, the same man might adopt a suggestive, predatory manner while talking to a female secretary, but a cold, formal manner while talking to a male colleague. A businesswoman may adopt a cool, formal manner when at a board meeting (converging towards a masculine speech style), but a warm playful manner when talking to her children.

THE ROLE OF SELF-STEREOTYPING

But how do members of each sex know what to conform to, or how to enact a stereotype? And why do individuals differ in their interpretation and admiration of stereotypical attributes? The social identity explanation is that it is the identification or inclusion of self within the category which is responsible for stereotypical behaviour and that individual variation reflects differences between individuals in the cognitive representation of sex-stereotypes. Indeed, because of the multi-layered and textured nature of social identity, the fact that sex is subjectively salient does not mean that we can directly predict what an individual will do. For example, a man sitting in a bar, talking about women to other men may, *at that time*, perceive the most criterial distinguishing attribute to be male sexuality. His conversation may be replete with sexual innuendo and images of women as sexual objects. In a different setting, perhaps when playing with his young son, he may perceive 'maleness' to be best distinguished in terms of 'male' activity. His conversation may dwell on truck-driving, football, and fighting. In each of these cases the man is behaving normatively, not so much because he is responding to social pressure but because he conceives of himself in slightly different ways, as a man. The same may be said for women, for whom the norms also change greatly as they get older. It is normative for young women to be stereotypically sexual, for slightly older women to be stereotypically maternal, and for old women to be stereotypically asexual (Itzin 1986).

The fact that the norms of behaviour can differ for the two sexes is revealed in their typical responses to intergroup situations. Traditionally, it has been suggested, women stress communality among people (especially women), while men stress agency (for details of this distinction see Bakan 1966). This has been invoked to explain why female subjects are sometimes less discriminatory in experimental research (Williams 1984). However, agency and communion can be regarded as opposite sides of the same coin; social identification involves the psychological *differentiation* of one's own group from others. This may be achieved by agentically focusing on competitive comparisons between groups *and/or* by communally focusing on the cohesiveness within one's own group. That agency and communion are not sex-typed characteristics becomes clear in the case of collective protest. For example, the communion expressed among women at Greenham Common is balanced by their agency towards the (male) representatives of the dominant group, and again the agency expressed by striking male coal-miners against the police during the 1984–5 coal strike in Britain is complemented by camaraderie and communion among strikers. Also, there are wide variations between women in the sex-role orientation they adopt and in how strongly they identify with their group (Condor 1986). Those who identify with women and hold a radical sex-role ideology are most likely to engage in social competition with men, while those who identify but hold a traditional sex-role ideology are least likely to compete with men.

Sex identification does not directly affect all behaviour and is not fixed in content or degree. Rather, at different times and in different situations sex might be more or less salient. Certainly, some individuals find it generally to be more salient than do others, and one of the outstanding questions is still what it is that produces these differences. It seems plausible that those who hold social-change belief structures and perceive men's position to be illegitimate would find their sex to be more salient more often because there is greater potential to engage in positive differentiation. Beyond this general influence there will be important situational differences. While physical factors such as the number of males and females present and the numerical distinctiveness of one category, have been found to make sex salient (Taylor et al. 1978), the crucial process is psychological – the way those present are perceived. This will include oneself, of course, and helps us to explain why the same person can present a different self-image in different contexts. For example, a collection of individuals at a singles bar will perceive one another in terms of sex, while that same collection of individuals may perceive themselves in terms of nationality if news of war is announced. More subtly, as these extracts from an article in the women's magazine *Cleo* show, women may adopt and present a 'sexual' self to men ('there's something that appeals to most of them about a new woman who's slick, confident and beautifully dressed'), but a 'caring' self to women ('I let her know I've got the same problems she does – too much to do and too little time . . . children to pick up from school'). Similarly, a man might adopt different selves in each context ('I can be myself around women, whereas I have to put on a pose of toughness when I'm out with the guys') (*Cleo*, September 1986: 68). Finally, as we suggested above, 'sex' need not refer to all members of one's own sex, but may be defined purely in terms of a specific subgroup.

All of these possibilities should also make it clear why there may be no close correspondence between self-esteem and real world intergroup discrimination. Theoretically, differentiating in favour of one's own group is motivated by a desire or need for a positive self-image. However, this is not necessarily achieved by objective discrimination but by differentiation towards valued poles of specific dimensions. If the group norm is defined as 'co-operative', 'fair', or even 'generous', then salient social identity will be manifested in that way. In addition, it will not be all of one's social identifications which are enhanced but only those which are salient and which specifically relate to the evaluative dimensions being employed.

THE INTERPERSONAL DIMENSION

A fascinating aspect of relations between the sexes is that they exist simultaneously at both intergroup and interpersonal levels (Abrams and Condor 1984). While power and status differences between the sexes are often enormous, and are more global than are the differences between specific ethnic groups, it is also true that the marital relationship and heterosexual coupling are a fundamental feature of the organization of society. In contrasting social and personal identity, or group and interpersonal behaviour, social identity theory is ambiguous concerning the apparently simultaneous interpersonal and intergroup contours of heterosexual relationships.

One resolution of the issue might be to conceptualize salience (high/low) as being orthogonal to identity (personal/social), so that both aspects of identity could be salient simultaneously. This is precisely the manner in which Stephenson describes the position of industrial negotiators (Stephenson 1984; see Ch. 6 above). Another way to tackle the problem is to view the couple as a *group*, whose unity is defined by a particular form of reciprocity between members of different categories. For some couples this reciprocity may take the form of mutual reinforcement of traditional sex roles, while for others it may take the form of mutual bracketing-off from the intergroup distinction. In yet other couples there may be a deliberate transcendence of traditional roles, and an attempt to compensate for some of the imbalances at the intergroup level. It is interesting, however, that one of the traditional criterial attributes for members of both sexes is interest in attracting a member of the opposite sex, and this is strongly sanctioned by society (a superordinate 'group'). Individuals who depart from this concern are often stigmatized, assumed to be infertile or impotent, or regarded as asexual, while those who favour intragroup relationships are often stereotyped as possessing attributes of the opposite sex (e.g. effeminacy is stereotypical for male homosexuals, while masculinity, or 'butchness' is for lesbians).

In terms of heterosexual relationships, perceptions of one's partner at the intergroup and interpersonal levels may in some cases be incongruent, and lead to conflicts of expectations. Moreover, within each level there will be variations in the way these perceptions are interpreted and evaluated. For example, if the female partner holds a radical sex-role ideology, and views her situation *as a woman* as one of unjust oppression, it is likely that she will perceive the male partner stereotypically – as possessing the *exploitative* qualities of all men. The more salient is the intergroup level the more likely it is that the male will be perceived as a representative of a 'competitive' outgroup. Alternatively, if the female holds a traditional sex-role ideology she may place great value on her partner's stereotypically masculine behaviour, and indeed may strive to maintain her own traditional femininity in order to preserve mutually positive intergroup distinctiveness. She might agree with Raquel Welch that, 'most women feel the same way I do. They want men to behave in the classic way and dominate them' (*Cleo*, January 1986: 17). Similarly, a man holding a traditional sex-role ideology may generally behave in a highly masculine way to his partner, emphasizing her feminine sexuality. It is interesting to speculate what happens when the male, at the intergroup level, has a more radical sex-role orientation than the female, and there is still plenty of scope for research and theory to be developed in this area.

These intergroup perceptions are likely to have important consequences because they provide a structure and social context for the relationship at the interpersonal level. To the extent that these perceptions are balanced and compatible (e.g. both partners hold a similar sex-role ideology) there is no reason for direct conflict. However, congruity on one level will not always entail congruity on another (e.g. similar sex-role ideology does not involve compatibility in terms of personality), and differences in the salience of levels for each partner may be a source of misunderstanding and conflict (for example, where the female's personal identity is salient but she is subjected to unwelcome pressure to behave in a stereotypically feminine way by her male partner, or where the male refuses to comply with a request to engage in what he regards as 'women's work'). Finally, it is clear that the two levels are mutually influential and that the content and interpretation of one's perceptions are a continuing part of this process rather than simply preceding or resulting from it.

The example of the heterosexual couple also illustrates the point that intergroup contact is not sufficient to ameliorate differences between groups. In the case of sex, it is often argued that the traditional relationship simply reinforces and reifies the differences. Moreover, even though such relationships involve co-operative interdependence (of roles), there is no widespread generalization of affection between the sexes from the one-to-one level to the intergroup level. This point serves to emphasize that the relationship is mediated by subjective beliefs and ideology. In turn, the possession of particular beliefs also demands some explanation. One direction to be explored is the way that the cross-cutting and texturing of self-definition in terms of sex by other self-categories, such as age, mediates these beliefs (10 year olds are likely to be more concerned with intergroup differentiation between the sexes *per se*, whereas 16 year olds are particularly concerned with differentiation on dimensions concerned with sexuality – see Abrams and Condor 1984).

Theoretical advances

We have used the concrete example of relations between the sexes to help illustrate the way in which the different strands of the social identity approach intertwine to provide an integrated analysis of intergroup behaviour. We now move on to make some concluding remarks concerning the social identity approach as a whole – its accomplishments and its prospects.

The social identity approach advances our understanding of an array of phenomena and leads to a characterization of relationships between people which is distinctly different from that found in most of social psychology. First, intergroup relationships are not explained in terms of the personality characteristics, psychodynamics, or personal attitudes of individual group members. Nor are they, defined in terms of objective conflicts of interest between groups. The stereotyping which accompanies intergroup behaviour does not merely reflect faulty cognitive assimilation of empirical evidence. Instead, the intergroup relationship is explained in terms of the collectively held *subjective* perception of group membership, and is psychologically interpreted as one of conflict, difference, and so on. The stereotypes are part of a general process whereby intergroup relationships are sustained and justified to varying degrees. The functions of stereotyping are largely group-serving, and like much intergroup behaviour, do not always directly benefit the individual group member.

Second, the cohesiveness of the group, behaviour within the group, conformity to group norms, and collective group behaviour are not explained in terms of interpersonal dependence for need satisfaction or information. The group is conceived as being a psychological entity which specifies *a priori* to whom one is attracted, whose norms are to be conformed to, and the appropriate target of collective behaviour. That is, the process of self-categorization as a group member directs the search for information, the affective bonds with others, and the incorporation of norms to include the self.

Third, the nature of language and communication is not described as static or constraining, but as part of the process by which identity is symbolized to others and which defines relationships between groups. Moreover, throughout the analysis, society is not treated as an extraneous variable, the contribution of which is merely to provide content. The social identity approach tries to include society explicitly, as psychologically represented by the individual group member, in its analysis of the different forms taken by intergroup relations. It is because of the inseparability of the self from society (and hence groups in society) that the analysis extends from intragroup to intergroup relationships – something which has failed demonstrably with other extrapolations (for a review, see Billig 1976) that rely on intra-psychological processes (such as frustration, instinct) without inclusion of the social context as part of the explanation.

The social identity approach is vibrant and flourishing, and continues to provide an exciting impetus for the theorizing and research of a growing number of social psychologists. An increasing diversity of phenomena is being subjected to its analysis (e.g. intergroup contact, minority influence, leadership, interindividual attraction, second-language acquisition, power, multiple-group settings, conformity, salience), but perhaps we can identify a smaller number of areas in which some current and future theoretical initiatives are occurring.

One area concerns further exploration of the self-categorization underpinnings of social identity (e.g. Turner et al. 1987), and another the macro-social and ideological construction of social-belief systems and the content and meaning of specific intergroup contexts (e.g. Condor and Henwood 1986). The precise motivational status of self-esteem in social identity is also in need of some elaboration and clarification to specify its relationship to more specific goals, purposes, and social practices (e.g. Abrams and Hogg 1986). A fourth focus concerns differences in self-preservation contingent on self-conception as an individual or group member. Finally, there is the issue of the relationship between interpersonal and intergroup relations. Traditionally, they have been treated as separate, but there are instances when they appear to be closely intertwined, as in the sex example above, but also with regard to ethnographies of cultures in which interpersonal relations exist and are encouraged between hostile and antagonistic tribal subgroups.

Conclusion

The social identity approach emerges from a metatheoretical critique of psychological reductionism. It circumvents the individualism which is explicit to varying degrees in much of social psychology by placing the group in the individual and showing how the unit of analysis becomes transformed not only theoretically but also empirically. Social identification with groups is as psychologically real, and measurable, as is interpersonal attraction, reactance, frustration, performance anxiety or any other psychological phenomenon. In focusing on this transformation – from individual to group member – the approach opens the way for a more integrated and complete analysis of the social psychological functioning of individuals in society. By avoiding the reduction of groups to individuals, it allows us to conceptualize the *relationship* between individual and society, and to place theoretically the group within the individual.

Recommended reading

The general reading for this chapter is of course the preceding nine chapters of this book! For overviews of research and theory on the relations between the sexes we would recommend Archer and Lloyd (1982) and Deaux (1985). Social identity analyses of sex are to be found in Breakwell (1979), Condor (1986), Huici (1984), Smith (1985), Williams (1984), and Williams and Giles (1978). Smith's book in particular is also an excellent and scholarly overview of the topic in general.

References

Abèles, R.D. (1976) 'Relative deprivation, rising expectations, and black militancy', *Journal of Social Issues* 32: 119–37.

Abelson, R.P., Aronson, E., McGuire, W.J., Newcomb, T., Rosenberg, M.J., and Tannenbaum, P.H. (eds) (1968) *Theories of Cognitive Consistency: A Sourcebook*, Chicago: Rand-McNally.

Abrams, D. (1983) 'The impact of evaluative context on intergroup behaviour', paper presented at the Annual Conference of the Social Psychology Section of the British Psychology Society, Sheffield, September 1983.

Abrams, D. (1984) 'Social identity, self-awareness, and intergroup behaviour', University of Kent, unpublished doctoral dissertation.

Abrams, D. (1985) 'Focus of attention in minimal intergroup discrimination', *British Journal of Social Psychology* 24: 65–74.

Abrams, D. and Brown, R.J. (1986) 'Self-consciousness and social identity: a challenge to deindividuation theories of group process', University of Dundee, unpublished paper.

Abrams, D. and Condor, S. (1984) 'A social identity approach to the development of sex identification during adolescence', paper presented at the International Conference on Self and Identity, Cardiff, July.

Abrams, D. and Hogg, M.A. (1986) 'Social identity, self-esteem, and intergroup discrimination: a critical re-examination', Universities of Dundee and Melbourne, unpublished paper.

Abrams, D. and Manstead, A.S.R. (1981) 'A test of theories of social facilitation using a musical task', *British Journal of Social Psychology* 20: 271–8.

Abrams, D., Sparkes, K., and Hogg, M.A. (1985) 'Gender salience and social identity: the impact of sex of siblings on educational and occupational aspirations', *British Journal of Educational Psychology* 55: 224–32.

Abrams, D., Wetherell, M., Cochrane, S., Hogg, M.A., and Turner, J.C. (1986) 'Knowing what you think by knowing who you are: a social identity approach to norm formation, conformity, and group polarization', University of Dundee, unpublished paper.

Abramson, L.Y. and Alloy, L.B. (1981) 'Depression, non-depression, and cognitive illusions: a reply to Schwartz', *Journal of Experimental Psychology* 110: 436–47.

Adorno, T.W., Frenkel-Brunswik, E., Levinson, D.J., and Sanford, R.M. (1950) *The Authoritarian Personality*, New York: Harper.

Ajzen, I. (1974) 'Effects of information on interpersonal attraction: similarity vs affective value', *Journal of Personality and Social Psychology* 29: 374–80.

Alain, M. (1985) 'An empirical validation of relative deprivation', *Human Relations* 38: 739–49.

Albert, R.S. (1953) 'Comments on the scientific function of the concept of cohesiveness', *American Journal of Sociology* 59: 231–4.

Alexander, C.N., Zucker, L.G., and Brody, C.L. (1970) 'Experimental expectations and autokinetic experiences: consistency theories and judgemental convergence', *Sociometry* 33: 108–22.

Allen, V.L. (1965) 'Situational factors in conformity', *Advances in Experimental Social Psychology* 2: 133–75.

Allen, V.L. (1975) 'Social support for non-conformity', *Advances in Experimental Social Psychology* 8: 1–43.

Allen, V.L. and Wilder, D.A. (1980) 'Impact of group consensus and social support on stimulus meaning: mediation of conformity by cognitive restructuring', *Journal of Personality and Social Psychology* 39: 1116–25.

Allport, F.H. (1920) 'The influence of the group upon association and thought', *Journal of Experimental Psychology* 3: 159–82.

Allport, F.H. (1924) *Social Psychology*, Boston: Houghton-Mifflin.

Allport, G.W. (1954) *The Nature of Prejudice*, London: Addison-Wesley.

Allport, G.W. (1968) 'The historical background of modern social psychology', in G. Lindzey and E. Aronson (eds) *Handbook of Social Psychology*, vol. 1, 2nd edn, Reading, Mass.: Addison-Wesley.

Allport, G.W. and Postman, L.J. (1947) *The Psychology of Rumor*, New York: Holt, Rinehart, & Winston.

Alvy, K.T. (1973) 'The development of listener adapted communications in grade-school children from different social-class backgrounds', *Genetic Psychology Monographs* 87: 33–104.

Amir, Y., Sharan, S., Rivner, M., and Ben-Amir, R. (1979) 'Group status and attitude change in desegregated classrooms', *International Journal of Intercultural Relations* 3: 137–52.

Anderson, E. and Anderson, D. (1984) 'Ambient temperature and violent crime: tests of the linear and curvilinear hypotheses', *Journal of Personality and Social Psychology* 46: 91–7.

Andreski, S. (1971) *Herbert Spencer*, London: Nelson.

Andreyeva, G.M. and Gozman, L.J. (1981) 'Interpersonal relationships and social context', in S. Duck and R. Gilmour (eds) *Personal Relationships*, vol. 1, *Studying Personal Relationships*, London: Academic Press.

Apfelbaum, E. (1979) 'Relations of domination and movements for liberation: an analysis of power between groups', in W.G. Austin and S. Worchel (eds) *The Social Psychology of Intergroup Relations*, Monterey, Calif.: Brooks-Cole.

Archer, J. and Lloyd, B. (1982) *Sex and Gender*, Harmondsworth: Penguin.

Argyle, M. (1973) *Social Interaction*, London: Tavistock.

Argyle, M. (1975) *Bodily Communications*, London: Methuen.

Arkin, R.M. (1981) 'Self-presentation styles', in J.T. Tedeschi (ed.) *Impression Management Theory and Social Psychological Theory*, London: Academic Press.

Asch, S.E. (1951) 'Effects of group pressure upon the modification and distortion of judgements', in H. Guetzkow (ed.) *Groups, Leadership and Men*, Pittsburgh: Carnegie Press.

Asch, S.E. (1952) *Social Psychology*, Englewood-Cliffs, NJ: Prentice-Hall.

Asch, S.E. (1956) 'Studies of independence and conformity: 1. A minority of one against a unanimous majority', *Psychological Monographs* 70 (416): whole issue.

Aschenbrenner, K.M. and Schaefer, R.E. (1980) 'Minimal group situations: comments on a mathematical model and on the research paradigm', *European Journal of Social Psychology* 10: 389–98.

Ashmore, R.D. and Del Boca, F.K. (1981) 'Conceptual approaches to stereotypes and stereotyping', in D.L. Hamilton (ed.) *Cognitive Processes in Stereotyping and*

Intergroup Behaviour, Hillsdale, NJ: Erlbaum.

Back, K.W. (1951) 'Influence through social communication', *Journal of Abnormal and Social Psychology* 46: 9–23.

Backman, C. and Secord, P. (1962) 'Liking, selective interaction, and misperception in congruent interpersonal relation', *Sociometry* 25: 321–55.

Bakan, D. (1966) *The Duality of Human Existence*, Chicago: Rand McNally.

Bales, R.F. (1950) *Interaction Process Analysis: A Method for the Study of Small Groups*, Reading, Mass.: Addison-Wesley.

Ball, P., Giles, H., Byrne, J.L., and Berechree, P. (1984) 'Situational constraints on the evaluative significance of speech accommodation: some Australian data', *International Journal of the Sociology of Language* 46: 115–29.

Ball, P., Giles, H., and Hewstone, M. (1984) 'Second language acquisition: the intergroup theory with catastrophic dimensions', in H. Tajfel (ed.) *The Social Dimension: European Developments in Social Psychology*, vol. 2, Cambridge: Cambridge University Press.

Bandura, A. (1977) *Social Learning Theory*, Englewood-Cliffs, NJ: Prentice-Hall.

Banuazizi, A. and Movahedi, S. (1975) 'Interpersonal dynamics in a simulated prison: a methodological analysis', *American Psychologist* 30: 152–60.

Barber, T.X. (1973) 'Experimental hypnosis', in B.B. Wolman (ed.), *Handbook of General Psychology*, Englewood-Cliffs, NJ: Prentice-Hall.

Barlow, J.A. (1981) 'Mass line leadership and thought reform in China', *American Psychologist* 36: 300–9.

Barocas, R. and Gorlow, L. (1967) 'Self-report personality measurement and conformity behaviour', *Journal of Social Psychology* 71: 227–34.

Baron, R.A. and Ransberger, V.M. (1978) 'Ambient temperature and the occurrence of collective violence: the "long hot summer" revisited', *Journal of Personality and Social Psychology* 36: 351–60.

Barron, F. (1953) 'Some personality correlates of independence of judgment', *Journal of Personality* 21: 287–97.

Bartlett, F.C. (1932) *Remembering*, Cambridge: Cambridge University Press.

Bass, B.M. (1981) *Stogdill's Handbook of Leadership*, New York: Free Press.

Bauman, Z. (1978) *Hermeneutics and Social Science: Approaches to Understanding*, London: Hutchinson.

Baumeister, R.F. (1982) 'A self-presentational view of social phenomena', *Psychological Bulletin* 91: 3–26.

Baumeister, R.F. (1986) *Identity: Cultural Change and the Struggle for Self*, New York and Oxford: Oxford University Press.

Baumeister, R.F., Cooper, J., and Skib, B.A. (1979) 'Inferior performance as a selective response to expectancy: taking a dive to make a point', *Journal of Personality and Social Psychology* 37: 424–32.

Becker, H.S. (1963) *Outsiders*, New York: Free Press.

Beebe, L.M. and Giles, H. (1984) 'Speech accommodation theories: a discussion in terms of second language acquisition', *International Journal of the Sociology of Language* 46: 5–32.

Bem, S.L. (1981) 'Gender schema theory: a cognitive account of sex-typing', *Psychological Review* 88: 354–64.

Benedict, R. (1935) *Patterns of Culture*, London: Routledge & Kegan Paul.

Berger, P.L. and Luckmann, T. (1971) *The Social Construction of Reality*, Harmondsworth: Penguin.

Bergum, B.O. and Lehr, D.J. (1963) 'Effects of authoritarianism on vigilance performance', *Journal of Applied Psychology* 47: 75–7.

Berkowitz, L. (1954) 'Group standards, cohesiveness, and productivity', *Human Relations* 7: 509–19.

Berkowitz, L. (1962) *Aggression: A Social Psychological Analysis*, New York: McGraw-Hill.

Berkowitz, L. (1965) 'The concept of aggressive drive', *Advances in Experimental Social Psychology* 2: 301–29.

Berkowitz, L. (1972) 'Frustrations, comparisons, and other sources of emotion arousal as contributors to social unrest', *Journal of Social Issues* 28: 77–91.

Berkowitz, L. (1974) 'Some determinants of impulsive aggression: role of mediated associations with reinforcements for aggression', *Psychological Review* 81: 165–76.

Berkowitz, L. (1982) 'Aversive conditions as stimuli to aggression', *Advances in Experimental Social Psychology* 15: 249–88.

Berkowitz, L. and Le Page, A. (1967) 'Weapons as aggression-eliciting stimuli', *Journal of Personality and Social Psychology* 7: 202–7.

Berkowitz, L. and Walster, E. (eds) (1976) *Equity Theory: Toward a General Theory of Social Interaction*, vol. 9 of *Advances in Experimental Social Psychology*, New York: Academic Press.

Berlyne, D.E. (1979) 'Arousal: drive as an energizing factor', *Motivation and Emotion* 1(2): whole issue.

Bernstein, B. (1971) *Class, Codes and Control (Vol. 1): Theoretical Studies Towards a Sociology of Language*, London: Routledge & Kegan Paul.

Bernstein, M. and Crosby, F. (1980) 'An empirical examination of relative deprivation theory', *Journal of Experimental Social Psychology* 16: 442–56.

Berscheid, E. and Walster, E.H. (1978) *Interpersonal Attraction*, second edition, Reading, Mass.: Addison-Wesley.

Beynon, H. (1975) *Working for Ford*, London: English Universities Press.

Bierly, M.M. (1985) 'Prejudice toward contemporary outgroups as a generalized attitude', *Journal of Applied Social Psychology* 15: 189–99.

Billig, M. (1973) 'Normative communication in a minimal intergroup situation', *European Journal of Social Psychology* 3: 339–43.

Billig, M. (1976) *Social Psychology and Intergroup Relations*, London: Academic Press.

Billig, M. (1982) *Ideology and Social Psychology: Extremism, Moderation and Contradiction*, Oxford: Blackwell.

Billig, M. (1984) 'Political ideology: social psychological aspects', in H. Tajfel (ed.) *The Social Dimension: European Developments in Social Psychology*, vol. 2, Cambridge: Cambridge University Press.

Billig, M. (1985) 'Prejudice, categorization and particularization: from a perceptual to a rhetorical approach', *European Journal of Social Psychology* 15: 79–103.

Billig, M. and Tajfel, H. (1973) 'Social categorization and similarity in intergroup behaviour', *European Journal of Social Psychology* 3: 27–52.

Birdwhistle, R.L. (1974) 'The language of the body: the natural environment of words', in A. Silverstern (ed.) *Human Communications: Theoretical Explanations*, New York: Wiley.

Blake, R.R., Helson, H., and Mouton, J.S. (1956) 'The generality of conformity behaviour as a function of factual anchorage, difficulty of task and amount of social pressure', *Journal of Personality* 25: 294–305.

Blake, R.R. and Mouton, J.S. (1961) 'Reactions to intergroup competition under win/lose conditions', *Management Science* 7: 420–35.

Blake, R.R. and Mouton, J.S. (1962) 'The intergroup dynamics of win/lose conflict and problem solving collaboration in union–management relations', in M. Sherif (ed.) *Intergroup Relations and Leadership*, New York: Wiley.

Blakey, D. (1979) 'Affadavit re: the threat and possibility of mass suicide by members of the People's Temple', in report of a staff investigative group to the committee on Foreign Affairs, US House of Representatives, 15 May 1979, *The Assassination of Representative Leo J. Ryan and the Jonestown Guyana Tragedy*, Washington, DC:

Government Printing Office.

Blau, P.M. (1962) 'Patterns of choice in interpersonal relations', *American Sociological Review* 27: 41–55.

Bloom, L. (1970) *Language Development: Form and Function in Emerging Grammars*, Cambridge, Mass.: MIT Press.

Blumberg, H., Hare, P., Kent, V., and Davies, M. (eds) (1983) *Small Groups and Social Interaction*, New York: Wiley.

Bobo, L. (1983) 'Whites' opposition to busing: symbolic racism or realistic group conflict', *Journal of Personality and Social Psychology* 45: 1196–210.

Bolinger, D. (1975) *Aspects of Language*, 2nd edn, New York: Harcourt Brace Jovanovich.

Bond, C.F. (1982) 'Social facilitation: a self-presentational view', *Journal of Personality and Social Psychology* 42: 1042–50.

Bond, C.F. and Titus, L.J. (1983) 'Social facilitation: a meta-analysis of 241 studies', *Psychological Bulletin* 94: 265–92.

Bonner, H. (1959) *Group Dynamics: Principles and Applications*, New York: Ronald Press.

Borden, R.J. (1975) 'Witnessed aggregation: influence of an observer's sex and values on aggressive responding', *Journal of Personality and Social Psychology* 31: 567–73.

Borden, R.J. (1980) 'Audience influence', in P.B. Paulus (ed.) *Psychology of Group Influence*, Hillsdale, NJ: Erlbaum.

Borgida, E., Locksley, A., and Brekke, N. (1981) 'Social stereotypes and social judgment', in N. Cantor and J.F. Kihlstrom (eds) *Personality, Cognition and Social Interaction*, Hillsdale, NJ: Erlbaum.

Bornstein, G., Crum, L., Wittenbraker, J., Harring, K., Insko, C.A., and Thibaut, J. (1983) 'On the measurement of social orientations in the minimal group paradigm', *European Journal of Social Psychology* 13: 321–50.

Bourhis, R.Y. (1979) 'Language in ethnic interaction: a social psychological approach', in H. Giles and B. Saint-Jacques (eds) *Language and Ethnic Relations*, Oxford: Pergamon Press.

Bourhis, R.Y. and Genesee, F. (1980) 'Evaluation reactions to code switching strategies in Montreal', in H. Giles, W.P. Robinson, and P.M. Smith (eds) *Language: Social Psychological Perspectives*, Oxford: Pergamon Press.

Bourhis, R.Y., Giles, H., and Lambert, W.E. (1975) 'Social consequences of accommodating one's style of speech: a cross-national investigation', *International Journal of the Sociology of Language* 6: 53–71.

Bourhis, R.Y., Giles, H., Leyens, J.-P., and Tajfel, H. (1979) 'Psycholinguistic distinctiveness: language divergence in Belgium', in H. Giles and R.N. St Clair (eds) *Language and Social Psychology*, Oxford: Blackwell.

Bourhis, R.Y., Giles, H., and Rosenthal, D. (1981) 'Notes on the construction of a "Subjective Vitality Questionnaire" for ethnolinguistic groups', *Journal of Multilingual and Multicultural Development* 2: 144–55.

Bourhis, R.Y. and Hill, P. (1982) 'Intergroup perceptions in British higher education: a field study', in H. Tajfel (ed.) *Social Identity and Intergroup Relations*, Cambridge: Cambridge University Press.

Bovard, E.W. (1951) 'Group structure and perception', *Journal of Abnormal and Social Psychology* 46: 398–405.

Brandstätter, H. (1978) 'Social emotions in discussion groups', in H. Brandstätter, J.H. Davis, and H. Schuler (eds) *Dynamics of Group Decisions*, Beverly Hills, Calif.: Sage.

Branthwaite, A., Doyle, S., and Lightbown, N. (1979) 'The balance between fairness and discrimination', *European Journal of Social Psychology* 9: 149–63.

Breakwell, G. (1979) 'Woman: Group and identity?', *Women's Studies International*

Quarterly 2: 9–17.

Brehm, J.W. (1966) *A Theory of Psychological Reactance*, New York: Academic Press.

Brewer, M.B. and Kramer, R.M. (1985) 'The psychology of intergroup attitudes and behaviour', *Annual Review of Psychology* 36: 219–43.

Brewer, M.B. and Silver, M. (1978) 'Ingroup bias as a function of task characteristics', *European Journal of Social Psychology* 8: 393–400.

Brigham, J.C. (1971) 'Ethnic stereotypes', *Psychological Bulletin* 76: 15–38.

Brogan, H. (1973) *Tocqueville*, London: Fontana.

Brown, R. (1965) *Social Psychology*, New York: Free Press.

Brown, R. (1986) *Social Psychology*, 2nd edn, New York: Free Press.

Brown, R.J. (1978) 'Divided we fall: an analysis of relations between a factory workforce', in H. Tajfel (ed.) *Differentiation Between Social Groups*, London: Academic Press.

Brown, R.J. (1984a) 'The effects of intergroup similarity and cooperative *vs* competitive orientation on intergroup discrimination', *British Journal of Social Psychology* 23: 21–33.

Brown, R.J. (1984b) 'The role of similarity in intergroup relations', in H. Tajfel (ed.) *The Social Dimension: European Developments in Social Psychology*, Cambridge: Cambridge University Press.

Brown, R.J. and Abrams, D. (1986) 'The effects of intergroup similarity and goal interdependence on intergroup attitudes and task performance', *Journal of Experimental Social Psychology* 22: 78–92.

Brown, R.J. and Ross, G.F. (1982) 'The battle for acceptance: an investigation into the dynamics of intergroup behaviour', in H. Tajfel (ed.) *Social Identity and Intergroup Relations*, Cambridge: Cambridge University Press.

Brown, R.J. and Turner, J.C. (1981) 'Interpersonal and intergroup behaviour', in J.C. Turner and H. Giles (eds) *Intergroup Behaviour*, Oxford: Blackwell.

Brown, R.J. and Williams, J.A. (1984) 'Group identification: the same thing to all people?', *Human Relations* 37: 547–64.

Bruner, J.S. (1951) 'Personality dynamics and the process of perceiving', in R.R. Blake and G.V. Ramsay (eds) *Perception: An Approach to Personality*, New York: Ronald.

Bruner, J.S. (1957) 'On perceptual readiness', *Psychological Review* 64: 123–52.

Bruner, J.S. (1958) 'Social psychology and perception', in E.E. Maccoby, T.M. Newcomb, and E.L. Hartley (eds) *Readings in Social Psychology*, New York: Holt, Rinhart & Winston.

Bruner, J.S. and Goodman, C.C. (1947) 'Value and need as organizing factors in perception', *Journal of Abnormal and Social Psychology* 42: 33–44.

Bruner, J.S., Goodnow, J.L., and Austin, G.A. (1956) *A Study of Thinking*, New York: Wiley.

Burke, K. (1962) *A Grammar of Motives and a Rhetoric of Motives*, Cleveland, Ohio: World.

Burns, R. (1979) *The Self-Concept*, London: Longman.

Burnstein, E. and Vinokur, A. (1977) 'Persuasive argumentation and social comparison as determinants of attitude polarization', *Journal of Experimental Social Psychology* 13: 315–32.

Buss, A.H. (1980) *Self-Consciousness and Social Anxiety*, San Francisco: Freeman.

Buss, A.R. (1978) 'Causes and reasons in attribution theory: a conceptual critique', *Journal of Personality and Social Psychology* 36: 1311–321.

Byrne, D. (1969) 'Attitudes and attraction', *Advances in Experimental Social Psychology* 4: 35–89.

Byrne, D. (1971) *The Attraction Paradigm*, New York: Academic Press.

Byrne, D. and Wong, T.J. (1962) 'Racial prejudice, interpersonal attraction, and assumed dissimilarity of attitudes', *Journal of Abnormal and Social Psychology* 65: 246–52.

Caddick, B. (1981) 'Equity theory, social identity and intergroup relations', in L. Wheeler (ed.) *Review of Personality and Social Psychology*, vol. 2, London: Sage.

Caddick, B. (1982) 'Perceived illegitimacy and intergroup relations', in H. Tajfel (ed.) *Social Identity and Intergroup Relations*, Cambridge: Cambridge University Press.

Cairns, E. (1982) 'Intergroup conflict in Northern Ireland', in H. Tajfel (ed.) *Social Identity and Intergroup Relations*, Cambridge: Cambridge University Press.

Cairns, E. and Mercer, G.W. (1984) 'Social identity in Northern Ireland', *Human Relations* 37: 1095–102.

Campbell, A. (1971) *White Attitudes Toward Black People*, Ann Arbor, Mich.: Institute for Social Research.

Campbell, D.T. (1957) 'Factors relevant to the validity of experiments in social settings', *Psychological Bulletin* 54: 297–312.

Cannavale, F.J., Scarr, H.A., and Pepitone, A. (1970) 'Deindividuation in the small group: further evidence', *Journal of Personality and Social Psychology* 16: 141–7.

Cantor, N. (1981) 'A cognitive-social approach to personality', in N. Cantor and J.F. Kihlstrom (eds) *Personality, Cognition, and Social Interaction*, Hillsdale, NJ: Erlbaum.

Cantor, N. and Mischel, W. (1979) 'Prototypes in person perception', *Advances in Experimental Social Psychology* 12: 3–51.

Cantor, N., Mischel, W., and Schwartz, J. (1982) 'Social knowledge: structure, content, use and abuse', in A.H. Hastorf and A.M. Isen (eds) *Cognitive Social Psychology*, New York: Elsevier.

Cantril, H. (1941) *The Psychology of Social Movements*, New York: Wiley.

Caplan, N. (1970) 'The new ghetto man: a review of recent empirical studies', *Journal of Social Issues* 26: 59–73.

Caprara, G.V., Renzi, P., Amolini, P., d'Imperio, G., and Travaglia, G. (1984) 'The eliciting cue value of aggressive slides reconsidered in a personological perspective: the weapons effect and irritability', *European Journal of Social Psychology* 14: 313–22.

Carswell, E.A. and Rommetveit, R. (eds) (1972) *Social Contexts of Messages*, London: Academic Press.

Cartwright, D. (1968) 'The nature of group cohesiveness', in D. Cartwright and A. Zander (eds) *Group Dynamics: Research and Theory*, 3rd edn, London: Tavistock.

Cartwright, D. (1979) 'Contemporary social psychology in historical perspective', *Social Psychology Quarterly* 42: 82–93.

Cartwright, D. and Zander, A. (eds) (1968) *Group Dynamics: Research and Theory*, 3rd edn, London: Tavistock.

Carver, C.S. (1974) 'Facilitation of physical aggression through objective self-awareness', *Journal of Experimental Social Psychology* 10: 365–70.

Carver, C.S. (1979) 'A cybernetic model of self-attention processes', *Journal of Personality and Social Psychology* 37: 1251–81.

Carver, C.S. and Humphries, C. (1981) 'Havana daydream: a study of self-consciousness and the negative reference group among Cuban Americans', *Journal of Personality and Social Psychology* 40: 545–52.

Carver, C.S. and Scheier, M.F. (1978) 'The self-focusing effects of dispositional self-consciousness, mirror presence and audience presence', *Journal of Personality and Social Psychology* 36: 324–32.

Carver, C.S. and Scheier, M.F. (1981a) *Attention and Self-Regulation: A Control-Theory Approach to Human Behaviour*, New York: Springer-Verlag.

Carver, C.S. and Scheier, M.F. (1981b) 'A control systems approach to behavioural self-regulation', in L. Wheeler (ed.) *Review of Personality and Social Psychology*, vol. 2, London: Sage.

Charters, W.W.Jnr and Newcomb, T.M. (1952) 'Some attitudinal effects of experimentally increased salience of a membership group', in G.E. Swanson, T.M. Newcomb, and E.L. Hartley (eds) *Readings in Social Psychology*, New York: Holt.

Chomsky, N. (1957) *Syntactic Structures*, The Hague: Mouton.

Cialdini, R.B., Borden, R.J., Thorne, A., Walker, M.R., Freeman, S., and Sloan, L.R. (1976) 'Basking in reflected glory: three (football) field studies', *Journal of Personality and Social Psychology* 34: 366–75.

Cialdini, R.B., Cacioppo, J.T., Bassett, R., and Miller, J.A. (1978) 'The low-ball procedure for producing compliance: commitment then costs', *Journal of Personality and Social Psychology* 36: 463–76.

Cialdini, R.B., Petty, R.E. and Cacioppo, J.T. (1981) 'Attitude and attitude change', *Annual Review of Psychology* 32: 357–404.

Clark, H.H. and Clark, E.V. (1977) *Psychology and Language: An Introduction to Psycholinguistics*, New York: Harcourt Brace Jovanovich.

Clément, R. (1980) 'Ethnicity, contact and communicative competence in second language', in H. Giles, W.P. Robinson, and P.M. Smith (eds) *Language: Social Psychological Perspectives*, Oxford: Pergamon Press.

Clyne, M.G. (1981) '"Second generation" foreigner talk in Australia', *International Journal of the Sociology of Language* 28: 69–80.

Clyne, M.G. (1985) *Multilingual Australia*, 2nd edn, Melbourne: River Seine.

Coch, L. and French, J.R.P.Jnr (1948) 'Overcoming resistance to change', *Human Relations* 1: 512–32.

Codol, J.-P. (1975) 'On the so-called "superior conformity of the self" behaviour: twenty experimental investigations', *European Journal of Social Psychology* 5: 457–501.

Cohen, A.I. (1981) 'Group cohesion and communal living', in H. Kellerman (ed.) *Group Cohesion: Theoretical and Clinical Perspectives*, New York: Grune & Stratton.

Cohn, T.S. (1953) 'The relation of the F-scale to a response to answer positively', *American Psychologist* 8: 335.

Comte, A. (1877) *A General View of Positivism*, trans. J.H. Bridges, London: Routledge.

Condor, S.G. (1984) 'Womanhood as an aspect of social identity', University of Bristol, unpublished doctoral dissertation.

Condor, S.G. (1986) 'Sex role beliefs and "traditional" women: feminist and intergroup perspectives' in S. Wilkinson (ed.) *Feminist Social Psychology: Developing Theory and Practice*, Milton Keynes: Open University Press.

Condor, S.G. and Brown, R.J. (1986) 'Psychological processes in intergroup conflict', in W. Stroebe, A. Kruglanski, D. Bar-Tal, and M. Hewstone (eds) *The Social Psychology of Intergroup and International Conflict: Theory, Research and Application*, New York: Springer.

Condor, S.G. and Henwood, K.L. (1986) 'Stereotypes and social context', manuscript submitted for publication, University of Lancaster.

Cook, T.D., Crosby, F., and Hennigan, K.M. (1977) 'The construct validity of relative deprivation', in J.M. Suls and R.L. Miller (eds) *Social Comparison Processes*, Washington, DC: Hemisphere.

Cooley, C.H. (1902) *Human Nature and the Social Order*, New York: Schocken Books.

Cooper, J. and Croyle, R.T. (1984) 'Attitudes and attitude change', *Annual Review of Psychology* 35: 395–426.

Corder, S.P. (1981) *Error Analysis and Interlanguage*, Oxford: Oxford University Press.

Costanzo, P.R. (1970) 'Conformity development as a function of self-blame', *Journal of Personality and Social Psychology* 14: 366–74.

Cottrell, N.B. (1972) 'Social facilitation', in C.G. McClintock (ed.) *Experimental Social Psychology*, New York: Holt, Rinehart & Winston.

Cottrell, N.B., Wack, D.L., Sekerak, G.J., and Rittle, R.H. (1968) 'Social facilitation of dominant responses by the presence of others', *Journal of Personality and Social Psychology* 9: 245–50.

Couch, A. and Keniston, K. (1960) 'Yeasayers and naysayers: agreeing response set as a personality variable', *Journal of Abnormal and Social Psychology* 60: 151–74.

Crocker, J., Thompson, L.J., McGraw, K.M., and Ingerman, C. (1987) 'Downward comparison, prejudice, and evaluations of others: effects of self-esteem and threat', *Journal of Personality and Social Psychology* 52: 907–17.

Crook, J.H. (1980) *The Evolution of Human Consciousness*, Oxford: Clarendon Press.

Crosbie, P.V. (ed.) (1975) *Interaction in Small Groups*, New York: Macmillan.

Crosby, F. (1976) 'A model of egoistic relative deprivation', *Psychological Review* 83: 85–113.

Crosby, F. (1982) *Relative Deprivation and Working Women*, New York: Oxford University Press.

Crosby, F. (1984) 'Relative deprivation in organizational settings', *Research in Organizational Behaviour* 6: 51–93.

Crowne, D.P. and Liverant, S. (1963) 'Conformity under varying conditions of personal commitment', *Journal of Abnormal and Social Psychology* 66: 547–55.

Crutchfield, R.S. (1955) 'Conformity and character', *American Psychologist* 10: 191–8.

Cuff, E.C. and Payne, G.C.F. (eds) (1984) *Perspectives in Sociology*, 2nd edn, London: Allen & Unwin.

Davies, J.C. (1980) 'Biological perspectives on human conflict', in T.R. Gurr (ed.) *Handbook of Political Conflict*, New York: Free Press.

Davis, J.A. (1959) 'A formal interpretation of the theory of relative deprivation', *Sociometry* 22: 280–96.

Deaux, K. (1976) 'Sex: a perspective on the attribution process', in J.H. Harvey, W.J. Ickes, and R.F. Kidd (eds) *New Directions in Attribution Research*, vol. 1, Hillsdale, NJ: Erlbaum.

Deaux, K. (1985) 'Sex and gender', *Annual Review of Psychology* 36: 49–81.

Deaux, K. and Wrightsman, L.S. (1984) *Social Psychology in the 80s*, 4th edn, Monterey, Calif.: Brooks-Cole.

DeCharms, R. and Rosenbaum, M.E. (1957) 'The problem of vicarious experience', in D. Willner (ed.) *Decisions, Values, and Groups*, Elmsford, NY: Pergamon.

Deconchy, J.-P. (1984) 'Rationality and social control in orthodox systems', in H. Tajfel (ed.) *The Social Dimension: European Developments in Social Psychology*, vol. 2, Cambridge: Cambridge University Press.

de Saussure, F. (1955) *Cours de linguistique générale*, Paris: Payot.

Deschamps, J.-C. (1973–4) 'L'attribution, la catégorisation sociale et les représentations intergroupes', *Bulletin de Psychologie* 27: 710–21.

Deschamps, J.-C. (1977) 'Effect of crossing category membership on quantitative judgement', *European Journal of Social Psychology* 7: 122–6.

Deschamps, J.-C. (1982) 'Social identity and relations of power between groups', in H. Tajfel (ed.) *Social Identity and Intergroup Relations*, Cambridge: Cambridge University Press.

Deschamps, J.-C. (1983) 'Social attribution', in J. Jaspars, F.D. Fincham, and M. Hewstone (eds) *Attribution Theory and Research: Conceptual, Developmental and Social Dimensions*, London: Academic Press.

Deschamps, J.-C. (1984) 'Intergroup relations and categorical identification', in H.

Tajfel (ed.) *The Social Dimension: European Developments in Social Psychology*, vol. 2, Cambridge: Cambridge University Press.

Deschamps, J.-C. and Doise, W. (1978) 'Crossed category memberships in intergroup relations', in H. Tajfel (ed.) *Differentiation Between Social Groups*, London: Academic Press.

Deutsch, M. (1949) 'A theory of co-operation and competition', *Human Relations 2*: 129–52.

Deutsch, M. (1973) *The Resolution of Conflict*, New Haven, Conn.: Yale University Press.

Deutsch, M. and Gerard, H.B. (1955) 'A study of normative and informational influences upon individual judgment', *Journal of Abnormal and Social Psychology 51*: 629–36.

Diener, E. (1976) 'Effects of prior destructive behaviour, anonymity and group presence on deindividuation and aggression', *Journal of Personality and Social Psychology 33*: 497–507.

Diener, E. (1979) 'Deindividuation, self-awareness and disinhibition', *Journal of Personality and Social Psychology 37*: 1160–71.

Diener, E. (1980) 'Deindividuation: the absence of self-awareness and self-regulation in group members', in P.B. Paulus (ed.) *Psychology of Group Influence*, Hillsdale, NJ: Erlbaum.

Diener, E., Fraser, S.C., Beaman, A.L., and Kelem, R.T. (1976) 'Effects of deindividuation variables on stealing by Halloween trick-or-treaters', *Journal of Personality and Social Psychology 33*: 178–83.

Diener, E., Lusk, R., DeFour, D., and Flax, R. (1980) 'Deindividuation: effects of group size, density, number of observers, and group member similarity on self-consciousness and disinhibited behaviour', *Journal of Personality and Social Psychology 39*: 449–59.

Diener, E. and Srull, T.K. (1979) 'Self-awareness, psychological perspective and self-reinforcement in relation to personal and social standards', *Journal of Personality and Social Psychology 37*: 413–23.

Diener, E. and Wallbom, M. (1976) 'Effects of self-awareness on antinormative behaviour', *Journal of Research in Personality 10*: 107–11.

Dion, K.L., Miller, N., and Magnan, M.A. (1971) 'Cohesiveness and social responsibility as determinants of group risk taking', *Journal of Personality and Social Psychology 20*: 400–6.

Dipboye, R.L. (1977) 'Alternative approaches to deindividuation', *Psychological Bulletin 84*: 1057–75.

di Pietro, R.J. (1978) 'Culture and ethnicity in the bilingual classroom' in J.E. Alatis (ed.) *International Dimensions of Bilingual Education*, Washington, DC: Georgetown University Press.

Doise, W. (1969) 'Intergroup relations and the polarization of individual and collective judgements', *Journal of Personality and Social Psychology 12*: 136–43.

Doise, W. (1978) *Groups and Individuals: Explanations in Social Psychology*, Cambridge: Cambridge University Press.

Doise, W. (1982) 'Report on the European Association of Experimental Social Psychology', *European Journal of Social Psychology 12*: 105–11.

Doise, W. (1986) *Levels of Explanation in Social Psychology*, Cambridge: Cambridge University Press.

Doise, W., Csepeli, G., Dann, H.D., Gouge, C., Larsen, K., and Ostell, A. (1972) 'An experimental investigation into the formation of intergroup representations', *European Journal of Social Psychology 2*: 202–4.

Doise, W. and Dann, H.D. (1976) 'New theoretical perspectives in the experimental study of intergroup relations', *Italian Journal of Psychology 3*: 285–303.

Doise, W., Deschamps, J.-C., and Meyer, G. (1978) 'The accentuation of intra-category similarities', in H. Tajfel (ed.) *Differentiation Between Social Groups*, London: Academic Press.

Doise, W. and Sinclair, A. (1973) 'The categorization process in intergroup relations', *European Journal of Social Psychology* 3: 145–57.

Doise, W. and Weinberger, M. (1973) 'Représentations masculines dans différentes situations de rencontre mixtes', *Bulletin de Psychologie* 26: 649–57.

Dollard, J., Doob, L.W., Miller, N.E., Mowrer, O.H., and Sears, R.R. (1939) *Frustration and Aggression*, New Haven, Conn.: Yale University Press.

Donnerstein, E., Donnerstein, M., Simon, S., and Ditrichs, R. (1972) 'Variables in inter-racial aggression: anonymity, expected retaliation and a riot', *Journal of Personality and Social Psychology* 22: 236–45.

Douglas, A. (1957) 'The peaceful settlement of industrial and intergroup disputes', *Journal of Conflict Resolution* 1: 69–81.

Douglas, A. (1962) *Industrial Peacemaking*, New York: Columbia University.

Downing, J. (1958) 'Cohesiveness, perception and values', *Human Relations* 11: 157–66.

Druckman, D. (1978) 'Boundary role conflict: negotiation as dual responsiveness' in I.W. Zartman (ed.) *The Negotiation Process: Theories and Applications*, London: Sage.

Duck, S.W. (1973a) 'Similarity and perceived similarity of personal constructs as influences on friendship choice', *British Journal of Social and Clinical Psychology* 12: 1–6.

Duck, S.W. (1973b) *Personal Relationships and Personal Constructs: A Study of Friendship Formation*, London: Wiley.

Duck, S.W. (1977a) *The Study of Acquaintance*, Farnborough, Hants.: Saxon House.

Duck, S.W. (1977b) *Theory and Practice in Inter-personal Attraction*, London: Academic Press.

Duck, S.W. (1977c) 'Inquiry, hypothesis, and the quest for validation: personal construct systems in the development of acquaintance', in S.W. Duck (ed.) *Theory and Practice in Interpersonal Attraction*, London: Academic Press.

Duck, S. and Gilmour, R. (eds) (1981) *Personal Relationships (Vol 1): Studying Personal Relationships*, London: Academic Press.

Duckitt, J. (1983) 'Culture, class, personality, and authoritarianism among white South Africans', *Journal of Social Psychology* 121: 191–9.

Dunn, J. (1984) 'Early social interaction and the development of emotional understanding' in H. Tajfel (ed.) *The Social Dimension: European Developments in Social Psychology*, vol. 1, Cambridge: Cambridge University Press.

Durkheim, E. (1933) *The Division of Labour in Society*, trans. G. Simpson, New York: Macmillan (first published in 1893).

Duval, S. (1976) 'Conformity on a visual task as a function of personal novelty on attitudinal dimensions and being reminded of the object status of self', *Journal of Experimental Social Psychology* 12: 87–98.

Duval, S. and Hensley, V. (1976) 'Extensions of objective self-awareness theory: the focus of attention-causal attribution hypothesis', in J.H. Harvey, W.J. Ickes, and R.F. Kidd (eds) *New Directions in Attribution Research*, vol. 1, Hillsdale, NJ: Erlbaum.

Duval, S. and Wicklund, R.A. (1972) *A Theory of Objective Self-Awareness*, New York: Academic Press.

Eagly, A.H. (1978) 'Sex differences in influenceability', *Psychological Bulletin* 85: 86–116.

Eagly, A.H. and Himelfarb, S. (1978) 'Attitudes and opinions', *Annual Review of Psychology* 29: 517–54.

Eckstein, H. (1980) 'Theoretical approaches to explaining collective political violence', in T.R. Gurr (ed.) *Handbook of Political Conflict*, New York: Free Press.

Edmonds, V. (1964) 'Logical error as a function of group consensus: an experimental study of the effect of erroneous group consensus upon the logical judgments of graduate students', *Social Forces* 43: 33–8.

Edwards, J. (1979) *Language and Disadvantage*, London: Edward Arnold.

Edwards, J. (1985) *Language, Society and Identity*, Oxford: Blackwell.

Eiser, J.R. (1980) *Cognitive Social Psychology*, London: McGraw-Hill.

Eiser, J.R. (1983) 'Attribution theory and social cognition', in J. Jaspars, F.D. Fincham, and M. Hewstone (eds) *Attribution Theory and Research: Conceptual, Developmental and Social Dimensions*, London: Academic Press.

Eiser, J.R. (1986) *Social Psychology: Attitudes, Cognition and Social Behaviour*, Cambridge: Cambridge University Press.

Eiser, J.R. and Stroebe, W. (1972) *Categorization and Social Judgement*, London: Academic Press.

Eiser, J.R. and van der Pligt, J. (1984) 'Attitudes in a social context', in H. Tajfel (ed.) *The Social Dimension: European Developments in Social Psychology*, vol. 2, Cambridge: Cambridge University Press.

Eisman, B. (1959) 'Some operational measures of cohesiveness and their interrelations', *Human Relations* 12: 183–9.

Elliot, A.J. (1981) *Child Language*, Cambridge: Cambridge University Press.

Elms, A.C. (1975) 'The crisis of confidence in social psychology', *American Psychologist* 30: 967–76.

Elms, A.C. and Milgram, S. (1966) 'Personality characteristics associated with obedience and defiance toward authoritative command', *Journal of Experimental Research in Personality* 1: 282–9.

Emler, N.P. (1984) 'Differential involvement in delinquency: toward an interpretation in terms of reputation management', in B.A. Maher and W.B. Maher (eds) *Progress in Experimental Personality Research*, vol. 13, New York: Academic Press.

Erikson, E. (1959) *Identity and the Life Cycle*, New York: International Universities Press.

Ervin-Tripp, S.M. (1969) 'Sociolinguistics', *Advances in Experimental Social Psychology* 4: 91–165.

Espinoza, J.A. and Garza, R.T. (1985) 'Social group salience and interethnic cooperation', *Journal of Experimental Social Psychology* 21: 380–92.

Exline, R.V. (1957) 'Group climate as a factor in the relevance and accuracy of social perception', *Journal of Abnormal and Social Psychology* 55: 382–8.

Exner, J.E. (1973) 'The self-focus sentence completion: a study of egocentricity', *Journal of Personality Assessment* 37: 437–55.

Eysenck, H.J. (1954) *The Psychology of Politics*, London: Routledge & Kegan Paul.

Farr, R.M. (1980) 'Homo loquens in social psychology', in H. Giles, W.P. Robinson and P.M. Smith (eds) *Language: Social Psychological Perspectives*, Oxford: Pergamon Press.

Farr, R.M. and Moscovici, S. (eds) (1984) *Social Representations*, Cambridge: Cambridge University Press.

Fellman, J. (1974) 'The academy of the Hebrew language', *International Journal of the Sociology of Language* 1: 95–103.

Fenigstein, A., Scheier, M.F., and Buss, A.H. (1975) 'Public and private self-consciousness: assessment and theory', *Journal of Consulting and Clinical Psychology* 43: 522–7.

Ferguson, C.K. and Kelley, H.H. (1964) 'Significant factors in over-evaluation of own groups' products', *Journal of Abnormal and Social Psychology* 69: 223–8.

Festinger, L. (1950) 'Informal social communication', *Psychological Review* 57:

271–82.

Festinger, L. (1954) 'A theory of social comparison processes', *Human Relations* 7: 117–40.

Festinger, L. (1957) *The Theory of Cognitive Dissonance*, Stanford, Calif.: Stanford University Press.

Festinger, L. (1980) 'Looking backwards', in L. Festinger (ed.) *Retrospections on Social Psychology*, New York: Oxford University Press.

Festinger, L., Pepitone, A., and Newcomb, T. (1952) 'Some consequences of deindividuation in a group', *Journal of Abnormal and Social Psychology* 47: 382–9.

Festinger, L., Schachter, S., and Back, K. (1950) *Social Pressures in Informal Groups*, New York: Harper & Row.

Fiedler, F.E. (1971) *Leadership*, New York: General Learning Press.

Fiedler, F.E., Chemers, M.M., and Mahar, L. (1976) *Improving Leadership Effectiveness: The Leader Match Concept*, New York: Wiley.

Fiedler, F.E., Warrington, W.G., and Blaisdell, F.J. (1952) 'Unconscious attitudes as correlates of sociometric choice in a social group', *Journal of Abnormal and Social Psychology* 47: 790–6.

Fine, M. and Bowers, C. (1984) 'Racial self-identification: the effects of social history and gender', *Journal of Applied Social Psychology* 14: 136–46.

Firestone, S. (1970) *The Dialectic of Sex: The Case for Feminist Revolution*, London: The Women's Press.

Fishman, J.A. (1968) *Language Loyalty in the United States*, The Hague: Mouton.

Fishman, J.A. (1972) *The Sociology of Language*, Rowley, Mass.: Newbury House.

Fiske, S.T. and Taylor, S.E. (1984) *Social Cognition*, Reading, Mass.: Addison-Wesley.

Flowers, M.L. (1977) 'A laboratory test of some implications of Janis' group-think hypothesis', *Journal of Personality and Social Psychology* 35: 888–96.

Folger, R., Rosenfield, D., Rheaume, K., and Martin, C. (1983) 'Relative deprivation and referent cognitions', *Journal of Experimental Social Psychology* 19: 172–84.

Forgas, J.P. (ed.) (1981) *Social Cognition: Perspectives on Everyday Understanding*, London: Academic Press.

Forward, J. and Williams, J. (1970) 'Internal–external control and black militancy', *Journal of Social Issues* 26: 75–92.

French, J.R.P. (1941) 'The disruption and cohesion of groups', *Journal of Abnormal and Social Psychology* 36: 361–77.

French, J.R.P. and Raven, B.H. (1959) 'The bases of social power', in D. Cartwright (ed.) *Studies in Social Power*, Ann Arbor, Mich.: University of Michigan.

Freud, S. (1922) *Group Psychology and the Analysis of the Ego*, London: Hogarth Press.

Froming, W.J. and Carver, C.S. (1981) 'Divergent influences of private and public self-consciousness in a compliance paradigm', *Journal of Research in Personality* 15: 159–71.

Froming, W.J., Walker, G.R., and Lopyan, K.J. (1982) 'Private and public self-awareness: when personal attitudes conflict with societal expectations', *Journal of Experimental and Social Psychology* 18: 476–87.

Fromkin, H.L. (1972) 'Feelings of interpersonal undistinctiveness: an unpleasant affective state', *Journal of Experimental Research in Personality* 15: 159–71.

Fromm, E. (1941) *Escape from Freedom*, New York: Farrar & Rinehart.

Gardner, R.C. (1979) 'Social psychological aspects of second language acquisition', in H. Giles and R.N. St Clair (eds) *Language and Social Psychology*, Oxford: Blackwell.

Gardner, R.C. (1981) 'Second language learning', in R.C. Gardner and R. Kalin (eds) *A Canadian Social Psychology of Ethnic Relations*, Toronto: Methuen.

Gardner, R.C. (1982) 'Language attitudes and language learning', in E.B. Ryan and H. Giles (eds) *Attitudes Towards Language Variation: Social and Applied Contexts*, London: Edward Arnold.

Gardner, R.C. and Lambert, W.E. (1972) *Attitudes and Motivation in Second Language Learning*, Rowley, Mass.: Newbury House.

Garfinkel, H. (1967) *Studies in Ethnomethodology*, Englewood Cliffs, NJ: Prentice-Hall.

Geen, R.G. and Gange, J.J. (1977) 'Drive theory of social facilitation: twelve years of theory and research', *Psychological Bulletin* 84: 1267–88.

Gerard, H.B. and Hoyt, M.F. (1974) 'Distinctiveness of social categorization and attitude toward ingroup members', *Journal of Personality and Social Psychology* 29: 836–42.

Gergen, K.J. (1971) *The Concept of Self*, New York: Holt, Rinehart & Winston.

Gergen, K.J. (1973) 'Social psychology as history', *Journal of Personality and Social Psychology* 26: 309–20.

Gergen, K.J. (1982a) *Toward Transformation in Social Knowledge*, New York: Springer-Verlag.

Gergen, K.J. (1982b) 'From self to science: what is there to know?', in J. Suls (ed.) *Psychological Perspectives on the Self*, Hillsdale, NJ: Erlbaum.

Gergen, K.J. and Gergen, M.M. (1981) *Social Psychology*, New York: Harcourt Brace Jovanovich.

Gibbons, F.X. (1978) 'Sexual standards and reactions to pornography: enhancing behavioural consistency through self-focused attention', *Journal of Personality and Social Psychology* 36: 976–87.

Gibbons, F.X., Carver, C.S., Scheier, M.F., and Hormuth, S.E. (1979) 'Self-focussed attention and the placebo effect: fooling some of the people some of the time', *Journal of Experimental Social Psychology* 15: 263–74.

Giles, H. (ed.) (1977) *Language, Ethnicity and Intergroup Relations*, London: Academic Press.

Giles, H. (1978) 'Linguistic differentiation in ethnic groups', in H. Tajfel (ed.) *Differentiation Between Social Groups*, London: Academic Press.

Giles, H. (ed.) (1984) 'The dynamics of speech accommodation', *International Journal of the Sociology of Language* 46, whole issue.

Giles, H., Bourhis, R.Y., and Taylor, D.M. (1977) 'Towards a theory of language in ethnic group relations', in H. Giles (ed.) *Language, Ethnicity and Inter-group Relations*, London: Academic Press.

Giles, H. and Byrne, J.L. (1982) 'The intergroup model of second language acquisition', *Journal of Multilingual and Multicultural Development* 3: 17–40.

Giles, H. and Johnson, P. (1981) 'The role of language in ethnic group relations', in J.C. Turner and H. Giles (eds) *Intergroup Behaviour*, Oxford: Basil Blackwell.

Giles, H. and Powesland, P.F. (1975) *Speech Style and Social Evaluation*, London: Academic Press.

Giles, H., Robinson, W.P., and Smith, P.M. (1980a) 'Social psychological perspectives on language: prologue', in H. Giles, W.P. Robinson, and P.M. Smith (eds) *Language: Social Psychological Perspectives*, Oxford: Pergamon Press.

Giles, H., Robinson, W.P., and Smith, P.M. (eds) (1980b) *Language: Social Psychological Perspectives*, Oxford: Pergamon Press.

Giles, H. and Saint-Jacques, B. (eds) (1979) *Language and Ethnic Relations*, Oxford: Pergamon Press.

Giles, H. and Smith, P.M. (1979) 'Accommodation theory: optimal levels of convergence', in H. Giles and R.M. St Clair (eds) *Language and Social Psychology*, Oxford: Blackwell.

Giles, H., Smith, P.M., Browne, C., Whiteman, S., and Williams, J.A. (1980)

'Women speaking: the voice of feminism', in S. McConnell-Ginet, R. Borker, and N. Furman (eds) *Women and Language in Literature and Society*, New York: Praeger.

Giles, H., Smith, P.M., Ford, B., Condor, S., and Thakerar, J.N. (1980) 'Speech style and the fluctuating salience of sex', *Language Sciences* 2: 260–82.

Giles, H. and St Clair, R.N. (eds) (1979) *Language and Social Psychology*, Oxford: Blackwell.

Giles, H. and Street, R.L. (1985) 'Communicator characteristics and behaviour', in M.L. Knapp and G.R. Miller (eds) *Handbook of Interpersonal Communication*, London: Sage.

Glaser, A.N. (1982) 'Drive theory of social facilitation: a critical reappraisal', *British Journal of Social Psychology* 21: 265–82.

Goffman, E. (1959) *The Presentation of Self in Everyday Life*, Garden City, NY: Doubleday-Anchor.

Goffman, E. (1968) *Asylums*, London: Pelican.

Golembiewski, R.T. (1962) *The Small Group: An Analysis of Research Concepts and Operations*, Chicago: University of Chicago Press.

Goodacre, D.M. (1951) 'The use of a sociometric test as a predictor of combat unit effectiveness', *Sociometry* 14: 148–52.

Gramsci, A. (1971) *Selections from the Prison Notebooks*, trans. and ed. G. Nowell Smith and Q. Hoare, London: Lawrence & Wishart.

Greenberg, J. (1983a) 'Overcoming egocentric bias in perceived fairness through self-awareness', *Social Psychology Quarterly* 46: 152–6.

Greenberg, J. (1983b) 'Self-image *vs* impression management in adherence to distributive justice standards: the influence of self-awareness and self-consciousness', *Journal of Personality and Social Psychology* 44: 5–19.

Greene, J. (1972) *Psycholinguistics: Chomsky and Psychology*, Harmondsworth: Penguin.

Greenwald, A.G. (1982) 'Is anyone in charge? Personalysis *vs* the principle of personal unity', in J. Suls (ed.) *Psychological Perspectives on the Self*, vol. 1, Hillsdale, NJ: Erlbaum.

Griffitt, W. (1974) 'Attitude similarity and attraction', in T.L. Huston (ed.) *Foundations of Interpersonal Attraction*, New York: Academic Books.

Gross, E. (1954) 'Primary functions of the small group', *American Journal of Sociology* 60: 24–30.

Gross, N. and Martin, W.E. (1952) 'On group cohesiveness', *American Journal of Sociology* 57: 546–64.

Guerin, B. (1983) 'Social facilitation and social monitoring: a test of three models', *British Journal of Social Psychology* 22: 203–14.

Guerin, B. (1986) 'Mere presence effects in humans: a review', *Journal of Experimental Social Psychology* 22: 38–77.

Guerin, B. and Innes, J.M. (1982) 'Social facilitation and social monitoring: a new look at Zajonc's mere presence hypothesis', *British Journal of Social Psychology* 21: 7–18.

Guimond, S. and Dubé-Simard, L. (1983) 'Relative deprivation theory and the Quebec Nationalist Movement: the cognitive–emotion distinction and the personal-group deprivation issue', *Journal of Personality and Social Psychology* 44: 526–35.

Gundlach, R.H. (1956) 'Effects of on-the-job experiences with negroes upon racial attitudes of white workers in union shops', *Psychological Reports* 2: 67–77.

Gurney, J.N. and Tierney, K.J. (1982) 'Relative deprivation and social movements: a critical look at twenty years of theory and research', *The Sociological Quarterly* 23: 33–49.

Gurr, T.R. (1970) *Why Men Rebel*, Princeton, NJ: Princeton University Press.

Hagstrom, W.O. and Selvin, H.C. (1965) 'The dimension of cohesiveness in small groups', *Sociometry* 28: 30–43.

Hamilton, D.L. (ed.) (1981) *Cognitive Processes in Stereotyping and Intergroup Behaviour*, Hillsdale, NJ: Erlbaum.

Haney, C., Banks, C., and Zimbardo, P. (1973) 'Interpersonal dynamics in a simulated prison', *International Journal of Criminology and Penology* 1: 69–97.

Hansell, S. (1984) 'Cooperative groups, weak ties, and the integration of peer friendships', *Social Psychology Quarterly* 47: 316–28.

Hardy, K.R. (1957) 'Determinants of conformity and attitude change', *Journal of Abnormal and Social Psychology* 54: 289–94.

Hare, A.P. (1962) *Handbook of Small Group Research*, New York: Free Press.

Hargreaves, D.H. (1967) *Social Relations in a Secondary School*, London: Routledge & Kegan Paul.

Harré, R. (1977) 'The ethogenic approach: theory and practice', *Advances in Experimental Social Psychology* 10: 283–314.

Harré, R. (1979) *Social Being: A Theory for Social Psychology*, Oxford: Blackwell.

Harré, R. (1983) *Personal Being*, Oxford: Blackwell.

Harvey, J.H. and Smith, W.P. (1977) *Social Psychology: An Attribution Approach*, St Louis, Louisianna: Mosby.

Harvey, J.H. and Weary, G. (1984) 'Current issues in attribution theory and research', *Annual Review of Psychology* 35: 427–59.

Haugen, E. (1977) 'Linguistic relativity: myths and methods', in W.C. McCormack and S.A. Wurm (eds) *Language and Thought: Anthropological Issues*, The Hague: Mouton.

Heaven, P.C.L. (ed.) (1980) *Authoritarianism: South African Studies*, Bloemfontein: DeVilliers.

Heaven, P.C.L. (1983) 'Individual *vs* intergroup explanations of prejudice among Afrikaners', *Journal of Social Psychology* 121: 201–10.

Heider, F. (1958) *The Psychology of Interpersonal Relations*, New York: Wiley.

Heider, F. and Simmel, M. (1944) 'An experimental study of apparent behaviour', *American Journal of Psychology* 57: 243–9.

Heine, P. (1971) *Personality in Social Theory*, Chicago: Aldine.

Helfrich, H. (1979) 'Age markers in speech', in K.R. Scherer and H. Giles (eds) *Social Markers in Speech*, Cambridge: Cambridge University Press.

Henchy, T. and Glass, D.C. (1968) 'Evaluation apprehension and the social facilitation of dominant subordinate responses', *Journal of Personality and Social Psychology* 10: 446–54.

Henriques, J., Holloway, W., Urwin, C., Venn, C., and Walkerdine, V. (1984) *Changing the Subject: Psychology, Social Regulation, and Subjectivity*, London: Methuen.

Henry, A. and Short, J. (1954) *Suicide and Homicide*, Glencoe, Ill.: Free Press.

Herzlich, C. (1973) *Health and Illness: A Social Psychological Analysis*, London: Academic Press.

Hewstone, M. (ed.) (1983) *Attribution Theory: Social and Functional Extensions*, Oxford: Blackwell.

Hewstone, M. and Brown, R.J. (eds) (1986) *Contact and Conflict in Intergroup Encounters*, Oxford: Blackwell.

Higgins, E.T. (1976) 'Social class differences in verbal communicative accuracy: a question of "which question?"', *Psychological Bulletin* 83: 695–714.

Higgins, E.T. (1981) 'The "communication game": implications for social cognition and persuasion', in E.T. Higgins, C.P. Herman, and M.P. Zanna (eds) *Social Cognition: The Ontario Symposium*, vol. 1, Hillsdale, NJ: Erlbaum.

Higgins, E.T., Fondacaro, R., and McCann, C.D. (1981) 'Rules and roles: the "communication game" and speaker–listener processes', in W.P. Dickson (ed.) *Children's Oral Communication Skills*, New York: Academic Press.

Higgins, E.T., Klein, R., and Strauman, T. (1984) 'Self-concept discrepancy theory: domain of self and standpoint of self as cognitive dimensions of the self-concept', paper presented at the International Conference on Self and Identity, Cardiff, July.

Higgins, E.T., McCann, C.D., and Fondacaro, R. (1982) 'The "communication game": goal-directed encoding and cognitive consequences', *Social Cognition* 1: 21–37.

Higgins, E.T. and Rholes, W.S. (1978) '"Saying is believing": effects of message modification on memory and liking for the person described', *Journal of Experimental Social Psychology* 14: 363–78.

Hilgard, E.R. (1973) 'The domain of hypnosis: with some comments on alternative paradigms', *American Psychologist* 28: 972–82.

Hinde, R.A. (1979) *Towards Understanding Relationships*, London: Academic Press.

Hinde, R.A. (1982) *Ethology: Its Nature and Relations with Other Sciences*, London: Fontana.

Hogg, M.A. (1985a) 'Masculine and feminine speech in dyads and groups: a study of speech style and gender salience', *Journal of Language and Social Psychology* 4: 99–112.

Hogg, M.A. (1985b) 'Cohesión de grupo', in C. Huici (ed.) *Estructura y Procesos de Grupo*, vol 1, Madrid: Universidad Nacional de Educación a Distancia; English MS entitled 'Group cohesiveness'.

Hogg, M.A. (1987) 'Social identity and group cohesiveness' in J.C. Turner, M.A. Hogg, P.J. Oakes, S.D. Reicher, and M. Wetherell, *Rediscovering the Social Group: A Self-Categorization Theory*, Oxford and New York: Blackwell.

Hogg, M.A. and Abrams, D. (1985) 'Review of, H. Tajfel (Ed.), "The Social Dimension: European Developments in Social Psychology (Vols. 1 and 2). (1984)"', *Journal of Language and Social Psychology* 4: 51–60.

Hogg, M.A., Abrams, D., and Patel, Y. (1987) 'Ethnic identity, self-esteem and occupational aspirations of Indian and Anglo-Saxon British adolescents', *Genetic, Social, and General Psychology Monographs*, in press.

Hogg, M.A., Joyce, N., and Abrams, D. (1984) 'Diglossia in Switzerland? A social identity analysis of speaker evaluations', *Journal of Language and Social Psychology* 3: 185–96.

Hogg, M.A. and Turner, J.C. (1985a) 'Interpersonal attraction, social identification and psychological group formation', *European Journal of Social Psychology* 15: 51–66.

Hogg, M.A. and Turner, J.C. (1985b) 'When liking begets solidarity: an experiment on the role of interpersonal attraction in psychological group formation', *British Journal of Social Psychology* 24: 267–81.

Hogg, M.A. and Turner, J.C. (1987a) 'Social identity and conformity: a theory of referent informational influence', in W. Doise and S. Moscovici (eds) *Current Issues in European Social Psychology*, vol. 2, Cambridge: Cambridge University Press.

Hogg, M.A. and Turner, J.C. (1987b) 'Intergroup behaviour, self-stereotyping and the salience of social categories', *British Journal of Social Psychology*, 26: 325–40.

Hogg, M.A. and Turner, J.C. (1987c) 'Polarized norms and subjective frames of reference: investigations of self-categorization theory of group polarization', University of Melbourne, unpublished paper.

Hogg, M.A., Turner, J.C., Nascimento-Schulze, C., and Spriggs, D. (1986) 'Social categorization, intergroup behaviour and self-esteem: two experiments', *Revista de Psicología Social* 1: 23–37.

Hollander, E.P. (1958) 'Conformity, status, and idiosyncracy credit', *Psychological Review* 65: 117–27.

Hollander, E.P. (1985) 'Leadership and power', in G. Lindzey and E. Aronson (eds) *Handbook of Social Psychology*, vol. 2, 3rd edn, New York: Random House.

Hollander, E.P. and Willis, R.H. (1967) 'Some current issues in the psychology of conformity and nonconformity', *Psychological Bulletin* 68: 62–76.

Hollingsworth, H.L. (1935) *The Psychology of the Audience*, New York: American Books.

Homans, G.C. (1961) *Social Behaviour: Its Elementary Forms*, New York: Harcourt Brace and World.

Horkheimer, M. and Flowerman, S.H. (1950) 'Foreword', in T.W. Adorno, E. Frenkel-Brunswik, D.J. Levinson and R.M. Sanford, *The Authoritarian Personality*, New York: Wiley.

Hormuth, S.E. (1982) 'Self-awareness and drive theory: comparing internal standards and dominant responses', *European Journal of Social Psychology* 12: 31–45.

Hornstein, H.A. (1972) 'Promotive tension: the basis of prosocial behaviour from a Lewinian perspective', *Journal of Social Issues* 28: 191–218.

Hornstein, H.A. (1976) *Cruelty and Kindness: A New Look at Aggression and Altruism*, Englewood Cliffs, NJ: Prentice-Hall.

Horwitz, M. (1953) 'The recall of interrupted group tasks: an experimental study of individual motivation in relation to group goals', *Human Relations* 7: 3–38.

Hovland, C. and Sears, R. (1940) 'Minor studies in aggression VI: correlation of lynchings with economic indices', *Journal of Psychology* 9: 301–10.

Hudson, R.A. (1980) *Sociolinguistics*, Cambridge: Cambridge University Press.

Huici, C. (1984) 'The individual and social functions of sex role stereotypes', in H. Tajfel (ed.) *The Social Dimension: European Developments in Social Psychology*, vol. 2, Cambridge: Cambridge University Press.

Husband, C. and Saifullah Khan, V. (1982) 'The viability of ethnolinguistic vitality: some creative doubts', *Journal of Multilingual and Multicultural Development* 3: 193–205.

Huston, T.L. (ed.) (1974) *Foundations of Interpersonal Attraction*, New York: Academic Press.

Huston, T.L. and Levinger, G. (1978) 'Interpersonal attraction and relationships', *Annual Review of Psychology* 29: 115–56.

Hyman, H.H. and Sheatsley, P.B. (1954) '"The Authoritarian Personality" – a methodological critique', in R. Christie and M. Jahoda (eds) *Studies in the Scope and Method of 'The Authoritarian Personality'*, New York: Free Press.

Hyman, H.H. and Singer, E. (eds) (1968) *Readings in Reference Group Theory and Research*, New York: Free Press.

Hymes, D. (1967) 'Models of the interaction of language and social setting', *Journal of Social Issues* 23: 8–28.

Israel, J. and Tajfel, H. (eds) (1972) *The Context of Social Psychology: A Critical Assessment*, London: Academic Press.

Itzin, C. (1986) 'Media images of women: the social construction of ageism and sexism', in S. Wilkinson (ed.) *Feminist Social Psychology: Developing Theory and Practice*, Milton Keynes: Open University Press.

Jaccard, J. (1981) 'Towards theories of persuasion and belief change', *Journal of Personality and Social Psychology* 40: 260–9.

Jackson, J.M. (1959) 'Reference group processes in a formal organization', *Sociometry* 22: 307–27.

Jackson, J.M. and Latané, B. (1981) 'All alone in front of all those people: stage fright as a function of number and type of co-performers and audience', *Journal of Personality and Social Psychology* 40: 73–85.

Jackson, J.M. and Padgett, V.R. (1982) 'With a little help from a friend: social loafing and the Lennon-McCartney songs', *Personality and Social Psychology Bulletin* 8: 672–7.

Jackson, J.M. and Williams, K.D. (1985) 'Social loafing on difficult tasks: working collectively can improve performance', *Journal of Personality and Social Psychology* 49: 937–42.

Jacobs, R.C. and Campbell, D.T. (1961) 'The perpetuation of an arbitrary tradition through several generations of a laboratory microculture', *Journal of Abnormal and Social Psychology* 62: 649–58.

Jahoda, G. (1961) *White Man*, London: Oxford University Press.

Jahoda, M. (1959) 'Conformity and independence: a psychological analysis', *Human Relations* 12: 99–120.

James, J. (1953) 'The distribution of free-forming small group size', *American Sociological Review* 18: 569–70.

James, W. (1890) *The Principles of Psychology*, New York: Holt, Rinehart, & Winston.

James, W. (1892) *Psychology*, London: Macmillan.

Janis, I.L. (1971) 'Groupthink', *Psychology Today* 5: 43–6.

Janis, I.L. (1972) *Victims of Groupthink: A Psychological Study of Foreign Policy Decisions and Fiascoes*, Boston: Houghton-Mifflin.

Jaspars, J.M.F. (1980) 'The coming of age of social psychology in Europe', *European Journal of Social Psychology* 10: 421–9.

Jaspars, J.M.F. (1986) 'Forum and focus: a personal view of European social psychology', *European Journal of Social Psychology* 16: 3–15.

Jaspars, J.M.F., Fincham, F.D., and Hewstone, M. (eds) (1983) *Attribution Theory and Research: Conceptual, Developmental and Social Dimensions*, London: Academic Press.

Jellison, J. and Arkin, R. (1977) 'Social comparison of abilities: a self-presentation approach to decision making in groups', in J.M. Suls and R.L. Miller (eds) *Social Comparison Processes: Theoretical and Empirical Perspectives*, Washington: Hemisphere.

Jennings, H.H. (1947) 'Sociometric differentiation of the psychegroup and the sociogroup', *Sociometry* 10: 71–9.

Johnson, D.W. and Johnson, R.T. (1982) 'The effects of cooperative and individualistic instruction on handicapped and non-handicapped students', *Journal of Social Psychology* 118: 257–68.

Johnson, D.W. and Johnson, R.T. (1984) 'The effects of intergroup cooperation and intergroup competition on ingroup and outgroup cross-handicap relationships', *Journal of Social Psychology* 124: 85–94.

Johnson, D.W., Maruyama, G., Johnson, R.T., Nelson, D., and Skon, L. (1981) 'Effects of cooperative, competitive, and individualistic goal structures on achievement', *Psychological Bulletin* 89: 47–62.

Johnson, R.D. and Downing, L.L. (1979) 'Deindividuation and valence of cues: effects' in prosocial and antisocial behaviour', *Journal of Personality and Social Psychology* 37: 1532–8.

Jones, E.E. (1964) *Ingratiation*, New York: Appleton-Century-Crofts.

Jones, E.E. and Berglas, S. (1978) 'Control of attributions about the self through self-handicapping strategies: the appeal of alcohol and the role of underachievement', *Personality and Social Psychology Bulletin* 4: 200–6.

Jones, E.E. and Davis, K.E. (1965) 'From acts to dispositions: the attribution process in person perception', *Advances in Experimental Social Psychology* 2: 219–66.

Jones, E.E. and Gerard, H.B. (1967) *Foundations of Social Psychology*, New York: Wiley.

Jones, E.E., Gergen, K.J., and Davis, K. (1962) 'Some reactions to being approved or disapproved as a person', *Psychological Monographs* 76(521): whole issue.

Jones, E.E. and Nisbett, R.E. (1972) 'The actor and the observer: divergent perceptions of the causes of behaviour', in E.E. Jones, D.E. Kanouse, H.H. Kelley, R.E. Nisbett, S. Valins, and B. Weiner, *Attribution: Perceiving the Causes of Behaviour*, Morristown, NJ: General Learning Press.

Jones, E.E. and Pittman, T.S. (1982) 'Toward a general theory of strategic self-presentation', in J. Suls (ed.) *Psychological Perspectives on the Self*, Hillsdale, NJ: Erlbaum.

Jones, E.E., Rhodewalt, F., Berglas, S., and Skelton, J.A. (1981) 'Effects of strategic self-presentation on subsequent self-esteem', *Journal of Personality and Social Psychology* 41: 407–21.

Jones, E.E. and Sigall, H. (1971) 'The bogus pipeline: a new paradigm for measuring affect and attitudes', *Psychological Bulletin* 76: 349–64.

Jung, C.G. (1946) *Psychological Types, or the Psychology of Individuation*, New York: Harcourt Brace.

Jung, C.G. (1972; *Four Archetypes: Mother, Rebirth, Spirit, Trickster*, trans. R.F.C. Hull, London: Routlege & Kegan Paul.

Kandel, D.B. (1978) 'Similarity in real-life adolescent friendship pairs', *Journal of Personality and Social Psychology* 36: 306–12.

Katz, D. and Braly, K. (1933) 'Racial stereotypes in one hundred college students', *Journal of Abnormal and Social Psychology* 28: 280–90.

Kellerman, H. (ed.) (1981) *Group Cohesion*, New York: Grune & Stratton.

Kelley, H.H. (1952) 'Two functions of reference groups', in G.E. Swanson, T.M. Newcomb, and E.L. Hartley (eds) *Readings in Social Psychology*, 2nd edn, New York: Holt, Rinehart, & Winston.

Kelley, H.H. (1967) 'Attribution theory in social psychology', in D. Levine (ed.) *Nebraska Symposium on Motivation*, Lincoln, Nebraska: University of Nebraska Press.

Kelley, H.H. and Michela, J.L. (1980) 'Attribution theory and research', *Annual Review of Psychology* 31: 457–501.

Kelley, H.H. and Thibaut, J. (1978) *Interpersonal Relations: A Theory of Interdependence*, New York: Wiley.

Kelly, G.A. (1955) *The Psychology of Personal Constructs*, New York: Norton.

Kelly, G.A. (1970) 'A brief introduction to personal construct theory', in D. Bannister (ed.) *Perspectives in Personal Construct Theory*, London: Academic Press.

Kelman, H.C. (1958) 'Compliance, identification and internalization: three processes of opinion change', *Journal of Conflict Resolution* 2: 51–60.

Kelman, H.C. (1961) 'Processes of opinion change', *Public Opinion Quarterly* 25: 57–78.

Kelvin, P. (1984) 'The historical dimension of social psychology: the case of unemployment', in H. Tajfel (ed.) *The Social Dimension: European Developments in Social Psychology*, vol 1, Cambridge: Cambridge University Press.

Kiesler, C.A. and Kiesler, S.B. (1969) *Conformity*, Reading, Mass.: Addison-Wesley.

Kihlstrom, J.S. (1985) 'Hypnosis', *Annual Review of Psychology* 36: 385–418.

Kinder, D.R. and Sears, D.O. (1981) 'Symbolic racism *vs* threats to the good life', *Journal of Personality and Social Psychology* 40: 414–31.

Kinney, E.E. (1953) 'Study of peer group social acceptability at the fifth-grade level at a public school', *Journal of Educational Research* 47: 57–64.

Kipnis, D.M. (1961) 'Changes in self concepts in relation to perceptions of others', *Journal of Personality* 29: 449–65.

Klimoski, R.J. (1978) 'Simulation methodologies in experimental research on negotiation by representatives', *Journal of Conflict Resolution* 22: 61–77.

Knowles, E.S. (1982) 'From individuals to group members: a dialectic for the social sciences', in W. Ickes and E. Knowles (eds) *Personality, Rules and Social Behaviour*, New York: Springer-Verlag.

Knowles, E.S. and Brickner, M.A. (1981) 'Social cohesion effects on spatial cohesion', *Personality and Social Psychology Bulletin* 7: 309–13.

Kormorita, S.S. and Lapworth, C.W. (1982) 'Cooperative choice among individuals vs groups in an n-person dilemma situation', *Journal of Personality and Social Psychology* 46: 1044–57.

Kramarae, C. (1981) *Women and Men Speaking: Frameworks for Analysis*, Rowley, Mass.: Newbury House.

Kramer, C. (1977) 'Perceptions of female and male speech', *Language and Speech* 20: 151–61.

Kraut, R.E. and Higgins, E.T. (1984) 'Communication and social cognition', in R.S. Wyer Jnr and T.K. Srull (eds) *Handbook of Social Cognition*, vol. 3, Hillsdale, NJ: Erlbaum.

Krech, D., Crutchfield, R.S., and Ballachey, E.L. (1962) *Individual in Society*, New York: McGraw-Hill.

Kruglanski, A.W. (1975) 'The human subject in the psychology experiment: fact and artifact', *Advances in Experimental Social Psychology* 8: 101–47.

Kushner, T. (1981) 'The status of arousal in recent social facilitation literature', *Social Behaviour and Personality* 9: 185–90.

Labov, W. (1970) 'Language in social context', *Stadium Generale* 23: 30–87.

Lakoff, R. (1975) *Language and Woman's Place*, New York: Harper & Row.

Lambert, W.E. (1967) 'The social psychology of bilingualism', *Journal of Social Issues* 23: 91–109.

Lambert, W.E. (1974) 'Culture and language as factors in learning and education', in F. Aboud and R.D. Meade (eds) *Cultural Factors in Learning*, Bellingham, Washington: Western Washington State College Press.

Lambert, W.E. (1979) 'Language as a factor in intergroup relations', in H. Giles and R.N. St Clair (eds), *Language and Social Psychology*, Oxford: Blackwell.

Lambert, W.E., Hodgson, R.C., Gardner, R.C., and Fillenbaum, S. (1960) 'Evaluation reactions to spoken language', *Journal of Abnormal and Social Psychology* 60: 44–51.

Landman, J. and Manis, M. (1983) 'Social cognition: some historical and theoretical perspectives', *Advances in Experimental Social Psychology* 16: 49–123.

Lange, A. (1971) 'Frustration–aggression: a reconsideration', *European Journal of Social Psychology* 1: 59–84.

LaPiere, R.T. (1934) 'Attitudes vs actions', *Social Forces* 13: 230–7.

Larrain, J. (1979) *The Concept of Ideology*, London: Hutchinson.

Latané, B. (1981) 'The psychology of social impact', *American Psychologist* 36: 343–56.

Latané, B. and Nida, S. (1980) 'Social impact theory and group influence: a social engineering perspective', in P.B. Paulus (ed.) *Psychology of Group Influence*, Hillsdale, NJ: Erlbaum.

Latané, B.; Williams, K., and Harkins, S. (1979) 'Many hands make light the work: causes and consequences of social loafing', *Journal of Personality and Social Psychology* 37: 822–32.

Latané, B. and Wolf, S. (1981) 'The social impact of majorities and minorities', *Psychological Review* 88: 438–53.

Leach, E. (1982) *Social Anthropology*, London: Fontana.

Le Bon, G. (1908) *The Crowd: A Study of the Popular Mind*, London: Unwin (first published in French in 1896).

Le Bon, G. (1913) *The Psychology of Revolution*, New York: Putnam.

Lefebvre, H. (1968) *The Sociology of Marx*, New York: Columbia University Press.

Lemaine, G. (1966) 'Inégalité, comparison et incomparabilité: Ésquisse d'une théorie de l'originalité social', *Bulletin de Psychologie* 20: 24–32.

Lemert, E.M. (1951) *Social Pathology*, New York: McGraw-Hill.

Lemyre, L. and Smith, P.M. (1985) 'Intergroup discrimination and self-esteem in the minimal group paradigm', *Journal of Personality and Social Psychology* 49: 660–70.

Lerner, M.J. (1970) 'The desire for justice and reactions to victims', in J. Maccoby and L. Berkowitz (eds) *Altruism and Helping Behaviour*, New York: Academic Press.

Lewin, K. (1943) 'Psychology and the process of group living', *Journal of Social Psychology* 17: 119–29.

Lewin, K. (1948) *Resolving Social Conflicts*, New York: Harper & Bros.

Lewin, K. (1952) *Field Theory in Social Science*, London: Tavistock.

Lifton, R.J. (1961) *Thought Reform and the Psychology of Totalism: A Study of 'Brainwashing' in China*, New York: Norton.

Linneweber, V., Mummenday, A., Bornewasser, M., and Loschper, G. (1984) 'Classification of situations specific to field and behaviour: the context of aggressive interactions in schools', *European Journal of Social Psychology* 14: 281–96.

Lippmann, W. (1922) *Public Opinion*, New York: Harcourt Brace.

Lock, A. (ed.) (1978) *Action, Gesture and Symbol: The Emergence of Language*, London: Academic Press.

Lock, A. (1980) *The Guided Reinvention of Language*, London: Academic Press.

Lord, C., Ross, L.D., and Lepper, M.R. (1979) 'Biased assimilation and attitude polarization: the effects of prior theories on subsequently considered evidence', *Journal of Personality and Social Psychology* 37: 2098–109.

Lord, R.G. (1977) 'Functional leadership behaviour: measurement and relation to social power and leadership perceptions', *Administrative Science Quarterly* 22: 114–33.

Lott, A.J. and Lott, B.E. (1961) 'Group cohesiveness, communication level and conformity', *Journal of Abnormal and Social Psychology* 62: 408–12.

Lott, A.J. and Lott, B.E. (1965) 'Group cohesiveness as interpersonal attraction', *Psychological Bulletin* 64: 259–309.

Lott, B.E. (1961) 'Group cohesiveness: a learning phenomenon', *Journal of Social Psychology* 55: 275–86.

Lyman, S.M. and Scott, M.B. (1970) *A Sociology of the Absurd*, New York: Appleton-Century-Crofts.

McCarthy, B. (1976) 'Agreement and friendship: affective and cognitive responses to attitudinal similarity–dissimilarity among same-sex friends', University of Lancaster, unpublished doctoral dissertation.

McCarthy, B. (1981) 'Studying personal relationships', in S. Duck and R. Gilmour (eds) *Personal Relationships (Vol. 1). Studying Personal Relationships*, London: Academic Press.

McDougall, W. (1921) *The Group Mind*, London: Cambridge University Press.

McGarty, C. and Penny, R.E.C. (1986) 'Categorization, accentuation and social judgement', Macquarie University, unpublished paper.

McGhee, P.E. and Teevan, R.C. (1967) 'Conformity behaviour and need for affiliation', *Journal of Social Psychology* 72: 117–21.

McGrath, J.E. (1966) 'A social psychological approach to the study of negotiation', in R. Bowers (ed.) *Studies on Behaviour in Organizations: A Research Symposium*, Athens, Georgia: University of Georgia Press.

McGrath, J.E. and Kravitz, D.A. (1982) 'Group research', *Annual Review of Psychology* 33: 195–230.

McGuire, W.J. (1968) 'Personality and susceptibility to social influence', in E.F.

Borgatta and W.W. Lambert (eds) *Handbook of Personality Theory and Research*, Chicago: Rand-McNally.

MacKenzie, W.J.M. (1978) *Biological Ideas in Politics*, Harmondsworth: Penguin.

Mackie, D.M. (1986) 'Social identification effects in group polarization', *Journal of Personality and Social Psychology* 50: 720–8.

MacKinnon, W.J. and Centers, R. (1956) 'Authoritarianism and urban, stratification', *American Journal of Sociology* 61: 610–20.

MacNeil, M.K. and Sherif, M. (1976) 'Norm change of subject generations as a function of arbitrariness of prescribed norms', *Journal of Personality and Social Psychology* 34: 762–73.

Mair, L. (1972) *An Introduction to Social Anthropology*, 2nd edn, Oxford: Clarendon Press.

Malinowski, B. (1926) *Myth in Primitive Psychology*, London: Kegan Paul.

Mann, L., Newton, J.W., and Innes, J.M. (1982) 'A test between deindividuation and emergent norm theories of crowd aggression', *Journal of Personality and Social Psychology* 42: 260–72.

Mann, S.H. (1977) 'The use of social indicators in environmental planning', in I. Altman and J.F. Wohlwill (eds) *Human Behaviour and Environment*, vol. 2, New York: Plenum.

Marchand, B. (1970) 'Answirkung einer emotional wertvollen und einer emotional neutralen Klassifikation auf die Schatzung einer Stimulusserie', *Zeitschrift Für Sozialpsychologie* 1: 264–74.

Markova, I. (ed.) (1978) *The Social Context of Language*, New York: Wiley.

Markus, H. (1977) 'Self-schemata and processing information about the self', *Journal of Personality and Social Psychology* 35: 63–78.

Markus, H. (1979) 'The effect of mere presence on social facilitation: an unobtrusive test', *Journal of Experimental Social Psychology* 14: 389–97.

Markus, H. and Nurius, P. (1984) 'Possible selves', paper presented at the International Conference on Self and Identity, Cardiff, July.

Markus, H. and Zajonc, R.B. (1985) 'The cognitive perspective in social psychology', in G. Lindzey and E. Aronson (eds) *The Handbook of Social Psychology*, 3rd edn, vol. 1, Reading, Mass.: Addison-Wesley.

Marlowe, D. and Gergen, K. (1969) 'Personality and social interaction', in G. Lindzey and E. Aronson (eds) *The Handbook of Social Psychology*, 2nd edn, vol. 3, Reading, Mass.: Addison-Wesley.

Marrow, A.J. (1969) *The Practical Theorist: The Life and Work of Kurt Lewin*, New York: Basic Books.

Martin, D.J., Abramson, L.Y., and Alloy, L.B. (1984) 'Illusion of control for self and others in depressed and non-depressed college students', *Journal of Personality and Social Psychology* 46: 125–36.

Martin, J. (1981) 'Relative deprivation: a theory of distributive injustice for an era of shrinking resources', in L.L. Cummings and B.M. Straw (eds) *Research in Organizational Behaviour*, vol 3, Greenwich, Conn.: JAI Press.

Martin, J. and Murray, A. (1983) 'Distributive injustice and unfair exchange', in K.S. Cook and D.M. Messick (eds) *Theories of Equity: Psychological and Sociological Perspectives*, New York: Praeger.

Marx, K. (1963) *Early Writings*, trans. and ed. T.B. Bottomore, New York: McGraw Hill (first published in German in 1844).

Maslach, C. (1974) 'Social and personal bases of individuation', *Journal of Personality and Social Psychology* 29: 411–25.

Maslach, C., Stapp, J., and Santee, R.T. (1985) 'Individuation: analysis and assessment, *Journal of Personality and Social Psychology* 49: 729–38.

Maslow, A.H. (1954) *Motivation and Personality*, New York: Harper.

Mead, G.H. (1934) *Mind, Self and Society*, Chicago: University of Chicago Press.

Mead, G.H. (1938) *The Philosophy of the Act*, Chicago: University of Chicago Press.

Mehrabian, A. (1971) 'Nonverbal communication', in J.K. Cole (ed.) *Nebraska Symposium on Motivation*, vol. 19, Lincoln, Nebraska: University of Nebraska Press.

Meltzer, M., Petras, J.W., and Reynolds, L.T. (1975) *Symbolic Interactionism: Genesis, Varieties and Criticisms*, London: Routledge & Kegan Paul.

Merton, R.K. (1957) *Social Theory and Social Structure*, New York: Free Press.

Mervis, C.B. and Rosch, E. (1981) 'Categorization of natural objects', *Annual Review of Psychology* 32: 89–115.

Michotte, A. (1963) *The Perception of Causality*, New York: Basic Books.

Mikula, G. (1984) 'Personal relationships: remarks on the current state of research', *European Journal of Social Psychology* 14: 339–52.

Milgram, S. (1974) *Obedience to Authority: An Experimental View*, New York: Harper & Row.

Miller, G.A. (1951) *Language and Communication*, New York: McGraw Hill.

Miller, N.E. and Brewer, M.B. (1984) *Groups in Contact: The Psychology of Desegregation*, New York: Academic Press.

Miller, N.E. and Bugelski, R. (1948) 'Minor studies in aggression: the influence of frustrations imposed by the ingroup on attitudes toward outgroups', *Journal of Psychology* 25: 437–42.

Miller, R.S. and Schlenker, B.R. (1985) 'Egotism in group members: public and private attributions of responsibility for group performance', *Social Psychology Quarterly* 48: 85–9.

Millett, K. (1969) *Sexual Politics*, London: Virago.

Milner, D. (1981) 'Racial prejudice', in J.C. Turner and H. Giles (eds) *Intergroup Behaviour*, Oxford: Blackwell.

Minard, R.D. (1952) 'Race relationships in the Pocahontas coalfield', *Journal of Social Issues* 8: 29–44.

Mischel, W. (1968) *Personality and Assessment*, New York: Wiley.

Mischel, W. (1969) 'Continuity and change in personality', *American Psychologist* 24: 1012–18.

Mischel, W. and Peake, P.K. (1983) 'Some facets of consistency: replies to Epstein, Funder, and Bem', *Psychological Review* 90: 394–402.

Moreno, J.L. (1934) *Who Shall Survive?* Washington, DC: Nervous and Mental Diseases Publishing Co.

Morley, I.E. and Stephenson, G.M. (1970) 'Formality in experimental negotiations: a validation study', *British Journal of Psychology* 61: 383–4.

Morley, I.E. and Stephenson, G.M. (1977) *The Social Psychology of Bargaining*, London: Allen & Unwin

Morris, W. and Miller, R.S. (1975) 'The effects of consensus-breaking and consensus-preempting partners on reduction of conformity', *Journal of Experimental Social Psychology* 11: 215–23.

Moscovici, S. (1961) *La Psychanalyse, son Image et son Public*, Paris: Presses Universitaires de France.

Moscovici, S. (1967) 'Communication processes and the properties of language', *Advances in Experimental Social Psychology* 3: 225–70.

Moscovici, S. (1972) *The Psychosociology of Language*, Chicago: Markham Publishing.

Moscovici, S. (1976) *Social Influence and Social Change*, London: Academic Press.

Moscovici, S. (1981) 'On social representation', in J.P. Forgas (ed.) *Social Cognition: Perspectives on Everyday Understanding*, London: Academic Press.

Moscovici, S. (1982) 'The coming era of representations', in J.-P. Codol and J. P. Leyens (eds) *Cognitive Analysis of Social Behaviour*, The Hague: Martinus Nijhoff.

Moscovici, S. (1983) 'On some aspects of social representations', paper presented at the symposium on 'Representations' of the American Psychological Association, Anaheim, Calif., August.

Moscovici, S. and Faucheux, C. (1972) 'Social influence, conformity bias and the study of active minorities', *Advances in Experimental Social Psychology* 6: 149–202.

Moscovici, S. and Mugny, G. (1983) 'Minority influence', in P.B. Paulus (ed.) *Basic Group Processes*, New York: Springer-Verlag.

Moscovici, S. and Zavalloni, M. (1969) 'The group as a polarizer of attitudes', *Journal of Personality and Social Psychology* 12: 125–35.

Mugny, G. (1982) *The Power of Minorities*, London: Academic Press.

Mulac, A., Incontro, C.R., and James, M.R. (1985) 'Comparison of the gender-linked language effect and sex role stereotypes', *Journal of Personality and Social Psychology* 49: 1098–109.

Mullen, B. (1983) 'Operationalizing the effect of the group on the individual: a self-attention perspective', *Journal of Experimental Social Psychology* 19: 295–322.

Mullen, B. (1984) 'Participation in religious groups as a function of group composition: a self-attention perspective', *Journal of Applied Social Psychology* 14: 509–18.

Muller, E.N. (1980) 'The psychology of political protest and violence', in T.R. Gurr (ed.) *Handbook of Political Conflict*, New York: Free Press.

Mummenday, A. and Schreiber, H.J. (1983) 'Better or just different? Positive social identity by discrimination against or by differentiation from outgroups', *European Journal of Social Psychology* 13: 389–98.

Myers, D.G. and Lamm, H. (1976) 'The group polarization phenomenon', *Psychological Bulletin* 83: 602–27.

Myers, D.G., Wojcicki, S.G., and Aardema, B. (1977) 'Attitude comparison: is there ever a bandwagon effect?', *Journal of Applied Social Psychology* 7: 341–7.

Nadler, A., Goldberg, M., and Jaffe, Y. (1982) 'Effect of self-differentiation and anonymity in group on deindividuation', *Journal of Personality and Social Psychology* 42: 1127–36.

Natalé, M. (1975) 'Convergence of mean vocal intensity in dyadic communication as a function of social desirability', *Journal of Personality and Social Psychology* 40: 827–30.

Newcomb, T.M. (1943) *Personality and Social Change*, New York: Holt, Rinehart, & Winston.

Newcomb, T.M. (1947) 'Attitude development as a function of reference groups: the Bennington study', in E.E. Maccoby, T.M. Newcomb, and E.L. Hartley (eds) *Readings in Social Psychology*, New York: Holt, Rinehart, & Winston.

Newcomb, T.M. (1953) 'An approach to the study of communicative acts', *Psychological Review* 60: 393–404.

Newcomb, T.M. (1960) 'Varieties of interpersonal attraction', in D. Cartwright and A. Zander (eds) *Group Dynamics: Research and Theory*, 2nd edn, Evanston, Ill.: Row Peterson.

Newcomb, T.M. (1961) *The Acquaintance Process*, New York: Holt, Rinehart, & Winston.

Newcomb, T.M. (1968) 'Interpersonal balance', in R. Abelson, E. Aronson, W. McGuire, T. Newcomb, M. Rosenberg, and P. Tannenbaum (eds) *Theories of Cognitive Consistency: A Sourcebook*, Chicago: Rand McNally.

Newcomb, T.M., Koenig, L.E., Flacks, R., and Warwick, D.P. (1967) *Persistence and Change: Bennington College and Its Students after Twenty-five Years*, New York: Wiley.

Newcomb, T.M., Turner, R.H., and Converse, P.E. (1956) *Social Psychology: The Study of Human Interaction*, New York: Holt, Rinehart, & Winston.

Newtson, D. and Czerlinsky, T. (1974) 'Adjustment of attitude communications for contrasts by extreme audiences', *Journal of Personality and Social Psychology* 30: 829–37.

Ng, S.H. (1981) 'Equity theory and the allocation of rewards between groups', *European Journal of Social Psychology* 11: 439–43.

Ng, S.H. (1982) 'Power and intergroup discrimination', in H. Tajfel (ed.) *Social Identity and Intergroup Relations*, Cambridge: Cambridge University Press.

Ng, S.H. (1984a) 'Equity and social categorization effects on intergroup allocation of rewards', *British Journal of Social Psychology* 23: 165–72.

Ng, S.H. (1984b) 'Social psychology and political economy', in H. Tajfel (ed.) *The Social Dimension: European Developments in Social Psychology*, vol. 2, Cambridge: Cambridge University Press.

Nisbett, R. and Ross, L. (1980) *Human Inference: Strategies and Shortcomings of Social Judgment*, Englewood Cliffs, NJ: Prentice-Hall.

Nixon, H.L. (1976) 'Team orientations, interpersonal relations, and team success', *Research Quarterly* 47: 429–33.

Nye, R.A. (1975) *The Origins of Crowd Psychology: Gustav Le Bon and the Crisis of Mass Democracy in the Third Republic*, London: Sage.

Oakes, P.J. (1987) 'The salience of social categories', in J.C. Turner, M.A. Hogg, P.J. Oakes, S.D. Reicher, and M. Wetherell, *Rediscovering the Social Group: A Self-Categorization Theory*, Oxford and New York: Blackwell.

Oakes, P.J. and Turner, J.C. (1980) 'Social categorization and intergroup behaviour: does minimal intergroup discrimination make social identity more positive?', *European Journal of Social Psychology* 10: 295–301.

Orive, R. (1984) 'Group similarity, public self-awareness, and opinion extremity: a social projection explanation of deindividuation effects', *Journal of Personality and Social Psychology* 47: 727–37.

Orwell, G. (1949) *Nineteen Eighty Four*, London: Secker & Warburg.

Osgood, C.E., Suci, G.J., and Tannenbaum, P.H. (1957) *The Measurement of Meaning*, Urbana, Ill.: University of Illinois Press.

Paivio, A. (1965) 'Personality and audience influence', in B. Maher (ed.) *Progress in Experimental Personality Research*, New York: Academic Press.

Pandit, P.B. (1978) 'Language and identity: the Punjabi language in Delhi', *International Journal of the Sociology of Language* 16: 93–108.

Park, B. and Rothbart, M. (1982) 'Perception of out-group homogeneity and levels of social categorization: memory for the subordinate attributes of in-group and out-group members', *Journal of Personality and Social Psychology* 42: 1031–68.

Parkin, F. (1971) *Class Inequality and Political Order: Social Stratification in Capitalist and Communist Societies*, London: MacGibbon & Kee.

Parsons, T. (1951) *The Social System*, New York: Routledge & Kegan Paul.

Paulus, P.B. (1983) 'Group influence on individual task performance', in P.B. Paulus (ed.) *Basic Group Processes*, New York: Springer-Verlag.

Pennington, D.F., Harary, F., and Bass, B.M. (1958) 'Some effects of decision and discussion on coalescence change and effectiveness', *Journal of Applied Psychology* 42: 404–8.

Penrose, L.S. (1952) *On the Objective Study of Crowd Behaviour*, London: H.K. Lewis.

Pepitone, A. (1981) 'Lessons from the history of social psychology', *American Psychologist* 36: 972–85.

Pepitone, A. and Reichling, G. (1955) 'Group cohesiveness and the expression of hostility', *Human Relations* 8: 327–37.

Perkins, T.E. (1979) 'Rethinking stereotypes', in M. Barrett, P. Corrigan, A. Kuhn, and J. Wolff (eds) *Ideology and Cultural Production*, London: Croom Helm.

Pessin, J. (1933) 'The comparative effects of social and mechanical stimulation on memorizing', *American Journal of Psychology* 45: 263–70.

Pettigrew, T.F. (1958) 'Personality and socio-cultural factors in intergroup attitudes: a cross-national comparison', *Journal of Conflict Resolution* 2: 29–42.

Pettigrew, T.F. (1967) 'Social evaluation theory', in D. Levine (ed.) *Nebraska Symposium on Motivation*, vol 15, Lincoln, Nebraska: University of Nebraska Press.

Popper, K. (1969) *Conjectures and Refutations*, 3rd edn, London: Routledge & Kegan Paul.

Porter, L.W. and Lawler, E.E. (1968) *Managerial Attitudes and Performance*, Homewood, Ill.: Richard D. Irwin.

Potter, J., Stringer, P., and Wetherell, M. (1984) *Social Texts and Context: Literature and Social Psychology*, London: Routledge & Kegan Paul.

Potter, J. and Litton, I. (1985) 'Some problems underlying the theory of social representations', *British Journal of Social Psychology* 24: 81–90

Prentice-Dunn, S. and Rogers, R.W. (1982) 'Effects of public and private self-awareness on deindividuation and aggression', *Journal of Personality and Social Psychology* 43: 503–13.

Prothro, E.T. (1952) 'Ethnocentrism and anti-negro attitudes in the deep south', *Journal of Abnormal and Social Psychology* 47: 105–8.

Pruitt, D.G. and Kimmel, M.J. (1977) 'Twenty years of experimental gaming: critique, synthesis and suggestions for the future', *Annual Review of Psychology* 28: 363–92.

Pryor, J.B., Gibbons, F.X., Wicklund, R.A., Fazio, R., and Hood, R. (1977) 'Self-focussed attention and self-report validity', *Journal of Personality* 45: 513–27.

Rabbie, J.M. and De Brey, J.H.C. (1971) 'The anticipation of intergroup cooperation and competition under private and public conditions', *International Journal of Group Tensions* 1: 230–51.

Rabbie, J.M. and Horwitz, M. (1969) 'Arousal of ingroup–outgroup bias by a chance win or loss' *Journal of Personality and Social Psychology* 13: 269–77.

Rabbie, J.M. and Wilkens, G. (1971) 'Ingroup competition and its effect on intragroup relations', *European Journal of Social Psychology* 1: 215–34.

Radcliffe-Brown, A.R. (1952) *Structure and Function in Primitive Society*, London: Cohen.

Radke, M. and Klisurich, D. (1947) 'Experiments in changing food habits', *Journal of American Dietetic Association* 24: 403–9.

Ramuz-Nienhuis, W. and van Bergen, A. (1960) 'Relations between some components of attraction-to-group: a replication', *Human Relations* 13: 271–7.

Raven, B.H. (1974) 'The comparative analysis of power and power preference', in J.T. Tedeschi (ed.) *Perspectives on Social Power*, Chicago: Aldine.

Raven, B.H. and French, J.R.P. (1958) 'Legitimate power, coercive power and observability in social influence', *Sociometry* 21: 83–97.

Raven, B.H. and Kruglanski, A. (1970) 'Conflict and power', in P. Swingle (ed.) *The Structure of Conflict*, New York: Academic Press.

Ray, J.J. (1980) 'Authoritarianism in California 30 years later – with some cross-cultural comparisons', *Journal of Social Psychology* 111: 9–17.

Ray, J.J. and Lovejoy, F.H. (1983) 'The behavioural validity of some recent measures of authoritarianism' *Journal of Social Psychology* 120: 91–9.

Razran, G. (1950) 'Ethnic dislikes and stereotypes: a laboratory study', *Journal of Abnormal and Social Psychology* 45: 7–27.

Regan, D.T. (1976) 'Attributional aspects of interpersonal attraction', in J.W. Harvey, W.J. Ickes, and R.F. Kidd (eds) *New Directions in Attribution Research*, vol. 2, Hillsdale, NJ: Erlbaum.

Reicher, S.D. (1982) 'The determination of collective behaviour', in H. Tajfel (ed.) *Social Identity and Intergroup Relations*, Cambridge: Cambridge University Press.

Reicher, S.D. (1984a) 'Social influence in the crowd: attitudinal and behavioural effects of deindividuation in conditions of high and low group salience', *British Journal of Social Psychology* 23: 341–50.

Reicher, S.D. (1984b) 'The St Pauls' riot: an explanation of the limits of crowd action in terms of a social identity model', *European Journal of Social Psychology* 14: 1–21.

Reicher, S.D. (1987) 'Crowd behaviour as social action', in J.C. Turner, M.A. Hogg, P.J. Oakes, S.D. Reicher, and M. Wetherell, *Rediscovering the Social Group: A Self-Categorization Theory*, Oxford and New York: Blackwell.

Reicher, S.D. and Potter, J. (1985) 'Psychological theory as intergroup perspective: a comparative analysis of "scientific" and "lay" accounts of crowd events', *Human Relations* 38: 167–89.

Rejai, M. (1980) 'Theory and research in the study of revolutionary personnel', in T.R. Gurr (ed.) *Handbook of Political Conflict*, New York: Free Press.

Rejai, M. and Phillips, K. (1979) *Leaders of Revolution*, Beverley Hills: Sage.

Roberts, D.F. and Bachen, C.M. (1981) 'Mass communication effects', *Annual Review of Psychology* 32: 307–56.

Robinson, J.P., Converse, P.E., and Szalai, A. (1972) 'Everyday life in twelve countries', in A. Szalai (ed.) *The Use of Time*, The Hague: Morton.

Robinson, W.P. (1972) *Language and Social Behaviour*, Harmondsworth: Penguin.

Robinson, W.P. (ed.) (1983) 'Plenary papers and symposium reviews: Second International Conference on Social Psychology and Language, Bristol, 18–22 July, *Journal of Language and Social Psychology* 2, whole nos. 2, 3, and 4.

Robinson, W.P. (1984) 'The development of communicative competence with language in young children: a social psychological perspective', in H. Tajfel (ed.) *The Social Dimension: European Developments in Social Psychology*, vol. 1, Cambridge: Cambridge University Press.

Rogers, C.R. (1951) *Client-Centered Therapy*, Boston: Houghton-Mifflin.

Rogers, C.R. (1969) *Encounter Groups*, London: Penguin.

Rohrer, J.H., Baron, S.H., Hoffman, E.L., and Swander, D.V. (1954) 'The stability of autokinetic judgements', *Journal of Abnormal and Social Psychology* 49: 595–7.

Rokeach, M. (ed.) (1960) *The Open and Closed Mind*, New York: Basic Books.

Rokeach, M. (1973) *The Nature of Human Values*, New York: Free Press.

Rokeach, M., Smith, P.W., and Evans, R.I. (1960) 'Two kinds of prejudice or one?', in M. Rokeach (ed.) *The Open and Closed Mind*, New York: Basic Books.

Roloff, M.E. and Miller, G.R. (eds) (1980) *Persuasion: New Directions in Theory and Research*, London: Sage.

Romaine, S. (1984) *The Language of Children and Adults*, Oxford: Blackwell.

Rommetveit, R. (1967) *Words, Meanings and Messages*, New York: Academic Press.

Rommetveit, R. (1969) *Social Norms and Roles*, 2nd ed, Oslo: Oslo University Press.

Rommetveit, R. (1974) *On Message Structure: A Framework for the Study of Language and Communication*, New York: Wiley.

Rosch, E. (1975) 'Cognitive reference points', *Cognitive Psychology* 7: 532–47.

Rosch, E. (1978) 'Principles of categorization', in E. Rosch and B.B. Lloyd (eds) *Cognition and Categorization*, Hillsdale, NJ: Erlbaum.

Rosen, H. (1972) *Language and Class: A Critical Look at the Theories of Basil Bernstein*, Bristol: Falling Wall Press.

Rosenberg, M.J. and Abelson, R.P. (1960) 'An analysis of cognitive balancing', in M.J. Rosenberg, C.I. Hovland, W.J. McGuire, R.P. Abelson, and J.W. Brehm, *Attitude Organization and Change*, New Haven, Conn.: Yale University Press.

Rosenhan, D.L. (1973) 'On being sane in insane places', *Science*, 179: 250–8.

Rosnow, R.L. (1980) 'Psychology of rumor reconsidered', *Psychological Bulletin* 87: 578–91.

Rosnow, R.L. (1981) *Paradigms in Transition: The Methodology of Social Enquiry*,

Oxford: Oxford University Press.

Ross, L. (1977) 'The intuitive psychologist and his shortcomings', *Advances in Experimental Social Psychology* 10: 174–220.

Rousseau, J.-J. (1968) *The Social Contract* trans. M. Cranston, Harmondsworth: Penguin (first published in 1762).

Rubin, Z. (1973) *Liking and Loving: An Invitation to Social Psychology*, New York: Holt, Rinehart, & Winston.

Rudé, G. (1964) *The Crowd in History: A Study of Popular Disturbances in France and England 1730–1848*, New York: Wiley.

Runciman, W.G. (1966) *Relative Deprivation and Social Justice*, Berkeley, Calif: University of California Press.

Rutter, D.R. (1985) *Looking and Seeing*, London: Wiley.

Rutter, D.R. and Robinson, B. (1981) 'An experimental analysis of teaching by telephone: theoretical and practical implications for social psychology', in G.M. Stephenson and J.H. Davis *Progress in Applied Social Psychology*, vol. 1, Chichester: Wiley.

Ryan, E.B., Hewstone, M.R.C., and Giles H. (1984) 'Language and intergroup attitudes', in J.R. Eiser (ed.) *Attitudinal Judgements*, New York: Springer-Verlag.

Sachdev, I. and Bourhis, R.Y. (1985) 'Social categorization and power differentials in group relations', *European Journal of Social Psychology* 15: 415–34.

St Claire, L. and Turner, J.C. (1982) 'The role of demand characteristics in the social categorization paradigm', *European Journal of Social Psychology* 12: 307–14.

St Clair, R.N. and Giles, H. (eds) (1980) *The Social and Psychological Contexts of Language*, Hillsdale, NJ: Erlbaum.

Sampson, E.E. (1977) 'Psychology and the American ideal', *Journal of Personality and Social Psychology* 35: 767–82.

Sampson, E.E. (1981) 'Cognitive psychology as ideology' *American Psychologist* 36: 730–43.

Sanders G.S. (1981) 'Driven by distraction: an integrative review of social facilitation theory and research', *Journal of Experimental Social Psychology* 17: 227–51.

Sanders G.S. and Baron, R.S. (1977) 'Is social comparison irrelevant for producing choice shifts?' *Journal of Experimental Social Psychology* 13: 303–14.

Sankoff, G. (1972) 'Language use in multilingual societies: some alternative approaches', in J.B. Pride and J. Holmes (eds) *Sociolinguistics*, Harmondsworth: Penguin.

Sarbin, T.R. and Scheibe, K.E. (eds) (1983) *Studies in Social Identity*, New York: Praeger.

Schachter, S. (1951) 'Deviation, rejection, and communication', *Journal of Abnormal and Social Psychology* 46: 190–207.

Schachter, S. (1959) *The Psychology of Affiliation*, Stanford: Stanford University Press.

Schachter, S., Ellertson, N., McBride, D., and Gregory, D. (1951) 'An experimental study of cohesiveness and productivity', *Human Relations* 4: 229–38.

Schank, R.C. and Abelson, N.P. (1977) *Scripts, Plans, Goals and Understanding: An Inquiry into Human Knowledge Structures*, Hillsdale, NJ: Erlbaum.

Scheff, T.J. (ed.) (1975) *Labelling Madness*, Englewood Cliffs, NJ: Prentice-Hall.

Scheidlinger, S. (1952) *Psychoanalysis and Group Behaviour: A Study in Freudian Group Psychology*, New York: Norton.

Scheier, M.F. (1976) 'Self-awareness, self-consciousness and angry aggression', *Journal of Personality* 44: 627–44.

Scheier, M.F. (1980) 'Effects of private and public self-consciousness on the public expression of personal beliefs', *Journal of Personality and Social Psychology* 39: 514–21.

Scheier, M.F. and Carver, C.S. (1977) 'Self-focused attention and the experience of emotion: attraction, repulsion, elation, and depression', *Journal of Personality and Social Psychology* 35: 625–36.

Scheier, M.F. and Carver, C.S. (1980) 'Private and public self-attention, resistance to change and dissonance reduction', *Journal of Personality and Social Psychology* 39: 390–405.

Scheier, M.F. and Carver, C.S. (1981) 'Private and public aspects of self', in L. Wheeler (ed.) *Review of Personality and Social Psychology*, vol. 2, London: Sage.

Schein, E.H., Schneier, T., and Barker, C.H. (1961) *Coercive Persuasion*, New York: Norton.

Scherer, K.R. (1980) 'Personality, emotion, psychopathology and speech', in H. Giles, W.P. Robinson, and P.M. Smith (eds) *Language: Social Psychological Perspectives*, Oxford: Pergamon Press.

Scherer, K.R. and Ekman, P. (eds) (1982) *Handbook of Methods in Nonverbal Behaviour Research*, Cambridge: Cambridge University Press.

Scherer, K.R. and Giles, H. (eds) (1979) *Social Markers in Speech*, Cambridge: Cambridge University Press.

Schlenker, B.R. (1984) 'Identities, identifications, and relationships', in V.J. Derlega (ed.) *Communication, Intimacy and Close Relationships*, New York: Academic Press.

Schlenker, B.R. (1985) *The Self and Social Life*, New York: McGraw-Hill.

Schneider, D. (1969) 'Tactical self-presentation after success and failure', *Journal of Personality and Social Psychology* 13: 262–8.

Schönbach, P., Gollwitzer, P.M., Stiepel, G., and Wagner, U. (1981) *Education and Intergroup Attitudes*, New York: Academic Press.

Schuler, H. and Peltzer, U. (1978) 'Friendly *vs* unfriendly non-verbal behaviour: the effects on partners' decision-making preferences', in H. Brandstätter, J.H. Davis, and H. Schuler (eds) *Dynamics of Group Decisions*, Beverly Hills, Calif.: Sage.

Scott, W.A. (1965) *Values and Organizations*, Chicago: Rand-McNally.

Scotton, C.M. (1980) 'Explaining linguistic choices as identity negotiations', in H. Giles, W.P. Robinson, and P.M. Smith (eds) *Language: Social Psychological Perspectives*, Oxford: Pergamon Press.

Scotton, C.M. and Ury, W. (1977) 'Bilingual strategies: the social functions of code switching', *International Journal of the Sociology of Language* 13: 5–20.

Secord, P.F. (1959) 'Stereotyping and favourableness in the perception of negro faces', *Journal of Abnormal and Social Psychology* 59: 309–15.

Secord, P.F. and Backman, C.W. (1964) *Social Psychology*, New York: McGraw-Hill.

Secord, P.F., Bevan, W., and Katz, B. (1956) 'The negro stereotype and perceptual accentuation', *Journal of Abnormal and Social Psychology* 53: 78–83.

Seeman, M. (1981) 'Intergroup relations', in M. Rosenberg and R.H. Turner (eds) *Social Psychology: Sociological Perspectives*, New York: Basic Books.

Segal, M.W. (1979) 'Varieties of interpersonal attraction and their interrelationships in natural groups', *Social Psychology Quarterly* 42: 253–61.

Semin, G.R. (1980) 'A gloss on attribution theory', *British Journal of Social and Clinical Psychology* 19: 291–300.

Semin, G.R. and Manstead, A.S.R. (1979) 'Social psychology: social or psychological?' *British Journal of Social and Clinical Psychology* 18: 191–202.

Shatz, M. (1983) 'Communication', in P.H. Mussen (ed.) *Handbook of Child Psychology (vol. 3): Cognitive Development*, New York: Wiley.

Shaw, M.E. (1964) 'Communication networks', *Advances in Experimental Social Psychology* 1: 111–47.

Shaw, M.E. (1981) *Group Dynamics: The Psychology of Small Group Behaviour*, second edition New York: McGraw-Hill.

Shaw, M.E., Rothschild, G., and Strickland, J. (1957) 'Decision process in communication networks', *Journal of Abnormal and Social Psychology* 54: 323–30.

Sherif, M. (1935) 'A study of some social factors in perception', *Archives of Psychology* 27(187): 1–60.

Sherif, M. (1936) *The Psychology of Social Norms*, New York: Harper & Bros.

Sherif, M. (1951) 'A preliminary experimental study of intergroup relations', in J.H. Rohrer and M. Sherif (eds) *Social Psychology at the Crossroads*, New York: Harper.

Sherif, M. (ed.) (1962) *Intergroup Relations and Leadership*, New York: Wiley.

Sherif, M. (1966) *In Common Predicament: Social Psychology of Intergroup Conflict and Cooperation*, Boston: Houghton-Mifflin.

Sherif, M. (1967) *Group Conflict and Cooperation*, London: Routledge & Kegan Paul.

Sherif, M., Harvey, O.J., White, B.J., Hood, W., and Sherif, C. (1961) *Intergroup Conflict and Co-operation: The Robbers Cave Experiment*, Norman, Oklahoma: University of Oklahoma Institute of Intergroup Relations.

Sherif, M. and Sherif, C.W. (1969) *Social Psychology*, New York: Harper & Row.

Sherif, M., White, B.J., and Harvey, O.J. (1955) 'Status in experimentally produced groups', *American Journal of Sociology* 60: 370–9.

Shomer, R.W. and Centers, R. (1970) 'Differences in attitudinal responses under conditions of implicitly manipulated group salience', *Journal of Personality and Social Psychology* 15: 125–32.

Shotter, J. (1984) *Social Accountability and Selfhood*, Oxford: Blackwell.

Siegel, A.E. and Siegel, S. (1957) 'Reference groups, membership groups, and attitude change', *Journal of Abnormal and Social Psychology* 55: 360–4.

Simard, L., Taylor, D.M., and Giles H. (1976) 'Attribution processes and interpersonal accommodation in a bilingual setting', *Language and Speech* 19: 374–87.

Simmel, G. (1955) *Conflict and the Web of Group-Affiliations*, New York: Free Press.

Singer, E. (1981) 'Reference groups and social evaluations', in M. Rosenberg and R.H. Turner (eds) *Social Psychology: Sociological Perspectives*, New York: Basic Books.

Singer, J., Brush, C., and Lublin, S. (1965) 'Some aspects of deindividuation: identification and conformity', *Journal of Experimental Social Psychology* 1: 356–78.

Sistrunk, F. and McDavid, J.W. (1971) 'Sex variables in conforming behaviour', *Journal of Personality and Social Psychology* 17: 200–7.

Skinner, M. and Stephenson, G.M. (1981) 'The effects of intergroup comparison on the polarization of opinions', *Current Psychological Research* 1: 49–61.

Smith, K.K. and White, G.L. (1983) 'Some alternatives to traditional social psychology of groups', *Personality and Social Psychology Bulletin* 9: 65–73.

Smith, M.J., Colligan, M.J., and Hurrell, J.J.Jnr (1978) 'Three incidents of industrial mass psychogenic illness', *Journal of Occupational Medicine* 20: 399–402.

Smith, P.M. (1979) 'Sex markers in speech', in K.R. Scherer and H. Giles (eds) *Social Markers in Speech*, Cambridge: Cambridge University Press.

Smith, P.M. (1980) 'Judging masculine and feminine social identities from content-controlled speech', in H. Giles, W.P. Robinson, and P.M. Smith (eds) *Language: Social Psychological Perspectives*, Oxford: Pergamon Press.

Smith, P.M. (1983) 'Social psychology and language: a taxonomy and overview', *Journal of Language and Social Psychology* 2: 163–82.

Smith, P.M. (1985) *Language, the Sexes and Society*, Oxford: Blackwell.

Smith, P.M. Giles, H., and Hewstone, M. (1980) 'Sociolinguistics: a social psychological perspective', in R.M. St Clair and H. Giles (eds) *The Social and Psychological Contexts of Language*, Hillsdale, NJ: Erlbaum.

Smith, T.W., Snyder, C.R., and Perkins, S.C. (1983) 'The self-serving function of hypochondriacal complaints: physical symptoms as self-handicapping strategies', *Journal of Personality and Social Psychology* 44: 787–97.

Snyder, C.R. and Fromkin, H.L. (1980) *Uniqueness: The Human Pursuit of Difference*, New York: Plenum Press.

Snyder, M. (1974) 'The self-monitoring of expressive behaviour', *Journal of Personality and Social Psychology* 30: 526–53.

Snyder, M. (1979) 'Self-monitoring processes', *Advances in Experimental Social Psychology* 12: 85–128.

Snyder, M. (1981) 'On the self-perpetuating nature of social stereotypes', D.L. Hamilton (ed.) *Cognitive Processes in Stereotyping and Intergroup Behaviour*, Hillsdale, NJ: Erlbaum.

Snyder, M. (1984) 'When belief creates reality', *Advances in Experimental Social Psychology* 18: 247–305.

Snyder, M. and Cantor, N. (1979) 'Testing hypotheses about other people: the use of historical knowledge', *Journal of Experimental Social Psychology* 15: 330–42.

Snyder, M. and Monson, T.C. (1975) 'Persons, situations and the control of social behaviour', *Journal of Personality and Social Psychology* 32: 637–44.

Snyder, M. and Swann, W.B. (1978) 'Behavioural confirmation in social interaction: from social perception to social reality', *Journal of Experimental Social Psychology* 14: 148–62.

Snyder, M., Tanke, E.D., and Berscheid, E. (1977) 'Social perception and interpersonal behaviour: on the self-fulfilling nature of social stereotypes', *Journal of Personality and Social Psychology* 35: 656–66.

Sole, K., Marton, J., and Hornstein, H.A. (1975) 'Opinion similarity and helping: three field experiments investigating the bases of promotive behaviour', *Journal of Experimental Social Psychology* 11: 1–13.

Spencer, H. (1896) *The Principles of Psychology*, New York: Appleton-Century-Crofts.

Sperling, H.G. (1946) 'An experimental study of some psychological factors in judgement', MA thesis, New School for Social Research, New York; summarized in S.E. Asch (ed.) (1952) *Social Psychology*, Englewood Cliffs, NJ: Prentice-Hall.

Stang, D.J. (1972) 'Conformity, ability, and self-esteem', *Representative Research in Social Psychology* 3: 97–103.

Stang, D.J. (1976) 'Group size effects on conformity', *Journal of Social Psychology* 98: 175–81.

Steiner, I.D. (1974) 'Whatever happened to the group in social psychology?', *Journal of Experimental Social Psychology* 10: 94–108.

Steiner, I.D. (1983) 'Whatever happened to the touted revival of the group?', in H. Blumberg, P. Hare, V. Kent, and M. Davies (eds) *Small Groups and Social Interaction*, vol 2, New York: Wiley.

Steiner, I.D. (1986) 'Paradigms and groups', *Advances in Experimental Social Psychology* 19: 251–89.

Stephenson, G.M. (1981) 'Intergroup bargaining and negotiation', in J.C. Turner and H. Giles (eds) *Intergroup Behaviour*, Oxford: Blackwell.

Stephenson, G.M. (1984) 'Interpersonal and intergroup dimensions of bargaining and negotiation', in H. Tajfel (ed.) *The Social Dimension: European Developments in Social Psychology*, vol. 2, Cambridge: Cambridge University Press.

Stephenson, G.M., Abrams, D., Wagner, U., and Wade, G. (1986) 'Partners in recall: collaborative order in the recall of a police interrogation', *British Journal of Social Psychology* 25: 341–3.

Stephenson, G.M., Brandstätter, H., and Wagner, U. (1983) 'An experimental study of social performance and delay on the testimonial validity of story recall', *European Journal of Social Psychology* 13: 175–91.

Stephenson, G.M. and Tysoe, M. (1982) 'Intergroup and interpersonal dimensions of social behaviour: the case of industrial bargaining', in G.M. Breakwell, H. Foot, and R. Gilmour (eds) *Social Psychology: A Practical Manual*, London: Macmillan/ BPS.

Stouffer, S.A., Suchman, E.A., DeVinney, L.C., Star, S.A., and Williams, R.M. Jnr (1949) *The American Soldier: Adjustment During Army Life*, vol. 1, Princeton, NJ: Princeton University Press.

Strauss, A.L. (1977) *Mirrors and Masks: The Search for Identity*, London: Martin Robinson & Co.

Stricker, L.J., Messick, S., and Jackson, D.N. (1970) 'Conformity, anticonformity, and independence: their dimensionality and generality', *Journal of Personality and Social Psychology* 16: 494–507.

Strickland, B.R. and Crowne, D.P. (1962) 'Conformity under conditions of simulated group pressure as a function of the need for social approval', *Journal of Social Psychology* 58: 171–81.

Strickland, L.H., Aboud, F.E., and Gergen K.J. (eds) (1976) *Social Psychology in Transition*, New York: Plenum Press.

Strozier, C.B. (1982) *Lincoln's Quest for Union: Public and Private Meanings*, New York: Basic Books.

Struhl, K.J. (1981) 'Ideology and social cohesion', in H. Kellerman (ed.) *Group Cohesion: Theoretical and Clinical Perspectives*, New York: Grune & Stratton.

Stryker, S. (1981) 'Symbolic interactionism', in M. Rosenberg and R.H. Turner (eds) *Social Psychology: Sociological Perspectives*, New York: Basic Books.

Suls, J.M. and Miller, R.L. (eds) (1977) *Social Comparison Processes: Theoretical and Empirical Perspectives*, Washington: Hemisphere.

Sumner, W.G. (1906) *Folkways*, Boston: Ginn.

Szasz, T. (1961) *The Myth of Mental Illness*, New York: Hoeber.

Tajfel, H. (1957) 'Value and the perceptual judgement of magnitude', *Psychological Review* 64: 192–204.

Tajfel, H. (1959) 'Quantitative judgement in social perception', *British Journal of Psychology* 50: 16–29.

Tajfel, H. (1963) 'Stereotypes', *Race* 5: 3–14.

Tajfel, H. (1969a) 'Social and cultural factors in perception', in G. Lindzey and E. Aronson (eds) *Handbook of Social Psychology*, vol. 3, Reading, Mass.: Addison-Wesley.

Tajfel, H. (1969b) 'Cognitive aspects of prejudice', *Journal of Social Issues* 25: 79–97.

Tajfel, H. (1970) 'Experiments in intergroup discrimination', *Scientific American* 223: 96–102.

Tajfel, H. (1972a) 'Social categorization', English manuscript of 'La catégorisation sociale', in S. Moscovici (ed.) *Introduction à la psychologie sociale*, vol. 1, Paris: Larousse.

Tajfel, H. (1972b) 'Some developments in European social psychology', *European Journal of Social Psychology* 2: 307–22.

Tajfel, H. (1972c) 'Experiments in a vacuum', in J. Israel and H. Tajfel (eds) *The Context of Social Psychology: A Critical Assessment*, London: Academic Press.

Tajfel, H. (1973) 'The roots of prejudice: cognitive aspects', in P. Watson (ed.) *Psychology and Race*, Harmondsworth: Penguin.

Tajfel, H. (1974) 'Intergroup behaviour, social comparison and social change', unpublished Katz-Newcomb lectures at the University of Michigan, Ann Arbor.

Tajfel, H. (ed.) (1978a) *Differentiation Between Social Groups*, London: Academic Press.

Tajfel, H. (1978b) 'Intergroup behaviour: I. Individualistic perspectives', in H. Tajfel and C. Fraser (eds) *Introducing Social Psychology*, Harmondsworth: Penguin.

Tajfel, H. (1978c) 'Intergroup behaviour: II. Group perspectives', in H. Tajfel and C. Fraser (eds) *Introducing Social Psychology*, Harmondsworth: Penguin.

Tajfel, H. (1981a) *Human Groups and Social Categories: Studies in Social Psychology*, Cambridge: Cambridge University Press.

Tajfel, H. (1981b) 'Social stereotypes and social groups', in J.C. Turner and H. Giles (eds) *Intergroup Behaviour*, Oxford: Blackwell, and in H. Tajfel, *Human Groups and Social Categories: Studies in Social Psychology*, Cambridge: Cambridge University Press.

Tajfel, H. (ed.) (1982a) *Social Identity and Intergroup Relations*, Cambridge: Cambridge University Press.

Tajfel, H. (1982b) 'Social psyschology of intergroup relations', *Annual Review of Psychology* 33: 1–39.

Tajfel, H. (ed.) (1984) *The Social Dimension: European Developments in Social Psychology*, Cambridge: Cambridge University Press and Paris: Editions de la Maison des Sciences de l'Homme, vols 1 and 2.

Tajfel, H. and Billig, M. (1974) 'Familiarity and categorization in intergroup behaviour', *Journal of Experimental Social Psychology* 10: 159–70.

Tajfel, H., Billig, M., Bundy, R.P., and Flament, C. (1971) 'Social categorization and intergroup behaviour', *European Journal of Social Psychology* 1: 149–77.

Tajfel, H., Sheikh, A.A., and Gardner, A.A., (1964) 'Content of stereotypes and the inference of similarity between members of stereotyped groups', *Acta Psychologica* 22: 191–201.

Tajfel, H. and Turner, J.C. (1979) 'An integrative theory of intergroup conflict', in W.G. Austin and S. Worchel (eds) *The Social Psychology of Intergroup Relations*, Monterey, Calif.: Brooks-Cole.

Tajfel, H. and Turner, J.C. (1986) 'The social identity theory of intergroup behaviour', in S. Worchel and W.G. Austin (eds) *Psychology of Intergroup Relations*, Chicago: Nelson-Hall.

Tajfel, H. and Wilkes, A.L. (1963) 'Classification and quantitative judgement', *British Journal of Psychology* 54: 101–14.

Tarde, G. (1901) *L'Opinion et la foule*, Paris: Libraire Felix Alcan.

Taylor, D.M. and Brown, R.J. (1979) 'Towards a more social social psychology?', *British Journal of Social and Clinical Psychology* 18: 173–9.

Taylor, D.M. and Jaggi, V. (1974) 'Ethnocentrism and causal attribution in a S. Indian context', *Journal of Cross-Cultural Psychology* 5: 162–71.

Taylor, D.M. and McKirnan, D.J. (1984) 'A five-stage model of intergroup relations', *British Journal of Social Psychology* 23, Special Issue on Intergroup Processes: 291–300.

Taylor, D.M., Meynard, R., and Rheault, E. (1977) 'Threat to ethnic identity and second language learning', in H. Giles (ed.) *Language, Ethnicity and Intergroup Relations*, London: Academic Press.

Taylor, S.E. (1981) 'A categorization approach to stereotyping', in D.L. Hamilton (ed.) *Cognitive Processes in Stereotyping and Intergroup Behaviour*, Hillsdale, NJ: Erlbaum.

Taylor, S.E., Fiske, S.T., Etcoff, N.L., and Ruderman, A.J. (1978) 'Categorical and contextual bases of person memory and stereotyping', *Journal of Personality and Social Psychology* 36: 778–93.

Tedeschi, J.T. and Norman, J. (1984) 'Social power, self-presentation and the self', in B. Schlenker (ed.) *Self and Identity*, New York: McGraw-Hill.

Tedeschi, J.T. and Reiss, M. (1981) 'Predicaments and verbal tactics of impression management', in C. Antaki (ed.) *Ordinary Language Explanations of Social Behaviour*, London: Academic Press.

Thakerar, J.N., Giles, H. and Cheshire, J. (1982) 'Psychological and linguistic parameters of speech accommodation theory', in C. Fraser and K.R. Scherer (eds) *Advances in the Social Psychology of Language*, Cambridge: Cambridge University Press.

Thibaut, J.W. and Kelley, H.H. (1959) *The Social Psychology of Groups*, New York: Wiley.

Thorne, B., Kramarae, C., and Henley, N. (eds) (1983) *Language, Gender and*

Society, Rowley, Mass.: Newbury House.

Tilly, C. (1978) *From Mobilization to Revolution*, Reading: Mass.: Addison-Wesley.

Tilly, C., Tilly, L., and Tilly, R. (1975) *The Rebellious Century 1830-1930*. Cambridge, Mass.: Harvard University Press.

Triandis, H.C. (1971) *Attitude and Attitude Change*, New York: Wiley.

Triandis, H.C. (1977) *Interpersonal Behaviour*, Monterey, Calif.: Brooks-Cole.

Tripathi, R.C. and Srivastava, R. (1981) 'Relative deprivation and intergroup attitudes', *European Journal of Social Psychology* 11: 313-18.

Triplett, N. (1898) 'The dynamogenic factors in pacemaking and competition', *American Journal of Psychology* 9: 507-33.

Trotter, W. (1919) *Instincts of the Herd in Peace and War*, London: Oxford University Press.

Trudgill, P. (1975) *Accent, Dialect and the School*, London: Edward Arnold.

Tucker, R.C. (1970) 'The theory of charismatic leadership', in D.A. Rustow (ed.) *Philosophers and Kings: Studies in Leadership*, New York: George Brazilier.

Turner, C.W., Simons, L.S., Berkowitz, L., and Frodi, A. (1977) 'The stimulating and inhibiting effects of weapons on aggressive behaviour', *Aggressive Behaviour* 3: 355-78.

Turner, J.C. (1975) 'Social comparison and social identity: some prospects for intergroup behaviour', *European Journal of Social Psychology* 5: 5-34.

Turner, J.C. (1978a) 'Social categorization and social discrimination in the minimal group paradigm', in H. Tajfel (ed.) *Differentiation Between Social Groups*, London: Academic Press.

Turner, J.C. (1978b) 'Social comparison, similarity and ingroup favouritism', in H. Tajfel (ed.) *Differentiation Between Social Groups*, London: Academic Press.

Turner, J.C. (1980) 'Fairness or discrimination in intergroup behaviour? A reply to Branthwaite, Doyle and Lightbown', *European Journal of Social Psychology* 10: 131-47.

Turner, J.C. (1981a) 'Some considerations in generalizing experimental social psychology', in G.M. Stephenson and J.M. Davis (eds) *Progress in Applied Social Psychology*, vol. 1, London: Wiley.

Turner, J.C. (1981b) 'The experimental social psychology of intergroup behaviour', in J.C. Turner and H. Giles (eds) *Intergroup Behaviour*, Oxford: Blackwell.

Turner, J.C. (1982) 'Towards a cognitive redefinition of the social group', in H. Tajfel (ed.) *Social Identity and Intergroup Relations*, Cambridge: Cambridge University Press and Paris: Editions de la Maison des Sciences de l'Homme.

Turner, J.C. (1983) 'Some comments on "the measurement of social orientations in the minimal group paradigm" ', *European Journal of Social Psychology* 13: 351-68.

Turner, J.C. (1984) 'Social identification and psychological group formation', in H. Tajfel (ed.) *The Social Dimension: European Developments in Social Psychology*, vol. 2, Cambridge: Cambridge University Press.

Turner, J.C. (1985) 'Social categorization and the self-concept: a social cognitive theory of group behaviour', in E.J. Lawler (ed.) *Advances in Group Processes: Theory and Research*, vol. 2, Greenwich, Conn.: JAI Press.

Turner, J.C. and Brown, R.J. (1978) 'Social status, cognitive alternatives and intergroup relations', in H. Tajfel (ed.) *Differentiation Between Social Groups*, London: Academic Press.

Turner, J.C. Brown, R.J., and Tajfel, H. (1979) 'Social comparison and group interest in ingroup favouritism', *European Journal of Social Psychology* 9: 187-204.

Turner, J.C. and Giles, H. (eds) (1981) *Intergroup Behaviour*, Oxford: Blackwell.

Turner, J.C., Hogg, M.A., Oakes, P.J., Reicher, S.D., and Wetherell, M. (1987) *Rediscovering the Social Group: A Self-Categorization Theory*, Oxford and New York: Blackwell.

Turner, J.C., Hogg, M.A., Turner, P.J., and Smith, P.M. (1984) 'Failure and defeat as determinants of group cohesiveness', *British Journal of Social Psychology* 23: 97–111.

Turner, J.C. and Oakes, P.J. (1986) 'The significance of the social identity concept for social psychology with reference to individualism, interactionism and social influence', *British Journal of Social Psychology* 25, Special Issue on the Individual-Society Interface: 237–9.

Turner, J.C., Sachdev, I., and Hogg, M.A. (1983) 'Social categorization, interpersonal attraction and group formation', *British Journal of Social Psychology* 22: 227–39.

Turner, R.H. (1974) 'Collective behaviour', in R.E.L. Faris (ed.) *Handbook of Modern Sociology*, Chicago: Rand-McNally.

Turner, R.H. and Killian, L. (1957) *Collective Behaviour*, Englewood Cliffs: NJ: Prentice-Hall.

Tyerman, A. and Spencer, C. (1983) 'A critical test of the Sherifs' robbers cave experiments: intergroup competition and cooperation between groups of well-acquainted individuals', *Small Group Behaviour* 14: 515–31.

Ulman, R.B. and Abse, D.W. (1983) 'The group psychology of mass madness: Jonestown', *Political Psychology* 4: 637–61.

van Knippenberg, A.F.M. (1978) 'Status differences, comparative relevance and intergroup differentiation', in H. Tajfel (ed.) *Differentiation Between Social Groups*, London: Academic Press.

van Knippenberg, A.F.M. (1984) 'Intergroup differences in group perceptions', in H. Tajfel (ed.) *The Social Dimension: European Developments in Social Psychology*, vol. 2, Cambridge: Cambridge University Press.

van Knippenberg, A.F.M. and Oers, H. (1984) 'Social identity and equity concerns in intergroup perceptions', *British Journal of Social Psychology* 23: 351–62.

Vanneman, R.D. and Pettigrew, T.F. (1972) 'Race and relative deprivation in the urban United States', *Race* 13: 461–86.

Vaughan, G.M. (1964) 'The transsituational aspect of conformity behaviour', *Journal of Personality* 32: 335–54.

Vaughan, G.M. (1978) 'Social change and intergroup preferences in New Zealand', *European Journal of Social Psychology* 8: 297–314.

Vickers, E., Abrams, D., and Hogg, M.A. (1987) 'The influence of social norms on discrimination in the minimal group paradigm', University of Dundee, unpublished paper.

Vinokur, A. and Burnstein, E. (1974) 'The effects of partially shared persuasive arguments on group-induced shifts: a problem-solving approach', *Journal of Personality and Social Psychology* 29: 305–15.

Vleeming, R.G. (1983) 'Intergroup relations in a simulated society', *Journal of Psychology* 113: 81–7.

Waddell, N. and Cairns, E. (1986) 'Situational perspectives on social identity in Northern Ireland', *British Journal of Social Psychology* 25: 25–32.

Wagner, U. and Schönbach, P. (1984) 'Links between educational status and prejudice: ethnic attitudes in West Germany', in N. Miller and M.B. Brewer (eds) *Groups in Contact: The Psychology of Desegregation*, New York: Academic Press.

Walker, I. and Pettigrew, T.F. (1984) 'Relative deprivation theory: an overview and conceptual critique', *British Journal of Social Psychology* 23: 301–10.

Watson, G. and Johnson, D. (1972) *Social Psychology: Issues and Insights*, Philadelphia: J.B. Lippincott.

Webb, J. (1982) 'Social psychological aspects of third party intervention in industrial disputes', University of Nottingham, unpublished doctoral dissertation.

Weber, M. (1930) *The Protestant Ethic and the Spirit of Capitalism*, London: Allen & Unwin.

Weber, M. (1958) *From Max Weber: Essays in Sociology*, ed. with an introduction by H.H. Gerth and C.W. Mills, New York: Oxford University Press. .

Weigert, A.J. (1983) *Social Psychology: A Sociological Approach Through Interpretive Understanding*, Notre Dame, Indiana: University of Notre Dame Press.

Wetherell, M. (1987) 'Social identity and group polarization', in J.C. Turner, M.A. Hogg, P.J. Oakes, S.D. Reicher, and M. Wetherell, *Rediscovering the Social Group: A Self-Categorization Theory*, Oxford and New York: Blackwell.

Wetherell, M., Turner, J.C., and Hogg, M.A. (1986) 'A referent informational influence explanation of group polarization', University of St Andrews and Macquarie University, unpublished paper.

Wheeler, L., Deci, E.L., Reis, H.Y., and Zuckerman, M. (1978) *Interpersonal Influence*, 2nd edn, Boston: Allyn & Bacon.

White, M.J. (1977) 'Counternormative behaviour as influenced by deindividuating conditions and reference group salience', *Journal of Social Psychology* 103: 75–90.

Wicklund, R.A. (1980) 'Group contact and self-focused attention', in P.B. Paulus (ed.) *Pschology of Group Influence*, Hillsdale, NJ: Erlbaum.

Wicklund, R.A. (1982) 'How society uses self-awareness', in J. Suls (ed.) *Psychological Perspectives on the Self*, vol. 1, Hillsdale, NJ: Erlbaum.

Wicklund, R.A. and Duval, S. (1971) 'Opinion change and performance facilitation as a result of objective self-awareness', *Journal of Experimental Psychology*, 7: 319–42.

Wieman, J.M. and Harrison, R.P. (1983) *Non-Verbal Interaction*, London: Sage.

Wilder, D. (1977) 'Perception of groups, size of opposition and social influence', *Journal of Experimental Social Psychology* 13: 253–68.

Wilder, D.A. (1984) 'Intergroup contact: the typical member and the exception to the rule', *Journal of Experimental Social Psychology* 20: 177–94.

Wilder, D. (1986) 'Social categorization: implications for creation and reduction of intergroup bias', *Advances in Experimental Social Psychology* 19: 291–355.

Williams, J.A. (1984) 'Gender and intergroup behaviour: towards an integration', *British Journal of Social Psychology* 23: 311–16.

Williams, J.A. and Giles, H. (1978) 'The changing status of women in society: an intergroup perspective', in H. Tajfel (ed.) *Differentiation Between Social Groups*, London: Academic Press.

Williams, K., Harkins, S., and Latané, B. (1981) 'Identifiability as a deterrent to social loafing: two cheering experiments', *Journal of Personality and Social Psychology* 40: 303–11.

Williams, R.M. Jnr (1947) *The Reduction of Intergroup Tensions*, New York: Social Science Research Council.

Wilson, P. (1982) *Black Death, White Hands*, Sydney: Allen & Unwin.

Wine, D. (1971) 'Test anxiety and direction of attention', *Psychological Bulletin* 76: 92–104.

Wine, D. (1980) 'Cognitive-attentional theory of test anxiety', in I.G. Sarason (ed.) *Test Anxiety: Theory Research and Application*, Hillsdale, NJ: Erlbaum.

Wittgenstein, L. (1953) *Philosophical Investigations*, Oxford: Blackwell.

Wolf, S. (1979) 'Behavioural style and group cohesiveness as sources of minority influence', *European Journal of Social Psychology* 9: 381–95.

Worchel, S. and Cooper, J. (1979) *Understanding Social Psychology*, 2nd edn, Homewood, Ill.: The Dorsey Press.

Wrightsman, L.S. (1977) *Social Psychology*, 2nd edn, Monterey, Calif.: Brooks-Cole.

Wundt, W. (1916) *Elements of Folk Psychology: Outlines of a Psychological History of the Development of Mankind*, London: Allen & Unwin.

Wyer, R.S. Jnr (1966) 'Effects of incentive to perform well, group attraction and group acceptance on conformity in a judgemental task', *Journal of Personality and*

Social Psychology 4: 21–7.

Wyer, R.S. Jnr and Srull, T.K. (eds) (1984) *Handbook of Social Cognition*, vol 3, Hillsdale, NJ: Erlbaum.

Yager, S., Johnson, R.T., Johnson, D.W., and Snider, B. (1985) 'The effect of cooperative and individualistic learning on positive and negative cross-handicap relationships', *Contemporary Educational Psychology* 10: 127–38.

Yinger, J.M. and Simpson, G.E. (1973) 'Techniques for reducing prejudice: changing the prejudiced person', in P. Watson (ed.) *Psychology and Race*, Harmondsworth: Penguin.

Zajonc, R.B. (1965) 'Social facilitation', *Science* 149: 269–74.

Zajonc, R.B. (1980) 'Compresence', in P.B. Paulus (ed.) *Psychology of Group Influence*, Hillsdale, NJ: Erlbaum.

Zander, A. (1979) 'The psychology of group processes', *Annual Review of Psychology* 30: 417–51.

Zimbardo, P.G. (1970) 'The human choice: individuation, reason and order vs deindividuation, impulse and chaos', in W.J. Arnold and D. Levine (eds) *Nebraska Symposium on Motivation 1969*, Lincoln, Nebraska: University of Nebraska Press.

Zimbardo, P.G. (1975) 'Transforming experimental research into advocacy for social change', in M. Deutsch and H.A. Hornstein (eds) *Applying Social Psychology*, Hillsdale, NJ: Erlbaum.

Author index

Subject index

HUMANITIES